D0302973

Calculating
compassion

Manchester University Press

HUMANITARIANISM
Key debates and new approaches

This series offers a new interdisciplinary reflection on one of the most important and yet understudied areas in history, politics and cultural practices: humanitarian aid and its responses to crises and conflicts. The series seeks to define afresh the boundaries and methodologies applied to the study of humanitarian relief and so-called 'humanitarian events'. The series includes monographs and carefully selected thematic edited collections which will cross disciplinary boundaries and bring fresh perspectives to the historical, political and cultural understanding of the rationale and impact of humanitarian relief work.

Illustrations

Contents

The right of Rebecca Gill to be identified as the author of this work has been asserted by her in accordance with the Copyright, Designs and Patents Act 1988.

Published by Manchester University Press
Oxford Road, Manchester M13 9NR, UK
and Room 400, 175 Fifth Avenue, New York, NY 10010, USA
www.manchesteruniversitypress.co.uk

Distributed in the United States exclusively by
Palgrave Macmillan, 175 Fifth Avenue, New York,
NY 10010, USA

Distributed in Canada exclusively by
UBC Press, University of British Columbia, 2029 West Mall,
Vancouver, BC, Canada V6T 1Z2

British Library Cataloguing-in-Publication Data
A catalogue record for this book is available from the British Library

Library of Congress Cataloging-in-Publication Data applied for

ISBN   978 0 7190 7810 1   hardback
First published 2013

The publisher has no responsibility for the persistence or accuracy of URLs for any external or third-party internet websites referred to in this book, and does not guarantee that any content on such websites is, or will remain, accurate or appropriate.

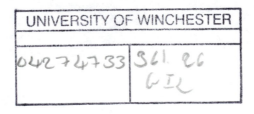
Typeset in 10.5/12.5pt Arno Pro
by Graphicraft Limited, Hong Kong
Printed in Great Britain
by CPI Antony Rowe Ltd, Chippenham, Wiltshire

Calculating compassion

Humanity and relief in war, Britain 1870–1914

Rebecca Gill

Manchester University Press

Manchester and New York

distributed in the United States exclusively by Palgrave Macmillan

Acknowledgements

I would like to take this opportunity to thank individuals and organisations for their generous assistance in the research and writing of this book. This book is based on a PhD thesis submitted to the University of Manchester, and I first wish to acknowledge the unflagging support, enthusiasm and insights of my PhD supervisor, Bertrand Taithe, without whom this project would never have got off the ground. Thanks are owed also to Peter Gatrell and John Horne, my two examiners, for their careful reading and comments.

Since starting work at the University of Huddersfield, I have been fortunate to benefit from a period of research leave. I would like to thank my colleagues in the History Department for making this possible and for their consistent support while I was writing this book.

Over the years, I have profited from the insight and erudition of Jo Laycock, Helen Dampier and Emily Baughan and I would like to express my gratitude for their willingness to share their research and knowledge with me. I would also like to thank David Taylor, Brian Walker and Stéphanie Prévost for taking the trouble to read drafts of this book.

Every attempt has been made to contact holders of copyright for the images and quotations from private papers that I have reproduced. For reproductions of illustrations and permission to reproduce photographs, acknowledgements are due to the British Library, the Library of Congress and the British Red Cross Museum and Archives. I wish to thank archivists at a number of institutions for making their collections available to me. These include the Wellcome Library (and the RAMC for making the Longmore papers publicly available); the London School of Economics library; the John Rylands Library, University of Manchester; the Bodleian Library (and the National Trust for making the Disraeli papers available for consultation); the Brotherton Library, University of Leeds; the Document and Sound Section at the Imperial War Museum; The National Archives; the British Red Cross Museum and Archives; and the Library of the Society of Friends, London. John Spencer of Bankfield Museum in Halifax was kind enough to furnish me with historical details of British Army uniforms.

Finally, a big thank you is owed to my husband, Andrew, whose love and encouragement made the writing of this book possible.

Abbreviations

BLPES	British Library of Political and Economic Science
BRCS	British Red Cross Society
CBRCC	Central British Red Cross Committee
COS	Charity Organisation Society
FWVRF	Friends War Victims' Relief Fund
ICRC	International Committee of the Red Cross
IWM	Imperial War Museum
JRL	John Rylands Library, University of Manchester
LSF	Library of the Society of Friends
NAS	British National Society for Aid to the Sick and Wounded in War
RAMC	Royal Army Medical Corps
SACC	South African Conciliation Committee
SCF	Save the Children Fund
TNA	The National Archives
VAD	Voluntary Aid Detachment

Introduction:
calculating compassion in war

'Pity and sympathy would have inclined me to carry liberality to its utmost limits, but I endeavoured to keep my heart in subjection to my head.'[1] With these words, Sir John Furley, founder member of the St John Ambulance Association and long-time champion of battlefield philanthropy, looked back on an eventful career. At the point of writing, he had undertaken voluntary action on behalf of wounded soldiers in the Franco-Prussian War of 1870–71, the Russo-Turkish War of 1877–78 and the South African War of 1899–1902. Photographs from the time show him resplendent in the ornamental uniform of the Order of St John, plumed helmet and an array of knightly paraphernalia suggesting venerable traditions and exalted lineage. In reality, the present incumbents of St John's Gate in Clerkenwell were able to date their origins back no further than the 1850s. Critics did not spare their jibes at this parvenu 'claptrap and mutual decoration crowd.'[2] Yet, for all that they were beset by mockery, pecuniary difficulties and rivalry, the Order of St John's attempt to revive a tradition of battlefield chivalry is an important strand in the history of modern relief work in Britain. It is with unravelling these rather tangled origins that this book is concerned.

Furley's attempt to subject heart to head resounded in many accounts of relief work in this period. Not all of these arose from the experience of organising assistance to wounded combatants. Others recounted missions to aid civilian populations caught perilously in the grip of war. Aid to the suffering in war was hardly new, of course, but an impulse to rationalise and organise was. Furley and his colleagues were only too happy to remind the public of the Hospitaller work carried out by the medieval Knights of St John during the crusades to the Holy Land. More recent examples included Florence Nightingale's famous mission to ameliorate conditions in British army hospitals during the Crimean War. The

---

[1] John Furley, *In Peace and War: Autobiographical Sketches*, Smith, Elder and Co., London, 1905, p. 64.

[2] Quoted in John F. Hutchinson, *Champions of Charity: War and the Rise of the Red Cross*, Westview Press, Oxford, 1996, p. 254.

Quakers, meanwhile, had been quietly providing assistance to non-combatants since the early 1800s. But by the late nineteenth century, a new generation of relief funds had arisen, singularly protesting their organisational proficiency, neutrality and impartiality, and trenchantly eschewing the partisanship and evangelism of earlier endeavours.

Accompanying Furley and his associates to the battlefields were a number of rival societies for the relief of war-time suffering. In theatres of war in nineteenth-century Europe – France, the Balkans – and in Britain's wars of empire – the Sudan, South Africa – enterprising men and women opened soup kitchens, carried stretchers, nursed the wounded and delivered food and clothing to the destitute. These years saw the now ubiquitous Red Cross emblem first make its appearance on the battle-field. Emblazoned on armbands and ambulance wagons, it symbolised the neutral status that medical staff and their patients were granted by the 1864 Geneva Convention. As will be seen, not all of those delivering aid were convinced that the flourishing Red Cross movement represented an unqualified good, or were agreed as to its purpose. At home, meanwhile, impromptu warehouses overflowed with a miscellany of donations. When the Franco-Prussian War flared across the Channel, society ladies squeezed their way through stacks of packing cases to oversee the sorting and shipping of Bovril and pyjamas, Benger's invalid food, blankets, soda water and bandages. These scenes were replicated with each new conflict. Volunteers of both sexes abounded, and *matériel* was distributed in unprecedented quantities; some of this provided welcome comfort, on occasion it proved essential to life.

Whether in warehouses at home or on foreign battlefields, volunteers did not always work in harmony, but many demonstrated great sense of purpose, and, on occasion, bravery. Some lost their lives, killed in shell attacks on hospitals or dying of typhus among crowded refugee encampments. Many more relished the esca-pades, camaraderie and even privations of war. We should not imagine that all were competent or compelled primarily by a sense of compassion: opportunities for adventure, pay and professional experience all proved a draw. Eminent surgeons rubbed shoulders with those qualified by little more than a few hasty days' observa-tion in a local hospital. Some were complete novices. Others were fresh from medical school, energetic and enthusiastic, but, as the most candid admitted, cavalier in their absolute power over the sick and wounded, and dangerously ill-equipped for battlefield surgery. Still others left businesses and professional occupations behind. Derision and suspicion abounded, of amateurism, profiteering, theft from cadavers and a ghoulish voyeurism; of civilising war, but in doing so, making it palatable. At the time of the Franco-Prussian War, Josephine Butler, sceptical of all things military, derided the 'graceful charity' involved in 'making bandages'.[3] In *Blackwood's*

[3] Quoted in Heloise Brown, *'The Truest Form of Patriotism': Pacifist Feminism in Britain, 1870–1902*, Manchester University Press, Manchester, 2003, pp. 64–65, 166.

Magazine another observer complained of 'Jew pedlars, camp-sutlers, neutral vendors of bad cigars and worse liquor . . . seen at Sedan wearing the Red Cross'.[4] Some of this criticism was justified.

In now largely unread tales of ambulance adventures and life amidst huddled refugee populations, a sidelight is thrown on the backwash of war.[5] In their pages, the squalor and misery of impromptu camps and temporary hospitals are gleaned, but so too are flashes of hope and idealism. The honing of relief workers' professional skill is documented and, just as important, an ability to extemporise in the face of war-time disorder. We learn of people and experiences not usually dwelt upon in standard military histories: of daring dashes across snow-topped Balkan mountains to reach the injured; of 'lady amateurs' accused of volunteering their services in search of hospital passions; and of the innovativeness of the British Red Cross personnel who accompanied Wolseley on his Nile expedition to rescue Gordon. The landscape of war opens out to include soldiers rendered *hors de combat* by their injuries and evacuated to the remnants of buildings or, if lucky, a well-ordered Red Cross hospital. We catch sight of those caught in devastating conflict and interned against their will in civilian camps, and of those despairing of whether to flee their homes or struggle for subsistence in ruined villages.

Such tales illuminate the diverse inspiration, impressive innovation and uneven efficacy of those pioneering individuals who rushed to offer some form of ameliora-tion. That they did so amidst chaos, broken communications and lost supplies is testament both to their endurance and the ad hoc nature of early relief efforts. Here in the backwash they joined journalists, tourists, consular officials, arms dealers and medical salesmen in the jostling peripatetic communities unique to war and disaster. Frequently, their motivation for aiding the wounded and vulnerable was met with suspicion by a press that was by turns prurient and censorious. But for being used to thinking of relief workers as modern-day saints, we ought not to be surprised that their arbitrary interventions were not always welcome or thought benevolent. Indeed, the question of motivation remains an apt one. There is too ready a willingness to collapse relief agencies' present-day concerns and dilemmas into the aspirations of this pioneering generation. Or to assume that aid organ-isations are simply timeless compassion given administrative form. Instead, ideals and aspirations varied, and they repay historical scrutiny. The novel refrain of neutrality and impartiality may have been heard over and again among late nineteenth-century relief workers, but it would be a mistake to assume that this arose from a common imperative or a shared response to human suffering. Many a time, instances of suffering that prompted Sir John Furley and his knights-errant to pity left others cold.

---

[4] Henry Brackenbury, 'Philanthropy in War', *Blackwood's Magazine*, February 1877, p. 167.

[5] This evocative phrase is taken from Ellen La Motte, *The Backwash of War: The Human Wreckage of the Battlefield as Witnessed by an American Hospital Nurse*, G. P. Putnam's Sons, London, 1916.

At the core of this book there rests an inquiry: why, at this historical juncture, did particular instances of war-time suffering move Furley and certain other contemporaries to action? Furley was far from unique in extolling the need to balance heart with head, pity with proficiency. How and why this was attempted also requires consideration. Doing so brings into focus the tentative emergence of relief work as a new vocational field. Here arose notions of scientific impartiality, routine 'emergency' practices and a plethora of new war-time roles. These gave shape to a field of endeavour still recognisable today. Not all war-time suffering occasioned such a response, however. Nineteenth-century relief workers did not assume a mandate to respond to *all* suffering in *all* wars. A rush of pity may have been felt for the Christian in the war-torn Balkans, but not for his Jewish or Muslim neighbour; a sympathetic outcry may be heard over the plight of Boers in concentration camps, but a segregation of concern may render silent the suffering of black inmates. All were not equal in the brotherhood of humanity. This begs the question, still pertinent today, of how the boundaries of compassion operated. The unashamedly selective nature of nineteenth-century relief work offers one crucial difference from the universal proclamations of modern-day aid agencies, but it has bestowed some troubling legacies and habits of mind, nonetheless.

Relief in war: mapping 'the field'

Some of the organisations that feature in this book are familiar: the St John Ambulance Association, the Save the Children Fund (SCF), the British Red Cross Society (BRCS) and the various committees of the Religious Society of Friends are with us today. Others lasting the duration of a single conflict are now more or less forgotten. With their foundation, relief work emerged as a discernible enterprise of modern war, the legacies of which are complicated and occasionally controversial. Though to be found proffering solidarity with the vulnerable or victimised in conflicts of unprecedented scale and ferocity, they were not simply bystanders at the birth of 'total' war; instead, they were integral to the medico-military infrastructure that made wars of attrition between large conscript and volunteer armies possible and palatable. They were also at the forefront of the relief, rehabilitation and resettlement of populations displaced or interned in wars which increasingly targeted civilian populations. For some, such as the British Red Cross, this assistance was in deliberate service to a military imperative: there was both virtue and advantage to be had in greater hospital efficiency and well-run internment camps. For others, including Quakers and radicals of all hues, relief in war was conceived as a protest at a militarised state and society and as constructive work towards international peace and freedom (though this did not preclude their endeavours from serving military imperatives, however unintentional). The emergence of organised relief work intersected with attempts at the rationalisation of philanthropy and social investigation at home, with anxieties over military capacity and with the rise of a crusading 'new' journalism.

It also contributed to wide-ranging political transformations. Among other things, this saw 'England's Mission' abroad debated, the War Office assert itself over an entrenched military elite and the entitlements of participatory citizenship pressed with ever greater vigour.

This book starts with the diverse motivations of this pioneering generation of relief workers in mind, rather than by assuming any shared humanitarian ideal. Here, attentiveness to the language in which relief workers couched their own sense of purpose is revealing. For the word 'humanitarian', so frequently coupled with relief work today, was largely avoided, its usage connoting a crankish disposition and a tendency to merciless inflexibility. As the *Oxford English Dictionary* notes, in the nineteenth century the term was 'nearly always *contemptuous*, connoting one who goes to excess in their humane principles'.[6] Thus, it could be said with admiration that the Prussians, 'confident in the support of their superiors', knew

> . . . nothing of the pusillanimous dread of the Press and fear of responsibility asserted to be traditional in the English Army; they are *humane* not *humanitarian*. The question with them is not, 'Can a man be removed with safety?' but, 'Will his removal give him a better chance of recovery than his remaining?' If so, though he may suffer seriously in transit, the suffering must be borne.[7]

The earliest use of the term to denote a set of vocational practices – that is, of the emergency relief of the wounded that we specifically associate with 'humanitarian aid' today – was during the Great War. In 1914 Sir James Cantlie, Harley Street doctor and prominent promoter of the Red Cross, founded the College of Ambulance and Humanitarian Corps in London, giving classes in first aid, home nursing, hospital remedies and hygiene.[8] Prior to this, many in the Red Cross movement in Britain referred simply to the 'aid and assistance' they offered to belligerent armies in the field. In doing so, they captured the subsidiary role that they envisaged for themselves vis-à-vis the regular army medical service. Quakers of this period, meanwhile, refused aid to soldiers but concentrated with renewed theological conviction on non-combatant relief. They tended to render their work a form of 'loving service'.[9] Even today, many Quakers reject the term 'humanitarian' for failing to capture the spiritual import that they attach to relief. But this period did include one defiantly positive appropriation of the term. Intersecting circles of radicals – Positivists, socialists and New Liberals – concerned with the wellspring of ethical

[6] Original italics.

[7] Comments of Dr Ball in *Report of the Operations of the British National Society for Aid to the Sick and Wounded in War During the Franco-Prussian War 1870–71 together with a Statement of Receipts and Expenditure and Maps, Reports and Correspondence*, Harrison & Sons, London, 1871, p. 20. [Hereafter NAS, *Report* (Franco-Prussian War).]

[8] See press cuttings in the papers of Sir James Cantlie, Wellcome Library, MS7930/16.

[9] For example, as used by Helen Harrison, veteran of relief work in Armenia and South Africa during the Boer War, quoted in Hope Hay Hewison, *Hedge of Wild Almonds: South Africa, the 'Pro-Boers' and the Quaker Conscience*, James Currey, London, 1989, p. 207.

acts in an age when a Christian God was a less ready spur to action invested the term with new scientific import.[10] Foremost among these were members of the Humanitarian League (founded 1891), such as Edward Carpenter, Frederic Harrison and Ramsay MacDonald. 'Humanitarianism' offered the possibility of a technocratic altruism based upon objectively adduced laws of moral action. It would be from these circles that one prominent strand of crusading relief work would emerge in this period, concerned with raising the public's moral consciousness and with 'rational' alleviation of suffering. But again, it would be a mistake to imagine that this 'humanitarian' work was the direct antecedent of present-day humanitarian relief, just as it would be erroneous to assume that it denoted universality of provision or was grounded in an understanding of individual human rights.[11] Far from it.

For many in this period, whether aiding soldiers or feeding civilians, the claims of humanity were deemed concomitant with patriotic loyalty and the enlightened but central role of the state. Full participation in humanity depended upon one's place in the scale of civilisation, fostered and promoted by a suitably progressive polity, rather than any inalienable human rights. By the same token, relief agencies tended to prioritise their European 'brothers' and 'sisters', busying themselves with those considered the most susceptible to their civilising example and calling upon government to intervene on their behalf. Thus, though early relief workers undertook novel transnational interventions, transferring resources and expertise across national borders and drawing attention to distant suffering, it would be far from accurate to assume that all adhered to 'internationalism' as carrying moral value, wished to be thought of as 'humanitarians' or considered that the claims of 'humanity' transcended the imperial or nation state.

This, then, is a complex field of endeavour, and one irreducible to a single ideal. 'Field' is used here not in the purloined anthropological sense that aid workers attach to 'going into the field' today, with its suggestion of an extant site of professional endeavour and its obliteration of the processes of identification and interaction, but in a meaning of the term inspired by another borrowing, this time from sociologist Pierre Bourdieu. Bourdieu's main preoccupation was the arena of artistic and literary production, but his notion of a vocational 'field' works equally well in other cases – in this instance, the coming into being of a field of organised relief work during the late nineteenth century. Particularly instructive is Bourdieu's insistence on a model that combines recognition of individual agency, innovation and virtue with an acknowledgement of the importance of social relations. He did not assume that vocational behaviour is purely autonomous, but nor did he assume that social structures simply determine behaviour in any mechanistic

---

[10] Stefan Collini, *Public Moralists: Political Thought and Intellectual Life in Britain, 1850–1930*, Oxford University Press, Oxford, 1993, pp. 84–85.

[11] Samuel Moyn, *The Last Utopia: Human Rights in History*, Harvard University Press, London, 2010, p. 4.

sense.[12] Rather, he emphasised *habitus* – an individual's habits of mind or dispositions, which, though apparently intuitive, are shaped by the social relations, institutional practices and distinguishing customs that define their professional field. *Habitus* both organises perceptions and influences future practice. As applied here, this theory of professional practice encompasses the processes of selection and models of delivery adopted in encounters with suffering strangers. But it also extends to domestic administrative arrangements and fund-raising and recruitment drives to encompass the span of how suffering was expressed, compassion represented and relief ministered.

Bourdieu situated the vocational field of endeavour within external relations of political and social power. He also analysed internal competition over the meaning and merit ascribed to individual or institutional actions (in this case the criticism that flew between rival relief organisations and animated the pages of the press). Crucially, he viewed the nature of such competition and critique as circumscribed, as self-perpetuating and as providing an important legitimating function for the field as a whole. To understand the field of relief, it therefore becomes necessary not only to consider the importance of competition and rivalry, but to look also for the philanthropic conventions and cultural assumptions – or habits of mind – that were so commonplace as to appear universal. This book highlights how, in the contest over how authentic knowledge of suffering was adduced and compassion best calculated, legitimacy was – and continues to be – bestowed on the value of relief work in principle. Rather than adjudicate between competing ethical positions, it investigates the historical context that made the very existence of these practices – and this ethical debate – possible.

In this period, the field of relief work was liable to be ad hoc in its interventions, its committees governed by small, often dynastic, and usually rivalrous, affiliations, and a traditionally gendered division of labour. Very quickly, like many of those running charitable organisations in this era, these committees came to value efficiency, and the standardisation of care, personnel and technique. But for individual volunteers, traditional notions of charitable service and intuitive acts of heartfelt compassion remained central to the value that they placed on their work, and featured no less prominently in fund-raising campaigns. It is not surprising that the most perspicacious relief workers felt acutely the difficulty of balancing heart and head, pity and routine, for these early volunteers were exporting the philanthropic conventions – and conflicts – of their age. Steeped in the Victorian culture of altruism and welfare reform, they were active at a moment when concerted efforts were being made to systematically investigate poverty and rationalise the provision of relief, and when calls for greater statutory intervention were beginning to be heard with

[12] Pierre Bourdieu, 'The Field of Cultural Production, or: The Economic World Reversed', in Pierre Bourdieu, *The Field of Cultural Production: Essays on Art and Literature*, ed. Randal Johnson, Polity Press, Cambridge, 1993.

greater frequency. Many advocates of war-time relief had direct experience of social intervention and inquiry amongst the metropolitan poor. Here, as abroad, they grappled with the appropriate response to suffering and with the duty of voluntary action. They also experienced some of the pleasures and rewards that came with venturing into the lives of the poor, and the peculiar glamour that attached itself to slumming and self-imposed privation found an echo in the escapades of war relief. New vistas for exploration and adventure came into view and offered the possibility for self-assertion and an antidote to the boredom of middle-class women's lives.[13]

This was the era in which the strictures of independence and 'self-help' and fears of the pauperising effects of unfettered and ill-coordinated charity motivated the Charity Organisation Society (COS) to consolidate domestic relief provision. A similar trend is observable in overseas relief. The necessity of accurate investigation was advocated; surveys and interviews were instigated. Eglantyne Jebb, founder member of the SCF, and herself a COS worker, was to bemoan the inefficiencies of foreign relief funds, and decry the lack of 'self help' among war victims. Kate Courtney, also an SCF founder member, had trained with the COS and had assisted Samuel Barnett in his settlement work in East London. Here she developed contacts and experience which would inform her campaigning work in the South African and First World wars. Like many, these women embodied the on-going tension between 'empathetic and scientific' approaches to human need.[14]

Unlike domestic hardship, which, however 'foreign' to middle-class observers, was also proximate, overseas relief work took place in difficult-to-reach and little-known areas. Part of this book involves consideration of how knowledge of this distant suffering arose. Here, the rise of investigative journalism was as crucial to the field of foreign relief as it was to dramatic exposés of exploitation and suffering at home. Newspapers of the period took to hiring foreign correspondents and utilising the new electric telegraph to provide on-the-spot reports. But pity and the impetus to ameliorative action were not simply a response to the immediacy of graphic reportage: the ties between the emerging fields of relief work and 'new' journalism were far closer and more knotted, as were the individual relationships between aid workers and their contacts in the press. Relief workers relied on journalists for intelligence and the setting of priorities when their own lines of communication were weak. But the reverse was true, and newspapers frequently followed where relief workers led. Press interest lent the new aid organisations valuable publicity, and relief agents' frequent 'letters to the editor' offered a means to public account-ability. But such publicity had its drawbacks: relief work had become a favourite topic in newspapers eager for eye-witness accounts of war, but equivocation existed over the propriety of these new ventures. Were relief agents as rigorously accountable

[13] Ellen Ross, 'Adventures among the Poor', in *Slum Travellers: Ladies and London Poverty, 1860–1920*, University of California Press, Berkeley, 2007.
[14] Seth Coven, *Slumming: Sexual and Social Politics in Victorian London*, Princeton University Press, Oxford, 2004, p. 92.

as they claimed, or, journalists asked, as neutral? Intimate accounts of suffering and its ministration were relished, but the same newspaper might well air suspicions of partiality and incompetence. And there was a fine line between publicity for a cause and criticism of existing provision. Advocating aid to British soldiers risked jealousy and suspicion among the military medical services – precisely those with whom co-operation was essential. In such cases, access might well be compromised. But was silence preferable? Diplomacy, tact and good relations with the press were thus crucial: and the role and etiquette of the relief worker took shape in response. Sometimes the journalist and the relief worker were one and the same person. The *Daily Telegraph's* reporter during the 1870–71 siege of Paris also allocated its relief fund, and this was by no means the only example. Graphic reportage sustained the granting of relief; but the reverse was also true.

Until after the Great War, the career relief worker was an exception. As well as journalism and charity work, overseas relief workers had a variety of peace-time occupations, as missionaries, politicians and scholars, as members of the military, or on the staff of teaching hospitals. This meant that they could mobilise friends and contacts in a number of influential circles. It also meant, of course, that the direction and form of relief owed much to the ebb and flow of wider political, professional and intellectual currents. Relief workers did not simply respond to these preoccupations: they contributed to the shaping of perceptions and knowledge, especially concerning appropriate involvement in foreign affairs. One key area of debate was the implication of emergent European nationalism. Was it a threat to the Continental balance of power, or did it offer the promise of self-determination and a new order of consensual and peaceful international relations? Ought Britain to intervene, and if so what was to be the nature of this intervention – and how might proffering relief assist in these contending processes of stabilisation and liberation? Equally animating was the expansion of empire, the fulfilment, it seemed, of Disraelian imperialism, yet dominated by contending visions of liberalism and the rise of colonial nationalism. While Red Cross personnel accompanied the British army in its imperial wars, other relief organisations, reaching out to their suffering 'sisters' in the colonies, challenged the nature of these imperial connections. And what was the appropriate response to wars that were now increasingly national or 'total'? New medical challenges were posed by rapid-fire weaponry, Krupp steel and other technological innovations, while antisepsis, sprung-wheeled stretchers and hospital trains contributed both to the capacities and to the demands experienced by voluntary organisations. Did relief workers form part of the first line of national defence – or was their purpose to soften international rivalries and remedy militarism at home?

Relief workers not only helped to shape the debate on foreign policy interventions, but also helped to ensure that these were held up as test cases of the morality of the political class. The politics of humanity and relief therefore were complex: spanning the implications for the intended recipients of aid, on the one hand, and the political aspirations of those at home, on the other. In many cases, relief workers provided the direct and 'impartial' knowledge of suffering which a new generation of tenacious journalists (W. T. Stead at the *Northern Echo*, in particular) used to stir moral agitation and hold politicians to account. Stead and his ilk demanded that the people's moral interests be represented; meanwhile, sympathetically minded states-men made attempts to capture the moral imagination and aspirations of a growing electorate – and used relief workers' testimony to lend authority to political pro-nouncements. Gladstone, famously, attempted to galvanise Liberal supporters over the treatment of distant Bulgarians and blessed relief agents then at work in the Balkans. Attendance at a protest meeting, subscription to a relief fund, bandage rolling or volunteer nursing, all could be seen as a personal and intuitive response to the suffering of others. But they also constituted participation in new moral communities and nourished emerging political identities that were all the more powerful because they rested on a sense of duty, 'higher ideals' and a feeling of solidarity. In this way, voluntary aid work could endorse claims of moral and participatory citizenship premised on public service to one's country, an appeal which held particular attrac-tion for the politically marginal or unenfranchised – female suffragists, especially.

This was true both of those such as the Order of St John, which advocated voluntary relief work with the British army as a patriotic duty, and those of 'progressive' views who advocated aid as a gesture of public-spirited solidarity with the oppressed. Of the latter, the Religious Society of Friends was prominent. For many Quakers relief work was an expression of theological commitment. Whether at home or abroad, they participated in many of the relief committees and instances of practical aid work under discussion. In tracing both their compulsion to do so and their distinctive methods of distribution and accountability it is possible to observe the importance of relief work to how Quakers viewed themselves in this period, and also that the legacy of their approaches and practices has endured to the present. The challenges of grappling with the demands of modern war, of implementing new approaches to poverty and of reckoning with the upheaval of a 'Quaker Renaissance' in theology all underpinned Quaker relief in this period. For Quakers, as for others in the late nineteenth century, relief work became an arena in which wider ideas and identities were forged and contested.

Moral progress or condemned to repeat?

In recent years, much has been written about the unlooked-for consequences of modern relief work, or the 'paradox of humanitarian action', to quote the title of one of the most lucid books on this topic. Its author, Fiona Terry, has analysed the con-tribution that foreign aid can make to the fighting strength of a belligerent, whether a state or ethnic group.[15] In fact, qualms as to the wider ramifications of relief work

---

[15] Fiona Terry, *Condemned to Repeat? The Paradox of Humanitarian Action*, Cornell University Press, London, 2002.

existed from the foundation of the first permanent relief organisations, and were part-and-parcel of their origins. Florence Nightingale, for example, argued that the voluntary provision of medical aid diluted the state's responsibility to the wounded. The British National Society for Aid to the Sick and Wounded in War (NAS, forerunner of the British Red Cross) was itself not insensible to these issues. In 1871, following its first relief mission to the battlefields of the Franco-Prussian War, it ruminated whether

> the benevolent efforts of neutrals in relieving so large an amount of suffering [have] been instrumental in freeing combatants from these difficulties? . . . The Geneva Convention was intended solely for the relief of suffering. It was never intended to add a new element of efficiency to armies, still less to aid the victor. It appears doubtful whether it has not led to all three results.[16]

These anxieties, though never prominent, persisted. Following fresh outcry over the persecution of Christians in the Ottoman Empire in the early 1920s, the historian Arnold J. Toynbee complained about the preferential nature of such concern. The results of such selectivity were disastrous, he argued, for in 'giving way to moral indignation', the public was inclined to forget that in a plural population, 'the liberation of one Christian from Moslem rule' not only involves 'the subjection and oppression of ten Moslems on the spot' but often 'the massacre of two Christians at a distance' in revenge.[17]

As Terry herself points out, such paradoxes cannot be treated solely as the outcome of modern relief operations in 'complex' wars. Wars have never been simple, nor were aid operations ever straightforward.[18] Nevertheless, the consequences of moral outcries and relief work – in any period – are difficult to assess. Did they 'render war more easy', as Nightingale worried, or unwittingly endorse ethnic nationalism, as Toynbee alleged?[19] Moreover, was the tally of lives saved here but ruined elsewhere, as Toynbee suggested, a sufficient or practical moral calculus; and to what extent was the relief worker to be held responsible in such circumstances? These predicaments are notoriously hard to resolve. Significantly, however, the nineteenth- and early twentieth-century relief worker rarely experienced them as a paradox. Why? Take, for example, Emily Hobhouse. Having exposed the levels of civilian distress in British concentration camps during the Boer War, she was disappointed to find South African politicians turning her testimony of Boer suffering to political account in an era of escalating Afrikaner nationalism.[20] Yet, whatever the

---

[16] NAS, *Report* (Franco-Prussian War), p. 175.

[17] Arnold J. Toynbee, *The Western Question in Greece and Turkey: A Study in the Contact of Civilisations*, Constable & Co., London, 1922, p. 91.

[18] Fiona Terry, 'Humanitarian Action: Victim of Its Own Success?', *The Humanitarian Decade: Challenges for Humanitarian Assistance in the Last Decade and into the Future*, Vol. II, United Nations Office for the Coordination of Humanitarian Affairs, 2004, pp. 42–45.

[19] Florence Nightingale, quoted in Hutchinson, *Champions of Charity*, p. 350.

[20] Liz Stanley, *Mourning becomes . . . Post/Memory, Commemoration and the Concentration Camps of the South African War*, Manchester University Press, Manchester, 2006, p. 81.

unlooked-for consequences, she never regretted her interventions.[21] She remained confident that her work constituted the moral vanguard; by example, she trusted, others would follow her elevated lead.

A similar confidence permeates other contemporary accounts; indeed, their considerable aplomb amounts to a defining feature. This was, in part, a confidence grounded in class, the *habitus* of a social elite long used to occupying a role of authority and moral leadership, and to assuming that its values ought to be replicated and exported to those less fortunate. Thus is detectable the *noblesse oblige* of the 'lady bountiful', convinced that her work was beneficial and improving. But more than this, there existed a cosmic confidence in the inevitability of moral progress and the pre-eminent role of Western civilisation in improving the fortunes of others, and here aid agencies and their representatives considered themselves at the fore. Whatever the unlooked-for consequences of aid, we find faith that relief would exemplify the brotherliness and compassion which would tame the spirits of war, temper cruelty and exploitation and foster world peace.

Today within the social elites which still tend to dominate relief organisations a confident assurance in the possibility of doing good still abounds, as does conviction that there exists a moral duty toward suffering strangers. Nevertheless, the twentieth century's 'total' wars and genocides (with the Rwandan genocide operating as a particular watershed), external critiques from journalists and academics and a rapidly professionalising aid sector have all contributed to greater self-reflexivity and a fundamental challenge to such cosmic progressivism.[22] The work of Fiona Terry is a case in point. Since the 1960s and 1970s, this has been coupled with a realisation that non-Western societies appear resilient to the export and replication of Western values and practices, and that assumptions about the inevitability of mono-linear 'development' are ill founded. The assumption of cumulative progress in which the West would be model and vanguard has thus been questioned (if not obliterated). So too has that unshakeable Victorian confidence that the relief worker had a role in the transformative evolution of humane sensibilities to the point where all human cruelty and suffering would evaporate and armed conflict be civilised to the point of anachronism. As baldly put by one International Committee of the Red Cross (ICRC) official in Rwanda, '[w]e work in the context of war, and there will always be war'.[23] In the light of this newly austere realism, it is not surprising that the

[21] Ryrie Van Renan (ed.), *Emily Hobhouse: Boer War Letters*, Human & Rousseau, Cape Town, 1984, p. 31; Ruth Fry, *Emily Hobhouse: A Memoir*, Foreword by General Right Hon. J. C. Smuts, Jonathan Cape, London, 1929, pp. 162–163.

[22] For example, former president of Médecins Sans Frontières (France) Jean-Hervé Bradol speaks of the need to overcome the 'illusion that humanity is inexorably progressing toward an ideal society', for in the name of the 'common good' it allows for the 'sacrifice' of certain peoples in need and prevents humanitarian organisations from recognising their fundamental duty to 'save as many lives as possible', 'The Sacrificial International Order and Humanitarian Action', in Fabrice Weissman (ed.), *In the Shadow of 'Just Wars': Violence, Politics and Humanitarian Action*, Cornell University Press, Ithaca, NY, 2004, p. 21.

[23] Unattributed quote in David Rieff, *A Bed for the Night: Humanitarianism in Crisis*, Vintage, London, 2002, p. 323.

unwelcome consequences of 'doing good' have now made themselves felt as dilemmas less readily subsumed by the greater good. To quote Terry once again, it is recognised that 'at an intrinsic and practical level, the paradoxes of humanitarian action will persist': that aid agencies are, to some extent, 'condemned to repeat'.[24]

Histories of relief work: lineages and legacies

Today, responses to these dilemmas are far from consistent, as would be expected in a field that is diverse and at times disputatious. Many have called upon the authority of history in an attempt to resolve them. Fiona Terry's methodical use of historical case studies is relatively rare. On the basis of her computation of the exploitation of aid from the Cold War onwards, she argues for a 'vigilant' ethic by which relief agencies withdraw when aid does more harm than good. This would better serve the ideal 'that people should not suffer' and the 'conviction that all people have equal rights by virtue of their membership in humanity', including 'protection' of life.[25] This is criticised by those for whom humanitarian imperatives dictate that saving life must come first. To do otherwise and withdraw aid is, in the words of Hugo Slim, 'doing evil that good may come'.[26]

Terry is not alone in appealing to history to argue for the ideals of relief work to be reclaimed or reconfigured. In many of these accounts, the presence of a consistent, foundational humanitarian ideal runs like a golden thread, linking early relief ventures to those of the present. This tendency is most commonly found in institutional histories whose authors celebrate its gradual unfurling to new areas of concern, from soldiers in the nineteenth century to refugees, children and maimed civilians in the twentieth.[27] However, to some observers this golden thread has become tarnished in recent decades. They point in particular to relief agencies' involvement in political advocacy and their yoking to a human rights agenda as clouding the purity of their initial vision of saving life first. These, they claim, leave relief organisations open to manipulation by states which, unwilling to risk military involvement, maintain credibility by endorsing humanitarian relief efforts. For David Rieff, a prominent media commentator on such issues, the humanitarian ideal of 'human solidarity' and 'of helping people when they most desperately need help' is best served by a return to the principled neutrality of the Swiss-born Henri Dunant and the ICRC in Geneva.[28] Dunant is remembered now for *Un Souvenir de Solferino*, his recollection of impromptu relief efforts on the Lombardy battlefields

[24] Terry, *Condemned to Repeat?*, p. 224.

[25] *Ibid.*, pp. 233–234, 240, 244, 245.

[26] Quoted in *ibid.*, p. 206.

[27] For example, Anon., *The Ceaseless Challenge: Souvenir of the Red Cross Centenary 1863–1963*, [The Society], London, 1963; Dame Beryl Oliver, *The British Red Cross in Action*, Faber and Faber, London, 1966. See the work of John F. Hutchinson for a critical attempt to rewrite this narrative, in particular his *Champions of Charity*.

[28] Rieff, *A Bed for the Night*, p. 27.

in 1859. He was one of the main instigators behind the international conferences at which the 1864 Geneva Convention was eventually signed. Dunant thus assumes the place of a 'founding father', while *Un Souvenir de Solferino* and the Geneva Convention amount to the Red Cross movement's sacred texts, 'establish[ing] the legitimacy of a neutral third party on the battlefield – the aid givers'.[29] Rieff concludes his account with a plea for the restoration of the clarity of Dunant's vision.

Yet retracing the golden thread to the time of Dunant and the signing of the Geneva Convention brings us face to face not with the purity of single-minded purpose but, rather, with multiple creeds and various interpretations of neutrality and impartiality. The British case also suggests the extent to which the ICRC and the Geneva Convention were but minor influences on the shaping of aid practices and the new vocation of relief work. The 1864 Geneva Convention explicitly did not contain reference to voluntary aid organisations (despite Rieff's assertion to the contrary). This was ensured by the role of British representatives at the preliminary conferences in Geneva who were keen to protect the regular army medical services from interference. Some measure of British disdain is captured in confidential reports written by delegates at later International Conferences of Red Cross Societies. Here, the ICRC was characterised as an 'irresponsible Committee of Swiss gentlemen' who 'perform no function that is of real importance'.[30] This was not the only view, of course, though interestingly it was held by most members of the executive of the NAS and its successor, the British Red Cross, for whom contact with the ICRC in this period was minimal and at arm's length. Those who did take a more idealistic view of the laws of war as heralding a new era of international co-operation were usually derided as sentimental cranks, or 'Utopian fanatics' as another confidential British briefing put it.[31]

Dunant's *Un Souvenir de Solferino* was not available in English translation until 1947. Early histories of the British Red Cross attributed the Society's origins as much to Florence Nightingale as to Henri Dunant (ironic, in some respects, given her scepticism of Dunant's scheme of voluntary aid on the battlefield, but in other respects unwittingly accurate once her attempt to imprint her own vision upon the NAS is known). In Britain, few early relief workers made mention of Dunant in their memoirs.[32] More influential was the legacy of medical failings in the Crimean War, of which the first Chair of the NAS, Lt Col Robert Loyd Lindsay V.C., had direct and unhappy experience. It is only in later histories that Dunant was canonised as a founding father. Here he was retrospectively accorded a visionary role and was held

---

[29] *Ibid.*, p. 69.

[30] Confidential Report on the Seventh International Conference of Red Cross Societies, 1902, p. 27, TNA, Foreign Office, Ardagh papers, PRO 30/40/3.

[31] Major General Ardagh to Senator Sir James Gowan, 29.7.1899, TNA, Foreign Office, Ardagh papers, PRO 30/40/3.

[32] A. K. Loyd *An Outline of the History of the British Red Cross Society from its Foundation in 1870 to the Outbreak of the War in 1914*, [The Society], London, 1917, p. 6; Mary Francis Billington, *The Red Cross in War: Woman's Part in the Relief of Suffering*, Hodder and Stoughton, London, 1914, p. 21.

to have promulgated the universalist ideal of a much later generation: of 'organiz[ing] human kindness to deal with all human suffering wherever it may be found', as the introduction to the 1947 English translation of *Un Souvenir de Solferino* had it.[33] When, today, we are exhorted to recapture Dunant's spirit of neutrality and the universality of his vision, it is important too to remember that the Red Cross was but one of several new aid organisations established at this time. Some, such as those of the Religious Society of Friends, or those founded to provide aid in the Balkans and South Africa, understood the impartial distribution of relief and the non-partisan nature of their endeavours to be fully compatible with advocacy of other commitments, whether pacifism, interventionism or vocal championing of the rights and duties of humanity. The golden thread thus has a tendency to unravel. Attention to these tangled origins allows us to contextualise current assertions and debates and to inquire into the genuinely novel aspects of today's field of relief. Indeed, it is the very thing that is strikingly novel – the premise of a shared humanitarian ideal, universal in its conception of a duty towards all sufferers in all war and disaster – that is often and erroneously assumed to be foundational.

Moreover, when allusions to the purity of past ideals are invoked to further present-day polemic this can tend to obscure the complex legacy of more workaday assumption and practice. This book's central purpose is to bring to the fore these long-standing, if neglected, vocational practices and habits of mind, and inquire into both their origin and their contemporary relevance. For today's relief projects do not simply echo those of the past; rather, they are part of a continuous fabric, an inherited iconography of suffering and the conventions of humane response upon which the urgency of ameliorative action is grounded. If the archetypal twenty-first-century subjects of fund-raising campaigns resemble their nineteenth-century forebears in both their passivity and gendered innocence, this is not surprising, given that such representations have permeated our culture, in text and vision, for well over a century, the only difference being that they are much more likely today to be black than white.[34] The association of innocence with such images is so pervasive that it conditions the mind-set of relief workers, who are, for example, less likely to treat women as potential perpetrators of violence. In the name of doing good, this imperative to intervene in order to save innocents replicates those found in colonial and nineteenth-century philanthropic contexts. However, the very notion of urgency, so central to the vocation of relief work, can tend to preclude any consideration of these historical continuities and, with them, the moral implications of such habits of mind. The immediacy of the pull upon an 'instinctual pity', and frantic responses to periodic emergency, seen simply as the practical administration of compassion, thus appear timeless.

[33] Major General Sir John Kennedy, Introduction in H. Dunant, *A Memoir of Solferino*, Cassell & Co., Ltd., London, 1947, unpaginated.

[34] Erica Burman, 'Poor Children: Charity Appeals and Ideologies of Childhood', *Changes: Journal of Psychology and Psychotherapy*, Vol. 12, 1994, 29–36.

And yet, repetitive images of undifferentiated suffering may mean that aid agencies struggle to maintain the appropriate attention for their causes. Thus, for example, in cases where abject suffering is used to publicly address political crimes, physical amelioration can deflect from political injury. Whether this then leads some to inflate impressions of suffering to 'emergency' levels was, as will be seen, to trouble relief workers during the 1899–1902 South African War, and continues to do so today. Meanwhile, those deemed not to be in crisis, or lacking full membership of humanity to appear less abject in their suffering, may miss out. Another implication of these customary behaviours is that, in some cases, they have been learnt equally by recipient as by donor. Looking at strategies used to secure aid, war correspondent Linda Polman resolutely rejects the image of recipients as passive entities. Though overlooking just how long lived such images are, she shows how some recipients are adept at managing their self-presentation to conform to Western expectations of suffering and helpless innocence.

> They've had more than half a century to study and test the mechanisms that prompt the Western aid world to act. Victims' groups are increasingly likely to have a highly developed understanding of how the humanitarian aid world works . . . Most refugee camps have televisions that can pick up CNN, so refugees see how 'we' portray victims.[35]

These stereotypes fulfil the Western prophesy of rescuing innocents, fortifying aid relationships which have changed little since the nineteenth century. They also cast into doubt the extent to which impartiality based on a genuine assessment of need alone, so central to relief workers' ethos and to their legitimacy, is achievable. For all the stress on ethical clarity urged, in their different ways, by Terry and Rieff, a *habitus* which consistently prioritises the donor's ethical position and relies upon representational strategies which risk compromising knowledge of human need defies Terry's call for a 'free exchange and dialogue' between aid agencies and populations in distress.[36] There is also a fundamental question pertaining to the influence of ethics on practice. While not wishing to call into question the validity of their ethical positions – which are self-consciously modest in their attempt to adjust to a 'second-best-world' – faith in the influence of ethical rigour to minimise the unlooked-for consequences of relief work has to be weighed against the influence of institutional prerogatives and customary behaviours. Just as a history of religion could never be limited to the study of theology alone, a history of relief work needs to go beyond ethics and ideals, to consider relief workers' own sense of purpose, the very various interpretation of first principle and the accumulation of unwritten convention and practices, as well as the diversity of responses by intended beneficiaries. Then, as now, the meaning of ideals and mandates differed within and between central and local committees, temporary hired staff and volunteers. The new field of

---

[35] Linda Polman, *War Games: The Story of Aid and War in Modern Times*, Viking, London, 2010, p. 146.
[36] Terry, *Condemned to Repeat?*, p. 243.

relief work to emerge in the nineteenth century was shaped as much by the mixed considerations of publicity and ideas of propriety, of philanthropic sentiment and 'scientific' efficiency, and by external challenges and pressures, as by a set of consistent values. Relief work was never simply the instrumentalisation of a shared ideal, nor can unlooked-for consequences be addressed by an appeal for ethical clarity alone.

A history of relief practices: an outline of sources and structure

If it is instructive to pay attention to the origins of relief work as a vocation in more depth, then new sources are required and old ones need to be returned to in new ways. Conceived as a rapid, organised but temporary response to a shortfall in existing provision or to a disruption to the normal means of subsistence, relief work turned upon the virtues of adaptability and innovation. An ethos of urgency, improvisation and self-sacrificing endurance quickly emerged. This was not always conducive to scrupulous record keeping. On the other hand, notions of account-ability – to self, to one's organisation and to donors – could give rise to carefully crafted statistical reports and personal accounts, the 'on the hoof' style of which lent a certain authenticity – and authority. Institutional archives contain many such reports, alongside committee minutes, correspondence and personal testimony, all of which provide insight into relief workers' practice and perceptions. The archives of the BRCS and the Library of the Society of Friends in London have been central to the writing of this book. Here can be discovered the administrative meticulous-ness of the Quaker's account to a domestic committee and the untiring 'watchful-ness' of the self as they encountered war, every minute spent profitably in bringing nearer the Kingdom of God on earth. Read aloud and circulated at Quaker meetings such accounts prompted further donations and emulations. Meanwhile, the reports of the BRCS, and its forerunner, the NAS, imitate government blue books, full of statistical renderings of relief operations and endorsements by members of the military hierarchy. Frequently, however, when placed alongside collections of personal letters by Red Cross personnel, we find this carefully crafted impression of proficiency and official blessing undercut.

Fund-raising and recruitment literature as well as the published recollections of individual relief workers demonstrate that this was a sphere of endeavour shaped as much by words and images as by frenetic deeds. Unsurprisingly, given the high number of aspirant writers to volunteer themselves, aid work was often styled a response to the human condition which required empathetic qualities and refined sensibilities. Tropes from picturesque travel writings infused many Victorian accounts. Later, literary relief workers of the Great War would aspire to a spare modernism.[37] Whether purposefully – and certainly some writers were acknowledged

---

[37] See Angela Smith, *The Second Battlefield: Women, Modernism and the First World War*, Manchester University Press, Manchester, 2000.

publicists – or unintentionally, one effect was to open up an imaginative vista which made relief in war and empire cognoscible and appealing. In Wilkie Colllins' tale of the redemptive power of Red Cross work in *The New Magdalen*, or in the evocative depiction of her 'dear little bell tent' by real-life nurse Dosia Bagot, relief work in these accounts became an edifying test of the self, for some spiritually purifying perhaps, but also romantic and glamorous.[38]

For the professional nursing lobby, however, these products of the 'enterprising society woman's pen' seemed yet further evidence of the dilettantism of the 'lady amateur'.[39] Certainly, it is worth stressing that the field of relief work emerged in close and not always harmonious connection with the professionalisation of nursing, as well as army reform and controversial theological transformations. Investigating these literary, professional and religious cross-currents therefore requires a wide range of sources, from popular travelogues to religious tracts, and from nursing journals to government inquiries. But, in a certain sense, relief work had its own quintessential character, mystique even, something derived from the adrenaline and camaraderie of war and its intimation of human extremes and, as such, resistant to purely theoretical training. As Red Cross advocate Sir James Cantlie remarked, 'How was first aid to be learned? Not at the hospitals. No surgeon in a hospital was a first-aider unless he had learned it outside . . . And what had first-aiders to do? The great charm about it all was that they had to learn to improvise everything.' Thus, should one find oneself lacking bandages: '[t]he ashes of a burnt handkerchief were necessarily sterilised and made excellent dressings'.[40] This was an ethos that could not be taught, it was said. But, by the time of First World War, such were the demands for a supply of efficient voluntary paramedics and amateur nurses that the disciplining of intuition became an imperative. With this came the rise of the relief workers' 'etiquette guide', in which the proprieties of the aid relationship were enumerated. With their strictures on dress code and deference to one's superiors, the historian is bequeathed one source of how heart was thought best subjected to head.

This book owes a number of intellectual debts to the scholarship of others, in particular to John F. Hutchinson's work on the early days of the Red Cross movement, Anne Summers's study of women's participation in the military nursing services, Eugenio Biagini's history of the idea of humanity and its place in British politics and Martti Koskenniemi's history of nineteenth-century international law. Together, archival sources and these historical monographs provide insight into relief ventures in a series of armed conflicts: in France (1870–71), in the Ottoman Empire (1876–78) and in British colonial wars in the Sudan (1883–84) and South

[38] Wilkie Collins, *The New Magdalen*, Sutton Publishing, Stroud, 2001 [1873]; Dosia Bagot, *Shadows of the War*, Edward Arnold, London, 1900, p. 35.

[39] The quote is taken from *The Nursing Record*, Vol. XXIV, No. 627, 7.7.1900.

[40] *Nursing Times*, 5.2.1914, cutting in Wellcome Library, Sir James Cantlie papers, MS7922/13.

Africa (1899–1902). A brief glance is cast forward to the Great War and beyond. These conflicts form both the chronology and the structure of the book, which is divided into three parts, each of which dwells on a particular facet of aid work, while also revealing continuities and connections across the period as a whole. Thus, what have previously been studied as distinct interventions are brought together to disclose wider networks, emergent practices and concerns.[41] Of course, an exclusive focus on war relief itself obscures a further level of interconnectedness, and, for reasons of space, this book does not cover peace-time disasters, civilian first aid, missionary activities and campaigns over colonial atrocities. This, then, is a fractional history, consciously so, because it makes no claim to be an all-encompassing history of relief work in war time or peace, and eschews the possibility of detecting the origins of a singular 'humanitarian ideal'. Instead, it delineates something else: idealism and conviction, certainly, but also rivalry and backbiting, historical contingency and the play of external pressure and influence.

The first part of this book explores the inauguration of the NAS at the outbreak of the Franco-Prussian War in 1870 under the figurehead of Loyd Lindsay, a well-connected Crimean veteran thought dashing by his admirers and a perennial liability by his detractors. At the fore of his critics stood the dogged but always diplomatic Sir John Furley and his associates at the Order of St John (Furley's criticisms did not stand in the way of cordial relations or Furley's employment as an NAS commissioner). The commencement of the Franco-Prussian War also saw the foundation of a Friends War Victims' Relief Fund (FWVRF), dedicated to ameliorating civilian distress and established by Quakers as a deliberate alternative to voluntary aid to soldiers. In this war Britain remained neutral, but in cabinet discussion and the pages of the press Gladstone advocated participation on the grounds of upholding the Public Law of Europe – significant because this saw him advocate the 'moral interventionism' with which he would later be identified and in the virtue of which certain relief agencies of the period concurred. Chapter 1 explores the origins of the Geneva Convention and British negotiations over its final form, stressing the legacy of the Crimean War on British attempts to reform the welfare of the common soldier. Turning then, on the one hand, to the news of suffering coming from France via a press eager to chase military hospital scandals and, on the other hand, to some of the domestic anxieties and concerns of the year 1870, it considers the factors determining the priorities of aid agencies at work in the Franco-Prussian War. Chapter 2 traces the delivery of aid by the NAS and FWVRF in France and their experimental introduction of rapid-response medicine and attempts at 'self help' among the peasantry. Examining the personal recollections of relief workers, it

---

[41] For agitation over Armenia see Akaby Nassibian, *Britain and the Armenian Question 1915–1923*, St. Martin's Press, New York, 1984; for Bulgaria see Richard Shannon, *Gladstone and the Bulgarian Agitation 1876*, Thomas Nelson & Sons Ltd., London, 1963 and Ann Pottinger Saab, *Reluctant Icon: Gladstone, Bulgaria and the Working Classes, 1876–1878*, Harvard University Press, Cambridge, MA, 1991; for protests over the South African War, see Arthur Davey, *The British Pro-Boers, 1877–1902*, Tafelberg, Cape Town, 1978.

considers how they imbued their new vocation with meaning as a benevolent but rational form of intervention, often in the face of hostility and suspicion.

Part II sees the revival of the NAS for work in the Balkans during a period of nationalist violence and Ottoman counter-insurgency which culminated in the Russo-Turkish War of 1877–78. Here a hesitant NAS was joined once again by the Quakers, as well as by a number of temporary relief agencies directed and staffed by individuals familiar with the terrain and sympathetic, more often than not, to the cause of the insurgents. The advocacy of 'moral interventionism' in the Ottoman Empire, both military and philanthropic, had political ramifications not only in the Balkans but also at home, where Gladstone's dramatic invocation of a brotherhood of humanity sought to capture and mould the people's 'moral interests'. Chapter 3 analyses how, as part of wider networks of affiliation and concern, these relief workers competed to present knowledge of suffering in a region little known in Britain, helping to shape impressions of 'aggressor' and 'victim' that would inform one of the era's biggest political convulsions: the 'Bulgarian atrocities' agitation. In doing so, they put 'Bulgaria' on the map, if only as an administrative district for relief, but in consequence recognising Christian nationalist claims to autonomy and the Russian *casus belli*. Notions of historic Christian nations suppressed by Turkish despotism and of a natural antipathy between the region's Muslims, Christians and Jews informed the scope of these relief ventures, but alienated some at home from a brotherhood of humanity that they perceived as extending full membership only to Christians. Chapter 4 focuses on the delivery of aid and the politics of administering relief to civilians, refugees and soldiers in this region of insurgency and state violence, considering some of the various and contested understandings of neutrality that ensued.

The final part of this book follows the staff of relief committees as they dispensed aid in British colonial wars. Chapter 5 examines the critiques of British policy in the Boer War (1899–1902) emanating from intersecting circles of Quakers, New Liberals and ethicists, and considers these groups' offer of aid to Boer civilians. Inspired by Gladstone's vision of an ethical polity founded on the duty to protect the right of humanity to self-determination, and committed to international co-operation, these turn-of-the-century progressives were concerned to give genuine representation to the people's moral interests at home and abroad, free of the warping effects of corruption, drink, want and oppression. Where they differed from Gladstone was in the conviction that an ethical polity would be realised though 'scientific' human-itarianism: objective study of the laws of human society would provide both surer basis for intervention to alleviate its wants and greater reason in public affairs. Where some also departed was in their conviction that genuine representation of the people's moral interests must also include women. Progressive women in Britain launched an attack upon the war's conduct and argued that remedying women's political exclusion would help to tame the spirits of war. Kate Courtney, Emily Hobhouse and Barbara Bradby inaugurated a relief mission to aid their Boer 'sisters' and forge a model of empathy and friendly co-operation. This saw an intensification of an association between female compassion, women's suffrage and the delivery of overseas aid which would, with different emphases, become a salient feature of the field of relief.

Chapter 6 concentrates on the methodologies – and controversies – of relief for Boer inmates of British concentration camps in South Africa and on the implications of this relief for its intended recipients during and after the war. Though viewed sympathetically by Quaker communities at home, this work clashed, on occasion, with that of individual Quaker relief workers. But controversy flared most publicly when Emily Hobhouse came into conflict with Millicent Garrett Fawcett and the 'Ladies Committee' charged with reporting on conditions in the camps. The chapter ends with British relief workers' segregation of concern in South Africa and with consideration of Hobhouse's Boer Home Industries scheme, her work of 'reconstruction' following the end of the war. Here some of the racial, class and gender assumptions that underpinned Hobhouse's emancipatory project come into focus.

The final chapter concentrates on aid to British soldiers. It commences with the attempt to rescue Gordon in the Sudan, dwelling on the troubling nature of press publicity that ensued, as well as the professional jealousy of the army medical services and internal fissures within the voluntary aid movement. These continued with the creation of a BRCS, which in 1905 subsumed the NAS to become part of the anti-invasion preparations of the Edwardian period. This chapter concludes with analysis of a newly feminised Red Cross, considered in terms both of the preponderant number of female recruits and of the popular maternal image of the organisation found in fiction, Voluntary Aid Detachment (VAD) 'etiquette guides' and fund-raising posters. This feminisation contributed to a profitable ambiguity which obscured the shift towards an increasingly militarised British Red Cross, while keeping alive traditions of intuitive, voluntary service. This book closes by tracing continuities in vocational practices and dispositions to emerging areas of concern in the post-war period, in particular child welfare, and briefly considers their implication for relief work today.

Part I

A new vocation:
British relief in war – France, 1870–71

1

The origins of British relief in war

A memorial watercolour commemorates Lieut Col Robert Loyd Lindsay's service during the Franco-Prussian War.[1] Straight-backed, golden-haired and imposing, Loyd Lindsay strides away from a gutted house, his soldierly bearing conferred by long and distinguished service in the British army. At first glance, one would assume that he was on campaign. Closer scrutiny reveals the blue 'undress' uniform of a British officer, his red sash worn over the left shoulder to indicate that he is not on active service, and a red cross adorning a flag where one might have expected a military standard. For this painting marked a novel kind of battlefield valour: the provision of neutral relief to the sick and wounded. The epitome of nobility to his admirers (some thought him a latter-day King Arthur), Loyd Lindsay stood proudly at the helm of a new organisation, the British National Society for Aid to the Sick and Wounded in War.

Established on the day that war was declared between Prussia and France, the NAS claimed allegiance to the newly signed Geneva Convention of 1864. Under its aegis, Loyd Lindsay and his fellow volunteers, many of them champions of military reform at home, sought to provide roving medical assistance to soldiers of each side, predicated upon an impartial assessment of need and irrespective of the recipient's nationality. The NAS was not, however, the only British organisation proffering aid in war-torn France that year, though it was to prove one of the most enduring. It was joined by a newly established and similarly long-lived Quaker agency, the FWVRF – devoted to the relief of the civilian population – and a host of temporary funds which formed and disbanded over the course of the war.

To understand why foreign soldiers and French civilians were considered worthy subjects of organised relief, some background is needed, both to events in Britain in the year 1870 and to some more long-standing anxieties and concerns. Of particular

---

[1] Painted by war artist Robert Thomas Landells. Landells was commissioned by the *London Illustrated News* to cover the Franco-Prussian War. He combined this with service with the Prussian Red Cross in the winter campaign in the Loire.

1 Watercolour painting by Robert Thomas Landells depicting Colonel Robert Loyd Lindsay, chairman of the British National Society for Aid to the Sick and Wounded in War and Mr Whittle, both on foot, at Versailles.

importance was the intersection of movements for 'civilising' warfare through the codification of international law and the legacies of medical failings in the Crimean War (1853–56). For it was here that new sites of intervention began to be postulated, not least by newspaper correspondents buoyed by their success in the Crimea and eager for the next circulation-boosting hospital scandal. Many of those involved in the NAS were themselves veterans of the Crimean debacle. For Sir Thomas Longmore, leading military surgeon of the day and the British government's delegate to the conferences at which the Geneva Convention was negotiated, these deficiencies had stimulated a lifelong interest in improving medico-military efficiency. It had also made him wary of interference by well-intentioned amateurs. His objectives were therefore rather circumscribed in comparison to the expansive hopes of the conveners of the Geneva conferences, who, confident that they were distilling the humane essence of Western civilisation, wished to see a formal role in war accorded to the civilian volunteer.

All this, of course, left cold many of those Quakers explicitly opposed to the principle of providing relief to soldiers. It was no coincidence that 1870 saw the intensification of Quakers' previous efforts in war relief. The FWVRF was conceived as a sally at the Red Cross movement, but it also came at a time when Quakers were publicly accused of introspection and complacency – criticisms which would soon be heard emanating from within Quaker circles. In time, relief work became an important way of enacting renewed theological and ethical commitment, and one of the defining Quaker testimonies against war. In parliament, meanwhile, the possibility of a moral intervention in the Franco-Prussian War was echoed by the prime minister, though this was unpopular, and, when subsequently Gladstone declared the country neutral, the dispatch of medical supplies represented the extent of British involvement on the battlefield.

Over the course of 1870–71, a nascent field of war-time relief began to emerge, one which saw divergent outlooks between – and within – organisations as to the function and morality of aid in war. Whatever the idealist interpretation of international law as the 'spirit' of western civilisation, or the technical delimitation of scope imposed by the medico-military establishment, here amidst the battlefields and siege towns of France a flourishing voluntary aid movement arose with little affiliation to Geneva or the regular medical services and a perennially ambivalent notion of neutrality. Another significant feature was already in evidence, for the Franco-Prussian War displayed well the tangled relationship between the new breed of investigative reporter and the pioneering relief worker. Relief work, then, was never simply a practical response to news of suffering, nor merely an embodiment of legal protocols, but arose in part from existing preoccupations and concerns. This takes us to the early days of August 1870 and anxieties over Gladstone's handling of military restructuring, on the one hand, and criticism of the Quakers over the Education Act, on the other. For it was in response to these immediate anxieties that British men and women first journeyed to France to deliver relief.

Wounded soldiers, international law and the legacy of the Crimea

While risk of injury has always been part of the fortunes of war, the late nineteenth century saw, simultaneously, a surge in the effectiveness and status of medico-military arrangements and the ascension of the suffering of the common soldier into a moral cause. It would, of course, be easy to follow the lead of institutional histories, such as those written to celebrate the work of the Red Cross, and see this as a triumph of Western civilisation and, in particular, the vision of one man, the Swiss champion of battlefield philanthropy, Henri Dunant. Certainly Dunant's role in drafting proposals for the impartial treatment of the wounded in war, which would – after substantial negotiation – become the text of the first Geneva Convention, should not be overlooked. Dunant was author of a slim book called *Un Souvenir de Solferino* (1862) and had devoted himself to winning accord for its proposal for greater voluntary aid in times of war. In its pages, Dunant recounted his horror at witnessing the fate of soldiers left to die for want of adequate care after the 1859 battle between the Austrian and French armies at Solferino. Taking inspiration from the local Piedmont women who had tended French and Austrian soldiers without thought of nationality, he proposed the formation of voluntary agencies for the amelioration of wounded troops:

> Would it not be possible, in time of peace and quiet, to form relief societies for the purpose of having care given to the wounded in wartime by zealous, devoted and thoroughly qualified volunteers?[2]

In 1862, Dunant had approached the Geneva Society for Public Utility for assistance in realising his vision of battlefield chivalry. The Society's chairman, Gustave Moynier, a lawyer by training but wealthy enough to bypass the bar and devote himself to philanthropic good works and academic law, convened a conference in 1863 to discuss Dunant's proposals. He then facilitated the congress at which the final text of the Geneva Convention was signed. But, however cogent their ideal of battlefield philanthropy, it would have had little effect had it been ignored by European governments. After all, unsolicited proclamations and resolutions regarding charitable hobbyhorses were two-a-penny, and calls for war-time wounded to be rendered neutral and succoured by volunteers were not unique. The question, therefore, is why a voluntary code concerning the protection and care of wounded soldiers achieved widespread accord at this particular juncture. Indeed, of all the directives issued by the international law fraternity in this era – and this was a period of increasing activity in this regard – the Geneva Convention and other laws of war were the only ones formally acceded to by the Great Powers. To understand this widespread acquiescence, it is necessary to place the signing of the Geneva Convention within the context of medico-military concerns and, for the British, of

---

[2] Dunant, *Un Souvenir de Solferino*, quoted in Hutchinson, *Champions of Charity*, p. 18.

the particular interest in this issue that followed the Crimean War. But it is necessary first to understand something of the workings and assumptions of international lawyers in this period.

International law was undergoing a transformation at this time in both its professional practices and its premises. The optimistic consensus that international law was an irresistible force of civilisation reached its apogee in the period 1870–1914.[3] This buoyant outlook found increased coherence in new professional institutes and journals and drew in sympathetic barristers and legal academics, such as the British lawyer John Westlake.[4] It is important to understand the meaning of 'law' for these professionals, for it was not equivalent to the rules of a sovereign state, nor was transgression subject to sanction. Rather, akin to the 'laws of nature', 'law' here referred to observable phenomena and their correct codification, derived, in this instance, from discerning inquiry into the characteristics of contemporary Western society. The basis of international law thus rested on the erudition of its practitioners to capture the Hegelian spirit of Western civilisation and to standardise it in coherent form. Thus was offered the possibility of a rational, Europe-wide code to replace national discrepancies. How was this spirit to be adduced? Not, as in the natural sciences, by experiment or vast programmes of classification, nor by reference to extant treatises or diplomatic conventions, but by 'scientific' contemplation of the jurist's own conscience as the exemplar of progressive public opinion. After all, international lawyers, devoted to such enlightened goals, were surely at the forefront of civilisation and the best indicators of its values.[5]

'In external law it is science, or rather the conscience of humanity that is the source, the tribunal and the sanction of positive law', proclaimed one of the most prominent lawyers of the period.[6] In this sense, international law was self-determining, and it is no surprise to find that its adherents were ardent supporters of national liberation to ensure the most authentic expression of a people's spirit, and with it a surer basis of law. Nonetheless, there were parameters to such expansive aspirations. The popularity of evolutionary theory was in evidence in lawyers' assumptions that Europe had progressed further than other, more barbarous regions, and likewise evinced a more advanced spirit. International law was the manifestation of Western civilisation and could not necessarily be applied elsewhere. In practice, however, the boundaries of Europe were far from agreed. The universality of Natural Law, which

---

[3] Casper Sylvest, 'The Foundation of Victorian International law', in Duncan Bell (ed.), *Victorian Visions of the Global Order: Empire and International Relations in Nineteenth-Century Political Thought*, Cambridge University Press, Cambridge, 2007, p. 52.

[4] John Westlake (1828–1913) was barrister at Lincoln's Inn, and from 1887 Whewell Professor of International Law at Cambridge. He was a member of the British government's 'Balkan Committee', 1905–13.

[5] The following discussion of international law is indebted to Martii Koskenniemi, *The Gentle Civilizer of Nations: The Rise and Fall of International Law 1870–1960*, Cambridge University Press, Cambridge, 2001, pp. 51–55.

[6] Rolin-Jaequemyns, 'De l'étude de la legislation comparée et de droit international', quoted in *ibid.*, p. 16.

had earlier dominated, and which had allowed for all to be included in its province, gave way to a hierarchical exclusivity: international law was international to only the extent that the virtues of civilisation were deemed to hold sway. These assumptions are everywhere in evidence in the hopes attached to the Geneva Convention and the establishment of the Comité International in Geneva as its self-appointed custodian.

The signing in Geneva in August 1864 of a convention 'for the Amelioration of the Condition of the Wounded in Armies in the Field' was met with a degree of self-satisfaction all round. The Swiss, in particular, were gratified by what seemed to be an endorsement of their pacifist and progressive credentials. The final text of the Geneva Convention comprised ten articles, all concerned with the status of those deemed temporarily extraneous to combat by virtue of a wound or illness, and their carers. All personnel proffering aid were to seek official recognition from the belligerent armies. Articles 1 and 2 stipulated that ambulance staff (when on duty) and medical facilities be treated as neutral; Article 6 that wounded combatants be 'collected and cared for' irrespective of nationality and that evacuation parties and their personnel also be considered neutral. Inhabitants of a war zone who chose to proffer aid to the wounded stood to benefit from the 'neutrality which humane conduct will confer', through partial exemption from requisitioning (Article 5). A red cross emblem was to be worn on an armband by all those caring for the wounded and displayed prominently on all medical vehicles, hospitals and private homes containing injured soldiers (Article 7). Of the signatories, all of whom represented European states, twelve acceded immediately, but a number of others, including Britain, deferred ratification. Britain acceded to the Geneva Convention a year later, in 1865.

The Geneva Convention, intended to apply to those rendered *hors de combat*, was one of several attempts to codify the laws of war in this period. There was nothing new in the regularisation of military conduct. The novelty lay in the formalisation and revival of customs previously extemporised by warring generals. The Geneva Convention was followed in 1874 by the Brussels Conference on the Proposed Rules for Military Warfare. Convened by the Russians, it established a series of protocols respecting the customary law of armed combat on land and at sea. These received formal ascension at the First and Second Peace Conferences held in the Netherlands in 1899 and 1907. However, if those in uniform were now afforded a degree of legal protection, the position of non-combatants under international law (and the respective status of 'irregulars' and armed civilians) was rather more opaque. The most important statement concerned with the treatment of civilians came in the preamble to the first Hague Convention of 1899. Its author, the Russian jurist Fedor Fedorovitch Martens, sought to assert the principle of restraint in war. He had, however, to confront the fact that a precise agreement of terms was politically unobtainable. His compromise, the 'Martens' Declaration' remained a general statement of principle:

[I]t is right to declare that in cases not included in the present arrangements, populations and belligerents remain under the protection and empire of the principles of international law, as they result from the usages established between civilised nations, from the laws of humanity, and the requirements of the public conscience.[7]

Encapsulated within this statement was the nebulous principle that international law conveyed a spirit of civilisation irreducible to specific circumstance, type of weaponry or opponent. This proved a potent ideal. For Martens and a generation of like-minded lawyers, peace activists, religious groups and campaigning journalists eager to banish the 'war spirit' through arbitration and a reduction of the most barbaric of weapons, these developments appeared as proof that armed combat would soon be civilised out of existence. War, if fought at all, was to assume the status of a duel between gentlemen, and no personal animosity brought to bear on the exchange. One of those for whom the laws of war betokened a new spirit of humanity was the firebrand journalist W. T. Stead. Stead was no pacifist. But, like many others on the nineteenth-century peace and international law circuits, he was convinced that he was witnessing the landmark triumph of ethical imperatives over unrestrained military might.

Presided over by Moynier, the Comité International (better known from the 1880s as the International Committee of the Red Cross), saw itself as tending to this bloom of Western civilisation. It may have codified the wishes of European powers, but it did not take it upon itself to issue edicts or sanctions. After all, the spirit of the age hardly required a sovereign authority – European soldiers and their commanders, themselves members of Western civilisation and beholden to its advances, were subject to an increasingly enlightened public opinion. In their service to humanity, the custodians of international law considered themselves above politics and, in this sense, neutral, having proceeded according to a 'scientific' impartiality.[8] This neutrality provided the means by which the authority and legitimacy of international law were ensured. It was also a political necessity. The Great Powers were unlikely to ratify international laws if they were threatened with sanctions or embarrassment. Should a prominent power such as Britain or France refuse to recognise such laws, the authority of the ICRC and its self-mandated role as 'conscience' of Western civilisation would lack credibility. Two levels of Red Cross neutrality thus came into being. The technical status of neutrality, acting as a blanket of immunity, was afforded to wounded soldiers and their carers in order to ensure optimum treatment and recovery. This appeared to betoken a moral evolution of concern on behalf of 'suffering humanity'. For the Comité International, busy tending such pleasing evidence of progress and ready to codify similar advances, 'scientific' institutional neutrality underwrote its role as the rational conduit of the European conscience.

[7] Martens' Declaration (preamble to The Hague Convention of 1899), quoted in Geoffrey Best, *Humanity in Warfare: The Modern History of the International Law of Armed Conflicts*, Methuen, London, 1983, p. 166.
[8] Koskenniemi, *Gentle Civilizer*, p. 61.

This was not of itself a moral quality, though the ICRC's quietude as an institution, of remaining 'above the fray', has often been assumed to betoken a moral stance.

The attitude of the Comité is illuminated in its response to breaches of the Geneva Convention in the Franco-Prussian War. Rather than condemnation, there came a quest for greater clarity: the European 'conscience' had obviously been inadequately codified in existing provisions. Moynier led the call for a collective effort of rationalisation.[9] As Casper Sylvest notes, 'an evolutionary framework . . . hardly allowed for setbacks'.[10] It thus fell to others – particularly journalists – to hold governments to account before the court of public opinion. Throughout the Franco-Prussian War the press was shrill in its denunciation of the abuse of the red cross emblem and contraventions of the Geneva Convention. Grisly stories of Red Cross workers pilfering from cadavers and allegations of profiteering abounded. In later conflicts, W. T. Stead whipped up similar outrage to indict the British government of war-time abuse. Yet, as this might suggest, journalists were more likely to assume the role of incensed prosecutor than of neutral adjudicator. And their diatribes often assumed a highly political or propagandist character. Thus the public's instruction in international law – driving forth the 'spirit of the age' that international lawyers took such pride in adducing – was as likely to arise from campaigning journalists and the vitriol of propagandists as it was from the writings of distinguished jurists.

The final draft of the Geneva Convention did not simply embody the ideals of the international law fraternity. It was the product of purposeful negotiation and compromise. The initial congress had revealed European governments' scepticism as to the efficacy of independent agents on the battlefield. Any overt reference to such bodies was subsequently removed so as to ensure international acceptance of what were ultimately rather minimalist undertakings. Signatory states, it seemed, had little to lose in recognising the neutrality of those stretchered out of combat situations (though the precise status of a temporarily 'neutral combatant' would later prove contentious). Nevertheless, despite this careful limitation of scope, the Red Cross emblem soon took on a life of its own. Almost immediately, a mushroom-ing number of relief organisations, many without official accreditation, took up the notion of 'Genevan neutrality' and extended it beyond the ten formally adopted Articles, into something much more amorphous. This was precisely what British government delegates had been at pains to avoid.

For signatory nations, the appropriate rationalisation and standardisation of provision for the wounded and their carers had obvious benefits. The British government sent representatives to the Geneva congresses to ensure that this was achieved without challenge to existing medico-military provision, and because to

---

[9] Ultimately, Moynier would come to lead the call for an international war crimes court: Daniel Marc Segesser, '"Unlawful Warfare is Uncivilised": the International Debate on the Punishment of War Crimes, 1872–1918', *European Review of History*, Vol. 14, No. 2, June 2007, 215–234.

[10] Sylvest, 'Victorian International Law', p. 60.

have refused would have created a bad impression. This ought not to suggest a lack of concern for the war wounded; far from it. But rather, that concern for troop welfare arose from an appreciation of British interests. For this was a period in which medico-military arrangements were under scrutiny following the scandals of the Crimean War, and the effective husbandry of the nation's fighting force was part of a wider reformist agenda within modernising circles in the army and the War Office. This coincided with developments in antisepsis, pain relief and other medical advances. Standards and hopes were raised, and with them the threshold of what was deemed 'unnecessary' suffering in war. Nevertheless, unregulated voluntary endeavours, and the application of civilian standards, were not always welcomed by army medical officers.

The British delegates to the preliminary congress were Sir Thomas Longmore, the pre-eminent military surgeon of his day, and his colleague at the new military hospital at Netley, Dr Rutherford. They were under strict orders to restrict the scope of the Convention. Their negotiating position is instructive. The new protocols emanating from Geneva were to be adopted only so far as they coincided with existing attempts to rationalise the army medical services. Longmore's telegrams and letters from Geneva reveal, for instance, that the granting of neutrality to casualties and hospital staff was acceded to only on the grounds that it did not conflict with British army provision. However, the proposal to create teams of independent medical volunteers, first aired at the preliminary conference of 1863, was to be emphatically opposed. Longmore reassured London that

> there is no intention of discussing at this Congress the question of Volunteer assistance or of any modifications of the . . . management of the existing military hospital system of any country.[11]

The central proposal of Dunant's *Un souvenir de Solferino* was thus summarily dropped. Longmore arrived at the 1864 meeting in Geneva briefed with a specially prepared memorandum entitled 'Army Medical Regulations'. This described, point by point, the organisation of the British medical services and was intended to head off any suggestion that civilian involvement was necessary. Its author was Florence Nightingale, witness to the failings of army medical provision in the Crimea and advocate of War Office reform, particularly the training of female military nurses. Her counsel was routinely called upon. Unregulated, autonomous and amateur volunteers would, she argued, only divest governments of their proper responsibility (and trained nurses of their vocation) and spread confusion where order was most needed. Of Dunant's scheme for independent voluntary aid on the battlefield she was scathing. In a letter to Longmore, a regular correspondent, she summarised her opposition:

---

[11] Sir Thomas Longmore, letter to Major General Sir E. Lugard, Under-Secretary of State for War, Wellcome Library, RAMC, Longmore papers, LP/22/3.

I am more than ever convinced that Governments should be made responsible for their own Sick and Wounded – that they should not decline Volunteer, private, benevolent effort but that, exactly in the measure that this is *incorporated* in, *not* substituted for Government organisations (for sick and wounded).[12]

Longmore, for his part, endorsed such sentiments. Describing himself as 'trouble-some', he was another veteran of Crimean deficiencies not afraid to speak his mind.[13] He also represented the increasing erudition and technical skill observable in milit-ary surgeons of the period. His publications and voluminous pamphlet collection illuminate the emergence of a Europe-wide circle of practitioners eager to improve the recovery and retention rates of an army in the field through systematic treatment and evacuation procedures. Longmore himself became a widely quoted authority on the treatment of gunshot wounds.[14] Foreign conflicts were opportunities to observe such developments. That these men felt themselves to be on the cusp of important discoveries and unprecedented circumstances is palpable: permeating their writings is an awareness of the changing nature of war and weaponry and of the possibilities of innovations in medicine and sanitation. Longmore could find no virtue in authorising civilian agencies to enter into what was becoming a highly specialised area of expertise. A lecture to the Royal United Service Institution in 1866 was an opportunity to clarify that the sole purpose of the Geneva Convention was to grant neutrality to the injured and to authorised medical staff. Any question of independent volunteer assistance was to be dismissed, for it would 'lead to inter-ference with that unity and supremacy of control which is so essential for military discipline and success'.[15] Volunteers would be permitted onto the battlefield, but only as adjuncts of the regular army medical services.

I have dwelt upon the special purpose of the Congress, because it was supposed by some persons that the question of independent volunteer attendants, which had been discussed, as I have already mentioned, in the former assembly of 1863, was again to be opened and discussed in the Congress of 1864. This erroneous supposition led to the Congress being regarded with suspicion, and even with positive disapprobation, by some who would doubtless have regarded it very differently had no such views been entertained by them.[16]

The emergence of the treatment of the war wounded as a subject of international legal disquisition had thus occasioned cautious – and closely demarcated – interest from the British government. Yet, for the moment, Longmore's warning of the need

---

[12] Letter from Florence Nightingale, 14.7.1867, Wellcome Library, RAMC, Longmore papers, 1139 Box 251, 93/1–118.
[13] Quoted in Sir Neil Cantlie, *A History of the Army Medical Department*, Vol. 2, Churchill Livingstone, London, 1974, p. 406.
[14] Sir Thomas Longmore, *Gunshot Injuries*, 2nd edn, Longmans, Green and Co., London, 1895 [1861].
[15] Sir Thomas Longmore, 'On the Geneva Convention of August the 22nd 1864', A Lecture Delivered at the Royal United Service Institution, printed by Harrison and Sons, St Martin's Lane, London, p. 5.
[16] *Ibid.*, p. 15.

for an appropriately subordinate volunteer corps went unheeded, and his worst fears instead were realised. In place of due deference and tight regulation arose an autonomous, impromptu voluntary aid movement which prized the virtues of independence and amateurism (in the best Victorian sense of disinterestedness and fair play) above all. The outbreak of the Franco-Prussian War saw the foundation of a resolutely independent NAS with the distinguished Loyd Lindsay at its helm. Sniping in the wings were John Furley and other members of the recently revived Order of St John, now able to count Sir Thomas Longmore among their associates.

July 1870: Britain remains neutral, but the press go to war . . .

For the British public, news of relief efforts in war-torn France would provide the only source of British gallantry and derring-do after the shock of the initial Prussian invasion had ebbed and the Gladstone government had settled upon a policy of neutrality. Press interest in Cabinet discussion quickly dissipated once Britain had committed herself to non-intervention. This policy occasioned little dissent; yet the opposition, where it did exist, is worthy of note for the particular vision of moral intervention that it invoked. Curiously, one of the most tenacious critiques of the government's stance came from the prime minister himself. Gladstone advocated a policy that would have seen Britain assume, in concert with other Great Powers, the role of defender of the 'public law of Europe'. He liked to envision Britain, and himself, in the moral vanguard. Intervention was justified, he thought, when moral precepts, as embodied in treaties or other international conventions, were ignored or contravened. Having, to this end, surprised parliament by negotiating new treaties to safeguard the neutrality of Belgium from French or Prussian incursion, Gladstone sought to persuade Cabinet of its responsibility to enforce them, and also of the important balance-of-power considerations at play. What he envisaged was not the pragmatic neutrality endorsed by his Cabinet, nor Bright and Cobden's principle of non-intervention, but an 'active' neutrality alert to attacks against the moral order of Europe. When, at the close of the war, Bismarck proposed to annex Alsace and Lorraine, Gladstone was incensed, though his Cabinet remained unmoved.[17]

The only other consistent critics of British government policy were a small group of moralists known as the Positivists, prominent amongst whom was Frederic Harrison, a specialist in international law. These British followers of Auguste Comte preached that the social order, now in a period of such tangible flux, was to be reconfigured according to 'scientifically' adduced moral laws (adduced, that is, in much the same way as the laws of civilised warfare).[18] Here too, a putative community of

[17] Richard Shannon, *Gladstone: Heroic Minister, 1865–1898*, Penguin, London, 1999, p. 89, and see A. J. P. Taylor, *The Trouble Makers*, Pimlico, London, 1993 [1957], chapter 3.

[18] H. S. Jones, *Victorian Political Thought*, Macmillan, Basingstoke, 2000, pp. 82–83.

Western European nations mutually bound by ethical precepts was invoked; a union that, after some initial wavering, was to exclude Germany on the basis of her 'uncivilised' militarism. In 1871, with France lying prone under the weight of German aggression, and wearying of Gladstone's fulminations, the British Positivists demanded British military intervention, though no one cared much to listen.[19]

Thus, despite Gladstone's rhetorical concerns and the marginal objections of the Positivists, the only British interventions in the Franco-Prussian War would be of the charitable kind. Deprived of an army in the field, but attuned nevertheless to the circulation-boosting potential of suffering soldiers and medical deficiencies, newspaper editors took up the cause of voluntary aid with gusto. Their forte was the colourful – gory, even – vignette of hospital life in which the common soldier assumed the status of stoic repository of the nation's honour. A new line in ambulance adventure stories took hold. Press interest generated the funds that made such voluntary efforts possible: the NAS had no need for a fund-raising appeal. Newspaper editors were fixated on medical arrangements and the experience of the rank and file, in the hope of emulating Sir William Russell's exposé of medical deficiencies in the Crimea. Prior to Russell's famous reports, news of a battle and the fate of the troops had arrived through the War Office's official dispatches: by the time that they appeared in the press, sometimes after a lag of weeks, they amounted to done deeds and casualty lists. Now, however, the rise of investigative journalism in Britain coincided with a loosening of military censorship (which would last until the South African War of 1899–1902). Journalists were able to follow the army's progress in the field. In the chaos of the Franco-Prussian War, press freedom knew no bounds.

In his analysis of the 'new humanitarian narratives' of the late eighteenth and early nineteenth centuries, Thomas Laqueur postulates a 'causal link' between representations of suffering and the origins of modern humanitarian responses: 'a particular cluster of humanitarian narratives created "sympathetic passions" – bridging the gulf between facts, compassion and action'.[20] Newspaper accounts of war-time suffering undoubtedly stimulated donations, but making any such 'causal link' requires caution. Sympathetic volunteers did not simply respond to reports of suffering; as will be seen, the impetus to provide battlefield aid predated the Franco-Prussian War and was motivated by a variety of special interests not necessarily 'humanitarian'. These champions of battlefield philanthropy were instrumental in the creation of new narratives of suffering and were thus involved in legitimating and reproducing the grounds of their own interventions. It is worth bearing in mind too the lack of a unanimous response: Quakers, for example, though exposed to these narratives, felt no compulsion to aid wounded combatants. These far from

---

[19] Frederic Harrison, *Autobiographic Memoirs*, Vol. II (1870–1910), Macmillan & Co. Ltd., London, 1911, pp. 2–12.

[20] Thomas Laqueur, 'Bodies, Details and the Humanitarian Narrative', in Lynn Hunt (ed.), *The New Cultural History*, University of California Press, Berkeley, 1989, pp. 177 and 179.

straightforward links between reports of suffering and attempts at its amelioration, and between individual journalists and relief workers, were an integral part of the origins of relief work, and remain so today.

The roving journalist reported on events that were still unfolding. The triumphs and tribulations of the ordinary soldier were lent a compelling immediacy. As noted by one journalist in the Franco-Prussian War,

> The system of newspaper correspondence, the mass of picturesque and minute detail . . . is so great, that the majority even of unlettered readers have brought vividly before their eyes the suffering of individuals like themselves, day by day . . . and our sympathies have been brought forth almost as if our own flesh and blood had been sufferers.[21]

During the course of 1870–71 newspapers gave between one and two pages daily to the conflict. Initially, owing to the assumption of French provocation, sympathy lay with the Prussians. This would shift as news of Prussian victories and the suffering of the French population sank in, especially during the siege of Paris. Editors competed for sensational exclusives and encouraged their correspondents to make use of the new electric telegraph to provide the most up-to-date information. The *Daily News* could boast that its report from Rezonville was 'not only the first detailed report of that great battle which has reached this country, but the first letter of a Special Correspondent which an English newspaper has ever published as received in full by telegraph from the seat of war.'[22] For the duration of the war, the *Daily News* was locked in a successful battle for circulation with *The Times*, whose manager, Mowbray Morris, was disappointed to find his chief correspondent, Sir William Russell, unable to repeat his Crimean success.[23] With an eye for ineptitude and corruption, journalists extended their scope to contraventions of the newly minted laws of war, and scrutiny of some rather discordant interpretations of the new Geneva Convention took place. Grisly revelations of red-cross-wearing ruffians stealing from the dead soon emerged. Governments and public bodies were held publicly to account. Following a particularly graphic depiction of a wounded soldier, *Good Words* urged that

> so deep a conviction of these horrors will now arise among the governed as to compel their governors to remember that the cause must indeed be a holy one which can justify such atrocious defacement of God's image as our new weapons of destruction accomplish in its worst form – and every means of negotiation, [and] every appeal to what has been called the 'police of Europe', should be exhausted.[24]

---

[21] Anon., 'What England Has Done for the Sick and Wounded', *Good Words*, c.1870, cutting in BRCS Archive, D/Wan/1/3/5.

[22] *Daily News*, 23.8.1870.

[23] See R. Perkins, 'The Life and Times of Lt Col Sir Nicolai Elphinstone Bart', unpublished manuscript, BRCS Archive, T2 Elph.; Stephen Koss, *The Rise and Fall of the Political Press in Britain*, Hamish Hamilton, London, 1981, p. 193.

[24] Anon., 'What England Has Done for the Sick and Wounded'.

The urgency of the situation in ill-prepared French hospitals was stressed by the *Daily News*: 'it must be remembered that every day lost in forwarding means of relief may cost hundreds of lives'.[25] NAS volunteers frequently attested to the effects of such reports. 'English people', Loyd Lindsay reflected, 'could not have endured to hear of the suffering incidental to these events without endeavouring to do something themselves towards relieving them.'[26] But the press was not merely an impartial observer. Existing together on the peripheries of conflicts in unfamiliar localities, the new breed of war correspondent and the relief worker were locked in a mutually dependent and, at times, mutually antagonistic relationship. Reporters for *The Times*, *Daily Telegraph* and *Daily News* commanded funds raised by their newspapers and directed relief workers to areas where need appeared to be most pressing. In turn, relief workers drew upon their privileged access to the battlefield and siege towns to supply newsworthy information, and in some cases acted as newspaper correspondents in their own right. Thus it was that Mowbray Morris urged the director of the NAS depot at Tours, Lt Col Sir Nicolai Elphinstone, to act as *The Times* correspondent, the better to compete with the *Daily News*.[27] But, however heartrending these reports of suffering, a number of domestic anxieties and concerns were to prove equally compelling reason to journey across the Channel that autumn.

The foundation of the British National Society for Aid

On 4 August 1870, Willis' Rooms on Piccadilly played host to the inauguration of the NAS. The month previously, on 15 July, war between Prussia and France had been declared. That same day, Captain Burgess, a member of the Order of St John of Jerusalem, Anglia, had written to *The Times* to invite interested parties 'to meet and to consult' as to how they can best further the cause of humanity at this crisis'.[28] For Burgess and many of those present, this was the culmination of attempts, so far thwarted, to found a voluntary aid society in the years since the signing of the Geneva Convention. These would-be knights-errant, bearing the distinctive white cross (or *crâchat*) of the Order of St John, were at the forefront of a Victorian fascination with medieval chivalry. Their vision was of a band of battlefield gallants operating as the official adjuncts of the army's regular medical services. The tenacious John Furley, friend and ally of Sir Thomas Longmore and one of the leading members of the Order, had devoted years to drumming up support. When Prussia had invaded Denmark in 1864, Furley had taken it upon himself to bestow aid upon the wounded. The rapid provision of war-time aid was to become his life's work.

[25] *Daily News*, 10.9.1870.
[26] 'Letter to the local committees and to the subscribers of the National Fund for aid to the sick and wounded in war, By Col. Loyd Lindsay', 12.1.1871, BRCS Archive, D50/A1.
[27] Perkins, 'The Life and Times of Lt Col Sir Nicolai Elphinstone Bart.', p. 17.
[28] *The Times*, 16.7.1870.

In 1858 the Order of St John, dissolved at the time of the Reformation, had been re-established in Britain. Instruction on correct insignia and titles, and the ordaining of an organisational memory, were instituted through a succession of lectures, statutes and histories. The Order chose to renounce both its military traditions and its Catholic connections and to fashion a new identity for its members as Protestant philanthropists.

> The sacred name of Charity should alone be inscribed on the banner of our future Knights – the schemes of political ambition be 'parcel of the past'. The noble emulation of doing good should be the sole guiding principle of the English Langu[e] of the Order of St John.[29]

To this end, it set about acquiring charitable causes. The Order's philanthropic ambitions were not, however, matched by its financial wherewithal. Having been forced to put its attempt at domestic charity to one side, it proposed a new quest: the Order would renew its war-time Hospitaller tradition. Many members of the revived Order existed in the ambit of the military and a role in this connection married a strong sense of tradition with a contemporary interest in extending the country's paramilitary services. John Furley was an enthusiastic member of the Volunteer Movement established after the Crimea. It was in this capacity that he had first become acquainted with Loyd Lindsay. When Longmore and Dr Rutherford attended the third Red Cross conference, held in Berlin on 22 April 1869, it was Furley who would accompany them, and it was Furley, rather than Loyd Lindsay (who viewed the NAS as a resolutely British institution and kept the ICRC at arm's length), who would continue to represent Britain at ICRC meetings in the future.[30] In the weeks leading up to the Berlin Conference, Furley and Burgess had been hard at work establishing a Provisional Committee to inquire into the foundation of a permanent voluntary aid society.

The 1869 Berlin Conference, to which a number of Continental National Red Cross Societies were already able to send delegates, was to impress upon Furley the urgent need for a British branch of the movement. Later that year, Burgess, acting as Secretary to the new Provisional Committee, convened a private meeting to discuss the formation of a society to aid the wounded in war, to which Loyd Lindsay, as well as Longmore, was invited. Earlier attempts to interest the government in such a scheme had failed, but the new Committee scored two important successes: Longmore continued his involvement in an advisory capacity, corresponding with both Burgess and Furley on the subject (and by 1871 appears to have been made a member of the Order of St John), and the Army Medical Department agreed to a

---

[29] *The Statutes of the Sovereign and Illustrious Order of St John of Jerusalem, Anglia*, printed by John E. Taylor, London, 1864, p. 32.

[30] The year 1869 also saw Furley engaged in translating Gustave Moynier and Louis Appia's book, *La Guerre et la Charité*, in the hope of rousing British interest in the formation of an aid society; see Furley to Longmore, 4.6.1869, Wellcome Library, RAMC, Longmore papers, 1139/L/44/1b.

meeting. But the War Office and Army Medical Department remained, as yet, unswayed. Only when a European war loomed a year later did the idea gain influential support, if only minimal government assistance.

The meeting in Willis' Rooms on 4 August took place on the day that the first guns sounded across the Channel. Suddenly, with a war between two of Europe's mightiest states pending, the welfare of the ordinary soldier – British as well as French and Prussian – gained a new significance. Britain lay exposed to charges of lagging behind her Continental neighbours in the organisation of voluntary aid. These concerns were heightened not by news of suffering, for this would come later (indeed, Burgess mistakenly prophesised that 'we shall probably . . . not hear of the mass of individual suffering'), but by a more generalised anxiety: how well prepared was Britain, should she be embroiled in this or similar crisis? 'Every country in Europe, except Britain has its "Société de secours aux blessés et malades militaires" ', Burgess urged in his letter to *The Times*. 'Now is our opportunity to form a strong British "Society of help for the Sick and Wounded" '. Burgess had followed up this letter with an approach to Loyd Lindsay to spearhead the proposal. This was an acknowledgement both of the colonel's interest in troop welfare, and of his con-siderable social cachet. Loyd Lindsay was quick to endorse Burgess's plan for the foundation of a national aid society. A few days later he seconded, and over-shadowed, Burgess's letter to *The Times* with one of his own, advertising the £1,000 that he had already deposited in Coutts Bank for the purpose.

Loyd Lindsay had retired a hero from the British army, having won the Victoria Cross for outstanding valour in the Crimea. He had very nearly not returned, having contracted dysentery and come close to death in a British army hospital. He was fortunate: as Nightingale later showed, many of his colleagues succumbed to this preventable and treatable condition, owing to inadequate medical provision. Corus-cating in his denouncements at the time, Loyd Lindsay would remain ever sceptical of the reformist proclamations of the medico-military authorities. Since leaving the army, he had been comfortably settled on a large estate in Berkshire by his father-in-law, where he had taken up the life of a gentleman farmer, and became a stalwart of the local Volunteers. In 1865 he was elected Conservative Member of Parliament for Berkshire. He had not forgotten his earlier brush with incompetent medical officers, and, in the House of Commons and on various committees of inquiry, took up the question of army reform and soldiers' welfare with alacrity. In the records of the NAS, one detects the influence of an old soldier able to appreciate the value of unsolicited 'comforts' and the chivvying of public concern. But he was determined that such efforts would not interfere with the government's own duty of care. As his wife, Harriet Loyd Lindsay, would recall,

> He was convinced that had there been a well-managed Red Cross Society at the commencement of the Crimean war much suffering would have been averted and many lives saved. What he saw and experienced during that campaign impressed itself

deeply on his mind; he realised that however well organised an Army Medical Service may be, it never has been, and never will be, able to cope adequately with the sudden emergencies of war on a large scale, and he held that voluntary organisations, unimpeded by official restrictions, are alone capable of giving auxiliary relief and of providing extra comforts and luxuries with the requisite promptitude and rapidity. He felt, moreover, that the British people would always insist on taking personal share in alleviating the suffering of their soldiers, and that some recognised and authorised channel through which public generosity could flow, was a matter of paramount importance.[31]

In a matter of days after the foundation of the NAS was announced, Loyd Lindsay could advertise the patronage of the Prince of Wales, to whom he had served as equerry.[32] Indeed, Loyd Lindsay's establishment contacts, which bestrode the worlds of high finance, politics and the military, coloured the outlook of the NAS for a generation. His interests and social standing (consolidated through marriage to the daughter of millionaire banker Lord Overstone) had brought him into the fold of the shires gentry, who would later play such a prominent role in the British Red Cross movement. Each edition of *The Red Cross*, the Society's journal, was graced by such a personage. In opposition in parliament, he was turned to by his party leader, Disraeli, to speak on military affairs, and it was in this connection that he was known to the public. Gladstone's first ministry saw Loyd Lindsay immersed in deliberations over one of the biggest root-and-branch reforms of the military that the country had ever seen. Broadly in favour of the proposals of Edward Cardwell, Secretary of State for War, he had, at Disraeli's prompting, nonetheless spoken out against abolition of purchase in the army. The winter of 1870–71 found Loyd Lindsay in London and busy, overseeing the NAS's work in France from offices in St Martin's Place and debating the implications of Cardwell's reforms in the House of Commons. News of the swift and devastating campaign wrought by the German armies gave these exchanges extra frisson. Many came to see the virtue of modernising the British forces, but there were qualms too that Gladstone's efficiencies risked crippling their effectiveness.

Loyd Lindsay's father-in-law was one of those to express disgruntlement. Lord Overstone, generous patron of many charitable and civic causes, had assumed a place on the Executive Committee of the NAS and would occupy an influential behind-the-scenes role until his death in 1883. 'The state of our Army I fear is ridiculous,' he grumbled the day after war broke out in August 1870.[33] As Overstone's faith in Gladstone dwindled, his alarm at Prussian supremacy grew. In July 1871 he voted against a second reading of the Army Regulation Bill in the Lords. 'I trust that

---

[31] Harriet Wantage [Lady Wantage], *Lord Wantage, V.C., K.C.B. A Memoir by His Wife*, Smith, Elder & Co, London, 1907, p. 172.

[32] *The Times*, 25.7.1870.

[33] Lord Overstone to G. W. Norman, 5.8.1870, in D. P. O'Brien (ed.), *The Correspondence of Lord Overstone*, Vol. 3, Cambridge University Press, Cambridge, 1971, p. 1202.

Gladstone-Cobdenism has now come to an end', he griped to Lord Granville, Gladstone's Foreign Secretary,

> – I have always looked upon it as an unfortunate and dangerous delusion. May Providence protect and preserve us! But it would be presumptuous to hope for this, unless we first do justice to ourselves, and learn a solemn lesson from the works of Bismarck and of Moltke.[34]

Crimean deficiencies, military restructuring, a question mark over Gladstone's competence, and Prussian military success, all sharpened interest in the foundation and subsequent endeavours of the NAS. At that first meeting in Willis' Rooms, Loyd Lindsay was elected Chairman, Burgess retained his position as Secretary, and a further twenty members of the Order of St John joined the Committee. John Furley left for France the following day, in the company of Dr William MacCormac. From this time onwards, the NAS had an independent existence from the Order of St John, and members of the two organisations would continue in uneasy collaboration.

The founders of the NAS, unlike those of the Comité International, took for granted that war was an eternal feature of human relations. For Loyd Lindsay and his fellow NAS Committee members, the carnage wrought only a short distance away across the Channel by the innovative use of railways, Krupp steel and breech-loading rifles was a source of grave concern. For these men, with their military connections, the moral course of action was to alleviate the 'unnecessary' suffering of those defending their country's honour. 'Believing . . . in the continued prevalence of war among nations', Loyd Lindsay expressed shock that 'the most barbarous and cruel indifference to the wants and sufferings of the soldiers who were fighting their country's battles abroad, was almost universally displayed'.[35] While impartiality was assured on the grounds that aid would be provided for all sides in this and subsequent conflicts, an important caveat was written into the new society's resolutions. 'Aid and assistance of the Society [would] be given in the first instance to the Sick and Wounded of our own Armies should we unfortunately be engaged in War.'[36] After the initial correspondence in *The Times*, the NAS made no further appeal. The beneficiary of unsolicited subscriptions, it presented itself merely as the conduit of spontaneous public sympathy, neither manipulating the public sentiment nor pursuing a dogmatic agenda. As Loyd Lindsay would attest in his subsequent report on NAS work in France, 'the Committee were drawn almost unintentionally and unconsciously into the discharge of duty of enormous magnitude and responsibility'.[37] The publicity afforded by its agents' frequent letters to the press went unacknowledged.

---

[34] Overstone to Granville, 20.1.1871, in O'Brien, *The Correspondence of Lord Overstone*, p. 1205.
[35] Loyd Lindsay, 'Lecture to Royal United Service Institution: "On Aid to the Sick and Wounded in War"', Harrison and Sons, London, 1871, p. 3.
[36] NAS, *Report* (Franco-Prussian War).
[37] *Ibid.*, p. 24.

The Friends War Victims' Relief Fund

Not everyone greeted the formation of the NAS as an advancement of humanity. For Quakers, efforts to improve medico-military efficiency were anathema; the Geneva Convention was merely a 'humane system of mutual slaughter.'[38] On 7 October, at the Meeting for Suffering in London, the FWVRF for non-combatants was opened, 'soliciting contributions towards the relief of the suffering.'[39] Funds were to be directed at the peasantry of Northern France whose livelihoods had been destroyed, neglected or depleted by requisitioning. The FWVRF, it was hoped, would help to counteract the popularity of voluntary organisations for the aid of soldiers. Joseph Crosfield (as Clerk, the individual invested with the considerable responsibility of surmising decisions taken at the Quakers' Yearly Meetings) was appointed Chairman of the Executive Committee. His comments upon its inauguration can be taken as representative:

> The well-known views of the Society of Friends on all questions relating to the War have made it difficult for many of them to co-operate with perfect satisfaction in the efforts now being made for the benefit of 'sick and wounded *Soldiers*'. Nevertheless, the principles they profess, as a Christian body, prompt them without reserve, and with willing hearts, to extend help to the peasantry and other non-combatants who are suffering in person or property from the present War.[40]

December 1870 saw Quakers convening at the Mansion House to publicise the work of their new fund. Mr Robert Spence Watson, a Newcastle solicitor fresh from distributing relief around Metz, appealed to his countrymen for support. He appropriated Gladstone's invocation of Britain's moral rather than military role in the conflict. 'This surely was a work worthy of the support of England, which still enjoyed the blessing of peace, and another meaning might yet be given to our "benevolent neutrality".'[41] Like the prime minister, the Quakers aspired to be facilitators of international peace and friendship (though, unlike Gladstone's case, this was not to be underwritten by the threat of multilateral military action). W. E. Forster MP, scion of a Quaker family and immersed at the time in debates over his new Education Bill, found time to send a letter of support (enclosing £100 for the Fund). He emphasised that, naturally, at an operational level, strict impartiality would be maintained: 'the Friends ... had undertaken the superintendence of the fund, their principles guaranteeing the most complete neutrality'. Florence Nightingale sent her blessing, moved by the 'sufferings of the starving, stripped, and burnt-out peasants' in this 'most terrible of all earthly wars.'[42] The FWVRF

---

[38] Gilbert Venables, *Is War Unchristian?*, Hodder and Stoughton, London, c.1872.

[39] FWVRF Minute Book, 7 October 1870, LSF, WVRC/1870/M1.

[40] Joseph Crosfield, leaflet announcing initial appeal, undated, stuck and bound into the FWVRF Minute Book, LSF, WVRC/1870/M1.

[41] *The Times*, 8.12.1870.

[42] *Ibid.*

was keen to co-operate with other agencies whose mandate did not conflict with its own. Resources, personnel, information and administrative channels were shared with the *Daily News*'s Fund on Behalf of the Distressed Peasantry of North-Eastern France, the Mansion House Fund to aid those caught in the siege of Paris, and Lord Vernon's Peasant Farmers Seed Fund.[43] Upon their arrival in France, Quaker agents were instructed to establish communication with Mr Bullock, an expatriate businessman administering the *Daily News*'s Fund in France. He was to inform them of the areas most in distress. The Quakers also carried letters of introduction to Mr McLean, *The Times*'s special correspondent at Metz. Once again, journalists operated as an informal information bureau for agents who lacked other sources of up-to-date intelligence. Often they inadvertently determined operational priorities.

Whereas previous Quaker relief efforts had been the private ventures of individual Friends, the FWVRF was the first 'corporate' Quaker relief agency. This was a watershed moment in the history of the Religious Society of Friends. The Fund was formed at a time of theological transition within the Society, one that saw the beginnings of the ascendancy of individual conscience over scriptural authority. Nevertheless, Quakers had a long history of advocacy and assistance on behalf of those in distress, and relief work in the Franco-Prussian War caught the tail end of an earlier engagement with evangelical social reform. Quakers had, in the past, provided relief in Germany, Greece, Finland and Ireland during times of war and exceptional hardship. Indeed, two of those commissioned by the FWVRF, James Hack Tuke and Joseph Crosfield, could draw directly on experience of relieving distress in the Irish famines. For Tuke, work in France represented a diversion from on-going concerns in Ireland. Here he continued to undertake experiments in mixed farming, using methods that he now redeployed in France in 1870–71.[44] Friends were known for their contribution to the movement to abolish slavery and for their concern for the moral treatment of prisoners and the mentally infirm. Methods deployed to rehabilitate prisoners and treat the mentally disturbed, particularly those which rested on purposeful occupation and self-sufficiency, but also on community co-operation and moral leadership, would find an echo in their provision of relief in war long after the hold of evangelicalism had slackened.

For Quakers, aid in war, as in other instances of distress, was an act of Christian service. Suffering had a particular resonance with their own sense of history as a sect persecuted for its singular religious conviction and refusal to bear arms following the Restoration in the seventeenth century. The very name of the annual Meeting for Suffering, convened initially to organise assistance for needy brethren, provided a constant reminder of the Quakers' early history of oppression and charitable

[43] FWVRF Minute Book, 7 October 1870, LSF, WVRC/1870/M1.
[44] John Ormerod Greenwood, *Quaker Encounters: Friends and Relief*, Vol. I, William Sessions Ltd., York, 1975, pp. 36–37.

endeavour. Nevertheless, one needs to be wary of assuming that the Quakers can claim an unmixed pedigree of consistently 'speaking truth to power' or of articulating a strict pacifism from the time of their founder, Charles Fox. Indeed, while Quakers had long sought the relief of suffering in war-time, and done so in pursuit of Christian ideals, attitudes towards war and the meaning and methods connected to its amelioration and abolition varied over time. Relief in the Franco-Prussian War occurred at a time when the Quakers' peace testimony was a received and largely unexamined article of faith. Moving testimonies of relief work in France combined virulent anti-war polemics with a disconcerting fascination with Prussian militarism (in contrast, the French were deemed to be rather effete and desultory). War was something to be denounced for standing in the way of the Kingdom of God, but, for evangelicals, it was also something that could be visited upon the sinful. Pacifism, however, had yet to assume a central place in Quaker identity.

In the autumn of 1870, absolutist pacifism and the large-scale relief programmes with which Quakers were identified by the time of the Great War – and the public accord which these would bestow – were still a long way in the future. Indeed, commencement of the FWVRF's work in France was to coincide with hostile sideswipes against the Quakers in *Blackwood's Magazine*. Debates over the implications of Forster's Education Act, one of the Gladstone ministry's other landmark reforms, were still rumbling (the Bill received royal assent on 9 August 1870). The Quakers, like other non-conformist denominations, feared that the Act would extend the influence of voluntary (usually Anglican) schools at their expense. On the eve of their Mansion House Meeting *Blackwood's* alleged that,

> the lazy Quaker shirks military service and public duties, and tries to escape public burdens that they may give himself up to ease and the accumulation of wealth. He throws on other men all the hard and dangerous work of the world, and thrives at their expense, isolating himself from all their interests, passions, fortunes, and living to only his own sect.[45]

This stung the Quakers to issue the following rebuttal in *The Times*:

> [t]he meeting convened yesterday at the Mansion House by the Society of Friends in aid of the war victims might alone furnish a sufficient reply to [these] sharp and unmerited charges. . . . [F]or more than half a century some of the most active and successful organisations of a philanthropic and patriotic nature have been mainly directed and supported by the Society of Friends.[46]

Subsequent editions of *The Times* featured letters from France detailing Friends' work amidst the destitute peasantry. FWVRF agent Samuel Capper became a regular correspondent. New Year 1871 was greeted by Friends with an appeal for peace and an address entitled 'War and Christianity':

[45] Quoted in *The Times*, 9.12.1870.
[46] *The Times*, 9.12.1870.

The awful conflict is still going on between men acknowledging the same Father in Heaven, and who still avow allegiance to Him who said 'By this shall all men know that ye are My disciples, if ye have love one to another.' (John, xiii, 35)

When we think of all the agony of this mutual slaughter . . . we are ready to exclaim, – Is this Christianity? . . . And if the strongest possible negative must be given to [this] question, the inquiry may well arise, – Upon whom does the guilt of these tremendous iniquities fall? It is not for us to pass judgement upon the actors in this vast tragedy. This responsibility can only be measured by the Great Searcher of hearts.[47]

An appeal to the authority of scripture and a degree of political diffidence (war tends to be blamed on a 'war spirit' to be countered through Christian love) were characteristic of Quaker thinking at this time. The editor of *The Times*, for one, professed himself unconvinced, if not of the sincerity of Quaker beliefs, then of their idealism.

[O]ne is tempted to be impatient with an appeal which simply recounts our difficulties and failures, without affording the least indication how to overcome them. . . . [T]here is no doubt how men ought to act; but the problem is how to deal with men acting as they do. The question is not whether it is the duty of individuals to practice forgiveness and mercy, but whether, if individuals fail to do so, Rulers and 'Higher Powers' are to suffer injustice and violence to reign uncontrolled.[48]

Here was the quintessential argument against pacifism, but also the point of departure for Loyd Lindsay's efforts to mitigate such regrettably frequent calls to arms.

Over the course of the next half century, relief work would, for some Quakers, provide a response to the kind of criticisms levelled by *The Times* and *Blackwood's*, providing a sphere of benevolent service, participatory citizenship and model of brotherly love through which they hoped to inspire harmonious international relations. For this reason, Quaker aid to civilians was consistently conceived as a means rather than simply an end. Relief work would become important, not as the manifestation of any 'right' to immunity or aid, nor of any value attached to neutral humanitarianism, but because it was born of repeated acts of conscience and a commitment not simply to oppose war but to also undertake constructive work for peace. In this respect, it contributed to Quakers' invigorated pledge to undertake Christian service in society at large, the better to realise the Kingdom of God on earth.

Like their fellow relief workers at the newly founded NAS, the FWVRF would aspire to a strict operational impartiality based on an objective assessment of need; but not all members of the Religious Society of Friends attached the same signific-ance to institutional neutrality. Increasingly, as the century wore on, younger and

[47] 'War and Christianity', *The Times*, 9.1.1871.
[48] *The Times*, 11.1.1871.

more radical Friends felt compelled to speak out against the political causes of war-time suffering and to pinpoint those responsible for the reigning 'war spirit'. Though they were as likely to render such intimations of conscience 'above' politics as were international lawyers, many Quakers would find that their compulsion to bear witness to suffering called forth an engaged response of a kind which made political neutrality impossible. Thus it was that the NAS and the Quakers would be both brought together and separated by their impulse to ameliorate suffering in war. The following chapters follow them, first to France, then to the Balkans and beyond.

2

Accounting for compassion:
British relief in the Franco-Prussian War, 1870–71

Relief workers' accounts from the Franco-Prussian War reveal genuine concern, often at personal cost, to ameliorate the affliction of injured soldiers and of civilians wracked by siege and agricultural disruption. From their inception, the NAS and the FWVRF faced very different challenges: the one had to contend with dispensing aid to moving (and, in the French case, ad hoc) armies, the other with a stationary population subject to siege and requisitioning. Both witnessed scenes of unprecedented human suffering wrought by new quick-fire weaponry and heavy artillery. That they felt themselves to be dealing with destruction on a scale never before witnessed is tangible. The NAS apprehended 'the vast preparations which were being made for the destruction of life' in 'a contest more tremendous than any which had taken place within the memory of man'.[1] The Quakers spoke of 'fearful ravages, inseparable from the presence of large armies in the field', and the suffering of 'the innocent and helpless . . . the aged, the women and the children'.[2]

British relief agents responded with alacrity and innovation. Opportunities were taken to observe and to test new ideas and methods – whether the latest theories in battlefield medicine or contemporary models of social investigation and poverty relief. However, as well as satisfying their own conscience and expectations, relief workers had to comply with the wishes of supporters, be accountable to donors, fend off press suspicion and secure access to the battlefield from the respective military authorities. They did so by expressing a careful calibration of concern which betokened a response at once benevolent and proficient. Compassion and spontaneity were crucial, but heart was to be kept firmly in subjection to head. As NAS Chairman Loyd Lindsay confidently announced, 'it is possible to be as precise in the administration of relief to wounded and sick men in war as it is to be in ordinary

---

[1] NAS, *Report* (Franco-Prussian War), p. 3.
[2] Leaflet distributed at the start of war and bound into the Minute Book of the FWVRF, 1870–1871, LSF WVRC/1870/M1.

mercantile transactions'.[3] Or as one reviewer put it, 'spontaneity might be regarded as the central light' of relief in war,

> each man knows what he has to do, with out an order. Therein lies the sympathetic character of the work; it is not the learning that asserts itself, but the philanthropic heart. It bleeds sometimes; but the clear head retains its sway.[4]

Thus it was that amidst the wounded and prisoners of war, destitute peasants and famished inhabitants of siege towns, British agents developed models of rapid-response medicine and 'self-help' relief which gave the field of relief some of its most recognisable features. Meanwhile, in their reports and personal reminiscences they invoked an ethos of discriminating compassion which rendered aid work account-able to self, supporters and the general public – and ultimately, for some, to God.

Administering the gift

The enthusiastic involvement of the South German states did much to ensure that Prussia was able to execute swift defeats upon the French armies in Eastern France between 4 August and 2 September. First Metz was besieged, and then Napoleon III was forced to surrender at Sedan. Yet the fighting continued. In Paris, a provisional government of liberals and radicals invoked the tradition of *levée en masse*. Gambetta, the French prime minister, escaped besieged Paris in October and attempted to raise a 'people's army' on the Loire. Fighting continued for a further five months and Paris eventually fell on 28 January 1871. Henceforth, the war would be between superior German conscript armies and French 'irregular' forces. 'After 2 September', wrote A. J. P. Taylor, 'the Franco-German war became the first war of nations; the rules of civilized warfare broke down, and the pattern of twentieth-century warfare was created.'[5] That the inauguration of the Red Cross movement coincided with the extremes of this first total 'war' was more than a regrettable irony. As Bertrand Taithe and Jean H. Quataert have shown, participation in the new Continental Red Cross societies was conceived primarily as service to the nation-state and became an important part of popular mobilisation in this and future wars.[6] Meanwhile, transgressions of the newly minted laws of war gave substance to accusations of enemy barbarity and provided a new dimension to war-time propaganda and fear. Repeated contraventions of the Geneva Convention were reported by British

[3] NAS, *Report* (Franco-Prussian War), p. 151.
[4] Review of 'William MacCormac, Notes and Recollections of an Ambulance Surgeon', *British Medical Journal*, 23.8.1871.
[5] A. J. P. Taylor, *The Struggle for Mastery in Europe*, Oxford, Oxford University Press, 1971 [1954], p. 211.
[6] Bertrand Taithe, 'The Red Cross in the Franco-Prussian War: Civilians, Humanitarians and War in the "Modern Age"', in Roger Cooter *et al.* (eds), *War, Medicine and Modernity*, Stroud, Sutton Publishing, 1998; Jean H. Quataert, 'German Patriotic Women's Work in War and Peace Time, 1864–90', in Stig Förster and Jörg Nagler (eds), *On the Road to Total War: The American Civil War and the German Wars of Unification, 1861–1871*, Cambridge, Cambridge University Press, 1997.

observers commissioned by the Gladstone government to survey the belligerents' medical and sanitary arrangements or affiliated to the NAS in France.[7] The lessons not only of Prussian military might, but also of superior German standards of hygiene, voluntary provision and medical administration were not lost on these observers. At home, initial exasperation at Napoleon's provocation of Prussia turned quickly to sympathy for French sufferings. As early as 10 September, the *Daily News* was reporting that 'from the immense quantity of wounded that were lying in the hospitals, and the large number of dead horses and other pestilential matter, typhus of a very malignant character had broken out'. By 17 October, and the launch of its own relief fund, it was describing how 'plain unmistakeable famine is advancing with fearfully rapid strides, with pestilence in its wake'. The suffering of the peasantry left 'one old blind woman . . . burning a soldier's boot on her hearth for want of fuel'. By 8 November the lack of medicine, disinfectant and tonics for treating French wounded was being deplored.

The NAS was inundated with donations, and offers of help on a scale surpassing even that of the Patriotic Fund in the Crimean War. Of the £297,000 collected during the course of the war, £200,000 was received by the end of September.[8] The majority of cash gifts were attributed to private individuals; however, records also show that subscription lists were opened in nearly every military regiment and every ship in the Channel Fleet and that donations were received from 5,824 churches after an appeal by the Archbishop of Canterbury.[9] At the Society's headquarters, organisational capacities were strained by a flood of agents' telegrams, the jumble of *matériel* and calls paid by impromptu volunteers. Squeezing his way up the stairs to visit Loyd Lindsay, one visitor found 'the staircase, halls etc. were crowded with cases full of bandages, old linen, lint for the wounded'.[10] The three houses in St Martin's Place lent to the NAS by the government quickly proved insufficient, and a disused workhouse and the vaults of St Martin's Church were commandeered for use as a warehouse.

All were new to the provision of voluntary aid, especially on such an escalating scale. No plan or even precedent existed. Forced to improvise, the scope and extent of the NAS's involvement grew to keep pace with rapidly accumulating funds. Reports of suffering continued to fill newspaper columns and the public expected 'something to be done'. Doing something, whether sending out a new ambulance or venturing into a siege town, provided journalists with tales of valiant battles against pain and death, gave rise to fresh accounts of suffering and renewed public expectation.

---

[7] See the confidential 'Reports from Medical Officers, on the War between France and Germany in 1870–1871', TNA, WO 33/23. The author of one of these reports, Deputy Inspector General J. H. Ker Innes, was attached to an NAS ambulance and corresponded directly with Lord Overstone.

[8] Using The National Archives' online currency converter, £297,000 in 1870 would now have a spending worth of £13,572,900.

[9] NAS, *Report* (Franco-Prussian War), pp. 3–24.

[10] Diary, Wellcome Library, Thomas Weldon Trench papers, MS7846/43.

Aid to the wounded in war quickly developed its own momentum. Loyd Lindsay, his wife Harriet and father-in-law Lord Overstone, forced to decamp to their London residence, unexpectedly found themselves amidst a flurry of activity. 'The fact is, the business of this Sick and Wounded Fund completely overwhelms us,' Lord Overstone dashed off to a friend.

> The public sympathises with the movement far beyond our anticipation – and the contributions pour in so rapidly and to so large an amount that it has been found necessary to enlarge the sphere of operation – and to undertake duties which were not at first in contemplation.[11]

Twelve thousand packages were received, opened, sorted, repackaged and sealed with lists of contents, and four tons of goods were dispatched each day to the Continent (train and freight companies provided free transport) for a total of 188 days. The press cheered a country united by a burst of self-sacrificing generosity. *Good Words* noted donations from

> two hundred national schools; widow's mites, such as 'five shirts, two new', from a coachman's wife; lint and bandages made up in our own hospitals, forgetful of their own needs; . . . a day's pay of the officers and privates of several regiments and ships' companies; mill girls, school children and teachers working in their spare hours; . . . Dissenting chapels in the hills, people who give not of their abundance, but of their necessities.[12]

The first act of the Executive Committee, on which sat, among others, the Earl of Shaftesbury, Baron de Rothschild and Sir Harry Verney (brother-in-law of Florence Nightingale), was to establish two working committees. An all-male Working Committee would be put in charge of recruiting volunteers, managing monetary donations and collating information from France. A Ladies Committee would take responsibility for supervising the reception, storage and packaging of provisions. Both committees comprised wealthy, aristocratic, royal or otherwise distinguished patrons, many drawn from Loyd Lindsay's own circle. Harriet Loyd Lindsay oversaw the Ladies Committee, on which sat Princess Christian, Lady Augusta Stanley and Florence Nightingale. Florence Nightingale, recruited as an advisor by both the NAS and the Army Medical Services, and sceptical of impromptu voluntary efforts, was eager to impress her own vision of medico-military reform upon proceedings. Almost daily, letters flew between her and Sir Harry Verney, who sought her advice on the selection of nurses and the general workings of the Executive Committee.[13] The recruitment of a small number of upper-class female war nurses owed much to

[11] Overstone to Norman, 11.9.1870, in O'Brien, *The Correspondence of Lord Overstone*, p. 1203.

[12] Anon, 'What England Has Done for the Sick and Wounded', p. 38; also *The Standard*, 7.10.1870 (cuttings in BRCS Archive, Wantage papers, D/Wan/1/3/5).

[13] The extent to which Nightingale was still considered the figurehead of war relief is apparent in the hundreds of applications that she received from women anxious to become NAS nurses, despite the fact that her name was not mentioned in the publicity. Wellcome Library, Florence Nightingale papers, MS 9004/5.

Nightingale's legacy and, though initially controversial, would launch relief work as a new sphere of female activity. In total, the NAS engaged 110 people to distribute aid and provide medical assistance, comprising 62 surgeons, 16 nurses and 32 agents responsible for running depots in France.

Elsewhere in London, Quakers were also to be found busy sorting and packing. However, in contrast to the NAS's initially ad hoc endeavours, long-established Quakerly practices and close networks of kin and kind provided the FWVRF with a structure that could be adapted for the collection and administration of relief. Quakers could also call upon direct experience of dispensing aid to a destitute domestic population, including the tribulations of relief work in the Irish famines. The FWVRF comprised 53 members, who met weekly, and an Executive Committee that met daily for two to five hours for the duration of the war. As with the NAS, a Ladies Committee was responsible for storing and packing material goods and overseeing the sewing of garments, employing poor women in London's East End to do so. September saw an FWVRF appeal read out in austere Friends' Meeting Houses up and down the country, and small congregations began to send in their donations to the central committee. At the larger Meetings, local committees were established to appeal for and collate donations from Friends and non-Quakers alike. The Manchester Committee, for example, mirroring the FWVRF, was responsible for organising public meetings, canvassing subscriptions amongst the leading merchants of the city, distributing pamphlets and advertising in the local newspaper.[14] The Executive Committee in London circulated bi-weekly reports, enlivened by heart-rending letters from agents in France, to these local committees. These reports had the dual function of raising funds and reassuring Friends that their donations were being wisely spent. No doubt the appending of subscription lists arranged in descending order of amounts provided an extra fillip to Quaker generosity. In total, £75,690 was raised by the Society of Friends for the alleviation of non-combatant suffering in France.

The FWVRF employed 41 commissioners – 33 men and 8 women, 11 of whom were non-Quakers. To distinguish its personnel from the Red Cross, the FWVRF issued its agents with a distinctive red and black double star. The majority were men of business, offering their services for a few months at a time or for as long as their businesses could manage.[15] Quaker women had a long tradition of voluntary work;

---

[14] 'Report of the Committee to raise subscriptions in aid of the "War Victims' Relief Fund"', Minutes of the Manchester Preparative Meeting for the first 5 months of 1871, Manchester Central Library, M85/5/1/10. A total of £2,523 was raised and £100 worth of clothing donated in Manchester.

[15] For written accounts of Quaker relief work see, Robert Spence Watson, *The Villages Around Metz*, J. M. Carr Printing Works, Newcastle, c.1872; James Hack Tuke, *A Visit to Paris in the Spring of 1871 on Behalf of the War Victims' Fund of the Society of Friends*, F. B. Kitto, London, 1871; Samuel Capper, *Wanderings in War Time. Being the Notes of Two Journeys taken in France and Germany in the Autumn of 1870 and the Spring of 1871*, Richard Bentley and Son, London, 1871; John Bellows, *The Track of War Around Metz and the Fund for the Non-Combatant Sufferers*, Trubner and Co., London, 1871; and William Jones, *Quaker Campaigns in Peace and War*, Headley Brothers, London, 1899.

however, the Franco-Prussian War saw their elevation to the role of independent, unchaperoned relief workers for the first time. These included Christine Majolier Alsop and M. A. Marriage Allen, both of whom had experience of missionary and charitable work, and Elizabeth Barclay, a nurse. Richenda Elizabeth Reynolds and Augusta Fry, granddaughters of the prison reformer Elizabeth Fry, acted as agents in and around Metz, where they organised clothing distribution.[16]

Treatment of the wounded

Directed by the press to the neediest areas, the agents of the NAS and the Society of Friends concentrated their initial efforts in Eastern France. They situated their headquarters and central depots at Arlon, 40 miles from Sedan in neutral Belgium. Later, the NAS would follow the German army to the Loire and the environs of the French capital. After the lifting of the siege of Paris, the Quakers extended their endeavours from Alsace and Lorraine to the villages surrounding the capital and also, on the heels of the Loire campaign, to Orleans. Equipped with letters of introduction, medical and other provisions and the badges of their respective organisations, these intrepid men and women were left to fashion for themselves the most suitable roles and procedures. Receiving scant instruction from their domestic committees, NAS agents were entrusted to respect the neutrality and impartiality encoded in the Geneva Convention; and FWVRF commissioners to operate as fitted Quaker values. Each set of agents corresponded with their home committees and with the press. The letters of NAS agents reveal, after a period of rapid but uncoordinated effort, the gradual standardisation of medical aid through the development of evacuation protocols and convoy systems. Those of the Quakers reveal a more ready sense of purpose and the swift instrumentalisation of a system of indirect relief.

The bedraggled state of the French forces and the ragtag of militias and volunteers of vastly various quality posed particular problems. Sanitary arrangements had collapsed in the siege towns and epidemics tore through the new recruits, who, unlike the regular troops, had not been vaccinated. French medical officers, insufficient in number even before the war, were now overwhelmed by the number and severity of the sick and wounded.[17] New developments in weaponry caused novel kinds of injury – though it was noted that those unfortunate enough to encounter the new breech-loading *mitrailleuse* rarely survived. 'The scene on the battle-field was *unusually terrible*', recalled one NAS surgeon on surveying the human debris at Sedan, 'masses of coloured rags glued together with blood and brains, and pinned into strange

---

[16] See M. Braithwaite, *Memorials of Christine Majolier Alsop*, S. Harris and Co., London, 1881; M. A. M. Allen, *Simple Sketches of Christian Work and Travel*, Headley Bros., London, 1911; FWVRF Minute Book, 1870–1871, LSF, WVRC/1870/M1.

[17] Bertrand Taithe, *Defeated Flesh: Welfare, Warfare and the Making of Modern France*, Manchester University Press, Manchester, 1999.

shapes by fragments of bones.'[18] Those of the wounded who survived the battle were found languishing in improvised hospitals. After the battle of Sedan one British volunteer found scenes of torment in a church, the wounded suffering for want of anything but the most basic care:

> 'Who is there to look after these poor fellows,' I said. 'Is there nobody at night?' 'Nobody, Monsieur.' 'Not even to give them a cup of cold water?' 'Nobody, Monsieur.'
>
> While I was there the rations came round – two small pieces of very dry bread, a small lump of hard boiled horse flesh, and a small tin of soup.[19]

The numbers of French wounded in German hands strained German forces that were relying upon requisitioned provisions. 'I felt more than words can say', wrote the Quaker Robert Spence Watson on observing French prisoners with their 'hollow faces, thin, bent, and wasted frames' en route to Germany.[20] In the siege towns, lack of fresh food, poor sanitation and the rapid spread of communicable disease left the inhabitants struggling to survive. As the situation in Paris deteriorated and winter set in, residents weakened by lack of food consumed adulterated milk and bread and inhabited freezing apartments. The plight of bourgeois residents subject to egalitarian rationing elicited particular sympathy from the Quakers:

> people in well-to-do circumstances had suffered during the siege as much as, perhaps more, than the poor . . . people in that position, who are accustomed every day of their lives to certain luxuries, do suffer, when deprived of them, to a greater degree than those who are accustomed to live more hardily. And, seeing that the rations in Paris were distributed in equal quantity and quality to everyone alike . . . we cannot wonder that great suffering was produced among the class I have indicated.[21]

But disorganisation also presented opportunities. With large numbers of prisoners of war in German hands, and the disordered state of the French military, the British were not only welcome but were granted an unusual degree of latitude.

NAS volunteers either offered their services to existing French or German hospitals or formed complete ambulance units under the control of the Society. Having had no time to draw up plans for the distribution of relief, NAS ambulances (at the time the word referred to peripatetic field hospitals) and depots were generally improvised. 'Everything in wartime is à l'imprévu', reflected William MacCormac, surgeon at St Thomas' Hospital. Frustrated by the lack of command at the NAS, he joined British colleagues and veterans of the American Confederate Army to establish a semi-independent Anglo-American Ambulance.[22] Very quickly, it gained a reputation

[18] F. Creswell Hewett, *Recollections of Sedan*, Fowler & Co. (printer), Halifax, NS, 1877, p. 18.

[19] Thomas Weldon Trench to Loyd Lindsay, Sedan, 11.9.1870, Wellcome Library, Thomas Weldon Trench papers, MS 7846.

[20] Watson, *The Villages Around Metz*, p. 117.

[21] Tuke, *A Visit to Paris*, p. 8.

[22] William MacCormac, *Notes and Recollections of an Ambulance Surgeon. Being an Account of Work Done under the Red Cross during the Campaign of 1870*, J. and A. Churchill, London, 1871.

as a model of flexible medical provision. Such was their accumulating experience and efficiency that when practising 'alert' procedures they were able to pack up and move within 22 minutes.[23] This entrepreneurial spirit characterised the distribution of relief in the early days. Individuals joined ambulances at will or set up impromptu soup kitchens.[24] The autonomous NAS hospitals arrived complete with stretcher bearers, catering equipment, nurses, orderlies and dispensaries. The British government provided, at cost price, a portable hospital from Woolwich and met the Society's request for 12 medical officers to be seconded from the army medical services.[25] For *The Standard* this was one of the finest examples of 'practical Christianity' since the embarkation of missionary ships to Africa.[26] The Woolwich 'field' hospital (with 12 hospital marquees, 8 ambulance wagons, 27 members of the army hospital corps and provisions and bedding for 200 patients) was the first of its kind to be used by a British military staff. Its departure offered opportunity for a rehearsal.

The NAS committee in London received logistical information from its agents (from which an overview of relief provision was gradually constructed), but it had no effective means to control the distribution of aid once it had left the warehouse in London. It relied instead upon a series of depots founded in France by expatriate businessmen and their wives, for example at Amiens and Boulogne, which would telegraph their requirements to the Society in London.[27] Nevertheless, many agents were unaware of the location of depots, the contents of stores or where help was most needed.[28] Something – or someone – was needed to counter this haphazard arrangement. In August, the NAS applied to the Secretary of State for War and the Commander-in-Chief of the British army for the assistance of Capt. Henry Bracken-bury of the Royal Artillery, esteemed Professor of Military History at the Royal Military Academy, Woolwich. Brackenbury, a leading member of the reformist 'Wolseley ring', was busy casting an astute eye on proceedings for *The Standard*. With a staff of 32, Brackenbury acted as a roving commissioner responsible for logistics and communications, founding the depot at Arlon, laying down supply lines between hospitals in the district of Metz and the Ardennes and organising

---

[23] Norman Maclean 'The English Military Ambulance 1870 (The first field ambulance?)', typescript of article for *British Army Review*, Wellcome Library.

[24] For impromptu soup kitchens see the letters of Thomas Weldon Trench, Wellcome Library, Thomas Weldon Trench papers, MS7846; for unaffiliated doctors see Charles Ryan, *With an Ambulance in the Franco-German War, Personal Experiences and Adventures with Both Armies, 1870–1871*, John Murray, London, 1896, pp. 1–2.

[25] For example, see Surgeon-Major Porter's telegram from the War Office, Wellcome Library, Surgeon-Major Porter papers, MS 7843/878/97.

[26] *The Standard*, n.d., pasted into Porter's scrapbook, Wellcome Library, Surgeon-Major Porter papers, MS7841.

[27] *Red Cross Operations in the North of France, 1870–1872*. Printed for the Boulogne English Committee for Aid to the Sick and Wounded in War, Spottiswoode & Co., London, 1872.

[28] Dr Connolly, on arrival at Sedan, 'found no one at all connected with the Society . . . I met here *The Times* Special Correspondent, who advised me to go to Metz or thereabouts, as there is a great deal of work to be done there.' This was a common complaint; NAS, *Report* (Franco-Prussian War), p. 158.

provisions for starving and wounded troops after the siege of Metz had ended.[29] He quickly surmised that the most crucial factor was not the quantity of equipment but its accurate and swift deployment. 'The great questions now are depôts and transport. To have the stores at hand and the means of conveying them where wanted are the two first necessities of the moment.'[30] Though he bemoaned the lack of an 'Intelligence Department', Brackenbury's work amounted to the first systematisation of emergency aid. For the NAS, the model came quickly to be that of a military operation. Brackenbury took to styling himself the 'commander-in-chief', from whom [relief workers] get systematic instructions.'[31]

Those staffing the new ambulances ranged in experience and eminence. Distinguished surgeons worked alongside medical students and recent graduates eager for paid experience. The 21-year-old Charles Ryan took a break from studying in Dublin to offer his services as a medical volunteer, his sympathy for the French Republic piqued by news of French defeats. Pioneering female doctor Elizabeth Garrett, in Paris to pursue her training, also rushed to volunteer her services. Accompanying them was an assortment of individuals lacking any affiliation. The freelance Thomas Weldon Trench took to ministering to the souls of the wounded while distributing beef tea from a Fortnum and Mason hamper. Meanwhile, patients could expect to be nursed by a combination of trained and remunerated nurses and enthusiastic 'lady-amateurs'. Of the 16 nurses commissioned by the NAS, 8 were members of the All Saints' Sisterhood from University College Hospital.[32] The rest were upper-class women with varying degrees of hospital experience, joined by British women independently offering their services to the French or German Red Cross societies.

Details of these nurses are patchy, but of those for whom records remain, Emma Pearson and Louisa MacLaughlin, both trained nurses, worked at the battlefields of Saarbruch, Sedan and Orleans.[33] The Pearson family was involved in the Order of St John and is listed as participating in meetings to discuss voluntary aid prior to the Franco-Prussian War. Florence Lees, an ally of Florence Nightingale, worked in hospitals in Metz and Homburg, having joined the German Red Cross after Nightingale received a request from the Crown Princess of Prussia. Zepherina Veitch (Mrs Henry Smith) joined the Anglo-American Ambulance at Sedan, while Mrs Templer, on holiday in Germany at the outbreak of war, undertook 14 days' training and joined the German Red Cross. The rest included Clara Lowe, who had

[29] House of Commons Debates, 11.8.1871, *Hansard*, Vol. 208, cc. 1479–1492.
[30] Letter quoted in Wantage, *Memoir*, p. 180.
[31] NAS, *Report* (Franco-Prussian War), p. 63.
[32] Anne Summers, *Angels and Citizens: British Women as Military Nurses 1854 to 1914*, Threshold Press, Newbury, 2000, p. 115.
[33] Louisa MacLaughlin and Emma Pearson, *Our Adventures during the War of 1870*, 2 vols, Richard Bentley and Son, London, 1871. Emma Pearson, co-author of *Our Adventures during the War of 1870*, had already penned her experiences during the Italian Wars of Unification, *From Rome to Mentana*, Saunders, Otley and Co., London, 1868 and a three-volume romance, *One Love in Life*, Hurst and Blackett, London, 1874. MacLaughlin and Pearson were dismissed from the NAS for 'insubordination'; *Our Adventures* is largely an attempt at vindication.

experience of nursing the poor in the East End of London, Kate Neligan, who worked with the Anglo-American Ambulance after six weeks of training, and Anne Thacker, a Crimean widow, who trained as a nurse in 1870 and worked in the hospitals of Cologne. For practising nurses, war-time relief work provided rigorous training for hospital work at home and opportunities for professional advancement. As Mrs Henry Smith noted, 'There is one great advantage in my work here, viz., that I should not have seen such cases in ten years' work in London hospitals as I have seen in the short time I have been out.'[34]

If it was initially ad hoc, it should not be imagined that NAS medical treatment was amateur. On the contrary, many of those under NAS care benefited from treatment by world-leading experts. NAS volunteers included prominent military surgeons of the day, accompanied by doctors with the latest training in infection control and pain relief. One of these, Dr Davis of St Bartholomew's Hospital, instructing on ventilation and the use of disinfectants ('what he calls hygiene', one observer noted), was so proficient that the governor of Sedan made him Head Inspector at Pont-à-Mousson and placed everyone under his orders.[35] For specialists in military medicine and surgery, the Franco-Prussian War provided an unparalleled opportunity for the practical application of innovative techniques and technologies, and for close surveillance of developments in Continental warfare. This knowledge was relayed to colleagues at home in specialist publications complete with technical diagrams and exemplary instructions for the construction of replica machinery (such as the Prussian's new sprung-wheeled hospital transports). Lengthy and meticulous reports were forwarded directly to the War Office. Successive volumes of the *British Medical Journal* carried MacCormac's impressions of war-time surgery with the Anglo-American Ambulance; MacCormac's only quibble was that he had not had the chance to experiment with the use of carbolic acid 'and the opportunity now lost of giving it a sort of crucial trial does not frequently recur'.[36] Elsewhere, Sandford Moore, surgeon with the Woolwich ambulance, published his insights in *The Lancet* and in pamphlet form. 'Rare opportunities were . . . presented', he wrote, 'for the observation of the immediate treatment and removal of the wounded on the field . . . [and] the working of the wheeled transport, British and Prussian, the former of which had not been previously tried in European warfare.'[37] NAS surgeons recruited from Netley and the London teaching hospitals were concerned especially

---

[34] See 'Mrs Henry Smith: Obituary', 1.4.1894, and 'Letters by the Late Mrs Henry Smith', *Nursing Notes: A Practical Journal for Nurses*, 1.11.1894; Mrs H. Templer, *A Labour of Love under the Red Cross during the Late War*, Simpkin, Marshall and Co., London, 1872; Anne Thacker, *The Narrative of My Experience as a Volunteer Nurse in the Franco-German War of 1870–1*, Abbott, Jones and Co., Ltd., London, 1897; Summers, *Angels and Citizens*, pp. 115–118.

[35] Letters of Thomas Weldon Trench, 2.10.1870, Wellcome Library, Thomas Weldon Trench papers, MS7846.

[36] NAS, *Report* (Franco-Prussian War), p. 107.

[37] Sandford Moore, *Notes with a Prussian Sanitats Detachment in the Loire Campaign, 1870*, Pardon & Son, London, 1872, p. 6.

to keep up to date with treatments for wounds inflicted by the new artillery.[38] They gained a reputation for the successful use of hypodermic injections of morphia for gun-shot wounds. William MacCormac and J. H. Porter (Netley) were able to gain enough first-hand experience to establish themselves as two of the leading authorities in military medicine.

Unable to accompany the NAS, owing to ill-health, eminent Professor of Military Surgery Thomas Longmore was forced to observe such innovations at a distance. From his post at Netley, he scrutinised the burgeoning literature on emergency medicine. His observations fed directly into the reform of the British army's medical services. In particular, the critical role of early treatment was becoming evident: 'Early assistance in the field is of first importance', Surgeon-Major Porter noted in his *Surgeon's Pocket Book*.[39] The next line of treatment required proximate hospitals to which casualties could be rapidly transported. Specially designed conveyances were essential so as to ensure wounds were not exacerbated by jolty movement, and Longmore became a renowned expert in the construction and use of stretchers. He recognised that higher recovery rates were best ensured by a chain of treatment centres as close to the front as was practicable. This had the advantage that men could be kept close to the seat of war and returned once recovered.

This emphasis on 'rapid response' medicine characterised the work of NAS surgeons and medical staff, and also that of the newly created band of depot managers, roving agents, communications directors and amateur stretcher bearers. The clinical impartiality associated with medical ethics and necessary for detached professional observation aided rapid and non-discriminatory treatment, and an operational neutrality quickly arose that resonated with, but was not conferred by, the Geneva Convention. In fact, the legal status of British volunteers was far from clear. Longmore, for one, bemoaned the presence of so many freelancers. The priority of non-discriminatory emergency care was thus established, but this arose on the ground, in response to (British) military priorities, rather than through any article of international law or universal 'humanitarian' imperative. The collection of the wounded and administration of 'first aid', their transportation and the creation of 'overspill' capacity in hospitals adjacent to the front, became the special niche of the NAS and the Red Cross movement. Here they contributed to a transformation in military medicine which saw stationary hospitals replaced by 'first-aid', dedicated conveyances and a line of treatment centres which, depending on severity, passed the wounded from clearing station to field hospital, and from base hospital, via hospital trains and ships, home. Life-chances were duly raised;

---

[38] William MacCormac, *Notes and Recollections of an Ambulance Surgeon*; Henry Rundle, *With the Red Cross in the Franco-German War 1870–1871*, Werner Laurie, London, n.d; Hewett, *Recollections of Sedan*; notebook of Surgeon-Major J. H. Porter; Moore, *Notes with a Prussian Sanitats Detachment*; Wellcome Library, Sir Thomas Longmore papers, RAMC 1139.

[39] J. H. Porter, *The Surgeon's Pocket Book: Being an Essay on the Best Treatment of Wounded in War*, Griffin, London, 1875, pp. 3 and 20.

army efficiency increased. That such a contribution to troop welfare might further the capacity for war making did not, in principle, pose a dilemma. Instead, on-going concerns regarding Britain's relative military capacity rendered such outcomes compatible.

'Self help' amongst the needy

The Quakers, of course, balked at the possibility of making war easier, and restricted their assistance to non-combatants. Unlike the NAS's early improvisations, the Friends' distribution of relief to the French peasantry operated according to a familiar structure and unwritten code of practice; theirs was a modest operation, answerable to a small group of fellow believers rather than forced to keep pace with the public's munificence. Different from the impromptu emergency aid of the roving Red Cross ambulance, the Quakers calculated the requirements of recipients and established a hierarchy of need. Nevertheless, it should not be assumed that Quaker relief was streamlined or necessarily efficient: wastage, duplication and a lack of co-ordination was as much a feature of FWVRF work in France as it was that of the NAS, and Quaker agents were forced to adapt and improvise. A clear principle on the importance of assessing need and avoiding dependency did not of its own build systematic channels of distribution and administration in war. The first task of the FWVRF was to survey distress amongst the peasantry. 'We were to go out and make the road for ourselves', prominent solicitor (and later president of the National Liberal Association) Robert Spence Watson recalled, 'aiming more at getting information and organising the work of relief than actually setting about it'.[40] The affected areas were split into administrative units and relief was distributed via local residents' committees. Attention was initially focused on Alsace and Lorraine, where most of the early fighting had occurred, and here FWVRF agents worked alongside the *Daily News* Fund, based in Sedan.[41]

On advice from the *Daily News's* Mr Bullock, the FWVRF centred its operations in Metz, where an advance depot was formed to supplement its main depot in neutral Arlon. Together with the *Daily News*, FWVRF commissioners instigated a detailed information-gathering exercise to enable the value of relief for each local committee to be calculated. First, it issued a survey to all of the local mayors 'asking for information as to the numbers wanting tools, seed, clothing, bedding'.[42] Grants were then made to small local panels of mayors and *curés*. A second administrative layer of regional committees, known as *Societés de secours aux paysans*, countered local deficiencies or misappropriation of funds. These were comprised of local dignitaries, bishops and presidents of the local chambers of commerce.[43] After

[40] Quoted in Greenwood, *Quaker Encounters*, p. 50.
[41] *Daily News*, 10.10.1870.
[42] Tuke, *A Visit to Paris*, p. 16.
[43] Greenwood, *Quaker Encounters*, p. 52.

the siege of Paris had ended, and in a desire to avoid duplicating the chaos of the competing organisations in the Lorraine, a conference was held to divide the affected areas between the various agencies. It was agreed that the FVWRF would take responsibility for the *département* of the Seine, the *Daily Telegraph* Committee at Versailles would oversee relief in the *département* of Seine-et-Oise, the *Daily News* Fund would administer St Denis and the surrounding villages and the Lord Mayor's Fund would look after the city of Paris.[44]

This approach owed much to the experience of domestic philanthropy, and Friends' burgeoning interest in the methodologies of social science; indeed, it had been at a meeting of the Social Sciences Association that the formation of the FWVRF had been instigated.[45] The Franco-Prussian War represented a juncture in Quaker attitudes and practices. On the one hand, modern methods of social investigation were deployed; on the other, perceptions of the causes of distress were infused with conventional philanthropic moralising. Accordingly, effective relief was thought to be dependent upon the quality of inquiry, the ability to promote self-help and the possibility of generating spiritual reform. The Quakers, like Poor Law administrators, guarded against indiscriminate giving, in the belief that it would encourage dependency. Surveys, interviews and committees were in place to prevent misappropriation of funds. Unfettered relief was as bad as too little relief. As Samuel Capper opined, 'If you open soup-kitchens and distribute potatoes and flour, you infallibly lower the character of a population.'[46] FWVRF agents gave money and agricultural machinery in the form of unsecured loans or in return for work. Female commissioners established sewing groups and encouraged women to make garments in return for payment. These were modelled on similar Quaker schemes in Britain.[47] 'This giving out will have a desirable effect upon the people themselves, presents or gifts having a pauperizing effect,' Augusta Fry noted.[48] Quaker agents, imbued with the lessons of the Irish famines, advocated mixed farming and the consolidation of small plots of land. Encouraging thrift, prudence and industriousness, Friends urged the French peasant to embrace more Quakerly habits. To this end, they instituted 'model' farming practices, bringing over steam machinery and a range of seed varieties and encouraging the cultivators of small farms to co-operate in planting and harvesting. In their attentiveness to long-term subsistence, avoidance of dependency and the use of micro-credit

[44] *Daily News*, 10.10.1870; W. K. Session, *They Chose the Star. An Account of the Work in France of the Society of Friends War Victims Relief Fund from 1870–1875, during and after the Franco-Prussian War*, published by Friends Relief Services, 1944, p. 14; Tuke, *A Visit to Paris*, p. 8.
[45] Many Quakers were concerned with social questions such as the causes and cures for poverty and criminality. Session, *They Chose the Star*, p. 6.
[46] Capper, *Wanderings in War Time*, p. 159.
[47] Of the female Volunteers, M. A. Marriage Allen had worked in the Ragged Schools of London, and as a missionary, while Christine Majolier Alsop had helped the destitute of the East End at the Bedford Institute.
[48] Letter, dated Metz 19.12.1870, quoted in FWVRF, *Executive Committee Report*, December 1870, bound into FWVRF Minute Book, 1870–1871, LSF, WVRC/1870/M1.

arrangements, the FWVRF gave the new field of organised relief some of its most consistent features.

Some Friends combined self-help schemes with evangelism and attempts at spiritual conversion. But no consensus existed over the relationship between religion and philanthropy. As in society at large, attitudes to human suffering were in flux. Punitive attributions of want to individual (or national) moral failing co-existed with attempts to implement secular and impartial welfare practices. Keen to dispel 'a very common delusion, with regard to what are called *philanthropic* movements, such as this for aiding the War Victims', John Bellows, an FWVRF agent in France, regretted that

> Many people regard them as *religious works*, and inconsiderately praise those who are engaged in them as if they were fulfilling some Divine mission. They even quote Scripture in support of such a notion . . . All this is but false sentimentalism, calculated greatly to mislead those who seek after *reality* in the things which are of weightiest moment to all.[49]

Despite Bellows' assertions, Helen Hatton, historian of the Irish famines, is premature to suggest that by the mid-nineteenth century Quakers were exceptional in philanthropic circles for understanding mass poverty to be structural rather than the fault of the poor. Quaker aid 'was not directed to the inculcation of middle-class virtue as the cure for poverty', she writes, and 'nor would they tolerate "souperism", that use of philanthropy which made relief contingent upon a religious duty'.[50] Yet many Friends blamed France's troubles on a moral degeneracy occasioned by irreligion and feckless communards. Ten thousand copies of the Scripture in French were distributed by Quakers, as well as seventy thousand pamphlets proclaiming the destruction and demoralisation of France to be a form of divine retribution.[51] It was believed that these sufferings had opened the heart of the French peasant to the Quaker message. Now was considered an opportune moment to accelerate the Protestant missionary work already afoot in France.[52] As one female relief worker put it, 'There is certainly an open door in France at the present time for simple Gospel teaching.'[53] Aid may not have been contingent on religious conversion, but the Quakers' relief work in France intrinsically combined material and spiritual salvation. Sewing circles doubled as religious meetings. This evangelism met with negligible success, however; Quaker agents had no conversions to record.

---

[49] For his attempt to separate Quaker philanthropy from religious beliefs, see John Bellows, *The Track of War around Metz*, p. 5. Original italics.

[50] Helen Hatton, *The Largest Amount of Good. Quaker Relief in Ireland, 1654–1921*, McGill–Queen's University Press, London, 1993, p. 4.

[51] See Braithwaite, *Memorials of Christine Majolier Alsop*, p. 184.

[52] For Protestant missionary work in France see H. Bonar, *The White Fields of France; or, The Story of Mr McAll's Mission to the Working Men of Paris and Lyons*, James Nisbet and Co., London, 1880. Following the war, the Quakers would run a mission in France for working-class women. This was eventually taken over by McAll, see Greenwood, *Quaker Encounter*, p. 77.

[53] M. A. M. Allen, *Simple Sketches of Christian Work and Travel*, p. 32.

Thus it was that, whatever their differences, this most destructive of wars provided the opportunity for the FWVRF and the NAS to develop a novel experiment in the systematisation of relief. Reality, however, frequently fell short of intention. But equally, their criteria of success differed. The NAS recognised war as a regrettable inevitability. Thoughts as to British preparedness in any future conflict remained uppermost. The motives of the belligerents of 1870–71 were not judged (or at least not openly): aid to combatants was to be provided according to the criterion of need, irrespective of any test of worth. In practice of course, the lack of an organised system of distribution thwarted this impulse. To help rectify this deficiency and, one suspects, to dispense rapidly accumulating funds, Loyd Lindsay made a one-off payment of £20,000 to each army for the purpose of medical improvements. Yet clinical detachment notwithstanding, suffering also assumed a moral quality for these volunteer surgeons and nurses: wounded soldiers were invested with heroic qualities and their endurance was viewed as a test of the nation's moral fibre. 'This was the time to judge of the difference of character', volunteer nurse Mrs Templer remarked, 'no one had a better opportunity of doing so than I had'.[54] Even so, the hope was that British aid would help to overcome these national differences and foster greater understanding; recognition of suffering confirmed the humanity of wounded and carer alike. Such benevolence could be provident: '[s]eeds of goodwill' had been planted and international friendships of 'Christian brotherhood' had been cultivated, 'to bear good fruit hereafter'.[55] Longmore was not the only one to toast the 'Christian principle of international charity embodied in the [Geneva] Convention'.[56]

Quakers likewise viewed compassion for the afflicted as a tenet of the Christian faith. But for Quakers the moral quality of suffering assumed a different import. In this war a moral lesson was drawn from the French peasants' suffering, and yet the suffering of strangers, though to be deplored, provided the possibility of new friendships and, if not conversion, then the spread of a 'social gospel' of inimitably Quaker virtues. If, therefore, the success of the NAS was quantified in terms of recovery rates, then the measure of Quaker relief work lay not simply in the numbers relieved but in the quality of the relationship between donor and recipient. Self-help, thrift and peacefulness were best encouraged through example. Assessed numerically, the FWVRF aided relatively few: 'this relief has been but a drop in a bucket'.[57] Ultimately, however, the success or otherwise of the Friends' relief in France rested in hands more exalted than their own:

[54] Templer, *Labour of Love*, p. 124.

[55] Comments of Sir Vincent Eyre, Boulogne Depot Manager, in *Red Cross Operations in the North of France 1870–1872, Printed for the Boulogne English Committee for Aid to the Sick and Wounded in War*, Spottiswoode & Co., London, 1872, p. 35.

[56] Longmore, 'On the Geneva Convention', p. 12.

[57] *General Report of the Committee of the War Victims' Fund to the Meeting for Sufferings*, Minute Book, FWVRF, 1870–1871, (n.d. [c. May 1871]), p. 8, LSF/WVRC/1870/M1.

On a retrospect of their labours during the last seven or eight months, the Committee feel bound, with humble thankfulness, to record their deep sense of having been favoured with a better wisdom and a higher guidance than their own. Over and over again have they had to marvel at the way in which difficulties, apparently almost insuperable, have been met and overcome.[58]

Their work ended – after about eight months – not because the need had been met, but because they were exhausted, their businesses had been neglected and Quaker consciences had been sufficiently salved.[59]

Adventures in war time

The reasons why volunteers undertook relief work are not always possible to fathom. It would be churlish to suggest otherwise than that they had genuine concern for those suffering for want of medical attention or the means of subsistence, but this does not preclude the pull of other factors. Opportunities for honing professional expertise and for evangelism have already been noted. Relief workers' own accounts reveal the diffuse recompense of unsolicited giving, not least the chance for adventure on a par with soldiering or the Grand Tour. For roving with an ambulance offered a novel type of wandering in war time. Accounts written by NAS and FWVRF relief workers are alike animated by the pleasure felt at feeling part of a campaign and of participating in the dramas and hardships of life in war's wake. 'We were all eager to get to the front, impatient to know what the future held in store for us . . . Everything seemed vague and adventurous', recalled Henry Rundle, a surgeon with a German reserve hospital.[60] Descriptions of privation, camaraderie and self-sacrifice recalled the soldier's lot (they also dispelled notions of extravagant living on charitable funds). Volunteer nurse Florence Lees adopted the hard-bitten tone of an experienced campaigner:

One tin mug was used for all purposes for which plates, pots, or cups, or basins can be used; and cutlery consisted of a soldier's travelling knife, fork and spoon. But enough of these discomforts, with which all who go to war or follow the camp, must necessarily be familiar.[61]

Meanwhile, the young medical graduate Charles Ryan pondered upon 'the good that each of us was bound by duty to perform; the sacrifice of every personal consideration, and even our lives if necessary, in the grand and holy cause of the service to the wounded'.[62] That the glory of campaigning animates NAS accounts is hardly

---

[58] *General Report of the Committee of the War Victims' Fund to the Meeting for Sufferings*, Minute Book, FWVRF, 1870–1871, (n.d. [c. May 1871]), p. 2, LSF/WVRC/1870/M1.

[59] Greenwood, *Quaker Encounters*, p. 49.

[60] Henry Rundle, *With the Red Cross*, p. 25.

[61] Lees, 'In a Fever Hospital before Metz', *Good Words*, 1873, p. 322.

[62] Charles Ryan, *With an Ambulance*, p. 29.

surprising, given their milieu, but even FWVRF agents were not immune to the peculiar pleasures of war, or its scenic potential. Of the Prussians, John Bellows, a prominent Quaker publisher, noted, 'It is a wonderful sight to see them drill or march . . . so machine-like, and so perfect for the end are the whole arrangements.'[63] Robert Spence Watson likewise described scenes of 'wonderful picturesqueness'. Soon after leaving Briey, he began to meet Prussian troops:

> For an hour and a half the first division of the second army kept marching past us – artillery, cavalry, and infantry, in immense numbers, pouring forwards to Lille. It was a marvellous sight, and we got weary of saluting . . . There were about 40,000 of them, and their solidity and simplicity were singularly impressive.[64]

These tales of ambulance exploits and charitable endeavour could be read on a number of levels: as war-time adventure stories; as exposés of the inadequacies of military hospitals; as valorisations of the heroic suffering of the common soldier; as anti-war tracts; and as testimonies to the respectability and benevolence of the author. They routinely assert, none too politely, that 'cultivated' (and high-born) pity was worth more than routine professionalism. Certainly, it would seem, suffering required a humanistic imagination and a literary aesthetic in order to be fully apprehended; relief work, from the first, was also a literary enterprise. Without such portrayals its meaning was, if not open, then at least subject to unwelcome interpretation, especially by the new breed of war correspondent.

Aspersions in the press were rife; accusations of ghoulish battlefield tourism abounded. 'It seems to us', intoned the *Observer*, 'that nothing can be worse than for tourists to follow the track of armies, gratifying a mere lust for excitement which is not free from cruelty.'[65] The *Daily News* reported tales of imposture, theft from cadavers and voyeurism. It advocated that

> for the credit of the [red cross] badge something should be done to purge it of these ruffians, and also to prevent its adoption by every dilettante sightseer, whose sole object in visiting Sedan is to see the scene of the battle and prig a dead man's knapsack or helmet (all the more precious relic if it has blood upon it) to delight wherewithal the gaping domestic circle in Hackney or Clapham.[66]

For the NAS and its agents in France, the refutation of whisperings of dilettantism, mismanagement and, in extreme cases, fraud quickly became an imperative. Loyd Lindsay felt keenly the need to forestall further 'indignant responses' and to account for their presence on the battlefield.[67] While the Quakers' mission of Christian compassion could be comprehended in terms of traditional charitable

---

[63] Bellows, *Track of War*, p. 25.
[64] Watson, *The Villages around Metz*, p. 15.
[65] Quoted in David Lloyd, *Battlefield Tourism, Pilgrimage and the Commemoration of the Great War in Britain, Australia and Canada, 1919–1939*, Berg, Oxford, 1998, p. 20.
[66] *Daily News*, 24.9.1870.
[67] Loyd Lindsay, letter reproduced in NAS, *Report* (Franco-Prussian War), pp. 51–52.

impulses (at least in a war where Britain was neutral), the novel desire to offer impartial assistance to the wounded of foreign armies required some justification. Propriety and neutrality had to be embodied in practice and on paper. Women, in particular, had to dispel the spectre of the camp follower that hovered over female activity in war. The trained nurse could invoke the example of Florence Nightingale, but for the 'lady amateur', responsible for hospital ministrations and impromptu dashings to collect and distribute stores, the self-abnegating Crimean nurse only partly afforded a precedent: the self-assertion needed for battles with red tape and unhelpful officials, entrenched military custom and jealous medical officers required further elaboration. The impression is less of collegiate self-effacement than of a spirited individualism: these were personal acts of service to wounded men, rather than routine professional duties and the deference of a religious order. Mrs Templer, who nursed at Pont-à-Mousson and Sedan, recalled how she tried

> in every way possible to alleviate their sufferings – and who would not have done so if they had seen the poor suffering creatures as I did. Mine was a Labour of Love, and I tried as consciously as possible to fulfil the work I had undertaken.[68]

Typically, such tales turn on intuition, spontaneity, providence, pluck and derring-do: fears of a prior agenda are summarily dispelled. Nevertheless, the 'call of the wounded' required careful delineation. Suffering existed as an abstract moral quality in these accounts: the corporeal body and the intimate physicality of nursing work were absent. '[T]o give a detailed account of daily labours in hospitals would only be wearisome.'[69] Female volunteers appear kind but matronly, battling valiantly to uphold English standards in foreign lands. Mrs Templer emerges as a formidable nanny-figure: after brow-beating the medical officer in charge, she turned to her patients: 'poor creatures were quite like children and had to be managed in the same way'.[70]

Over and again, the authors of these accounts owned only that they were reproducing diaries or 'rough scribblings'.[71] In her 'simple work', Mrs Templer modestly claimed to 'have merely narrated circumstances as they really occurred'.[72] The impression is of a response to suffering that was both sincere and unpremeditated. John Bellows described how his notes 'were penned under all kinds of difficulties and without the remotest thought for publishing them'.[73] Unvarnished recollections by hard-bitten campaigners guarded against accusations of mawkishness or contrivance, but such apparent artlessness was at odds with the pains taken to establish the cultivated sensibility of the author. Here the crucial ability to moderate one's

---

[68] Templer, *A Labour of Love*, p. 92.

[69] MacLaughlin, *Our Adventures*, p. 328.

[70] Templer, *A Labour of Love*, p. 60.

[71] See for example, Bellows, *Track of War*, p. 4; Tuke, *A Visit to Paris*, p. 1; Watson, *The Villages around Metz*, p. 3; MacLaughlin, *Our Adventures*, p. v; Templer, *A Labour of Love*, p. vii.

[72] Templer, *A Labour of Love*, p. vii.

[73] Bellows, *Track of War*, p. 4. For similar see Tuke, *A Visit to Paris*, p. 1; Watson, *The Villages around Metz*, p. 3.

sympathy was suggested not only in the content but also in the form of these accounts, and this was no more important than in the case of the female volunteer. As one NAS nurse wished to establish, 'No idle curiosity brought us to the seat of war.'[74] But few references were made to Dunant or to the new laws of war: literary conventions instead gave meaning to new roles and practices. War is described with detached interest rather than ghoulish curiosity, its 'picturesque' qualities duly noted. Scenes of battles and the detritus of war are situated within pastoral vistas and historical landscapes. Their authors, they imply, were not mere battlefield tourists but had taste, delicacy and erudition. Coinciding with academic interest in landscape painting and the growing popularity of sightseeing tours, this appreciation of the picturesque implied a cultivated way of seeing and feeling.[75] Volunteer nurse Mrs Henry Smith distilled the essence of war in poignant scenes of suffering interposed with glimmers of beauty and renewal. Amidst the relics of the battlefield, she found abandoned 'a small looking-glass, and two flowers something like crocuses, growing up among the ruins'.[76] Here, fellow NAS nurses Pearson and MacLaughlin described the battle of Sedan:

> The meadows were fresh and green, the trees just stirred their branches to the slight summer breeze . . . smoke came from cannon and rifle, but the golden sunshine threw a halo over all and softened down the distant outlines, and that was our view of the great battle around Sedan . . . A battle is very pretty ten miles off.[77]

With these discerning, but apparently spontaneous and unvarnished, recollections, an impression of useless gushings or a sympathy that merged into partisanship was avoided. But so too was an appearance of rigidity or cold calculation. In accounting for their presence on a foreign battlefield, a refined pity was called forth, one modulated by the practical efficiency of the level-headed English lady and gentleman. The spontaneous heart thus was firmly held in check by a discriminating eye, a steady hand and an inimitable sense of fair play. Time and again, this need to balance heart and head was heard. It still is.

Inevitably, however, a disparity grew between those for whom the quality of mercy was paramount and those for whom professional training and regulation seemed equally imperative. Inevitably, too, competing attempts to appropriate the legacy and lessons of the NAS's work in the Franco-Prussian War saw its members split between those favouring Loyd Lindsay's vision of independent and impromptu charitable endeavour and those wishing to see greater incorporation into the army

---

[74] MacLaughlin, *Our Adventures*, p. 4.

[75] J. Buzard, *The Beaten Track: European Tourism, Literature and the Ways to Culture, 1800–1918*, Clarendon Press, Oxford, 1993; Malcolm Andrews, *The Search for the Picturesque: Landscape Aesthetics and Tourism in Britain, 1760–1800*, Scholar Press, Aldershot, 1989. For a particularly influential contemporary definition of the picturesque see, John Ruskin, *The Seven Lamps of Architecture* (5th edn), George Allen, Orpington, 1886 [1849].

[76] 'Letters by the Late Mrs Henry Smith', p. 143.

[77] MacLaughlin, *Our Adventures*, p. 203.

medical services. For Quakers, meanwhile, aid in a war in which Britain was neutral had occasioned little internal dissent. But, as Quakers discovered in the Boer War, and again in the Great War, knowledge of suffering did not call forth a unanimous response, nor did an intimation of the Kingdom of God generate consensus on how best to ameliorate earthly suffering. For the pull of heart and the considerations of head varied from one Quaker to another.

Appropriating the legacy

When the end of the Franco-Prussian War came, those who had proffered relief returned to teaching hospitals, military barracks and neglected businesses. In Britain, the peace was commemorated in rousing verse. 'England's Blazon; or, the Blood Red Cross', subtitled an 'International Hymn of Peace and Charity', sang the praises of a philanthropic army of valiant NAS surgeons:

> 'Glory' England spurns – but when
> 'Duty' calls her to the fight,
> Undismay'd will march her men
> Shouting, God defend the right!
> Lord of battles! Prince of Peace!
> Deign our humble cry to hear
> Make proud oppressor cease
> Smite the nations with Thy fear.[78]

Well-bred English chivalry was a force to be reckoned with. In parliament, Gladstone had wished for a similar role for British diplomacy. To this end, he undertook one more diplomatic foray, one that would foreshadow a reorientation of 'England's Mission' abroad in the decades to come, and with it open up the next chapter in the history of British relief work. With European attention elsewhere engaged, Russia had taken the opportunity to abrogate the Black Sea clauses which, following her defeat in the Crimea, had barred her from patrolling its border with the Ottoman Empire. The Eastern Question once again threatened. The Conference of London, January to March 1871, saved face all round (acknowledging the sanctity of treaties in principle, but allowing Russia to pursue its claims). But Gladstone's failure to 'Smite the nations with Thy fear' was one reason for his unexpected election defeat of 1874. On-going controversy over the Education Act, and his mishandling of the non-conformist vote, was another. The Balkan insurgencies of 1875–76, which revealed a further and more serious example of Russian ambitions in the region, found Gladstone out of office. But moral interventionism – and its appeal to non-conformists and the grass roots alike – this time held sway; and here relief workers' role in helping to reimagine Britain's international responsibilities was crucial.

---

[78] James Vaughn and John Makeham, 'England's Blazon; or, the Blood Red Cross', F. Pitman, London, 1871.

Loyd Lindsay's prominent experience of providing aid augmented his credentials as a spokesperson on military matters and the current state of the British forces.[79] As the situation in the Balkans deteriorated, he was to be found speaking with authority on the need for a modern reserve force. In 1871, the NAS published a report of its work during the Franco-Prussian War, authored by Loyd Lindsay but including numerous memoranda and correspondence from agents at the time. The report charts the systematisation of public indignation and pity into an organised plan of operations. Designed to demonstrate the business-like manner of NAS administration, it was, as *The Times* reported, 'a formidable folio volume, precisely like a Parliamentary Blue-book'.[80] The NAS it portrayed was civilian and independent, free of the stultifying effects of War Office bureaucracy. As Loyd Lindsay noted, 'one of the great advantages of voluntary societies is, that their agents can work untrammelled by military regulation'.[81] Featured letters from those who had worked in France concurred:

> [O]ne advantage of this extra-official assistance pleases me very much; it would be an excellent decentralising movement; it would induce a habit of reliance on individual effort and volunteer personal energies; it would help to break down the habit of waiting for government impulse before any improvement is attempted.[82]

Loyd Lindsay felt that he had been granted a mandate to administer the public's munificence in war. He was now anxious lest proposals to siphon off donations for other purposes would threaten the NAS's fund-raising *métier*. For it was not clear that this mandate extended to the creation of an organisation for the training of volunteers. '[T]he public mind . . . was not likely to respond to any elaborate organisation or preparation in time of peace,' he cautioned.[83] 'What was given was spontaneously given', and,

> [t]he funds and the gifts which were entrusted to the Committee were administered bearing in mind that the legitimate functions of the Society were of a subsidiary character, to assist in certain cases the efforts which the Governments and peoples of France and Germany were making for the relief of their own sick and wounded soldiers. To have undertaken generally duties of a wider extent would have been to go beyond what were understood to be the proper duties of the Society.[84]

---

[79] *The Times*, 3.10.1870.

[80] Mary Poovey, *Making a Social Body: British Cultural Formation, 1830–1864*, University of Chicago Press, Chicago, 1995, p. 117.

[81] NAS, *Report* (Franco-Prussian War), p. 152.

[82] Sir Vincent Eyre, Chief of the NAS's Boulogne Committee, in *Questions on the Operations of the British National Society for Aid to the Sick and Wounded in War, and Replies Thereto, by Various Members of the Society's Staff and Others: Being the Result of Their Experiences in the Franco-Prussian War, 1870–1871*, London, Harrison & Sons, 1871, question 30.

[83] Archie K. Loyd, *An Outline of the History of the British Red Cross Society from Its Foundation in 1870 to the Outbreak of War in 1914*, London, [The Society], 1917, p. 10.

[84] NAS, *Report* (Franco-Prussian War), p. 24.

Balking at suggestions from members of the Order of St John for a 'regimentalised' NAS, Loyd Lindsay limited activities on the close of the Franco-Prussian War to the establishment of a new Council (comprising Loyd Lindsay, Rothschild, Overstone and other distinguished names). It invested surplus funds (in railways and, somewhat providentially, in the armaments company Vickers) and applied for a charter of incorporation so that the Society could assume a permanent footing. This meant, of course, quashing the hopes of the Order of St John for the official incorporation of voluntary aid into the army medical services. John Furley could do little other than confide to Longmore his despair at 'Lindsay's rough and ready manner of finding doctors, nurses and ambulance directors at a moment's notice.'[85] Longmore, meanwhile, criticised the NAS's rather ambivalent position vis-à-vis both the army medical services and the Geneva Convention. Together, they sought to persuade Loyd Lindsay of the need for pre-concerted voluntary effort, formally subsumed into the hierarchy of existing army medical provision.

Lecturing at the Royal United Services Institute in 1871, Loyd Lindsay championed an efficient but strictly autonomous volunteer relief agency. A year later, Longmore returned to the Institute to clarify the proper function of such an organisation and its place in international law. Longmore had, as British delegate in Geneva, ensured that the Convention would not confer inviolability and neutrality on private individuals of an independent foreign aid society. He was now emphatic that the NAS had had no warrant for its activities in France. Medical volunteers ought to be 'under the supreme command of the war department' and given training in peace time.[86] Frustrated at Loyd Lindsay's attitude, members of the Order of St John resigned in protest. In 1874 they established a small 'Ambulance Department', with the aim of training war-time volunteers through civilian life-saving work in industrial and mining districts. *Neuss* litters (a type of stretcher), pioneered by the Germans in the Franco-Prussian War, were purchased in Berlin for the purpose.[87] Col Brackenbury, the adroit Professor of Military History praised for bringing order to NAS affairs in France, reflected upon a 'duty beyond that which I owed the Society – a duty to the people at large'. His resignation would now enable him to bring 'external pressure to bear to induce the Council to take up [the peace-time organisation of voluntary aid] as their most important avocation.'[88]

For the NAS's female volunteers and those with an interest in female war nursing, the lessons and legacies of their work in the Franco-Prussian War turned on similar points. It was widely agreed that female nurses had been useful, owing to their 'self

[85] Furley to Longmore, 24.11.1872, Wellcome Library, Sir Thomas Longmore papers, RAMC 1139 box 243, 44/9.

[86] Longmore, 'On the Geneva Convention of 1864', p. 12.

[87] In 1878 the 'Ambulance Department' became the St John Ambulance Association. Ronnie Cole-Mackintosh, *A Century of Service to Mankind: A History of the St John Ambulance Brigade*, Century Benham, London, 1986, p. 18; Order of St John, *Report of the Chapter, 1874*, Harrison and Son, London, 1874, p. 6.

[88] H. Brackenbury, 'Aid to the Injured', Proceedings of a public meeting of the Knights of St John of Jerusalem, A. W. and J. P. Jackson, Woolwich, 1878.

sacrifice' and 'natural feminine lightness and dexterity'.[89] But it was felt that women ought to remain as far from the front as possible. Assistant Surgeon G. W. McNalty spoke for many when he proclaimed that '[t]here is not place for the female nurse in the regimental ambulance'.[90] Others dissented. Here, the question of training was imperative, and both experienced nurses and military surgeons were canvassed on this point. The spectacle of 'English ladies rushing wildly over the country, sleeping sometimes in the open field, and writing thrilling letters home of their work and hardships' was more than Florence Nightingale's protégé Florence Lees could bear. 'They seemed to be under no authority and accountable to no one, although in some cases they asserted that they belonged to the English Society.'[91] This, then, was tacit endorsement of Nightingale's vision of a corps of professional nurses formally accompanying the army in war. Yet, as a voluntary society relying on public dona-tions, the NAS could not afford to turn down enthusiastic offers of unsolicited help. For the foreseeable future, tensions between the well-meaning lady amateur and the trained nurse would simmer.

Quick to pass into fiction, these selfless 'ministering angels' would eventually become the popular image of aid work. In many ways their portrayal was the antithesis of female emancipation. In Wilkie Collins' *The New Magdalen* (1873) and G. A. Henty's *A Tale of Two Sieges of Paris* (1895), female protagonists were able to redeem moral failings (prostitution and 'advanced views', respectively) through the self-sacrifice of Red Cross work. For proponents of the female vote, however, the Red Cross nurse achieved an altogether different significance. If the soldier had been elevated to a symbol of national virtue and his suffering glorified as a form of martyrdom, then the ministration to his wants could be conceived as a moral and patriotic duty earning reciprocal rights.[92] Thus, it became possible for suffragists to construe relief work in war as an act of citizenship on a par with military service. The death of one such nurse in the Franco-Prussian War prompted the suffragist *Victoria Magazine* to muse,

> We are of the opinion that if her blood was not literally spilt in the battlefield (which is what in some people's minds constitutes the right to Suffrage) her life was just as fairly lost by the means of the battlefield. Therefore her compeers have a right to be heard for the sake of all those noble women who have nursed the sick and wounded in war and at home.[93]

Yet the equation between relief work, national duty and citizenship had more than one resolution. Relief work did not have to be an equivalent to soldiering in order to enact valid grounds for citizenship. Following Sonya Rose, citizenship can

---

[89] NAS, *Report* (Franco-Prussian War), p. 174.

[90] NAS, *Report* (Franco-Prussian War), p. 174.

[91] Florence Lees, *Questions on the Operations of the British National Society for Aid to the Sick and Wounded in War*, p. 5.

[92] Anne Summers, *Angels and Citizens*, pp. 126–127.

[93] *Victoria Magazine*, XVII, 1871, p. 381. Quoted in Summers, *Angels and Citizens*, p. 127.

also be considered 'a moral category that refers to how persons should conduct themselves as members of the national community'.[94] For Quakers this had a particular appeal. Relief work could be both a testament against war and a testament to moral self-determination. *Blackwood's* caricature of staid Quaker complacency was thus to be rebutted. It would be just such a concept of 'moral' citizenship that Gladstone would come to invoke in his denunciation of Tory policy in the Balkans. Here converged an avowedly patriotic politics of humanity that would animate foreign affairs and networks of relief workers for over a generation. This is the subject of Part II.

[94] Sonya Rose, 'Women's Rights, Women's Obligations: Contradictions of Citizenship in World War II Britain', *European Review of History*, Vol. 7, No. 2, 2000, 277.

Part II

Knowledge of suffering and the politics of relief:
the Balkans, 1876–78

3

New humanitarian politics: 'victim' nations and the brotherhood of humanity

> Never, probably, have so many imperative demands been made upon the generosity of the British nation, and never has the cry for help met with a response so prompt and liberal. . . . The ordinary claims of the National Society for Aid to the Sick and Wounded are supplemented by a dozen rival organizations; the Stafford House Committee, Lady Strangford's Committee, the Russian Wounded Fund, the Turkish Compassionate Fund, collections on behalf of Bulgarians, Bosnians, Montenegrins, all these and many more find liberal patrons. At the same time the Indian Famine makes a thrilling appeal to the sympathies of the nation which rules India, and the Mansion House Fund has already received subscriptions to the amount of nearly £130,000. . . . It is to England that every nation in turn appeals in its hour of tribulation with a confident assurance that the appeal will be answered. It is to England that the victims of war and pestilence and famine look for aid.[1]

If, in surveying relief to the Balkans and India in 1877, the leader writer at *The Times* expressed his amazement at the dizzying amounts collected, he also revelled in a moment of national pride. English benevolence seemed without parallel. In total, approximately £250,000 was raised for those affected by war in the Balkans. Double that amount was eventually collected for victims of the Madras famine. That this was a 'white man's burden' appeared self-evident; that this was also a peculiarly 'English man's burden', shouldered with innate moral good sense, was no less apparent. Nevertheless, if aid in colonial famine appeared an act of mercy in the face of natural calamity, the plethora of funds for Balkan relief – and the relatively lower subscription rates – suggests a less straightforward sense of purpose. Indeed, though the alleviation of suffering strangers in the Balkans was the occasion for self-congratulation, there was little consensus on the moral and material purpose of such aid, or of what it said of British interests and values. It is with the elaboration of impending crisis in the Balkans – and the politics of humanity and relief in Britain – that this chapter is concerned.

[1] *The Times*, 12.9.1877.

In 1876–78 the fate of communities affected by separatist violence in the Ottoman Empire would see sympathy and material support for 'oppressed' Christians become, for some, a moral imperative. Others felt the need to stabilise and pacify a region of British strategic interest to be equally pressing. At the *Northern Echo*, W. T. Stead mobilised a series of protest meetings to denounce Ottoman barbarism and Tory inaction. Their litany of resolutions he faithfully reported as the spontaneous expression of the people's moral interests, and he appealed to Gladstone for their representation. Gladstone chose his moment. In his thunderous *Bulgarian Horrors and the Question of the East*, Gladstone advocated 'moral intervention' in the Balkans and proclaimed a rejuvenation of British politics based on universal values. Protestors were urged to donate money for the relief of the victims of oppression as an expression of solidarity with their fellow protestors and their suffering 'brothers' in South-Eastern Europe.

In this context, relief workers did more than give expression to the public's concern. For, in the production of knowledge about this little-known region, they were instrumental in equating communities of suffering Christians with oppressed national groups and in galvanising W. T. Stead and a network of sympathetic journalists, scholars and politicians with their first-hand evidence of atrocity. It was on this evidence that the Duke of Argyll, trenchant champion of freedom for the 'oppressed' Bulgarian nation, could argue that Britain had a right of intervention, born not of 'a duty or a right founded upon Treaty, but upon the general principles of humanity'.[2] Distinguished historians, many of whom, such as E. A. Freeman, were active in the agitation, gave credence to a vision of centuries-old Christian nations labouring under the yoke of Ottoman tyranny, a vision which ignored the plight of the region's Jews and Muslims. The insurrections having largely failed, it was on these historical and moral claims that Balkan nationhood rested. Thus, relief efforts in the Balkans ought best to be understood as integral to the mobilisation of concern, stimulating considerable public outrage, and informing the people's moral interests, on the one hand, but alienating others by what seemed erratic emotionalism and an exclusively Christian brotherhood of humanity, on the other. This was to have significance beyond the events of 1876–78, for the exposure of atrocity and provision of relief formed a template of a popular humanitarian politics that would animate broad strands of radicalism up to the outbreak of the Great War in 1914 and beyond.[3]

Upheaval in the Balkans

Little-known Rumelia – now part of modern-day Bulgaria – occupied the central swathe of the Ottoman Empire's Balkan territories and was home to a mixed population

---

[2] House of Lords Debates, 31.1.1878, *Hansard*, Vol. 237, c. 696. This was far from straightforward: the 1856 Treaty of Paris after the Crimean War had specified that intervention should be a common decision of all members of the Concert of Europe.

[3] Eugenio Biagini, *British Democracy and Irish Nationalism 1876–1906*, Cambridge University Press, Cambridge, 2007, pp. 34–44.

of Orthodox Christians, Jews, Muslims (Circassians resettled after the Crimean War and a number of 'Pomaks', or converts from Christianity). In June 1876, rumour of bloodshed in the region around Filibe (also known at the time by its Greek name Philippopolis, and today as Plovdiv) reached the offices of the *Daily News*. Januarius Aloysius MacGahan, the newspaper's most intrepid journalist, was despatched to investigate. To the *The Times's* chagrin, the *Daily News* was able to emulate its success in the Franco-Prussian war and to scoop its rival, this time with bloodcurdling reports of a massacre of Christians by Ottoman irregulars. By this point, the initial Bulgar insurrection which had occasioned such violence had been over for two months. News of the 'Bulgarian atrocities' first arrived in letters sent from the region's Christians to Robert College in Constantinople, an American missionary school with strong ties to the Bulgarian intelligentsia.[4] A year earlier, news of similar massacres had reached Britain following a rebellion in Bosnia. This earlier bloodshed had done little to perturb British readers, despite the best efforts of resident pro-Slav relief worker and educationalist Paulina Irby and the sympathetic historians E. A. Freeman and Arthur Evans. Events in Rumelia would, however, elicit a far more emotive response, though not immediately.[5] It would take until the start of autumn before the country was enlivened by petitions, indignant protest meetings, fund-raising drives and a rash of relief missions, not to mention the emergence from retirement of a splenetic Gladstone.

It is worth pointing out some of the complexities of the events that British protestors labelled the 'Bulgarian atrocities'. The image of a national liberation movement quashed by an oppressive regime, though having obvious dramatic appeal, was an over-simplification: though a Bulgarian independence movement existed, the extent to which it had widespread support – or sought complete political autonomy – is debatable. Those practising Bulgarian Orthodoxy were in a majority in most of the Rumeli provinces, but any equation between religious observance and a suppressed Christian 'nation' was questionable, to say the least.[6] Demographic flux made it impossible to equate a homogenous ethnic bloc with a specific territory, in keeping with contemporary ideas of nationhood in the West. Not only had the Ottomans resettled Muslim Circassians on the Danubian plain, but many Christians had fled to the Rhodope Mountains following a period of disorder between 1770 and 1820. This was accompanied by seasonal migrations of Bulgar Christians to tend harvests and visit the markets of Adrianople (Edirne) and Istanbul. However, from the 1820s, a revival of interest in a Bulgarian language, religion and the greatness of past empire had undeniably taken place. This renaissance – or *vüzrazhdane* – emerged at a time of economic and social change and was cultivated by an 'imagined

[4] Saab, *Reluctant Icon*, p. 83.
[5] Even late in the summer of 1876, the reliably Liberal *Huddersfield Examiner* was reporting, with little further comment, 'a horrible massacre' in the Balkan mountains. It praised the reticence of the Disraeli government in pursuing non-intervention; *Huddersfield Examiner*, 10 and 18.7.1876. Only following Stead's editorials and the first Darlington meeting would a protest meeting take place in Huddersfield, on 4 September 1876.
[6] See Saab, *Reluctant Icon*, p. 28, n. 37.

community' of journalists, writers, teachers, business owners and churchmen resident throughout the Ottoman Empire, in places such as Bucharest, Odessa and Istanbul. For most of this period, 'liberationist' activity was directed not at the Ottoman government but at the dominant Greek churchmen and layer of state functionaries routinely accused of venality.[7] Even so, historian of the Bulgarian intelligentsia Thomas Meininger notes the lack of a 'common ideological outlook'.[8] The Bulgarian Orthodox population as a whole was largely quiescent, and there was no Bulgarian revolutionary tradition. The aspirations of this nationalist minority varied: religious independence (from the oversight of the Greek patriarchate), a dual monarchy (on the model of Austria-Hungary), compliance with the 1856 *Hatt-i Hümayun* (an Ottoman proclamation promising minority rights to Christians following the Crimean War), a federation of free Balkan states and, among radicals and only late in the process, the creation of an independent Bulgarian nation.[9] In April 1876, on the coat-tails of a revolt instigated by Serb irredentists in the provinces of Bosnia and Herzegovina, Bulgarian rebels led by Lyuben Karavelov and Vasil Levski seized the moment. According to British consular sources, Christian peasants were threatened with plunder and arson if they refused to join the insurgency.[10] The actual revolt was a disappointment: communication was poor, military sense was lacking and the rebels had overestimated local support (in total only 10,000 took up arms).[11] The insurgency appears to have amounted to a slaughter of Muslims. It is estimated that 1,000 Muslim villagers were killed.[12]

Rumours of a Bulgarian uprising elicited brutal local reprisals. Violence occurred against Christians and against Muslims in the area. When the authorities did intervene, they were forced to rely upon ill-disciplined irregulars, the *Başibazuks*, and the arming of Circassians (the regular army was already deployed in Bosnia and could not be spared). There is little doubt that these irregulars extracted a ferocious penalty. Many were Bulgarian Muslims and feared further rebel violence. At the time, the number of Christian dead was reported to have reached 150,000; historians now put the figure at around 3,000.[13] In Batak, women and children were burnt to death in a church, a scene of such emotional charge that it was invoked repeatedly in the British press. It is difficult to determine the extent to which this violence was

[7] The Greek Orthodox Church dominated the Orthodox *millet* (religious community), which was one of six *millets* in the Ottoman Empire by 1860: the Jewish, the Orthodox, the Roman Catholic, the Gregorian Armenian, the Roman Armenian and the Protestant. On Easter Day 1860 the Bulgarian Church declared ecclesiastical independence after a decade of hostility between the Greek Church and a rising Bulgarian middle class, and it received official recognition from the Sultan in 1872. See Dennis Hupchick, *The Balkans from Constantinople to Communism*, Palgrave, Basingstoke, 2002, p. 243.

[8] Thomas A. Meininger, *The Formation of a Nationalist Bulgarian Intelligentsia, 1835–1878*, Garland Publishing Inc, London, 1987, p. 249.

[9] Crampton, R. J., *Bulgaria*, Oxford University Press, Oxford, 2007, p. 24.

[10] Sir Henry Elliot, 'Atrocities in Bulgaria July 15 1876', Bodleian Library, Disraeli papers, B/XVI/A/11.

[11] Crampton, *Bulgaria*, p. 92.

[12] Justin McCarthy, *Death and Exile*, Darwin Press, Princeton NJ, 1995, p. 60.

[13] Saab, *Reluctant Icon*, p. 24.

systematic and state sponsored. A degree of opportune local score settling in the context of regional ethnic tension seems to have been a factor.[14] The Ottoman authorities denied acts of repression and were slow to bring the perpetrators to justice – confirmation for many in Britain that the violence was ordered and condoned at the highest level. With news of such atrocities, Russian pan-Slavists had a welcome pretext for intervention. And it was precisely upon such international recognition that the insurgents, their rebellion now quashed, relied. Meanwhile, Serbian and Montenegrin rebels, backed by Russia, took the opportunity to challenge the Ottoman Empire, launching their attack in July 1876.

A blanket ceasefire in October 1876 brought little stability. Russia, having failed to reach agreement with the European powers and the Ottoman authorities over the protection of Christians, declared war upon the Ottoman Empire the following April and joined forces with Bulgarian Christian insurgents. With Britain's rival waging war in the name of oppressed Christians, and her Ottoman ally overstretched and out of favour, the prime minister faced a precarious diplomatic situation. Members of Disraeli's cabinet, not unsympathetic to Eastern Christian suffering, were wary of Russian expansionism. Disraeli, his hands tied, could not be seen to offer support to the Ottomans, and declared a state of contingent neutrality. He was reduced to hoping that a show of Royal Navy strength in the Turkish Straits would be his strongest card against the Russians. Popular Russophobia took the heat out of Gladstone's coruscating calls for intervention on behalf of the region's Christians, and dissenters focused instead on promoting absolute neutrality. Disraeli's nerve paid off: though the victorious Russians initially proposed a huge Bulgarian client-state (the preliminary Treaty of San Stefano), negotiations at the 1878 Great Power conference in Berlin resulted in a division between Eastern Rumelia, under the suzerainty of the Ottoman Sultan, and a dependent principality north of the Balkans, under Russian organisation.[15] (These would unite as an independent Bulgarian nation in 1885, after a successful rebellion against Turkey.) Disraeli, rather than Gladstone, was to oversee the making of a (deliberately truncated) Bulgarian nation and, on paper at least, to safeguard Christian minority rights through a policy of 'alert' non-intervention and international diplomacy; this was not a role that he either sought or would be thanked for.

---

[14] Ill-managed attempts by the Ottoman government to reform the administration of the Bulgarian provinces, in particular to address the question of inequality between Christians and Muslims, in the light of Great Power pressure during the 1856 Paris Peace Conference, had resulted in fresh territorial assertions and renewed religious tension. See Saab, *Reluctant Icon*, p. 24; Anne Pottinger Saab, 'The Doctor's Dilemma: Britain and the Cretan Crisis of 1866–69', *Journal of Modern History*, Vol. 49. No. 4, December 1977, 1386; Ussuma Makdisi, 'Reclaiming the Land of the Bible: Missionaries, Secularism and Evangelical Modernity', *The American Historical Review*, Vol. 102, No. 3, June 1997, 702.

[15] The Macedonian vilayets were returned to Turkey.

'Atrocities' and the origins of the agitation in Britain

'More than ever before', argues Gary J. Bass, 'British foreign policy was driven by pressure from below.'[16] Protests over atrocities in Bulgaria and allegations of Tory complicity were undoubtedly popular, though not universally so. Meetings, petitions and donations to relief funds had gone from a trickle in the late summer of 1876 to a torrent when, in 1878, a British military incursion seemed imminent.[17] Many others met to attest their support for Disraeli, and their anger over Russian machinations. Yet, despite Gary J. Bass's confident assertion of 'grass-roots' influence, the effect on foreign policy was far from straightforward. This was a protest which had been carefully cultivated. 'Pressure from below' was galvanised and guided by those wielding extra-parliamentary political influence, in particular a free press eager to be seen to hold the Establishment to account. Here, the representation of events in Bulgaria as a one-sided atrocity and the dramatisation of suffering were crucial; and the contribution of the relief worker to the production of this knowledge was vital. Many of those distributing food and medicine in 1876–78 were already busy working as army doctors, pamphleteers, travel writers, educationalists and champions of female military nursing. Their attempt at relieving distress brought with it a certain authority: that of the impartial witness. Both in alerting influential friends and sympathetic journalists to the meaning of suffering in the Balkans, and in then providing a stream of correspondence on their own missions to the area, they generated a continuous commentary on the region's woes. They were thus ministrants of a 'spontaneous' outpouring of compassion that they had themselves been instrumental in arousing.

Historians of the 'Bulgarian atrocities' have endorsed the spontaneity which British agitators at the time claimed to distinguish their activities. In doing so, they have sought to differentiate the 'out-of-doors' protest of 1876 from the direction that it was subsequently given from within governing circles. Robert Seton-Watson's scholarly interest in the region gave rise to the first academic study of British responses to the events of 1876, taken from a diplomatic perspective. It also inspired his own efforts in Balkan relief (with Arthur Evans he worked for the Serbian Relief Fund during the First World War). He celebrated the 'Bulgarian atrocities' agitation as an example of unmediated popular morality: 'the Government was faced by a spontaneous outburst of indignation throughout Britain, and this stands beyond

---

[16] Gary J. Bass, *Freedom's Battle: The Origins of Humanitarian Intervention*, Alfred A. Knopf, New York, 2008, p. 236.

[17] In September 1876, between 6,000 and 10,000 people listened to Gladstone give a speech on the Eastern Question at Blackheath; about 1,000 listened to protests at the National Conference in December 1876. A petition in support of non-intervention in the war between Russia and Turkey amounted to 220,000 signatories in May 1878. By 1877, the protesters faced a counter-protest by the 'jingos'. One meeting in support of Disraeli, in Sheffield in January 1878, recorded attendance by 30,000. Details of these and further numbers can be found in Saab, *Reluctant Icon*.

question, to the eternal credit of the country'.[18] Later historians have followed suit. Richard Shannon, author of another standard work on the agitation, offered corroboration, but was astute to the ideological function of such claims:

> The proudest and most reiterated claim of advocates was that it was 'spontaneous.' This claim, made with substantial justice, becomes elevated into something more pretentious: a mystique, a confession of faith in the absolute purity of the agitation, a kind of dogma of immaculate conception and virgin birth.[19]

Ann Pottinger Saab, writing on the composition of the agitation, has likewise dubbed the early months a 'spontaneous protest'.[20] Yet the public response of 1876 – however genuine the sympathy for the Bulgarians – was not unmediated, and it is necessary to reflect on the ways in which an appearance of spontaneity lends an outcry of this nature its credibility. That the call to aid oppressed humanity arose untrammelled from the purest of sentiments seemed to give rise to a naturally occurring moral consensus which in turn provided the 'moral mandate' to press for intervention.

Three prerequisites secured the success of the campaign and the simulacrum of spontaneity: the appropriate moral to be elicited from violence in this area had been helpfully – and dramatically – drawn; sympathisers were equipped with appropriate resolutions and courses of action; and a valid sphere of intervention was delineated. The transformation of sporadic protest into a mass agitation can be traced to the *Northern Echo*, a Darlington-based newspaper with a large circulation under the editorship of W. T. Stead. Stead, impresario of the melodramatic outcry and self-styled antagonist of 'old corruption', was on a personal mission to raise the profile of the *Echo* and thereby establish his own journalistic reputation.[21] Events in Bulgaria provided the ideal campaign. Although news of the occurrences had been reported in the national press before Stead's intervention, only two public meetings had taken place and neither had led to subsequent protests. In fulminous editorials, Stead mixed eye-witness accounts with historical allegories of a clash of civilisation and barbarism. The complex and bloody series of events in Bulgaria was quickly turned into a Manichean morality tale. Allegations of atrocity carried a potent symbolic charge, signalling the barbarity of cruel and gratuitous acts.[22] Atrocities were not simply the unregulated crimes of rampaging individuals, nor to be understood as

---

[18] Robert Seton-Watson, *Disraeli, Gladstone and the Eastern Question: A Study in Diplomacy and Party Politics*, Macmillan & Co., Ltd., London, 1935, pp. 72–73.

[19] Richard Shannon, *Gladstone and the Bulgarian Agitation 1876*, Thomas Nelson & Sons Ltd., 1963, London, pp. 13–14.

[20] Saab, *Reluctant Icon*, p. 2.

[21] See R. L. Shults, *Crusader in Babylon, W. T. Stead and the Pall Mall Gazette*, University of Nebraska Press, Lincoln, 1972.

[22] This discussion of 'atrocities' draws on J. Horne and A. Kramer, *German Atrocities: A History of Denial*, Yale University Press, New Haven, CT, 2001 and Stéphane Audoin-Rouzeau and Annette Becker, *14–18: Understanding the Great War*, Institut français du Royaume-Uni, London, 2004.

part of wider civil disturbances. Rather, they were acts of tyranny emanating from the depravity inherent to despotic institutions. As such, the atrocities stood for more than the crimes themselves: they stood for the corruption and evil at the heart of the Ottoman regime.

Stead's atrocity stories ran in parallel with – and were often drawn from – graphic exposés in the *Daily News*, which in early August 1876 began to publish the findings of its special correspondent, MacGahan. Reports of the kidnap of Christian women into Turkish harems, which tapped into fears of a white-slave trade and prefigured Stead's own investigation of child abuse in the 1880s, were designed to at once horrify and titillate. Allegations of slavery became a central motif of the agitation. In her pamphlet *The Martyrs of Turkish Misrule*, Millicent Garrett Fawcett denounced Ottoman tyranny and alleged that young girls had been forced into servitude.[23] The involvement of Anti-Slavery Society members such as Sir Thomas Fowell Buxton (grandson of the famous abolitionist) provided a living link with this earlier crusade, and it was to a protest of these proportions that the organisers of the agitation aspired. The affront to public morality presented by the sexual abuse of women and children and the accusations of a white-slave trade in young girls was of particular concern to female agitators in Britain. If the compassion that such stories aroused, and the desire to send food and clothing, were viewed as natural feminine responses, then the call to relieve suffering also provided roles in public life akin to those occupied by women in the anti-slavery movement. Liberals, eager to reinvigorate discussions of national morality, and amenable to women's contribution to grass-roots activism, extended a special role in this 'moral community' to women. Indeed, this was to be one of the distinctive features of 'feminine' liberalism.[24]

The Turks, Stead proclaimed, were guilty of 'crimes [that] have horrified the world'. He tried to persuade fellow atrocitarian the Duke of Argyll to put pressure on the government to intervene on grounds of 'violation of the laws of war'.[25] Failing to establish this precedent – the Duke of Argyll refused his request, arguing that the laws of war did not offer the necessary sanction – Stead continued to advocate intervention. Balkan Christians were to be granted their autonomy on moral grounds and in the name of civilisation. His editorials provided a potted history of this unfamiliar region and simplistically divided the Balkans into suppressed Christian

---

[23] Millicent Garrett Fawcett, *The Martyrs of Turkish Misrule, Containing a Supplement by Miss Irby Detailing the Work of the Bosnian and Herzegovinian Fugitives and Orphan Relief Fund*, The Eastern Question Association, Papers on the Eastern Question, no. 11, Cassell, Petter & Galpin, London, 1877. See also F. W. Chesson, *Turkey and the Slave Trade. A Statement of Facts*, The Eastern Question Association, Papers on the Eastern Question, no. 7, Cassell, Petter & Galpin, London, 1877. Prominent anti-slavery campaigners such as Sir Thomas Fowell Buxton and F. W. Chesson, the secretary of the Aborigines Protection Society, became involved in the new Eastern Question Association. For details of Stead's 'Maiden Tribute' see Judith Walkowitz, *City of Dreadful Delight: Narratives of Sexual Danger in Late-Victorian London*, Virago Press, London, 1992.

[24] Biagini, *British Democracy*, p. 42.

[25] *Northern Echo*, 7.9.1876; Stead to Freeman, 14.8.1877, JRL, E. A. Freeman papers, FA1/2/221.

nations under the heel of 'the filthy and immoral despotism of the Turks'.[26] Evoking
the 'free fraternity' of nations advocated by one of his heroes, the Italian nationalist
Guiseppe Mazzini, he advocated a British campaign in favour of revolutionary
nationalism in the Balkans.[27] National self-determination was the most natural,
humane and Godly ordering of human society. Stead encouraged his readers to
temper any notions of Balkan 'backwardness' with the knowledge that, in struggling
for liberty, the region's Christian community was progressing towards civilisation.

> With all their shortcomings, they represent the cause of progress, of humanity, of
> civilisation in Eastern Europe . . . They represent also the principle of nationality. Said
> Mazzini, a short time before his lamented death, 'The Slavonian family is in movement
> upon a zone extending from the North Sea to the Adriatic, and eager to proffer the
> word at the fraternal European banquet.'[28]

Stead sought not only to awaken the conscience of his readers, but to direct the
expression of their outrage in a series of public demonstrations. It would take only
one local organiser in each town and village to lead the way he counselled. The first
of these meetings was held in Darlington on 25 August. With the *Daily News* beginning a series of reports from the Rhodope Mountains on 22 August, presenting in
vivid detail the killing of Christians in Batak and elsewhere, Stead used his editorials
to prime the organisers in Darlington with a definite agenda and set of resolutions:

> The Darlington meeting – forerunner, as we hope it will be, of other meetings . . . at
> Middlesbrough, Stockton, Durham and the Hartlepools . . . has a clear and definite
> duty to perform. It has to give expression in the most unmistakable terms not only to
> the feelings of horror excited by the atrocities in Turkey, but also the indignation with
> which the conduct of our Government is regarded in the North. The resolution which
> expresses the horror and indignation with which the atrocities in Bulgaria are regarded
> should add to that expression of feeling a pre-emptory demand that our incapable
> ambassador at Constantinople should be immediately removed. We do not ask for
> a crusade against the Turk, but we have a right to insist, in the name of Humanity,
> Civilisation and Christianity, that the expulsion of the Turk from Europe should be
> recognised as one of the leading objects of English policy abroad.[29]

Stead's instructions were heeded, and the Darlington meeting dutifully adopted
all of his proposals. It also voted to elect a committee to collect funds for the relief of
the sick and wounded. These proclamations were then reported verbatim in the

---

[26] *Northern Echo*, 13.7.1876. For the common tropes of Turkish tyranny and sensuality see Asli Cirakman,
*From the 'Terror of the World' to the 'Sick Man of Europe': European Images of Ottoman Empire and Society from
the Sixteenth Century to the Nineteenth*, Peter Lang, Oxford, 2002; Andrew Wheatcroft, *The Ottomans: Dissolving
Images*, Penguin, London, 1993.

[27] For the influence of Mazzini in British radical and liberal circles see C. A. Bayly and E. Biagini (eds),
Guiseppe Mazzini and the Globalisation of Democratic Nationalism, 1830–1920, Proceedings of the British
Academy, Oxford University Press, Oxford, 2008.

[28] *Northern Echo*, 13.7.1876.

[29] *Northern Echo*, 23.8.1876.

Northern Echo as evidence of public outrage – a similar report appeared the same day in the *Daily News* (wired from its 'special correspondent', probably Stead). Stead then encouraged similar meetings in his circulation district, chiding towns that showed lack of enthusiasm, and duly reporting successful meetings in the *Northern Echo*. By 22 September, 47 meetings had been held in Stead's North-East. Soon, Stead could celebrate evidence of a rugged Northern independence. 'In thus taking the lead in England, we but asserted our ancient prerogative, and showed that, in the struggle for freedom, the North-Country now, as ever, led the van.'[30]

This circularity created a momentum whereby meetings were encouraged, announced and then covered in the newspaper as evidence of spontaneous activism. These in turn were reported in *The Times* and other national newspapers, stimulating yet further meetings and a litany of resolutions. The organisers of the two earlier meetings now saw the benefit of stimulating public demonstrations through a definite programme and replicated Stead's tactics, if remaining wary of the man himself.[31] Petitions sent to the Foreign Office by the organisers of local meetings repeated Stead's resolutions in formulaic fashion.[32] They created the impression, through the force of repetition, of a moral community united in outrage. Thus the simulation of a spontaneous public outcry was achieved, such that Stead could appear as merely an impartial chronicler when, in his words, 'the Democracy sprang to its feet by an instantaneous impulse'.[33] Stead now pressed an initially reluctant Gladstone to take up the campaign and represent the country's moral interests. Gladstone, still smarting from defeat at the last election, was susceptible. With each copy of the *Northern Echo* dispatched to Gladstone at his home in Hawarden, Stead enclosed a few lines of pleading and baiting:

> I send you by this post, copy of the *Northern Echo* of this day's date. It contains a report of one of the most enthusiastic meetings ever held in Darlington, on the subject of our Eastern policy. The warmest expressions of confidence were used concerning yourself and more than one speaker ventured to express a hope that you may yet consent to resume office in order to complete the work of the Crimean War, by the emancipation of the Christians from Turkish yoke. As this is the first in a series of similar meetings which will we hope result in arraying the North of England as one man against the pro-Turkish policy of the Govt [sic] we need hardly say how thankful we should be if you could lend us the sanction of your mighty name, in prosecuting our campaign against the policy of Lord Beaconsfield.[34]

[30] *Northern Echo*, 30.8.1876.
[31] See Canon Liddon's letter to the *Daily News*, 31.8.1876, which proposed a series of resolutions similar to Stead's titled 'What to insist on', and Freeman's letter 'Points for Public Meetings,' *Daily News*, 5.9.1876, quoted in Shannon, *Gladstone and the Bulgarian Agitation*, p. 86.
[32] General Correspondence Respecting Atrocities in Bulgaria, TNA, Foreign Office Papers, FO 78/2551–2556. Saab deduces that 35% of the petitions sent during the parliamentary recess in the summer of 1876 derived from the north of England, *Reluctant Icon*, p. 218, n. 32.
[33] Stead quoted in Seton-Watson, *Disraeli, Gladstone and the Eastern Question*, p. 72.
[34] Stead to Gladstone, 26.8.1876, British Library, W. E. Gladstone papers, Add. MS 44303, f.230.

The politics of humanity

Gladstone found irresistible the call to reinvigorate the moral life of the nation and pursue his vision of the fraternal global order. The seclusion of his bookish retirement offered him the role of the prophetic outsider, and provided opportunity for a rapid perusal of historical and ethnographical works on the Balkans in preparation for publication of *Bulgarian Horrors* in early August.[35] As early as July, Gladstone had sought an interview with Lady Strangford, a woman personally acquainted with the Balkans and soon to launch her Bulgarian Peasants Relief Fund, and he would continue to solicit the opinions of other experts on the region throughout the autumn, including Humphrey Sandwith, Paulina Irby and James Lewis Farley, all of whom were active on behalf of pro-Slav funds.[36] His visitors contributed the first-hand evidence and stirring details that would give Gladstone's political pronouncements their bite. Gladstone brought his influence to bear in return.[37] 'Miss Irby, after her long and self-sacrificing experience, speaks with the weight of dispassionate authority, to which neither I nor any correspondent of a public journal can pretend,' Gladstone proclaimed in the preface that he contributed to her book.[38] The majority of his reading consisted of missionary or theological works. Almost inevitably, they depicted an insurmountable divide between Christian and Muslim communities in the Balkans.[39] He was also sent, and read, the work of E. A. Freeman and fellow Turkophobe historians. The 1850s had seen Gladstone pronounce on behalf of an independent Romania; his reading matter of 1876 largely confirmed his existing views on the region.

Gladstone differentiated Islam from 'the Turk', arguing that it was not religion but mis-government which had resulted in such 'horrors' in Bulgaria, for the Turks 'represent everywhere government by force, as opposed to government by law'.[40] Reformist declarations, merely masquerades of civilisation, were to be set at nought, as was the Ottoman government's ratification of international conventions.[41] Faced with evidence of Ottoman brutality, Gladstone was willing to sanction the breach of sovereignty by Serbian and Montenegrin insurrectionists, on grounds of 'human

[35] Ruth Clayton Windscheffel, *Reading Gladstone*, Palgrave Macmillan, Basingstoke, 2008, pp. 211–214.

[36] H. C. G. Matthew (ed.), *The Gladstone Diaries, Vol. IX January 1875–December 1880*, Clarendon Press, Oxford, 1986; see, for example, entries for 10 June, 6 July, 11 July, 19 July, 16 August, 17 October, 14 December, 1876.

[37] See Gladstone's diary entries for 6.7.1876 and 17.10.1876. Gladstone drew openly on Paulina Irby and G. Muir Mackenzie, *Travels in the Slavonic Provinces of Turkey-in-Europe*, Daldy, Isbister & Co., London, 1877 (1st edn 1867) in his political writings; see in particular William Gladstone, 'Montenegro', *The Nineteenth Century*, Vol. 1, No. III, May 1877.

[38] Irby and Mackenzie, *Travels in the Slavonic Provinces*, p. xii.

[39] Gladstone's diary records the review of J. L. Farley's *Turks and Christians* (1876), J. H. Newman's *Lecture on the History of the Turks in Relation to Christianity* (1854), Rev. W. Denton's *Christians in Turkey* (1863) and D. R. Morier's *Turkey and the Christian Powers* (1876).

[40] William Gladstone, *Bulgarian Horrors and the Question of the East*, John Murray, London, 1876, p. 10.

[41] *Ibid.*, p. 29.

sympathies, broad, deep and legitimate'.[42] This was in keeping with international lawyers' exclusion of the Ottoman Empire from the 'family of nations' whose sovereignty was respected, on the basis that the government in Istanbul was insufficiently civilised to reciprocate shared rights and obligations (its derogation from the Treaty of Paris of 1856, which had included a commitment to protect Christian communities, was the most relevant case in point).[43] In cases such as this, where Christians were endangered and civilised standards threatened, the international law fraternity upheld 'moral intervention' in sovereign states.[44] Only a few, such as the Positivist Frederic Harrison, who considered the Russians more despotic than the Ottomans, demurred.[45] Gladstone advocated the use of the navy, in concert with other powers, to defend Christians in the region. He also wished to introduce measures to prevent the repetition of atrocity through adequate international policing. In *Bulgarian Horrors* the Turks were instructed to leave the region 'bag and baggage'. The phrase proved a slippery one. Those such as the Duke of Argyll took it as an endorsement of the expulsion of Muslims from the Balkans and the absolute independence of Christian successor states.[46] In time, Gladstone would explain that he advocated merely the withdrawal of administrative and military personnel within the context of continued Ottoman sovereignty in the region. In this way, morality and balance-of-power interests were to be made compatible. Regional security and friendly Balkan states would ensure against Russian intrigue and advance British interests in an area of strategic import. As Gladstone subsequently clarified:

> The fabric of the Turkish Empire has been so shaken, that the primary aim of its wisest friends should be to secure it against further shocks, and with this in view to establish relations between the Porte and its provinces as easy and elastic as may be.[47]

> [But] as to expelling the [Ottoman] Empire, I had said it should, if possible, be retained in the fullness of its territorial possessions; only with the substitution of tribute and suzerainty.[48]

Gladstone commended 'the people' for their spontaneous outcry, and bestowed upon them the moral interests necessary to defeat the ogre of Tory corruption. Yet

---

[42] *Ibid.*, p. 30.

[43] John Westlake, a British expert on international law, understood the 'family of nations' to have its origins in a European civilisation founded on ancient Greece and Rome. He argued in favour of the right to intervention on behalf of the region's Christians. John Westlake, *Memories of John Westlake*, Smith, Elder and Co., London, 1914.

[44] Gladstone, *Bulgarian Horrors*, p. 27.

[45] Harrison sought to include the Ottoman Empire in the 'family of nations'. He termed the 'Bulgarian atrocities' agitation a 'religious crusade', and predicted a bloody race war. Frederic Harrison, *Autobiographic Memoirs*, p. 119. See also Frederic Harrison, 'Cross and Crescent', *Fortnightly Review*, December 1876.

[46] Gladstone, *Bulgarian Horrors*, p. 38. Duke of Argyll (Sir George Campbell), 'The Resettlement of the Turkish Dominions', *Fortnightly Review*, April, 1878.

[47] William Gladstone, 'The Paths of Honour and Shame', *The Nineteenth Century*, Vol. 3. No. XIII, March 1878, 599.

[48] William Gladstone, 'Aggression in Egypt and Freedom in the East', *The Nineteenth Century*, Vol. 2, No. VI, August 1877, 163.

he believed that the moral cause of liberty and international justice required state action and could not be left in the hands of activists whose very spontaneity rendered them inconsistent and a threat to constitutional government. He spoke apologetically of 'rude irregular methods', and reflected in print that

> [T]he most essential or the noblest among all the duties of government, the exercise of moral control over ambition and cupidity, have been left to the intermittent and feeble handling of those who do not govern.[49]

Gary J. Bass lauds the influence of 'pressure from below', but Gladstone's politics of humanity was never democratic in intention, and he remained unswayed by the radical tradition of Mazzinian democratic nationalism.[50] Rather, it was the state's responsibility to teach the masses the lessons of 'self-denial and self-restraint'.[51] If the keynotes of Ottoman and Christian relations were to be order, gradualism and moderation, then in much the same way the British people were to be given an education in liberal governance and England was to extend its moral influence on the world stage. This was to be, he declared in the *Nineteenth Century*, 'England's Mission', and it was nowhere more important than in her colonies.

> [I]t is the welfare of these [colonial] communities which forms the great object of interest and desire; and if the day should ever come, when in their own view that welfare would be best promoted by their administrative emancipation, then and then only the Liberal mind of England would at once say, 'Let them flourish to the uttermost . . .'[52]

In intense, often fervent, interventions in the 'Bulgarian atrocities' agitation, Gladstone proposed a humane foreign policy, reining in tyrants and freeing the oppressed. His words reverberated in petitions and protest meetings across the land, but in Stead's North-country in particular. This expansive calling forth of the rights and duties of humanity had popular appeal, but it also required careful mastery. Stratford de Redcliffe, to whom *Bulgarian Horrors* was dedicated, shared many of its author's sentiments, but was astute to the potency of his rhetoric:

> I feel with him but I am far from being able to go at all times with him. Is there not a passage somewhere in Juvenal which points out the dangers of eloquence? The power of using language with persuasive effect is a charming and enviable quality, when the words fall from a honeyed lip . . . But it is also a steam engine, and may drag a train over a precipice as well as place it gently before the final station.[53]

Gladstone's ideals would be reasserted in the election campaign which returned him to front-bench politics in 1879–80, and his involvement in the 'Bulgarian

---

[49] William Gladstone, 'England's Mission', *The Nineteenth Century*, Vol. 4, No. XIX, September 1878, 570.
[50] Casper Sylvest, *British Liberal Internationalism, 1880–1930: Making Progress?* Manchester University Press, Manchester, 2009, p. 171.
[51] Gladstone, 'England's Mission', 570.
[52] *Ibid.*, 572.
[53] Quoted in, Wantage *Memoir*, p. 232.

atrocities' would inform his gradual conversion to Home Rule for Ireland.[54] In an age of expanding electorates and mounting demands for suffrage reform, the rights and duties of humanity also entered the lexicon of the political mainstream, providing a protean vocabulary for the assertion of a variety of as yet unrepresented moral interests and a range of emancipatory projects, ones which often owed little to Gladstone's concerns. Here, in the name of shared humanity, and in revulsion at venal Tory government, some Liberals saw the potential for disciplining grass-roots party activists. Joseph Chamberlain was quick to perceive the potential of the 'Bulgarian atrocities' agitation as a ready-made foundation for his nascent National Liberal Federation.[55] But Gladstone, dependent upon moral convulsion and inclined towards a 'crisis management style of leadership', frustrated attempts to institution-alise party networks and communications.[56]

In time, debates over how and when humanity was best advanced by emancipa-tion – particularly as this pertained to colonial communities – divided liberals amongst themselves, as controversy at the time of the Boer War would attest. For Gladstone's universalism rested on the consistency of values, but was understood as progressive and subject to differential application. Thus Bulgaria and India, and later Ireland and South Africa, ought all to benefit from liberal freedoms, but their different rates of development equated to different degrees of intervention and discounted the blanket granting of 'home rule'.

The authority of history and the bounds of humanity

For some, advocacy of the rights and duties of humanity offered a congenial form of moral citizenship, free of property or other qualification. For the non-conformist vote, recently estranged by the Education Act of 1870, it held particular appeal. The Quaker journal The Friend urged that 'Those who feel at liberty to use their influence and votes may throw their weight into the scale of an enlightened policy, recognising the claims of Christian civilisation.'[57] For some, however, this new humanitarian politics and the selective identification of Christian victims of 'oppression' rankled: was not such emotionalism in politics dangerously erratic, and what of the fate of Ottoman Jews and Muslims? Accusations emanating from some quarters that a 'Jewish conspiracy' sought to uphold the Ottoman Empire so as to ensure that debts would be redeemed alienated many in the Jewish community in Britain. The Rev. Greville Chester characterised Disraeli as the 'Jew Earl, Philo-Turkish Jew and Jew Premier', insinuating a link between the modern-day Jewish community and the 'bloodlust' of the Ottomans.[58] Historians such as E. A. Freeman, a respected,

---

[54] Biagini, British Democracy, pp. 40–41.
[55] See the report of Chamberlain's speech to the Birmingham Liberal Association, The Times, 24.10.1876.
[56] Saab, Reluctant Icon, p. 200.
[57] The Friend, 1.10.1877.
[58] Quoted along with many similar examples in Anthony Wohl, 'Dizzi-Ben-Dizzi: Disraeli as Alien', Journal of British Studies, Vol. 34, No. 3, July 1995, 378.

Oxford-educated gentleman scholar of medieval England with an intense interest in the Balkans, gave spurious intellectual validation to such prejudice. Yet Freeman's vituperative attack on Disraeli as an 'alien' interloper in British politics was not simply an example of his singular intemperance as some later historians have implied.[59] Indeed, Freeman's diatribes against Disraeli resonated within a prominent circle of historians and political activists, even if his flamboyant rhetoric alienated him, at times, from fellow atrocitiarians. Goldwin Smith, Regius Professor of Modern History at Oxford (1858–66), publicly questioned whether Jews could be patriots. James Bryce, historian, Liberal politician and champion of Eastern Christians, considered Disraeli to be 'not really an Englishman.'[60] Freeman's portrayal of Disraeli was more in keeping with the well-worn trope of the Jew as literary villain – usurious and dishonest – than reflective of any deep-seated anti-Semitism in the 'Bulgarian atrocities' agitation as a whole, and his attempt to rouse the public by tapping into English folk memory failed.[61] Indeed, such expressions were the province of social and intellectual elites and, as Richard Shannon notes, found none of the popular or official endorsement which met Dreyfus in France.[62] But in their pitting of Christian against Muslim and Jew, they demonstrated that all were not equal in the brotherhood of humanity, and this selectivity had implications both for domestic politics and for the scope of British intervention in the Balkans.

Gladstone was rankled by the lack of Jewish – and Catholic – participation in the agitation. He also recorded a 'strong suspicion that Dizzy's crypto-Judaism has had to do with his policy.'[63] But he was consistent in articulating the universal rights of humanity to live free of oppression (an article of faith which he would expand upon during the 1879 election campaign). He was, however, rather too sanguine in his expectation that self-determination in the Balkans would live up to his own liberal values. Disraeli, kept abreast of events in world Jewry through his friendship with the Rothschilds, was well aware of Jewish persecution in the newly independent Romania.[64] This may explain his desire to separate Christian persecution from the Eastern Question – though his glibness regarding news of atrocity would cost him dear – and his outrage at what he saw as Gladstone's opportunistic and dangerous merging of the two.

The Jewish community in Britain was divided between traditional support for the Liberal Party and knowledge that self-determination in the Balkans had resulted

---

[59] Seton-Watson, for example, implies that Freeman's anti-Semitism was merely a 'violent personal animus' towards Disraeli; Seton-Watson, *Disraeli, Gladstone and the Eastern Question*, p. 113; Shannon also passes over Freeman's anti-Semitism, depicting him as the 'representative of the golden era of Liberalism,' Shannon, *Gladstone and the Bulgarian Agitation*, p. 226.

[60] Goldwin Smith, 'Can Jews Be Patriots?' *Nineteenth Century*, Vol. 3, No. XV, May 1878; Colin Holmes, 'Goldwin Smith: A "Liberal" Anti-Semite', *Patterns of Prejudice*, Vol. 6, No. 5, September/October 1972; James Bryce, *Studies in Contemporary Biography* (1903), quoted in Wohl, 'Dizzi-Ben-Dizzi: Disraeli as Alien', p. 395.

[61] Anthony Julius, *Trials of the Diaspora: A History of Anti-Semitism in England*, Oxford University Press, Oxford, 2010.

[62] Shannon, *Gladstone and the Bulgarian Agitation*, p. 201.

[63] Quoted in Shannon, *Gladstone: Heroic Minister*, p. 183.

[64] Letters concerning Jews in Roumania, 15.6.1877, Bodleian Library, Disraeli papers, B/XVI/B/145.

in Christian 'tyranny' and Jewish persecution. Many in the Jewish community in Britain, unmoved by Gladstone's campaign, withdrew their support for the Liberal Party in the wake of the atrocities agitation.[65] It is telling, in this respect, to see the name of Moses Montefiore, leader of British Jews and a campaigner on behalf of oppressed Jewries abroad, on the subscription list of the Turkish Compassionate Fund (an agency sympathetic to Disraeli's foreign policy and founded to aid displaced Jews and Muslims in the Balkans). But it is equally telling to see Gladstone's name there too. The *Jewish Chronicle* was quick to caution against ethnic nationalism and to remind its readers that the strength of European civilisation rested upon its heterogeneity:

> If it be thought that nationality in the abstract, lacking support from other considerations, is entitled to independence, wherever if aspires after this boon, then we have declared ourselves favourable to the disintegration of every state in the civilised world and to the overthrow of every commonwealth in existence . . . consider such a country as England not as the British empire with its dependants all over the globe, but simply as the United Kingdom. Before all she would have to part with Ireland as the patrimony of a different race. But Ireland itself would have to be divided into two parts, according as it is inhabited by the original Irish or the Saxon immigrants. We should next have to bid farewell to the Welsh as of Celtish [*sic*] descent, and lastly, the highlands of Scotland would have to be separated from the lowlands. . . . As in England so it would be in every other country. Racial homogeneity nowhere exists in Europe.[66]

This was an account of patrimony and descent which found little favour with those advocating Balkan independence. E. A. Freeman, prominently Turcophobic and intensely partisan, and W. T. Stead, moral pundit and chief mobiliser, were only the most outspoken of a circle of journalists, relief workers, scholars and politicians for whom the history of Rumeli villagers seemed suddenly pressing. Stead brought crusading zeal; churchmen Bishop Fraser and Canon Liddon, and an influential group of Oxford historians including James Bryce, Goldwin Smith, William Stubbs and J. R. Green, brought a degree of intellectual legitimacy (and, on occasion, intemperate racial prejudice). They also brought contacts in the region and political connections. Through these networks, ideas, influence and money flowed. Able to draw on each other for information and publicity, they shored up one another's authority and offered mutual public endorsement. It was amongst this circle that the notion arose of an ethnically homogenous and wickedly oppressed Bulgarian nation, and a response concerned primarily with rescuing Christian victims began to take hold. Over and again, the distinguished pedigree of the Bulgarian nation was propounded. Though it was miserably oppressed, inevitable historical forces determined that it was only a matter of time before Bulgarians stood to gain their

---

[65] Geoffrey Alderman, *The Jewish Community in British Politics*, Clarendon Press, Oxford, 1983, p. 40; See also Niall Ferguson, *The House of Rothschild: The World's Banker, 1849–1999*, Viking, New York, 2000.
[66] *Jewish Chronicle*, 4.8.1876.

freedom once again. The relatively recent emergence of nationalism in the Rhodope Mountains, and the active hand of international politicians and British activists, were duly overlooked.

A sense of history was thus vital to the 'Bulgarian atrocities' agitation, and here the role of Freeman was pivotal. Freeman was not only an authority on South-Eastern Europe, but could draw upon contacts with relief workers in the region to lend his scholarship urgency and relevance. Freeman's crucial role in the agitation has been downplayed, perhaps because his scurrilous publications and overt anti-Semitism taint the notion of a 'virtuous passion'. As a consequence, his extensive collection of personal papers covering the period – comprising an on-going correspondence between relief workers in the field, journalists, fellow historians and politicians – has generally been ignored.[67] Freeman had been a persistent critic of British appeasement of the Ottoman Empire, pointing to a history of Turkish tyranny over Christians.[68] Events in Bulgaria seemed to offer perfect confirmation of his views. Freeman's initiation into the cause of Balkan liberation came through friendship with the Oxford archaeologist Arthur Evans (who would later become his son-in-law). Evans had built his reputation on historical scholarship of the region. The pair first met in 1875 in Dalmatia, where Evans was acting as correspondent for the *Manchester Guardian* and agitating on behalf of the Slavs.[69] It was their publicity for Balkan liberation that had first led W. T. Stead to the cause; and, when later Stead thought that his readers needed a quick primer on the history of Ottoman misrule, it was to Freeman that he would turn. Freeman brought more than historical learning to the debate. Historians in this period were thought to have a duty to propound upon the lessons of history and their moral for public life.[70] For Freeman and many of his fellow historians, the history of the Ottoman Empire pointed to the obligations of British citizens in the present.

In Freeman's most influential work, his voluminous *The Norman Conquest of England* (1867–79), William the Conqueror is portrayed as accelerating existing religious, legal and political liberties rather than imposing a 'Norman yoke'.[71] This was one of several epic monographs celebrating an unbroken history of constitutional

[67] However, a noteworthy exception is C. J. W. Parker, 'The Failure of Liberal Radicalism: The Racial Ideas of E. A. Freeman', *The Historical Journal*, Vol. 24, No. 4, December 1981. Freeman's papers, comprising scrapbooks, correspondence, proofs and reviews are held by the John Rylands Library, University of Manchester.

[68] He had been a vociferous critic of the British government's mediation on behalf of the Ottoman Empire during the Cretan crisis, when France had wished to form a protectorate over the Christians of the island. See W. R. W. Stephens, *The Life and Letters of Edward A. Freeman*, Macmillan & Co., London, 1895.

[69] Evans's highly partisan articles for the *Manchester Guardian* were collected in Arthur Evans, *Through Bosnia and Herzegovina on Foot During the Insurrection, August and September 1875, with an Historical Review of Bosnia and a Glimpse at the Croats, Slavonians, and the Ancient Republic of Ragusa*, Longmans, Green & Co., London, 1877.

[70] Reba Soffer, 'Nation, Duty, Character and Confidence: History at Oxford, 1850–1914', *The Historical Journal*, Vol. 30, No. 1, March 1987, 79.

[71] J. W. Burrow, *A Liberal Descent: Victorian Historians and the English Past*, Cambridge University Press, Cambridge, 1981, p. 158.

liberty that shaped the invention of English traditions in this period.[72] But this narrative also had implications for the Balkans. When applied to South-Eastern Europe, a history of national traditions, suppressed temporarily and anomalously by Turkish despotism, suddenly came into focus. In *The Eastern Question in Its Historical Bearings*, Freeman described the formation of Balkan nations between the seventh and ninth centuries, and their subjection to Turkish rule in the fourteenth century:

> In the course of the fourteenth century, comes the great change, the great and fearful change which is the source and cause of all we have to think of now, the coming of the Ottoman Turks. Hitherto nations had been pouring in one upon another, but they were nations which at least had some points of agreement . . . They were all Europeans; They were all Christians . . . But now came a people of another kind; a people who had nothing in common with the languages, the laws, the religions, the general civilisation of Europe – a people who were great simply as conquerors, who could not embrace the religion and civilisation of Europe.[73]

Owing to racial and religious disparity, the Turkish invasion, unlike the Norman Conquest, had never resulted in assimilation and continuity, remaining simply a 'yoke'. For Freeman, the European race or 'family' was determined by affiliations of language, race and culture.[74] Blood lineage and an accumulation of cultural traditions had resulted in a distinct European civilisation and an Aryan race. Nonetheless, the 'family' could be enlarged through adoption and assimilation, accounting for the presence of Slav members. Excluded from the Aryan race, however, and demonstrating no propensity for adoption, were the 'Semites' and the 'Turanians' (Turks), whose presence on 'Aryan' soil represented a considerable discrepancy. These ideas fuelled Freeman's elision of Disraeli's Jewish heritage with his pro-Ottoman policy:

> It will not do to have the policy of England, the welfare of Europe, sacrificed to Hebrew sentiment . . . we cannot sacrifice our own people, the people of Aryan and Christian Europe, to the most genuine belief in an Asian Mystery . . . [Disraeli] is the active friend of the Turk. The alliance runs through all Europe. Throughout the East, the Turk and Jew are leagued against the Christian.[75]

Like Gladstone, Freeman maintained a correspondence with pro-Slav relief workers in the Balkans, prominent among whom were Paulina Irby and Humphrey

---

[72] Other popular works included William Stubbs's *Constitutional History of England* (1874–78) and J. R. Green's *Short History of the English People* (1874). See Billie Melman, 'Claiming the Nation's Past: The Invention of an Anglo-Saxon Tradition', *Journal of Contemporary History*, Vol. 26, Nos 3–4, September 1991; Asa Briggs, *Saxons, Normans and Victorians*, Hastings and Bexhill Historical Association, 1966.

[73] E. A. Freeman, *The Eastern Question in Its Historical Bearings*, National Reform Union, Manchester, 1876, from an address delivered in Manchester, 15.11.1876.

[74] E. A. Freeman, 'Race and Language', *Contemporary Review*, Vol. 29, March 1877; Parker, 'The Racial Ideas of E. A. Freeman', 836–838.

[75] E. A. Freeman, *The Ottoman Power in Europe: Its Nature, Its Growth and Its Decline*, Macmillan & Co., London, 1877, p. xviii.

Sandwith. He was likewise to pepper his pronouncements with their descriptions of the victimisation of Christians and the dastardly conduct of 'the Turks'. Irby, a long-term resident and traveller in the Balkans, was an educationalist who had assisted Bosnian Christians fleeing to Austria after the uprising. Freeman's letters to the *Pall Mall Gazette* – to which Stead attributed his initial interest in Balkan affairs – reproduced many stories of Turkish brutality sent by Irby, his 'trustworthy English informant on the Bosnian frontier'.[76] Meanwhile, the footloose and impulsive Sandwith had worked as a surgeon with the Serbian army, returning to the region during the Russo-Turkish War with donations for a hospital in Bucharest, given a generous boost by Freeman. As seasoned experts and impartial professionals, Irby and Sandwith had the credibility to identify acts of 'atrocity' and determine the interpretation of events for a British audience. Christian activists and educationalists such as Irby were particularly liable to equate religious communities with submerged nations, an impression reinforced by their selective encounters, for they were barred from attempting to convert the Muslim population. Irby joined missionaries, active in the region since the late 1860s, in promoting Christian communities and instilling Western ideas of nationalism.[77] In Sarajevo, she reported how she had imbued her educational work with nationalist propaganda: 'we are now giving them for reading books New Testaments and National Songs'.[78] These missionary accounts, written from the perspective of a subject people cruelly martyred, were the primary conduits of information on European Turkey available to the British reading public.

Sandwith's evidence of atrocity, meanwhile, was more physical, based on the privileged access to the wounded that was accorded to international doctors. In one letter to Freeman, Sandwith described how 'the other day I examined a poor woman shot through the thighs deliberately by a Turk'.[79] In another he related how, in contravention of the laws of war, the 'Servian wounded were killed and flags of truce fired on'.[80] Such 'brutalities', he averred, 'are all done systematically by order. I do not mean to say that the details of every abomination are directed by the Porte, but I do mean to say that the Turkish commanders have general orders to strike terror into the Servian population.'[81] He actively encouraged Freeman's use of these letters in Britain: 'I want you to draw your slashing weapon and quote largely from this letter giving my name if you like.'[82] To Gladstone, Sandwith stressed that the atrocities emanated from the highest level of government: '[e]very massacre that has broken out has been the result of orders from Constantinople.' In addition, he emphasised

---

[76] Stead to Freeman, 26.3.1878, JRL, E. A. Freeman papers, FA1/2/222. The substance of a letter by Irby describing Turkish atrocities reappears in Freeman's letter to the *Pall Mall Gazette*, 24.4.1876.

[77] For details of missionary endeavour in the Ottoman Empire see Makdisi, 'Reclaiming the Land of the Bible'.

[78] Irby to Freeman, 8.3.1879, JRL, E. A. Freeman papers, FA1/2/139b.

[79] Sandwith to Freeman, Belgrade, 30.9.1876, JRL, E. A. Freeman papers, FA1/2/187.

[80] Sandwith to Freeman, Widdin, 12.8.1876, JRL, E. A. Freeman papers, FA1/2/178a.

[81] Sandwith to Freeman, Belgrade, 6.9.1876, FA1/2/181a.

[82] *Ibid.*

the ease with which the Balkans could form independent states: '[i]f the Turks were suddenly to disappear there would be no anarchy. The Christians of Turkey are already organised for all practical parochial Government.'[83] In turn, the parameters of relief missions and aid workers' selective collection of intelligence owed much to having absorbed the historical and moral lessons of their scholarly associates in Britain. In his public writings, Sandwith drew on a familiar narrative to argue that the Balkans contained two irreconcilable races that required partition in order to ensure peace:

> In all other countries conquerors have begun their government in . . . tyrannical fashion, but time has modified and softened their tyranny, and by degrees the conquerors have become blended with the conquered. Not so Turkey; as time went on, a governing class has been formed, at once the most tyrannical, the most corrupt, the most debased, and the most addicted to foul and unmentionable vices that the world has yet seen.[84]

Irby likewise viewed Ottoman rule as tyrannous and bestowed an anachronistic nationhood onto the ethnically and religiously mixed Rumeli provinces, commenting that Bulgarian 'nationality must be of tough material which give not way' under rule from Constantinople.[85] Irby and her colleague G. Muir Mackenzie's account of Christian educational endeavours and refugee relief, *Travels in the Slavonic Provinces*, described the 'national' histories of each Christian community from pre-Ottoman times to the present. Turkish rule was represented as nothing other than an unfortunate interlude. In 1877, at the height of the Bulgarian and Serbian conflicts, Irby's publisher sought to reissue her account with additional information on these two regions. In preparation, Irby approached Freeman for scholarly advice, and marked her intention of consulting the work of other Slav historians.[86] Meanwhile, she approached Gladstone to write a preface for the new edition.[87] In fulfilling this commission, he eulogised Irby's account of her work in the Balkans and recorded its role in corroborating his own understanding of the region.

> Here, much more than in any other work I have been able to discover, is exhibited to view without passion or prejudice, as well as without reserve, the normal state of life among the subject races, the standing relation both between them and their government, and likewise between them and those Mohammedans, mainly descended from renegades, who are at once their fellow-subjects and their masters.[88]

---

[83] Sandwith to Gladstone, River Drina, Serbia, 25.12.1876, British Library, Gladstone papers, Add. MS 44452, f. 278.
[84] Humphrey Sandwith, *Shall we Fight Russia? An Address to the Working Men of Great Britain*, Cassell, Rebler & Galpin, London, n.d.; see also, Humphrey Sandwith, *England's Position with Regard to Turkey and the Bulgarian Atrocities*, D. Marples & Co., Liverpool, n.d.
[85] Irby and Mackenzie, *Travels in the Slavonic Provinces*, p. 73.
[86] Irby to Freeman, JRL, Freeman Papers, FA1/2/142.
[87] Irby to Gladstone, 5.4.1877, British Library, W. E. Gladstone papers, Add. MS 44454, f.22. Sandwith had written a preface for Irby's pamphlet 'Bosnia in 1875', Foreign Office Pamphlets, No. 76, 1876.
[88] Gladstone, Preface to Irby and Mackenzie, *Travels in the Slavonic Provinces*, p. ix.

Aid to 'historic' Balkan nations was taken up by a number of agencies with broadly liberal sympathies, including the Quakers. They were supported and promoted by this wider network of historians, churchmen and journalists, who urged the public to donate to their funds. One result of their emphasis on Christian subject nations was to overlook the presence of Jews and Muslims in these lands – and of their suffering once they were forced to flee. The following chapter investigates the implications of this for the bestowal of relief in the Balkans. The blanket immunity afforded by Britain's abstention from the Franco-Prussian War had concealed the ambiguous status of British aid workers and the extent to which they operated at their own discretion. Aid during a period of insurgency and war in the Balkans exposed a number of fissures, and little agreement as to the purpose and meaning of neutrality in such a context.

Neutrality and the politics of aid in insurgency: British relief to the Balkans, 1876–78

> I desire to perform yet one other duty, by reminding my countrymen that measures appear to be most urgently required for the relief of want, disease, and every form of suffering in Bulgaria. Lady Strangford has, with energetic benevolence proposed to undertake this work.[1]

So closed *Bulgarian Horrors*, Gladstone's vehement denunciation of Turkish crimes and Tory complicity. Many of the public meetings convened to express solidarity with 'oppressed' Balkan nations had duly made offerings of relief, many to Lady Strangford's fund. Elsewhere, a number of rival committees sprang up to provide medical aid to Ottoman or Russian troops. The NAS, after initial hesitation, launched its own mission to the Balkans following the Serbian declaration of war against the Ottoman Empire in 1876, and again during the Russo-Turkish War of 1877–78. In Britain this surge of relief would occasion considerable political interest, and controversy, but it would be too simplistic to claim that aid to the distressed peasant or wounded combatant in the Balkans fractured along party lines. A more accurate assessment would be that, in an age of suffrage reform, concern for the oppressed, displaced or injured overseas was not only reflective but also constitutive of emerging political configurations, and an expression of concern for Eastern 'brothers' was also often a demand that the people's moral interests be represented at home. Yet, for those offering aid, Lady Strangford included, overseas relief was less clearly a question of political solidarity than a site of enhanced opportunity. Strangford herself wished to advance the argument for female war nursing. This did not prevent Gladstone's adoption of her for the cause. Nor did it prevent the delivery of relief from having political implications for the Balkan region. This chapter is concerned with how the treatment of wounded combatants and the alleviation of distress among civilian populations – some forced to flee for their lives – contributed, however unwittingly, to the contending processes of liberation and stabilisation in a weakening Ottoman Empire.

[1] Gladstone, *Bulgarian Horrors*, p. 39.

In such a tumultuous political situation, the question of neutrality hovered over British relief efforts in the Balkans. The work of those agencies, such as Strangford's Bulgarian Peasant Relief Fund, which were ostensibly needs led but which targeted specific civilian groups, would meet the censure of those for whom neutrality and impartiality meant equality of provision for all sides. Col Henry Brackenbury, the logistical mastermind of NAS operations in the Franco-Prussian War, was once again casting his astute eye on proceedings, this time for *Blackwood's Magazine*. He was caustic in his assessment of funds such as Strangford's, deeming them dangerously partisan. The NAS did not, however, escape similar censure. Critics of the NAS Chairman, Conservative MP Loyd Lindsay, insinuated that he had transgressed the principle of neutrality in making known his disapproval of the Balkan rebels. The fact was that this plethora of largely self-mandated organisations was able to determine its own sphere of action, conditional upon only the (formal or informal) rights of access established with a belligerent army. Unsurprisingly, despite pressing need, achieving consensus and co-operation between agencies proved elusive; compared with the Franco-Prussian War a few years earlier, the protracted conflict in South-Eastern Europe saw a pronounced sense of rivalry – and far fewer donations. In the midst of Balkan upheavals, the remit of relief agencies and the meaning – and importance – of neutrality were contested, had quickly morphed and would continue to be extemporised.

Relief to 'oppressed nations'

Lady Strangford, helped along by Gladstone's patronage, administered one of the most prominent funds to aid suffering Christians in the Balkans, concentrating her efforts on those in the Rumeli district. Similar funds proliferated. Some were founded at the time of the initial uprisings in Bosnia in 1875, others to assist Rumeli Christians in 1876 following news of the 'Bulgarian atrocities' and still others to ameliorate abject civilian suffering during clashes between the Ottoman army and Serbian, Bulgarian and Russian forces. Those already established by the time of the 'Bulgarian atrocities' were given added impetus by public remonstrance on behalf of the Christians in Rumelia. Paulina Irby and Priscilla Johnston's fund to aid Christian refugees fleeing Bosnia for Austrian Slavonia received a particular boost. Irby was in England when the 'Bulgarian atrocities' agitation broke out and was quick to attest to the suffering of Christians across the Balkans in the pages of the *Daily News*.[2] It was she who pressured the Chairman of the Order of St John, Sir Edmund Lechmere, to inaugurate an Eastern War Sick and Wounded Fund, granting it £515 from her own fund and attending its first meeting.[3] Influential public backers lent their endorsement. Florence Nightingale forwarded Irby's correspondence to *The Times*;

[2] *Daily News*, 1.7.1876.
[3] Dorothy Anderson, *The Balkan Volunteers*, Hutchinson & Co., Ltd., London, 1968, p. 10; Order of St John, *Report of the Chapter 1877*, Harrison and Son, London, 1877, p. 10.

Gladstone gave a public talk on her work at the height of the 'Bulgarian atrocities' campaign.[4] Her chief ally, the historian E. A. Freeman, opened his own pro-Slav fund through the pages of *The Times*, raising £5,000 for Serbian and Bulgarian non-combatants, and continued to donate funds to Irby's venture.[5] Millicent Garrett Fawcett included a supplement detailing the work of Irby and Johnston's Bosnian and Herzegovinian Fugitives and Orphan Relief Fund in her *The Martyrs of Turkish Misrule*. It included the following appeal:

> One has only to attempt to realise what must be the condition of 200 000 people who have been burned out of house and home, and who have fled for their lives from a pitiless enemy, to see that they must necessarily be in want of everything that separates man from beast . . . The one help that every one is free to offer is to send money, food, and clothes, to keep the old men, women, and children alive while their sons and husbands and fathers are fighting against an intolerable enemy.[6]

Though rarely stated so bluntly, relief to Christians became a practical expression of support for the Balkan insurgents, or at the very least a show of solidarity with the 'oppressed'. Many such agencies proclaimed strict impartiality in the provision of relief – and congratulated themselves on a magnanimity born of Christian tolerance. Nevertheless, while such aid rarely discriminated on the ground, the geographical boundaries of relief operations favoured Christian populations.

This was not truer than it was for the Quakers. In the tradition of their recent work in France, Quakers bestowed aid on non-combatants, ostensibly with no thought to faith or allegiance. Nevertheless, relatively few Quakers felt a clear calling to aid those suffering in the Balkans, and those that did favoured aid to fellow Christians. Clearly, the blanket immunity afforded by Britain's neutrality in 1870–71 contrasted with the political maelstrom that now accompanied events in the East. Quakers' traditional loyalty to the Liberal Party was given a fillip by John Bright's deputation to the Foreign Office to urge non-intervention – an 'honourable neutrality' – and to caution the British government against facilitating, by force or otherwise, Turkish dominance.[7] 'Friends everywhere', the editor of Quaker journal *The Friend* reported, 'have been united with their fellow-citizens in bringing their influence to bear upon the Government.'[8] Nevertheless, not all supported non-intervention. Samuel Capper, veteran of Quaker relief in the Franco-Prussian War, wanted to see 'these fiends of lust and cruelty . . . publicly hanged', and advocated a military occupation of Bulgaria in concert with the other Great Powers.[9]

---

[4] See, for instance, reproduction of Irby's letter to Nightingale in *The Times* 13.3.1876.
[5] See Shannon, *Gladstone and the Bulgarian Agitation*, p. 38.
[6] Fawcett, *Martyrs of Turkish Misrule*, p. 18.
[7] Greenwood, *Quaker Encounters*, p. 82; *Daily News*, 15.7.1876. The 1856 Treaty of Paris had stipulated that the Concert of Europe guaranteed Turkish independence. The Russian invasion meant that other members of the Concert were legally entitled to support Turkey – a situation which found most atrocitiarians in England campaigning in favour of neutrality.
[8] *The Friend*, 2.10.1876.
[9] Letter to *Daily News*, 19.8.1876.

Quakers had a prior connection with relief missions to the region: they had supported Irby's earlier educational work in Bosnia.[10] Unsurprisingly, most viewed events in the Rhodope Mountains as straightforward examples of the oppression of Christians. William Jones, another veteran of Quaker relief in France, described them as 'horrible cruelties committed upon the peaceable inhabitants of Central Turkey'.[11] Like many, the Quakers conflated state or paramilitary violence with the activities of the Muslim population of the region in general, and with Conservative policy at a distance. This perpetuated a widespread tendency in the Liberal press: 'The Moslem Atrocities in Bulgaria' ran one typically inflammatory *Daily News* headline.[12] For Quakers in the 1870s, still dominated by evangelicalism, attempts to reconcile Christians and Muslims did not appear particularly pressing, and aid to Muslim 'oppressors' was unappealing. *The Friend* directed Quakers to their conscience:

> Those who feel at liberty to use their influence and votes may throw the weight into the scale of an enlightened policy, recognising the claims of *Christian* civilisation. All of us have been taught to answer the question, 'Who is my neighbour?' May our sympathies be kept alive, and we shall not lack channels for their exercise.[13]

September 1876 saw the foundation of the Friends War Victims' Fund for Non-Combatant Sufferers in Eastern Europe. The Fund declined to send out Quaker agents and refused co-operation with other agencies. Erstwhile colleagues at the Mansion House Fund were rejected on the grounds that that Fund's administration was being overseen by Henry Elliot, the British Ambassador allegedly responsible for ignoring atrocities in Bulgaria. Meanwhile, it was doubted that Lady Strangford's 'judgement and powers of administration will prove equal to her zeal'.[14] Instead, Quakers bequeathed their donations to James Long, veteran of Friends' relief in France though not himself a Quaker, and agent of his own Manchester and Salford Bulgarian Relief Committee. A further grant was made to Paulina Irby and Priscilla Johnson's Bosnian fund.

Long's centre of operation was Tatar Bazardjik, between Filibe and the Rhodope Mountains. The majority of his work consisted of rebuilding ruined villages, with the assistance of Alsatian carpenters previously employed to carry out reconstruction work during the Franco-Prussian War. Long's sympathies ensured that, though nominally impartial, the bulk of aid found its way to Christians. Once again, aid was reserved for non-combatants. As in France, efforts were made to avoid pauperism, and the roots of distress were understood as moral and not just physical. As the Report of the Friends War Victims' Fund commented,

---

[10] Greenwood, *Quaker Encounters*, p. 81.
[11] Jones, *Quaker Campaigns*, p. 220.
[12] *Daily News*, 8.7.1876 and 2.8.1876.
[13] *The Friend*, 1.10.1877. Original italics.
[14] Quoted in Greenwood, *Quaker Encounters*, p. 82.

In carrying on his work, James Long could not avoid remarking that the true source of the sufferings of the population of the vast Ottoman Empire is rather moral than material. In this belief [he] has made it one of his principal objects to provide or rebuild schools . . . and arrangements have been made for teaching the first elements to thousands of children who have hitherto been brought up in much ignorance and idleness.[15]

The Alsatian carpenters supervised local peasants and all labour was financially remunerated to avoid charity and foster self-help.[16] 'By the payment of fair wages for this useful and necessary work, the distribution of succour ministered to no spirit of idleness or pauperism, but on the contrary preserved the self-respect of the population.'[17] The majority of reconstructed villages were Christian, although some Muslim villages were rebuilt. In total £6,763 was collected, and 4,709 people were rehoused through Quaker assistance. Vincent Kennett-Barrington, veteran of NAS relief in the Franco-Prussian War, and now in the region to assist Lady Strangford, observed that Long's altruism brought certain dividends. 'Seems to be doing well in building for the poor and in buying land for himself. Cunning old boy.'[18]

It was with some satisfaction that the Quaker William Jones, reprising the role of commissioner from the days of the Franco-Prussian War, could report of his visit to Bulgaria that 'thanks to these new habitations, habits of decency will be intro-duced into these remote mountain villages.'[19] These familiar philanthropic values found adherents in other relief programmes. The Quakers may have doubted Lady Strangford's aptitude, but would have concurred readily with her desire to avoid pauperising the local population. As Strangford herself declared,

> I believed the truest kindness was to encourage them in self-improvement, not to force them into it; – I wanted to replace them where they were previously, and so assist them to develop their own advancement from *within* – not to clothe them with a false sense of advancement from *without* . . . I resolved firmly that the money I had brought should not be given in alms if it could be avoided; the people should be enabled to help themselves – that is, those who were better off should help those below them – they should work for each other.[20]

Lady Strangford, politically Conservative, widow of a British diplomat in Constantinople and rival of Florence Nightingale, was one of the first Lady

---

[15] Friends War Victims' Fund, 'Report from the Committee of the War Victims' Fund for Non-Combatant Sufferers in Eastern Europe, 1877', *Yearly Meeting Proceedings*, [The Society], London, 1877, p. 55.

[16] Friends War Victim Relief Fund, 'Report from the Committee of the War Victims' Fund'; Greenwood, *Quaker Encounters*, p. 83.

[17] Greenwood, *Quaker Encounters*, p. 54.

[18] Kennett-Barrington, 'Diary', January 1877, quoted in Peter Morris (ed.), *First Aid to the Battlefront: Life and Letters of Sir Vincent Kennett-Barrington (1844–1903)*, Alan Sutton, Stroud, 1992, p. 129. It appears that Long purchased the freehold of the new houses built with monies of the Relief Fund.

[19] Report to the War Victims' Committee, quoted in *The Friend*, 4.3.1877.

[20] Strangford raised £28,891. Viscountess Strangford, *Report of the Expenditure of the Bulgarian Peasant Relief Fund with a Statement of Distribution and Expenditure*, Hardwicke & Brogue, London, n.d., p. 3.

Commanders of the Order of St John. She was known for her schemes to encourage female war nursing, and her efforts at caring for the needy in this and subsequent conflicts garnered her cause considerable publicity. In any case, aid to wounded Christians resonated with the Order's appropriation of a medieval Hospitaller tradition. Strangford had herself received the order of the Holy Sepulchre from the patriarch of Jerusalem to mark her ancestors' involvement in the crusades.[21] Two years before the 'Bulgarian atrocities', she had offered to re-establish the Order's presence in the Holy Land with a grant for a hospital in Damascus.[22] Following the creation of the Eastern War Victims' Fund by the Order of St John, Lady Strangford – omitted from the founding committee – instigated her own relief mission to the region, at the urging of W. E. Forster MP.[23] Forster was one of only two MPs to have visited the region (the other was Sir George Campbell, the Duke of Argyll) and the first to press Disraeli in the House of Commons over his laconic dismissals of early reports of atrocities. Strangford was adamant that no assistance would be granted to the Turk, 'in distribut[ing] gifts to Bulgarians who are all and, only Christians . . . I am going to Philippopolis to my Bulgarian friends and every piaster that I give away will pass from me into Bulgarian hands.'[24]

Others members of the Order of St John active in the Balkans included the intrepid Emma Pearson and Louisa MacLaughlin, who five years previously had nursed with the NAS at Sedan. Following an earlier dispute with Loyd Lindsay and accusations of insubordination, they now worked with James Lewis Farley's League in Aid of the Christian *Rayahs* in Turkey. Echoing Irby's recollections of relieving Bosnian fugitives, Pearson, MacLaughlin and Lady Strangford all favoured topographical and historical reflection. Their reports and publications abound with potted ethnographic accounts of the peoples subjugated to Turkish rule. Pearson and MacLaughlin were able to observe at first hand that '[t]o all thinking persons who really know Servia and the Serbs, it is clear her best hope lies in independence. She has all the elements of national prosperity.'[25] Lady Strangford found that 'the Bulgarian is a curious mixture of industry and thrift with laziness and apathy; at one time he appears so Oriental, at others so Western.'[26] Such ambivalence was typical. But here lay the possibility of reform and reclamation. Characterising herself 'as a supporter to Turkey', but writing in her capacity as the 'Bulgarian nation['s] . . . one English friend', Strangford had begged Disraeli to remonstrate with the Ottoman sultan following news of events in Bulgaria in June 1876.[27] A year later she was to be

[21] Elizabeth Baigent, entry for Smythe [*née* Beaufort], Emily Anne, Viscountess Strangford, Dictionary of National Biography Online.

[22] Order of St John, *Report of the Chapter, 1874*, Harrison and Son, London, 1874, p. 6.

[23] Anderson, *Balkan Volunteers*, p. 13.

[24] *The Times*, 29.9.1876.

[25] Louisa MacLaughlin and Emma Pearson, *Service in Servia under the Red Cross*, Tinsley Brothers, London, 1877, p. 15.

[26] Strangford, *Report*, p. 3.

[27] Strangford to Disraeli, 25.6.1876, Bodleian Library, Disraeli papers, B/XVI/B/113.

found closing her Bulgarian Peasant Relief Fund report with a rousing entreaty: 'May God grant them independence and freedom'.[28] This, however, required self-determination rather than the diplomatic intervention of foreign powers favoured by Gladstone:

> May God grant them . . . freedom to work out for themselves their own development – the only sure method of attaining it. If they can do this, all their faults – the hardness of character, poorness of sentiment, and apathy of heart, even the love of drink, will pass away like morning clouds; and the nation will shine out, refined by education, clothed with the greater sweetness, unselfishness, generosity, and keener intelligence which always accompanies true civilisation.[29]

Clearly, Strangford thought herself an impartial observer of inevitable historical progress. She was unlikely to have considered that in the minds of the British public and the Rumeli peasant her methods of delivery and boundaries of operation gave credence to the idea of an implicitly Christian Bulgarian nation.

First Strangford turned to the provision of food and clothing, then to the running of hospitals in Batak and Panagiurishte (locations of the original insurgency). With the assistance of Bulgarian school teachers (a profession at the forefront of nationalist activity), Strangford mapped out a sphere of relief which divided the country into six geographical districts and then delegated to them the distribution of food and garments. Later, she recruited Bulgarian women from the mission college at Samokov to assist in nursing.[30] Prior to the arrival of James Long, she was one of the very first British visitors to Filibe. She was thus reliant on the few English-speaking residents with prior interest in the region, namely journalists and missionaries. Strangford and Long were not, however, the only distributors of relief: Filibe's foreign consuls had organised a local Relief Committee (a large grant from Russia was supplemented by donations from E. A. Freeman), and a similar committee in Constantinople – the Central Relief Committee – had sent an agent-in-chief to the region. To the north of the Balkan range, American and Scottish Bible societies distributed food, clothing and Protestant tracts.[31]

Following her arrival in October 1876, Strangford's first impressions were made in the company of the *Daily News* correspondent MacGahan and the head of the American mission at Samokov, Rev. J. F. Clarke. At Filibe she was greeted with a civic reception and a day of celebration. Like Irby, whose gravestone in Sarajevo would become the site of an annual memorial service, Strangford was welcomed in acts of communal gratitude as something of a national heroine.[32] 'In the larger

---

[28] Strangford, *Report*, pp. 25–26.
[29] *Ibid.*, pp. 25–26.
[30] *Ibid.*, p. 8.
[31] Anderson, *Balkan Volunteers*, p. 51.
[32] Irby's place in the pantheon of national heroines meant that each year, for several years, a commemoration service was held at her gravestone in Sarajevo on the anniversary of the day that Archduke Ferdinand was shot.

towns, such as Karlovo, Sopot, Eski-Zaghra and Slimnia, my visit became a fete for the whole town, crowds of persons waited patiently several hours by the roadside to receive us.'[33] Bulgarian independence came not as the result of a victorious rebellion, but through international diplomacy. The Bulgarian nation was created rather than liberated, and, for this reason, the boundaries of compassion and the parameters of British aid operations carried a particular significance. For, whatever the intentions of individual aid workers, they bestowed surrogate diplomatic recognition and contributed a vital organ of publicity. In their interpretation of the nature and cause of suffering, and in their conflation of religious observance with a 'victim' nation, British relief workers helped to consecrate the idea of a nation born in blood.

Disraeli, unable to come to the aid of the Turks and despairing at the onslaught of 'merciless humanitarians', was forced to reconcile himself to endorsing a territorially reduced but autonomous Bulgaria.[34] He could not afford a repeat of the agitation. Partition began to look inevitable. Though dismissive at first, and consistent in refusing the moral lesson of the agitators, he nevertheless took their reports of atrocity as auguries of Ottoman weakness. This was not the strategic disaster that it might have been: the recent purchase of shares in the Suez Canal saw a concomitant decline in the importance of the Balkans for the security of India. Nevertheless, he attached no special import to self-determination. Apprised of the fate of Jews in the Romanian successor-state, Disraeli was less than sanguine about the divisive consequences of a similar agitation on behalf of the Bulgarians. Those championing aid to 'suppressed' Christian nations largely ignored the many Muslim and Jewish residents of the Rumeli provinces who were forced to flee their homes in the wake of allied Balkan insurgents and Russian forces. Indeed, many more Christians, Jews and, preponderantly, Muslims would die as a result of widespread persecution and revenge attacks than had Christians at the time of the original 'Bulgarian atrocities'.

Refugees

The villages in Rumelia upon which Strangford and Long focused their concern had, by the spring of 1877, begun to return to normal (or, more precisely, with new hospitals and schools, to have gone through a small-scale process of modernisation). Additional aid was now thought unnecessary. Indeed, when the Central Relief Committee surveyed the distribution district it found many of those presumed killed by Ottoman irregulars to have returned from hiding in the mountains. Mortality figures were revised downwards; predictions of years of devastation made by W. E. Forster, Strangford and MacGahan now seemed exaggerated.[35] Yet, in a

---

[33] Strangford, *Report*, p. 23.

[34] Quoted in Bass, *Freedom's Battle*, p. 277.

[35] Anderson, *Balkan Volunteers*, p. 71. The Central Relief Committee reported a new figure of 3,700 Christians killed (about one third the figure estimated by the British consulate in September 1876).

matter of months these regions would again become the focus of international aid operations. For, in the direct path of the warring factions when conflict between the Russians and the Ottomans erupted in April 1877, they would experience severe population displacements and huge mortality.

The immense suffering accompanying such displacement generated a new relief effort. This was distinct from those efforts which earlier had assisted Christians around Filibe, such as those run by Strangford and Irby. Instead, it was initiated by agencies broadly supportive of the regional status quo and suspicious of Russian expansionism. Garlanded by distinguished aristocratic patrons and endowed by millionaire philanthropist Angela Burdett-Coutts, the Turkish Compassionate Fund emerged as one of the most prominent and wealthy of these new bodies. Founded to provide for fugitives of all faiths, its work was publicised in Edwin Arnold's journalism for the *Daily Telegraph*. It would raise £43,394. 'The [Russian] Emperor in his speeches had given to the campaign the semblance of a crusade', it was declared in the Report of the Turkish Compassionate Fund, 'and the subsequent proceedings of his officers speedily imparted to it the character of a war for the extermination of the Mussulmans in Europe.'[36] It was with aiding these displaced Muslim communities that the Turkish Compassionate Fund was most concerned. For the most part, recipients of this new relief effort were referred to as 'fugitives', but observers began to note the popularity of a new term: 'refugee'. As one relief worker noted, '"Refugees" was a new word then, but it has since become a verb, "I refugee", "he refugees".'[37] The neologism is significant. It marked the prevalence of a relatively new human condition: that of being deemed extraneous to an ethnically determined 'homeland', forced thus to seek sanctuary elsewhere. The currency of this English term is testimony to the role of British relief agencies in providing such 'refuge'. In an era of emerging nationalisms, the 'homeless' and 'unwanted' would become the archetypal new subject of relief campaigns, their amelioration an enduring area of aid agencies' intervention and expertise. Of course, relief workers were not simply bystanders at an unfolding tragedy. As Arnold J. Toynbee was to observe after the Great War, a new humanitarian politics that saw intervention in solidarity with 'victim' nations often succoured one victim but created another at a distance when less favoured groups were forced to flee.[38]

Unlike pro-Slav and Bulgarian relief funds, which relied on local connections, the Turkish Compassionate Fund worked closely with British diplomatic personnel. A similar arrangement was utilised by the Mansion House Fund, which used consular staff, rather than fielding its own agents, on grounds of which arrangement the Quakers had refused co-operation. In Istanbul this work was undertaken by

---

[36] W. Burdett-Coutts (ed.), *The Turkish Compassionate Fund: An Account of Its Origin, Working, and Results*, compiled by H. Mainwaring Dunstan, Remington & Co., London, 1883, p. 9.

[37] Burdett-Coutts, *Turkish Compassionate Fund*, p. 175.

[38] Arnold J. Toynbee, *The Western Question in Greece and Turkey: A Study in the Contact of Civilisations*, Constable and Co., London, 1922, pp. 90–91.

2 Photograph of orphans in the asylum of the Turkish Compassionate Fund at Filibe.

Sir Henry Elliot and his successor, Sir Henry Layard (famous for his excavation of Nimeh); in Edirne by Blunt, the British Vice-Consul; and in Albania by Mr Kirby Green.[39] Officially sanctioned relief served a dual function: on the one hand, suc-couring the needs of fleeing Bulgarian Christians, Tartars, Jews, Pomaks and Turks, thereby attempting to pacify a sphere of British interest; on the other, providing diplomatic leverage to counter the sultan's unmet calls for British (military) inter-vention. Though the sultan now considered the British to be unreliable allies, he chose to maximise the propaganda value of official British support, sending his thanks to the British government rather than to individual relief agencies and inviting the British ambassador and his wife to dine with him, 'a thing unknown in the annals of the Ottoman Empire.'[40]

Both the Fund's committee and the *Daily Telegraph* were sceptical of claims of unprovoked Turkish brutality during the initial April uprisings in the Rhodope Mountains, pointing instead to Russian intrigue and implicating pan-Slav pro-pagandists in the inter-ethnic violence of the region.

---

[39] These were the diplomats who had provided the British government with their disputed reports of events in Bulgaria. See, for example, the summary of consular dispatches to the Foreign Office, 'Atrocities in Bulgaria July 15 1876', Bodleian Library, Disraeli papers, B/XVI/A/11. Blunt's wife published an ethnographic work describing the 'so-called revolt' in the Rhodope Mountains. Fanny Blunt, *The People of Turkey: Twenty Years' Residence among Bulgarians, Greeks, Albanians, Turks and Armenians by a Consul's Daughter and Wife*, 2 vols, John Murray, London, 1878, pp. 10–11.

[40] Burdett-Coutts, *Turkish Compassionate Fund*, p. 183.

[T]he deliberate design of the war on the part of Russia was the depopulation of these districts, so that when the time should come for their being inhabited once more by Mussulmans, there should be none to put there. Subsequent events demonstrated only too clearly how thoroughly this end was attained.

They told also of the 'dastardly conduct of the Bulgarians'.[41] In the Turkish Compassionate Fund's report, ravished maidenhood, that evocative and eroticised image so favoured by W. T. Stead and his allies, was again savoured. Here the Muslim victim, passive and prone, becomes a subject of prurient concern to be appropriated, scrutinised for 'evidence' of atrocity and voyeuristically consumed. The author lingered on features which seemed to attest to the victim's European origins, her martyrdom depicted to arouse more than compassion:

> the flesh was still adhering to the almost skeleton remains, and what had not been devoured by dogs was quite fresh-looking . . . I cannot forget that woman's face. . . . Her face, which the dogs had respected and left intact, was almost strikingly beautiful, with a delicacy of outline and a perfect contour of cheek and chin that was only heightened by the pallor of death. Her mouth, which was small and beautifully formed, was slightly open, and her teeth visible, her eyes closed, and long fringed lashes lying on her cheek. There was just a faint expression of pain on the forehead, and her hair was lying all around her head like a rich brown wavy halo. She was entirely nude, and her throat had been cut with one clean, deep cut, which must have severed the jugular and windpipe immediately.[42]

Much of the work of the Fund centred on the large town of Filibe, the site, a year earlier, of Lady Strangford's relief efforts. It lay south of the Balkan mountains, on the road between Sofia and Edirne, and was both on the route of the Russian forces pushing towards Istanbul and the halting place for fleeing refugees. It had initially housed Christians fleeing from Ottoman reprisals after the insurgency, but latterly Muslims and Jews had congregated both here and in Edirne following the Russian advance on Plevna and the evacuation of Sofia, to the north. Many more refugees would find their way to Istanbul. The Turkish Compassionate Fund estimated the total number of refugees in the Ottoman capital to have reached 120,000. With the conscription of adult males into the Ottoman army, many of those aided were women and children. 'The Mosques in Stamboul are crowded with refugees,' Kennett-Barrington noted in a letter to his wife. 'Misery and starvation seem staring these poor people in the face and God knows who will help them.' Typhus and outbreaks of smallpox in the St Sophia mosque caused panic.

Kennett-Barrington, having broken with Lady Strangford and now working with the Stafford House Fund, organised the vaccination of 80,000 refugees and bought cows to stock a dairy and provide milk for Stafford House hospitals.[43] Material

---

[41] *Ibid.*, pp. 9 and 16.
[42] *Ibid.*, p. 12.
[43] Kennett-Barrington, letters to wife, 23.2.1878 and 25.2.1878, quoted in Morris, *First Aid to the Battlefront*, pp. 139–141.

assistance was granted according to the familiar principles of providential self-help: fabric was distributed for the making of clothing and to ensure against enforced idleness, and small grants of money were given for the purchase of necessities (this was considered suitable for Muslim women, for they were 'not likely to spend the money on drink').[44] Aid, to be effective, required a degree of cultural sensitivity. Relief in the home (most refugees were 'billeted' on resident co-religionists) was favoured over the establishment of hut encampments, which carried the same stigma as the workhouse in Britain. By November 1877 the total number of refugees in Filibe neared 20,000 and, as winter set in, need increased and employment on local farms dried up. The efforts of the Turkish Compassionate Fund thus redoubled and a soup kitchen for Muslims was established (on account of their seasonal fasting and the possibility of inter-communal tension, Christians were to be given raw provisions and a small cash allowance). Orphan children were provided for at a specially created 'asylum' in Filibe where, in addition to their material care, they were taught to read and write. The weakest amongst them, unable to digest regular nourishment, were revived with tinned 'milk food'. A photograph from the Fund's report shows well-ordered lines of neatly uniformed children: a testament to the merits of British charity, but also to the common humanity of Muslims, who were elsewhere portrayed as bloodcurdling fanatics.

During the course of 1877, concerned voices began to be raised in Britain. The hardship faced by the Muslim population was expounded upon (though it failed to generate the kind of public protest associated with the 'Bulgarian atrocities'). Newspapers reported armed attacks upon civilians. In January 1878 the House of Lords played host to a remarkable debate in which Britain's moral duty in the crisis was revisited – but this time from the perspective of the Muslim sufferer. The Earl of Pembroke and Montgomery rose to castigate the Duke of Argyll and to ask the Earl of Derby, the Foreign Secretary, a 'simple question of humanity', viz., what provision would be made for Muslims in the forthcoming peace negotiations? Advocating Great Power safeguards for Muslim 'civil rights under Christian rule', and 'not wish[ing] to sneer at Humanitarianism – indeed, this question has a purely human-itarian object', the Earl of Pembroke and Montgomery criticised those 'who raised the anti-Turkish cry in 1876', for not only were they reckless in 'hounding on Russia to a war that would cause more sin and suffering than half-a-century of Turkish misrule – but that . . . by so doing they were inevitably exposing the whole Mussulman population to the risk of expulsion or extermination'. However, if they were reckless then, they were 'apathetic now'. This apathy was born of two erroneous assump-tions. The first, that the resident Muslim population at large was responsible for the 'famous atrocities'. The second, the 'Darwinian view of the question', latterly raised by the Duke of Argyll in an address to the House on 17 January. The idea that 'this unfortunate race is being destroyed in consequence of their inferiority – not merely

---

[44] Burdett-Coutts, *Turkish Compassionate Fund*, p. 103.

by the forcible and most terrible means that we see at work, but by some subtle and mysterious law of Nature', represented a 'morally dangerous view'.[45]

March 1878, and the end of hostilities saw many refugees return to their homes under the ostensible protection of the Russian military authorities in Bulgaria. However, the cessation of hostilities and the signing of the Treaty of Berlin in 1878 failed to ameliorate their suffering. Refugees now numbered over 50,000 on the newly created border with Bulgaria and in the new province of Eastern Rumelia (despite explicit provision for Muslims in the first 'Minorities Treaty').[46] The Turkish Compassionate Fund continued its operations until 1882 and its report contained extracts from an investigation into the on-going level of distress in Filibe,

> I visited, during the time of my stay, a portion of the quarter (now in ruins) in which Turks had lived before the disasters. These houses, I was told, had been destroyed by the Bulgarians (not by the Russians) either for the sake of the wood, or to prevent the return of the Turks to them. In most instances nothing but bare walls and roof remained. Nevertheless, numbers of families were endeavouring to shelter themselves in what existed of their former homes.[47]

In the face of such mistreatment, and Russian obfuscation, many Muslims and Jews fled once again. British consuls were wont to draw unflattering comparisons with the treatment of peaceable Christians by the Ottoman state before the war.[48] It has been estimated that Muslims comprised 37% of the pre-war population; of these, 17% (260,000) had been killed or had died of starvation and disease, and 34% were permanent refugees by 1879.[49]

Wounded combatants

The NAS had lain dormant since the Franco-Prussian War. It had made inquiries as to the suitability of an aid mission to Spain in 1874 (the Third Carlist War) but, as, technically, this would have required both sides to be signatories of the Geneva Convention, this was dropped and the question of relief in a civil conflict lay unresolved.[50] This ambiguity persisted in 1876 when Serbia declared war on the Ottoman Empire; it may also have offered Col Loyd Lindsay a convenient screen for inaction. Loyd Lindsay's pro-Ottoman bias, unsurprising in a veteran of the Crimea and in keeping with that of his party, was strongly endorsed by his father-in-law, member of the NAS Council Lord Overstone. This may explain hesitancy, though it is equally possible that the diplomatic groundwork required in such a situation

[45] House of Lords Debates, 31.1.1878, *Hansard*, Vol. 237, cc. 691–697.

[46] Burdett-Coutts, *Turkish Compassionate Fund*, p. 140.

[47] *Ibid.*, p. 137.

[48] Report of British Vice-Consul Calvert, quoted in McCarthy, *Death and Exile*, pp. 84–85.

[49] McCarthy, *Death and Exile*, pp. 90–91.

[50] Col Loyd Lindsay to Earl of Derby, 5.5.1874, TNA, Foreign Office, Correspondence Respecting Geneva Convention, FO 83/760.

caused genuine delay.[51] Either way, the NAS was criticised for its apparent reluctance, and Loyd Lindsay was forced on the defensive when the Order of St John took the initiative in founding its pro-Serb, but nominally impartial, Eastern War Sick and Wounded Relief Fund.[52] The strength of feeling at the inauguration of this fund on 17 August was enough, apparently, to convince Loyd Lindsay that the public wished monies raised during the Franco-Prussian War to be spent on relieving Serbian and Ottoman wounded.[53] Florence Nightingale publicly sent her blessing and wished this new NAS venture 'Godspeed'.[54] To Lord Overstone, it seemed that the NAS had acquired an unwelcome public mandate to provide neutral relief in all conflicts. In private, he expressed his unease, being sceptical of the benefits of Red Cross work in a war such as was now unfolding in the Balkans. But the public's munificence had now to be administered, and recipients to be found. Nevertheless, if the 'fine impulses' of his son-in-law Loyd Lindsay were to be indulged, then a shrewd banker's eye must be kept on the curtailing of expenditure:

> I cannot say that I am an enthusiast in the cause of Neutral Aid to the Sick and Wounded of foreign armies. It is open to question on the ground both of policy and humanity. But we are in the situation of One who has money which we must spend. . . . Public sentiment would not permit the whole of our surplus fund, remaining over from the Franco German War to lie altogether idle under present circumstances – But I have resolutely resisted all proposals to stimulate public feeling and seek further contributions – by public meetings – local associations &c.[55]

The question of aid to Serbian wounded had crucial political ramifications. For acknowledging the Serbs as autonomous parties in negotiations over aid, or as signatory powers regarding international conventions, amounted to a form of diplomatic recognition. This was conceded by Lord Derby at the Foreign Office. Derby had earlier declined to answer a circular informing signatories of the Geneva Convention that Romania and Montenegro had acceded to the Convention, for risk of offending the Ottoman government, which had disputed the right of these principalities to claim full legal personality. The Geneva Convention, Derby griped, was 'being used for political objects to which the fussy eagerness of Switzerland in this matter readily lends itself'.[56]

[51] On 9 August 1876, just over a month after the declaration of war by Serbia (30 June), the Foreign Office confirmed to Loyd Lindsay that both Serbia and the Ottoman government were signatories of the Geneva Convention and that it would be advisable for the NAS to consider whether it wished the British government to request its diplomatic staff in Constantinople and Belgrade to ascertain whether neutral British aid would be welcome. TNA, Foreign Office, Correspondence Respecting Geneva Convention, FO 83/760.

[52] Wantage, *Memoir*, pp. 218–220.

[53] *Ibid.*, p. 220.

[54] *Ibid.*, p. 219.

[55] Lord Overstone, letter to Norman, 22.8.1876, in O'Brien, *The Correspondence of Lord Overstone*, p. 1291.

[56] Derby's comments appear on a letter received from diplomatic staff in Switzerland, c.July 1876, TNA, Foreign Office, Correspondence Respecting Geneva Convention, FO 83/760.

The Comité International saw things rather differently. Concern that war be 'civilised' in the Balkans and provision be made for the exodus of refugees accorded with the liberal sympathies of international lawyers in Geneva. Moreover, the Comité International had participated actively in the foundation of the Serbian and Montenegrin Red Cross Societies prior to national independence. Serbia and Montenegro, as principalities of the Ottoman Empire, had not been invited to ratify the Geneva Convention in 1864. However, during the wave of revolutions sweeping the Balkans and the attendant fleeing of Herzegovinan, Bulgarian and Bosnian Christians into neighbouring Montenegro and Serbia, the Comité International sought ratification of the Convention by the two principalities. The Montenegrins ratified on 29 November 1875 and the Serbians on 24 March 1876, and were thus bound by its laws when they declared war on Turkey in June 1876. On signing the Convention, the Montenegrin government requested direction in the administration of a relief programme from Geneva. Three delegates were duly despatched in December 1875, under orders to set up a Red Cross Society to aid refugees and those injured in the crisis in Herzegovina, and to promote recognition of the Geneva Convention during the uprisings. In Bulgaria, meanwhile, the Russians accompanied an alliance with Bulgarian insurgents in 1877–78 with an instrumental role in the foundation of a Bulgarian Red Cross.[57] Having one's 'own' Red Cross society announced one's modernity, civilisation and autonomy, and was thus of symbolic, not just practical, importance during the uprisings; indeed, the presidents of the new Red Cross societies had all been prominent in their respective independence movements.[58] In acknowledging the existence of 'national' aid societies in the Balkans, the ICRC publicly welcomed the Balkan states into the international brotherhood of civilised nations.

Loyd Lindsay was not so sure. He viewed the Serbian and Montenegrin uprisings as 'an insurrectionary conflict between people half barbarous, half civilised.'[59] Nevertheless, by 21 August 1876 Loyd Lindsay was journeying to Belgrade on behalf of a 'Turco-Servian Relief' Committee, an amalgam of two-thirds NAS Committee members and one third Order of St John. From the perspective of the rather impoverished Order of St John this was a marriage of convenience, the £20,000 of NAS funds now at their joint disposal barely compensating for the inertia of the NAS executive. From the start, this was an ill-starred union. Tensions were exacerbated when Loyd Lindsay took to publicly belittling the Serbian cause. Loyd

---

[57] The first Bulgarian Red Cross Society was founded on 25 October 1878 in Sliven. 'The Committee for Assistance to Refugees from Herzegovina' was founded in 1875 in Cetinje. This was the forerunner of the Montenegrin Red Cross, which was acknowledged by Geneva in 1876. The Serbian Red Cross was created on 6 February 1876 and accorded international recognition in the same year. For the history of the Bulgarian Red Cross see www.redcross.bg/history.html and www.usd.edu/dmhi/brc/brchistory.html. For the antecedents of the Yugoslav Red Cross see www.jck.org.yu/foundation/found.htm.

[58] In Bulgaria the President of the new Red Cross Society was Metropolir Seraphim, leader of the new national church of Bulgaria. In Serbia this role was fulfilled by the Rev. Mihajlo Jovanovic.

[59] Quoted in Anderson, *Balkan Volunteers*, p. 12.

Lindsay, considered dashing by many, but frustratingly inept and undiplomatic to those on the 'front line', was moved by the double desire of personally super-intending relief and 'studying on the spot' this latest permutation of the Eastern Question.[60] On arrival in the Balkans, Loyd Lindsay encountered a network of activists and sympathisers. The same names crop up at meetings, in letters to the press and in journalists' articles from the front: Paulina Irby, Emma Pearson, Louisa MacLaughlin, John Furley, Edmund Lechmere, Vincent Kennett-Barrington and Lady Strangford. All of these had connections with the Order of St John and many had worked previously with the NAS in the Franco-Prussian War. For them, Loyd Lindsay's autocratic methods rankled. Many also found his pro-Turkish leanings uncongenial. Even within the same family, ostensibly similar and 'impartial' relief work could provoke friction. Pro-Slav nationalist and refugee relief worker Paulina Irby was Lord Overstone's niece through marriage, but this did not prevent a degree of rancour. 'Lord Overstone was offensively ungracious to Sir E Lechmere [chair of the initial Eastern Sick and Wounded Fund] . . . also to his niece Miss Irby', noted an indignant John Furley.[61]

The blatant politicisation of much of the relief work in the Balkans not only strained existing tensions within the growing voluntary aid movement but also led to its proliferation. Once again, the *Daily News* kept a sceptical eye on Loyd Lindsay and his ministrations. Loyd Lindsay's critics, such as nurses Emma Pearson and Louisa MacLaughlin, fumed that his outspokenness was in clear contravention of his role as chair of a 'neutral' organisation.[62] For Loyd Lindsay, however, there appeared to be little inconsistency in providing medical aid to both sides with open political partisanship. In addition to the NAS, a number of other organisations jostled for public attention and a place in the field. Balkan Christians fighting the Ottoman Army or wounded in the insurgencies were aided by James Lewis Farley, a former employee of the Imperial Ottoman Bank. Farley had converted to the pro-Slav cause and founded the League in Aid of the Christian *Rayahs* in Turkey, following the Serbian rebellion in 1875. After the insurrection, he collected cash donations and provisions for the wounded of Dubrovnik, but, it is claimed, also used his fund as a cover to allocate money for the purchase of arms by insurgents.[63] It was with Farley's organisation that Pearson and MacLaughlin chose to affiliate.

Also operating freelance in the region was the surgeon Humphrey Sandwith. In receipt of some of E. A. Freeman's funds and a portion of those collected by the Mansion House, he combined assistance to wounded Serbian combatants with surrogate diplomacy. To Freeman, he accused Loyd Lindsay of indulging 'Turkish

---

[60] Wantage, *Memoir*, p. 220.
[61] Furley to Longmore 30.8.1876, Wellcome Library, RAMC, Sir Thomas Longmore papers, 1139/L/44/10b.
[62] MacLaughlin, *Service in Servia*, p. 141.
[63] Anderson, *Balkan Volunteers*, pp. 6–7.

proclivities at the expense of a charitable society'.[64] An associate of the Order of St John, Sandwith had been appointed to its provisional Eastern War Sick and Wounded Relief Fund. He was able to put his contacts in the Serbian camp at the disposal of Sir Edmund Lechmere, the leading light of the Order's by now some-what overshadowed mission to the region.[65] A self-styled 'honorary Conseiller d'Etat', Sandwith took leave from hospital work to (unsuccessfully) broker a peace deal between Serbia and the Porte and form an alliance against Russia and Austria in return for a Serbian mandate in Bosnia.[66] Falling in with Forbes, the *Daily News* cor-respondent, he was able to give privileged insider reports.[67] All this was reported back to an appreciative Freeman, whom he regaled with tales of Turkish 'barbarity' and instructions to forward details to the press. Sandwith would later make his own interventions in the 'Bulgarian atrocities' agitation, denouncing the Bulgarian massacres and 'slave raids' in *England's Position with Regard to Turkey and the Bulgarian Atrocities*, commending this most 'spontaneous', 'heartfelt' and 'universal' of move-ments in *The English People in Relation to the Eastern Question* and urging readers to stay true to the cause when Russian intervention loomed, in *Shall We Fight Russia?*[68]

The NAS's role in the Serbo-Turkish War proved controversial, on the grounds of its ineptitude as much as of its politicisation. Loyd Lindsay's instructions that a model hospital (the Katherine Hospital) be built in Belgrade – three days' travel from the front – was greeted with bewilderment and frustration. The side-lining of the wishes of the Order of St John to instead instigate a 'flying' hospital was a deficiency which 'no activity or zeal on the part of our energetic Associate, Mr Kennett-Barrington, could possibly remedy'.[69] The hospital was virtually empty for the duration of the war, filling up with the injured only after the Serbs' defeat forced a retreat to Belgrade. Vincent Kennett-Barrington, for the moment at work for the NAS, and revealing the initiative for which he was consistently praised, organised a convoy of carts and barges to transport the wounded to the hospital.

> The Servians seem to have forgotten that they could not fight without losing some wounded, and in consequence made no provision for their transport. I had two large ambulance waggons of the best design, an ambulance omnibus and carriage; besides convoys of country carts . . . with these I used to convey the wounded to the rear as far as Semandria, a town on the Danube. Thence I took them to Belgrade on a floating hospital. . . . The even motion of the barge was not even felt by the poor fellows inside, who required rest after a weeks [*sic*] torment of being jolted in country carts and waggons.[70]

[64] Sandwith to Freeman, 16.9.1876, JRL, E. A. Freeman papers, FA1/2/184.
[65] Sandwith to Freeman, Belgrade, 28.10.1876, JRL, E. A. Freeman papers, FA1/2/96.
[66] Sandwith to Freeman, 10.8.1876, JRL, E. A. Freeman papers, FA1/2/179; see Seton-Watson, *Disraeli, Gladstone and the Eastern Question*, pp. 118–119.
[67] Sandwith to Freeman, Belgrade, 16.9.1876, JRL, E. A. Freeman papers, FA1/2/184.
[68] Sandwith, *England's Position with Regard to Turkey*, p. 7; Sandwith, 'The English People in Relation to the Eastern Question', p. 490 (cutting in JRL, E. A. Freeman papers); Sandwith, *Shall We Fight Russia?*
[69] Order of St John in England, *Report of the Chapter*, 1877, p. 9.
[70] Kennett-Barrington to Fleetwood, 1.12.1876, in Morris, *First Aid to the Battlefront*, p. 125.

From the middle of October, deep snow fell in the mountains. Conditions were perilous. Four oxen had to be used to draw ambulance wagons over the churned tracks. Carts tumbled over on the inclines. On his last trip over the mountains in December, Kennett-Barrington found himself caught in a snowstorm between Kragnievatz and Oube. But for all Kennett-Barrington's efforts, for most observers, including the Serbians, the NAS hospital appeared but a hollow gesture. To *The Times*'s correspondent it was 'a fatal mistake, and I use the term in its literal sense'.[71] For many who might otherwise have been saved, the journey from the front proved too much. As Forbes of the *Daily News* remarked, 'the intervention of the N.A.S. at once arrested the relief efforts of other organisations, and the moral obligation rests on, and has been unfulfilled by, that Society of contributing real and effective, not sham and niggardly, succour'.[72] With criticism from all sides ringing in his ears, Loyd Lindsay was relieved to leave Belgrade for the Ottoman headquarters. He founded hospitals for the Turkish Army at Niš, at Sofia and in Albania.

On crossing enemy lines, Forbes accused Loyd Lindsay of spying for the Ottoman government.[73] This is unsubstantiated. He did, however, collect military intelligence for the British government. Throughout his visit, Loyd Lindsay corresponded with Disraeli and the Prince of Wales, who, he suggested, ought to write to the tsar to urge that he desist in his support of the Serbians. Overstone also took the liberty of forwarding Loyd Lindsay's letters, full of desultory Serbian peasants and intriguing Russians, to Disraeli, Granville and former ambassador to the Porte Stratford de Redcliffe (an old friend and correspondent). Loyd Lindsay wrote in the capacity of a privileged witness, passing on details of the condition of Serbian forces, first-hand observation of their military defeats and information gleaned from wounded Serbian officers. His letters to his Committee in London were published in *The Times*. The Serbian rebellion was a sham, he maintained, instigated by the Russians. 'It is quite as much the duty of England to exclaim against the wickedness of driving a people into rebellion against their will', he wrote, 'as it is to protest against the cruelties in Bulgaria'.[74] On his return to England, Loyd Lindsay took advantage of the authority granted to a privileged and 'impartial' observer to plead the merits of Disraeli's Eastern policy. At a meeting of Conservatives during the height of the 'Bulgarian atrocities' agitation, he repeated his contention that the Russians 'had promoted war in Servia'.[75] He also felt qualified to offer to accompany the British representative, Lord Salisbury, to the Great Power conference held at Constantinople in December 1876 (an offer that he was forced to retract when Lord Overstone fell ill). To Disraeli he wrote of

---

[71] Quoted in Anderson, *Balkan Volunteers*, p. 34.

[72] Quoted *Ibid.*, p. 33.

[73] This accusation was made by Archibald Forbes, the *Daily News* correspondent, and is reprinted in MacLaughlin, *Service in Servia*, p. 141.

[74] Loyd Lindsay to the Prince of Wales, Serbia, 5.9.1876, Bodleian Library, Disraeli papers, B/XVI/B/114.

[75] *Morning Post*, 7.11.1876, report of speech at the 'Abingdon Dinner'.

the special interest which circumstances connected with my recent visit to Turkey has caused me to take in the 'Eastern Question'. I have felt a strong desire to be on the spot during the proposed conference at Constantinople which cannot fail to be a period of deep interest and practical importance.[76]

War between Russia and Turkey seemed increasingly likely. During intense House of Commons debate on the merits of British policy, Loyd Lindsay reiterated his warning about Russian provocation in the face of calls for military intervention from the likes of Liberal MP Leonard Courtney. Having proffered intelligence to the Disraeli government and engaged in surrogate diplomacy, he was rewarded by promotion to the War Office, where, in August 1877, he was given the position of Financial Secretary.

For the Order of St John, personal frustrations at Loyd Lindsay's lack of fore-sight and maladroit interventions were compounded by the lack of government interest in the proper functioning of volunteer aid. A paper read before the General Assembly of the Order in June 1877 called, in a rather arresting phrase, for the formation of a 'Red Cross Army' to counter unregulated entrepreneurship and the general 'free-for-all' which now existed. The Geneva Convention had

> opened a floodgate . . . The streams of philanthropy pouring through innumerable different channels form one broad current which carries everything before it, and sometimes even threatens to upset the most elaborate military calculations.

> It seems to be the general opinion that any resolution passed at a meeting of private individuals interested in the mitigation and alleviation of the horrors of war, is equal in value to an article in the Convention of Geneva, which has received the assent of all the Governments of Europe. In fact a Red Cross flag or brassard, by whomever it may be raised or worn, is now regarded as superior to all treaties.[77]

Loyd Lindsay and the NAS Council loftily brushed such criticisms aside, and when war did break out between Russia and Turkey the actions of the NAS proved no less controversial. To Liberal observers it seemed that Loyd Lindsay was offering preferential treatment to the Turks. The NAS had charted a boat in the Black Sea, with the intention of distributing aid to the Eastern front (around Erzeroum), as well as via the Danube to the Russians in the Balkans. Initially, however, the Russians declined its help and the NAS focused its activities south of the Balkans. Later it would send supplies to aid Russian wounded in Bucharest. For its efforts, the NAS was greeted by an angry deputation comprising Leonard Courtney and other Liberal MPs, 'atrocitarians' such as William Morris, and prominent surgeons. They arrived at NAS headquarters in combative mood, protesting that 'it is most unlikely that the surgeons accompanying the ship or the stores contained in her can

---

[76] Loyd Lindsay to Disraeli, 11.11.1876, Bodleian Library, Disraeli papers, B/XVI/C/146.

[77] Anon., 'The proper sphere of volunteer societies for the relief of sick and wounded soldiers in war. A paper read before the General Assembly of the Order, 25 June 1977', Harrison and Co., London, 1877, pp. 5–7.

reach any other army but the Turkish army'. They then demanded that the NAS deliver aid to Montenegro, for, though a tributary state, it was 'fighting for freedom' and, by this reckoning, had earned the status of an autonomous recipient state.[78] The internal functioning of the NAS was also scrutinised and the deputation queried whether annual elections to the NAS Council had occurred as set out in its constitution. Loyd Lindsay responded that 'impartiality in the distribution of assistance does not necessarily involve equality in the amount of aid rendered to each party. It consists in the spirit in which the aid is rendered.'[79] This was his final word on the matter.

Once again, the NAS was not the sole operative in the field of combatant relief during the Russo-Turkish War. Leading liberal intellectuals, including the historians James Bryce, William Stubbs and E. A. Freeman and the High Churchman Canon Liddon, had opened a Russian Sick and Wounded Fund, employing the ubiquitous Humphrey Sandwith as surgeon (the public was told not to confuse this with Lewis Farley's new venture, the Sick and Wounded Russian Soldiers' Relief Fund, but often it did).[80] A certain rivalry between Freeman and Farley had developed and prevented co-operation. Following the fall of Plevna, it would be Turkish prisoners of war who would, ironically, stand most to benefit from these endeavours.[81] Added to these was Lady Strangford's new enterprise, the British Hospital and Ambulance Fund for the Sick and Wounded in War, which, though purposefully vague in its advertisements (which were featured, some might have thought incongruously, on the back cover of the Bulgarian Peasants Relief Fund's report), dealt primarily with Turkish wounded, first in Edirne, then in Sofia and finally in Istanbul.

Aid on the exclusive behalf of the Ottoman army came courtesy of the Stafford House Committee and a Turkish Wounded Soldiers' Relief Fund, which Stafford House eventually subsumed. Founded in December 1876 by the Duke of Sutherland, the Stafford House Committee was strongly Turcophile, with prominent establishment backing. It raised £22,517, of which £5,300 was donated by Indian Muslims.[82] It worked closely with the hierarchy of the NAS, which shared its political sensibilities, and was on good terms with the Turkish Compassionate Fund, into which some of its medical personnel drifted after the cessation of hostilities. Stafford House operations were divided between the two fronts, with surgeons staffing a Stafford House hospital in Erzeroum on the Eastern front, and providing roving transport and medical facilities on the lines from Istanbul to Edirne and west to Yamboli. After the fall of Plevna it assisted the wounded during the

---

[78] *Daily News*, 15.8.1877.

[79] Quoted in Anderson, *Balkan Volunteers*, p. 85.

[80] See Shannon, *Gladstone and the Bulgarian Agitation*, p. 174.

[81] Anderson, *Balkan Volunteers*, p. 107.

[82] See *The Graphic*, 18.5.1878; Vincent Kennett-Barrington, *Report of the Record and the Operation of the Stafford House Committee for the Relief of Sick and Wounded Turkish Soldiers*, Spottiswoode & Co., London, 1879.

Turkish retreat and finally concentrated its activities in Istanbul, aiding refugees and returning soldiers. For its pro-Turkish leanings, and with typical vituperation, Edward Freeman denounced the Stafford House Committee's operations as the 'synagogues of Satan' for 'patching up Turks "to do it again".'[83]

The question of neutrality

Not all approached the provision of relief in such a highly charged fashion; the promise of foreign escapades, and the enchantments of the Near East, attracted an altogether more louche coterie of young male doctors with an eye for adventure and the colourful account. George Stoker (brother of Bram), a young and, by his own admission, rather incompetent Stafford House doctor, could not resist evocative thoughts of 'harem life, beautiful Circassian slaves, jealous husbands, and unfaithful wives tied in sacks and cast into waters',[84] It is no coincidence that many of the medical personnel were recent graduates, unhindered by ties to medical practices and amenable to unrivalled medical experience in an exotic locale. For the youthful Charles Ryan, first encountered as a volunteer in the Franco-Prussian War and now to be found with the Turkish Army at Plevna and the Stafford House contingent at Erzeroum, this was the culmination of a rather desultory *Wanderjahr*.[85] The accounts of these doctors, replete with romantic Eastern scenes of seductive women and colourful bazaars, contain something of the attempts at ethnography and informative travelogue found in the work of the lady volunteer in the Balkans and the Franco-Prussian War. But there was no need to attest to a controlled sympathy here; they were paid to treat the wounded as efficiently as possible, and the rights or wrongs of the conflict and their proximity to the wounded required no elaboration. Instead, their tales were spiced with exoticisms for the delectation of the reader, and efforts at serious ethnography gave way to a ranking of Eastern beauties. Ryan quickly became intoxicated. 'During my stay in Stamboul I often walked through the bazaars, where solemn old Turks in baggy breeches sought to swindle me with polite decorum, and where the whole atmosphere breathed of the *Arabian Nights*.'[86] Gradually, however, the beginnings of an operational culture began to emerge. Those with acknowledged administrative expertise or medical training staffed relief ventures behind the lines, and often went between agencies and the different armies. Their impartiality was ensured less by a commitment to international conventions and more by professional detachment and, for some, genuine disinterestedness in the political situation. At the point of delivery an

[83] Freeman to [unidentified recipient], 24.3.1877, JRL, E. A. Freeman papers, FA1/8/1.

[84] George Stoker, *With 'The Unspeakables', or, Two Years Campaigning in European And Asiatic Turkey*, Chapman & Hall, London, 1878 p. 1.

[85] Charles Ryan, *Under the Red Crescent: Adventures of an English Surgeon with the Turkish Army at Plevna and Erzeroum, 1877–1878*, John Murray, London, 1897, p. 2.

[86] *Ibid.*, p. 16.

'urgentist' credo which married medical ethics and utilitarian administrative efficiency took hold.

The new 'urgentist' credo was exemplified in the work of Mr Vincent Kennett-Barrington. With a degree in law, but no aptitude for the bar, Kennett-Barrington made a name and a career for himself as a freelance aid worker. His contacts, discretion and evident administrative flair later enabled him to launch an international business career. Veteran commissioner for Loyd Lindsay's ill-fated hospital in Belgrade, as well as for Lady Strangford's Bulgarian Peasant Relief Fund, he had been involved in NAS work in France in 1870–71, and, in an independent capacity, during the recent Carlist War. By the end of the Russo-Turkish conflict, he was agent-in-chief for Stafford House. Here he was given a free hand (the Stafford House chairman, the Duke of Sutherland, did not feel the need to superintend in person) and was able to devise his own system of flexible relief provision. Whereas Loyd Lindsay had placed stress on establishing the Katherine Hospital in Belgrade as a 'model of good order and an object-lesson to the Servians', Kennett-Barrington had learned to value skilled extemporisation and good relations with the locals.[87] He co-ordinated a system of rapid-response relief, using integrated transport and moveable 'flying' hospitals of the sort advocated by Sir Thomas Longmore and other authorities. Roving commissioners like Kennett-Barrington were, like professional medics, paid (salaries during the Turco-Servian conflict had totalled 31% of NAS expenditure).[88] Kennett-Barrington's gift for logistics and energetic improvisation paid dividends. By creating an impression of interagency co-operation (though his agents would, at times, let slip the backbiting behind the scenes), proficient service and measurable success, he was able to win over influential figures in Ottoman governing and military circles and to put a model of 'systematised spontaneity' into practice with the Turkish Army.[89]

Kennett-Barrington's report for the Stafford House Committee, co-authored with committee member William MacCormac (latterly of the renowned Anglo-American Ambulance in the Franco-Prussian War), is illustrative of a statistical rendering of relief common (though in less exhaustive detail) to many agency reports of the period. Daily casualty and recovery rates were meticulously compared and plotted on pull-out graphs. Here is his characteristically dense summary for the period August–October 1877:

> during August 1877 the number of sick and wounded treated by the three sections of Stafford House and two of Lord Blantyre's was 3,884 the proportion of sick to wounded being as 1 to 10, and the average treated per day 412. In September the number of sections was increased to ten, and the number of different patients amounted to 11,534; relative proportion of sick to wounded remained the same as in August. The

[87] Letter quoted in Wantage, *Memoir*, p. 229.
[88] Morris, *First Aid to the Battlefront*, pp. 4–23.
[89] Anderson, *Balkan Volunteers*, pp. 141–153.

average under treatment per day was 981. During October, with the same sections the numbers treated fell off to 8,774, the sick being more than half as numerous again as the wounded, a result which is accounted for by the large number of sick treated by the Lom ambulances and transported by the Rustchuk-Varna railway section.[90]

Such detail served to stall any charges of inefficiency and to showcase Kennett-Barrington's considerable administrative talent. In circumventing the ethical and political positions taken by the various agencies in the Balkans – and working for a range of them irrespectively – Kennett-Barrington was able to devise a results-driven, highly proficient operation. If he also made a demonstrable contribution to the fighting strength of the Turkish army, as his report for Stafford House would seem to attest, this does not appear to have given him any qualms.

It is important not to mistake an individual for a trend, and certainly, as a career aid worker, Kennett-Barrington was at this stage a well-regarded exception. Nevertheless, the success of his ventures had important implications both for the purpose of aid and for the question of neutrality. His impressive statistics offered ample evidence of needs having been proficiently met. But others would query whether this was the appropriate measure of success for relief work in insurgency and foreign war. Col Henry Brackenbury RA, for one, thought not. Paid relief workers, he thought, though valued, ought best to remain subservient to the discretion of enlightened committee members.[91] The rather pompous Brackenbury (he insisted that his name be pronounced Whackenbaywe) was one of the leading minds in military reform in this period.[92] Widely prized for his perspicacity, Brackenbury had been hand picked by Sir Garnet Wolseley, the military's most influential reformer, to advance army modernisation. This was the same Henry Brackenbury who had been seconded from the British army to work as a self-styled 'commander-in-chief' of NAS operations in France in 1870–71, only to resign his membership in frustration at the Committee's lackadaisical approach to peace-time training. Unsurprisingly, NAS operations in Serbia had failed to mollify him: he denounced Loyd Lindsay and the Executive Council of titled dignitaries as an 'oligarchy' for ignoring the 'wishes of the more humble few' and for failing to seek regular subscribers to whom they would be accountable.[93] He aired his concerns publicly in the February 1877 edition of *Blackwood's Magazine*, at the critical point when the armistice between Turkey and Serbia was about to expire and the threat of Russian intervention loomed. Brackenbury's concern was twofold: to establish the merits of regulated civilian aid in British wars and to delineate an appropriate sphere of intervention in foreign conflicts.

---

[90] Kennett-Barrington, *Report of the Record and the Operation of the Stafford House Committee*, p. 10.
[91] Brackenbury, 'Philanthropy in War', p. 164.
[92] Ian F. W. Beckett, entry for Brackenbury, Sir Henry, Dictionary of National Biography Online.
[93] Brackenbury, 'Philanthropy in War', p. 169.

The significance of his critique derives from the astuteness with which he analysed the ambivalence, the dysfunction and the unintended consequences to which the sudden ballooning of war-time relief had given rise. His concerns, if not necessarily all his remedies, resonate rather startlingly with modern-day critiques, but it is his perspective, as one of those present at the inauguration of the voluntary aid movement, that is of most interest. Unlike the disenchantment of some recent commentators, for whom the wrongs of relief in war can be traced to the corruption of a pure ideal, Col Brackenbury had only to glance around him to perceive that British relief in war was less the preserve of collective idealism than the occupation of freelancers eager to appropriate the newfangled emblem of the Red Cross and the woolly appellation of 'neutrality' in pursuit of a variety of discordant ends. This state of affairs had been exacerbated by the contingent circumstances and ad hoc manner in which relief in war had been first instated in Britain. That British relief had been welcomed in 1870–71 owed more to the dishevelled state of French medico-military organisation and to the burden of an exceptionally large number of French wounded in Prussian hands than to any widespread agreement on the appropriate remit of overseas voluntary aid. At the time, this had concealed the NAS's self-mandated authority and questionable credentials. Moreover, as Britain had been neutral when large-scale aid operations had sprung up during the Franco-Prussian War, and both sides, as signatories of the Geneva Convention, had full national status, the potential for controversy engendered by relief in an insurgency or in an area of British strategic interest had been obscured.

For Loyd Lindsay and the NAS Committee, such ambiguities of international law were immaterial, for, as his wife and biographer noted, 'The influence of men such as England sends out has, indeed, done more to promote the cause of humanity in war than any conference or convocation.'[94] But for Brackenbury the ambiguities were threatening to affect Britain's relative medico-military strength, and to give rise to deleterious consequences in foreign conflicts. Firstly, the NAS, unlike the Continental Red Cross societies, had failed to seek regulation from the state or to create a trained corps of ambulance volunteers ready to assist Britain in any future war. Secondly, the amorphous and ill-defined nature of civilian aid in war had allowed numerous rival agencies to spring up and claim 'neutrality'. Now, with Disraeli playing a high-stakes game of 'wait and see' with respect to Russia's next move, the plethora of agencies at work in the Balkans was threatening to compromise Britain's state of contingent neutrality and 'every new philanthropic organisation which enters the field will add to the difficulty.'[95] The balance of power in the region, so critical to British concerns, was now off kilter. The 'action of both [pro-Slav and pro-Turkish] committees admits of plausible defence', with the friends of the Bosnian orphan pleading cold and hunger and the sympathisers of the Turkish

[94] Wantage, *Memoir*, p. 220.
[95] Brackenbury, 'Philanthropy in War', p. 150.

soldier pointing to the 'greatness of his sufferings', for, 'in short, there is no philanthropic effort made for the relief of suffering which does not *per se* commend itself to our minds', still,

> However praiseworthy in the abstract, the action of the one committee [Irby's Bosnian and Herzegovinian Fugitive and Orphan Relief Fund] is a direct support to men in rebellion against a friendly Power; while that of the Stafford House Committee is a deliberate gift of aid to the soldiers of one belligerent, to the direct detriment of the other, with whom we are, nominally at least, on terms of friendship and diplomatic alliance. Those, therefore, who subscribe to either fund, are clearly making themselves allies or enemies of Turkey in the existing struggle – are increasing the already grave difficulties of our diplomatists. . . . These may be thought extreme cases. Yet they are by no means exceptional.[96]

This was not, however, the only view on the matter. As Lady Strangford, founder of the Bulgarian Peasant Relief Fund, was said to have uttered, 'Is not humanity better than neutrality?'[97] In the cause of 'humanity', she declared 'do not let us permit so called political views . . . to interfere.'[98] For Lady Strangford, needs-led aid to civilians – not least when dispensed by a woman and on behalf of other women and children – was a universal response to human suffering. As such, it superseded political partiality, but could also render technical neutrality an unnecessary constraint. For Brackenbury, this amounted to the dangerous 'doctrine' that it was 'better to break the rules of international honour than to allow human beings to suffer privation.' Strangford, however, may well have taken this as an endorsement. This was – and remains – more than an abstract dilemma, and Brackenbury cited three practical considerations why: danger to aid workers' lives, expulsion of aid workers from the field and the possibility of affecting the outcome of a conflict. Would it be unwarranted, he pondered, in times of insurgency, if one of the belligerents 'promptly inflicted summary justice upon these agents for aiding and abetting rebellion'?[99]

How was such a situation to be remedied? Brackenbury recognised that once the public had knowledge of suffering in war, and had appropriated it as an area of interest and concern, such proprietorial obligations were unlikely to be easily renounced. Indeed, by and large, they ought to be celebrated as a gradual ripening of mercy and humanity. But, he cautioned, need alone ought not to be the criterion of intervention. Aid organisations must not provide aid exclusively to one side, however dire the conditions, nor seek to affect the outcome of a conflict. Instead, any advantage to a belligerent's war-making capacity ought to be cancelled out by ensuring that aid was bestowed in equal measure to the other side. Strictly impartial,

---

[96] *Ibid*, p. 151.
[97] Quoted in Anderson, *Balkan Volunteers*, p. 81.
[98] Quoted in *ibid.*, p. 80.
[99] Brackenbury, 'Philanthropy in War', p. 152.

equitable aid thus 'neutralised' its own power to influence the situation and functioned as an exemplar of English civility and compassion. This would affect a greater good: properly neutral aid in war represented the progress of humanity towards increasingly civilised accord, and functioned to advance harmony and reason in foreign relations.

> May we not dare to hope that the awful barbarism of nations armed, hand on sword, waiting but a word to close in deadly fight, is thus silently receiving its condemnation; ... and that, ... we may yet, ... see in the dim distance the light of the day when not brute force, but purer reason, shall reign triumphant in God's beauteous world?[100]

This was the moral foundation on which aid in a foreign war ought to be placed. But how was this carefully calibrated sphere of operation to be achieved? Brackenbury could offer no hard-and-fast rules, but only appeal to the discretion of committee members:

> Hence the vital necessity of such work being placed under the control of men of experience and judgment, whose position is a guarantee of the purity of their motives. Men who merely take service under a national aid society as they would under a contractor, for the sake of wages, valuable as they may be in carrying out definite orders, should not be trusted with discretionary powers. And the adventurer, who volunteers his services for the sake of what he can make indirectly, is carefully to be avoided.[101]

This then, was to be a self-regulating field, overseen by the delicacy, intuitive good sense and discretion of the amateur. Yet, given that individual relief agencies' sense of the 'greater good' veered between the expression of liberal solidarity with 'oppressed' peoples and aid to all sides in a conflict, there seemed to be little chance of a working consensus. Loyd Lindsay appeared satisfied with the purity of his motives and at ease with his conscience. Certainly, his wife and biographer had no qualms on his behalf. The different approaches of the Duke of Sutherland, Lady Strangford and Loyd Lindsay – convinced of the rectitude of their actions, and well-born amateurs all – hardly inspired confidence that the aid world would be amicably self-regulating. Only when the British military was convinced of the virtue of civilian aid did greater regulation of volunteers take place, and only in British wars, though, of course, any discretionary powers would be correspondingly lost.

For the moment, however, no trained corps of volunteers existed. Yet military modernisers such as Wolseley were beginning to note the potential for civilian aid.[102] In a letter to Loyd Lindsay from the time of the Balkan wars, Wolseley advocated the value of a purely voluntary agency in ensuring that the provisions of supplementary aid to the sick and wounded remained a public responsibility:

---

[100] *Ibid.*, p. 174.
[101] *Ibid.*, p. 165.
[102] Summers, *Angels and Citizens*, pp. 134–140.

I very much doubt if our government ever could render officially as much effective assistance to our sick and wounded as your Society could.

Looking at the subject also from a financial point of view, it is evident you could command any amount of money you asked the rich members of society to subscribe. In this way I think you could do the work better than our army administration could, and do it without adding to the cost of the war as charged against our Treasury.

However, I fully agree with you that the existence of your Society should not in any way lessen the energy of our Army Medical Department, and that the true province of the Society is to supplement the work done officially.[103]

Wolseley would stand to benefit from precisely such an arrangement in his controversial Egyptian campaign of 1884–85. Full oversight of civilian aid by the War Office would only arrive after the medico-military debacle of the Boer War. Nevertheless, in its persistent call for a trained corps of battlefield philanthropists, the clique surrounding Brackenbury, Longmore and Furley of the Order of St John did have a more immediate success. Disraeli's guarded neutrality would be replaced, within the year, by a tense situation in which British intervention seemed a real possibility. It was against a background of popular jingoism and Russophobia that the Order of St John took the opportunity of launching a nationwide St John Ambulance Association (founded in February 1878), which would train paramedical volunteers to deal with civilian accidents, with a view to war-time service.[104] By June 1878, 1,100 men and women had attended St John first-aid classes, and regional branches continued to spring up. A year later, approximately 2,000 people had completed the course in London alone.[105] The classes proved particularly popular with women. Anne Summers notes a popular desire for instruction in everyday accidents. But, as she also points out, many women 'saw themselves as budding war heroines, who might emulate the exploits of Florence Nightingale or Emily Strangford'.[106]

Meanwhile, the end of the Russo-Turkish War and the granting of greater autonomy in the Balkans saw a shift in British strategic thinking, as more partition seemed inevitable. The indirect lessons of the protest can be felt in the clauses of the Berlin Treaty that were concerned with those Christians, now vastly reduced in number, who remained in the Ottoman Empire. The new Foreign Secretary Lord Salisbury was particularly attentive to Armenian Orthodox populations living in Eastern Anatolia, a region which had been invaded by Russia with a view to annexation during the war. In laying claim to Cyprus and demanding that the Ottomans reform the treatment of Armenians, Lord Salisbury sought to secure British routes to India and prevent Russia from asserting her claims in the region, and also to avoid a repetition of the

---

[103] Quoted in Wantage, *Memoir*, pp. 243–244.
[104] Summers, *Angels and Citizens*, p. 141.
[105] *Ibid.*, p. 142.
[106] *Ibid.*, p. 142.

dangerous emotionalism of the 1876 protests.[107] However, the acquiescence of the Ottoman government to such a scheme was unforthcoming and the question of British responsibilities to Ottoman Christians lay unresolved. Subsequent events in the Ottoman Empire, particularly in Armenia and Macedonia, would continue to inspire moral outrage in Britain, triggering renewed flashpoints of dissenting protest. A potent stock of images – of slavery, rape and of a savagery lurking behind sham claims to civilisation – were at the emotional and ethical core of Liberal outcries over tyranny and oppression for a generation, and would stimulate many further public acts of conscience, including the provision of relief. They would also be used to denounce 'tyranny' closer to home. Twenty years later, many of those involved in the 'Bulgarian atrocities' would regroup to protest British military conduct in South Africa, with the question of neutrality to the fore once again. It is to these indignant protests that Part III turns.

---

[107] The Anglo-Turkish Convention of 1878, which granted Britain the occupation of Cyprus, and protection for Ottoman Christians, instituted a Defensive Alliance which was to be mobilised in case of an attack by Russia on the Eastern Ottoman front (via the Armenian provinces). This ambitious pact failed to materialise.

Part III

Boundaries of compassion:
humanity and relief in British wars, c.1884–1914

5

Scientific humanitarianism and British 'tyranny' in South Africa

In October 1899, Britain went to war against the two Boer Republics in the name of upholding the rights of British residents or 'Uitlanders'. When tense early days of unexpected defeats were followed by the relief of Mafeking in May 1900 many Britons savoured a long-awaited moment of jubilation. Crowds jostled on the streets to sing patriotic songs and partake in the general excitement. Critics of the war in South Africa, rejecting Britain's stated war aims and appalled at her conduct, recoiled. The Quaker John Wilhelm Rowntree detected 'an aspect of heathenism at the carnival of rejoicing'.[1] However, compared to the 'Bulgarian atrocities' agitation, now evoked with nostalgia, condemnation of Britain's role in South Africa was, for the most part, muted. But where it did exist, there was to be found a notable cross-over of individuals between this and the earlier protest, and allegations of slavery and tyrannous oppression hung over meetings denouncing the war against the Boers, just as they had over those to harangue the sultan and his British apologists. Once again, knowledge of distant suffering and efforts at its amelioration had implications both for the domestic aspirations of British agitators and for those for whom urgent relief and intervention was advocated (though not necessarily in ways anticipated by British sympathisers). This chapter focuses on how the politics of humanity and relief reverberated in 'progressive' circles in Britain, including those championing political representation for women.

To these veterans of the 'Bulgarian atrocities' agitation, and those fresh from recent campaigns over the Ottoman treatment of Christians in Armenia and Crete, the memory of Gladstone was never far away, his reputation as an icon of liberal internationalism soon to be sealed by Morley's celebrated biography.[2] Alongside the stalwarts of 1876, prominent among whom were Sheffield Liberal MP H. J. Wilson and the journalist W. T. Stead, stood younger apostles of humanity, many of whom

---

[1] Quoted in Hewison, *Hedge of Wild Almonds*, p. 121.
[2] Morley was researching his biography of Gladstone alongside intermittent participation in the anti-war agitation. See Sylvest, *British Liberal Internationalism*, p. 171.

had been infants at the time of Gladstone's rousing denunciations, but were well versed in his speeches nonetheless. Those keeping the Gladstonian flame alive faced popular disdain and raucous abuse but took comfort that their unanimity in opposition testified to a place in the vanguard. 'The best thing the *Manchester Guardian* had done in my time was to oppose the Boer War', ruminated its editor C. P. Scott to erstwhile ally Lloyd George, '[w]e were together there.'[3] Of course, for politicians such as Lloyd George, opposition to the war was a matter of adroit manoeuvring as well as genuine conviction; but Scott was right to remember the protest as a touchstone of progressive opinion around which 'advanced' Liberals, ethicists, egalitarians and Labour coalesced.

For many activists, reformers and intellectuals, opposition to the war in South Africa, and the delivery of relief, was an act of conscience which saw them marry a Gladstonian emphasis on moral intent to a newly 'scientific' humanitarianism. It also saw those in Britain who protested the rights and duties of humanity yoke their own emancipatory, liberationist and democratic struggles to an image of the down-trodden but fiercely independent Boers. This was no more apparent than in the articulation of a radical feminine critique which saw concern for suffering humanity as the natural preserve of female compassion, but as also exemplifying the need for self-determination, including the representation of women's moral interests in foreign affairs. Sympathy and practical relief for the Boers – especially those South African 'sisters' languishing in British concentration camps – was thus at once an ethical ideal 'above' political considerations and an implicit challenge to women's exclusion from parliamentary politics.

'Scientific' humanitarianism

As in 1876, opponents converged upon the questions of state violence, international conciliation and the right of a people to determine their future, free of coercion or manipulation, whether at home or abroad. At the core of this stood the vision of an ethical polity in which the rights and duties of humanity were sacred. Philosopher and *Manchester Guardian* journalist L. T. Hobhouse could write of 'the sovereign duty to a common humanity' and expect widespread accord.[4] Gladstone's legacy rested on his extension of classical liberal freedoms of contract and co-operation to embrace notions of Christian duties and civic virtues. But, by the turn of the century, thinkers such as L. T. Hobhouse and other 'new liberals' had taken to imbuing these ideals with an evolutionary logic and to arguing for the study of ethics as a branch of positive science. This spoke of wider trends in British intellectual and political life – what Stuart Jones has referred to as the attempt to foster 'an evolutionary

---

[3] C. P. Scott to Lloyd George, 1930, quoted in Stefan Collini, *Liberalism and Sociology: L. T. Hobhouse and Political Argument in England 1880–1914*, Cambridge University Press, Cambridge, 1979, p. 82. Scott and Lloyd George would diverge on subsequent foreign policy crises, especially following the Great War.

[4] Quoted in *ibid.*, p. 81.

science of ethics founded on a natural history of morals'.[5] The ethical polity would be achieved, these progressives argued, only when, through methodical and impartial intervention, intemperance, greed, cruelty, want and aggression and the corrupting effects of 'special interests' had been overcome. For some, this also extended to removing obstacles to women's political participation.

In a well-known chapter of her autobiography titled 'The Religion of Humanity', Beatrice Webb thus described a defining feature of late-Victorian social thought: the calling of science into the service of a humanist ethic.

> [T]he scientific method of reasoning, so it seemed to my practical mind, was not an end in itself; it was the means by which a given end could be pursued. . . . To what end, for what purpose, and therefore *upon what subject-matter* was the new faculty of the intellect to be exercised? . . . I suggest it was during the middle decades of the nineteenth century that, in England, the impulse of self-subordinating service was transferred, consciously and overtly, from God to man.[6]

Webb was one of a range of philosophers and moralists who thought altruism, the quality of public-spirited concern for the welfare of others (and a significant neologism of the period), offered a sounder basis for an ethical polity than did the vicissitudes of Christian compassion. Eschewing a technocratic calculation of utility or profitability, these thinkers instead cherished moral intent as the optimum criterion of personal or public action. 'They asked first not what would pay but what was true, what was right, and what was humane.'[7] These words, taken from Gilbert Murray's eulogy to his friends and fellow 'advanced' liberals Lawrence and Barbara Hammond, can be taken as representative of a veneration, among an extended circle, of ethics over efficiency. Nevertheless, such altruistic precepts were to be expounded in strict scientific fashion, and implemented according to impartial and rational methods. The point was that the insights of science would always be in subordinate service to, rather than replace, a higher ideal. In privileging altruism, such thinkers were not necessarily anti-Christian or secularist; indeed, their moral ideals and obligations were grounded in Christian teaching and rarely contested, and many also displayed an interest in establishing the truths which united all the world's religions.[8] It was, rather, that they could no longer hold up Christianity alone as a sufficient spur to moral action. In transferring the incentive from God to man, they preached a 'Religion of Humanity' which many in this period were drawn to profess.[9]

---

[5] Jones, *Victorian Political Thought*, p. 82.

[6] Beatrice Webb, *My Apprenticeship*, Longmans, Green & Co., London, 1926, pp. 142–143. Original italics.

[7] Quoted in Stewart A. Weaver, entry for Hammond, (John) Lawrence Le Breton, Dictionary of National Biography Online.

[8] Gregory Claeys, *Imperial Sceptics: British Critics of Empire, 1850–1920*, Cambridge University Press, Cambridge, 2010, p. 89.

[9] Collini, *Public Moralists: Political Thought and Intellectual Life in Britain, 1850–1930*, Oxford, Oxford University Press, 1993, pp. 84–85.

The 'Religion of Humanity' was a broad church and its congregation differed not least in their approach to a 'scientific' method of reasoning. L. T. Hobhouse provides an instructive example of one who undertook a serious scholarly attempt to bridge science and ethics. He is of particular interest here as leader writer for the anti-war *Manchester Guardian* during the South African War. Hobhouse, like many of his fellow philosophers, was preoccupied with establishing the basis of an ethical polity. Influenced by contemporary evolutionary theory, though applying its insights to human consciousness rather than to biological changes, he was convinced that man's moral evolution could be purposefully stimulated and advanced. To this end, he set about discovering empirical evidence for the consciously directed evolution of the human spirit. For L. T. Hobhouse, greater social co-operation, having overcome the baser drives leading to conflict and competition, seemed to be observable evidence of just such a development. In this schema, greater social interdependence became imbued with altruistic intent.[10]

Another tradition of 'humanitarian' thought in this period, though one ostensibly less teleological, was associated with the Positivists. These British followers of Auguste Comte asserted that an ethical system would be revealed through the objective observation of human society, or 'sociology'. These impartially adduced moral laws had informed the opposition of Frederic Harrison and his fellow Positivists to British policy during the Franco-Prussian War. They had also underwritten the Positivists' criticism of the emotionalism of the 'Bulgarian atrocities' agitators and would now decide their resistance to British policy in South Africa. Emily Hobhouse, L. T. Hobhouse's sister, admiring Harrison's grasp of foreign affairs and the zeal of his interventions, credited him with an inspirational role in stimulating the anti-war campaign. Though mocked for his adherence to a 'Religion of Humanity', which seemed to many in society at large as merely crankish, Harrison was widely prized among fellow progressives for his pugnacious denunciations of militarism and imperialism, his grasp of international law (he had been a professor of law for the Council of Legal Education) and his integrity.

These progressives frequented clubs for the study of ethics and intervened in public debates to expose bluster and hypocrisy and put forward the rational point of view. Many, including Harrison, congregated in the ranks of the Humanitarian League (1891–1919), where they prided themselves on being both agents in the evolutionary progress of mankind and an establishment for the foundation of a new 'moral science'. The League concerned itself with campaigns against organised cruelty, whether in the treatment of prisoners, animals or children. Among other causes, they campaigned against capital punishment, wished to see an end to blood sports and railed against 'murderous millinery' – the fashion for adorning women's hats with birds' plumage. The League's founder, the socialist, vegetarian and naturalist Henry Salt, was a man of strong feeling and conviction. Nevertheless, he took satisfaction

---

[10] Stefan Collini, entry for Hobhouse, Leonard Trelawny, Dictionary of National Biography Online.

in refusing to determine the path taken by the many 'advanced' individuals whom he brought together – preferring committees, dialogue and a democratic organisational structure. At the same time, he shared with his fellow Leaguers an intuitive moral certainty and an assumption of social leadership so deeply ingrained as to need little explication.

Henry Salt, like L. T. Hobhouse, was conscious of an innate but evolving human-itarian compassion which would overcome abuse, exploitation and struggle, but which was, by definition, impossible to institutionalise in any permanent system.[11] One step ahead of most their contemporaries (to whom they often appeared eccentric), the humanitarian took solace from occupying a place at the forefront of moral progress. Wryly captured in the title of Salt's reflections, this was to be the *Consolation of the Faddist*. 'It was our object', Salt reflected, 'to show that Human-itarianism is not merely a kindly sentiment, a product of the heart rather than of the head, but an integral portion of any intelligible system of Ethics or Social Science.'[12] Yet, secure in their own humane virtues, this interconnected group of fellow initiates all too readily took their own commitments as proof of the development of public mores and values. Much akin to the international law fraternity, their own human-itarian credentials were thus 'objectively' endorsed. This meant that there was little of the self-correction promised by a thoroughgoing 'positivist' science in instances where their outlook was curiously blinkered or troublingly inconsistent. And, when the public disappointed in its recidivist ways, it was the presence of obstacles to public enlightenment (such as educational deficiencies, corrupt government or a kept press) that was pointed to.

The Humanitarian League thus became a clearing house for a range of broadly progressive concerns expressed with the certainty of ethical conviction. To a greater or lesser degree, its members shared a commitment to the liberation and cultivation of the human spirit and the humane ordering of society to beget universal harmony and advancement. For many, this remained a quest for political liberty and an ethical polity, but for others this extended to the emancipation of the self from restrictive social and sexual conventions, with the help of Eastern spirituality, 'rational dress' and an artisan lifestyle. The months prior to the outbreak of war in South Africa found Humanitarian Leaguers agitating on a number of fronts. January 1899, for example, and the pages of their journal, *Humanity*, featured Leeds Quaker Isabella Ford advocating female suffrage 'on the humanitarian principle of *preventing* injustice instead of the philanthropic principle of merely trying to *palliate* it.'[13] A few months later saw the editor denouncing plans to use the exploding 'dum dum' bullet 'against a brave people whom we have shamefully wronged' in South Africa. This seemed to be 'a disquieting proof of the hypocritical spirit in which Governments

---

[11] Henry Salt, *Humanitarianism: Its General Principles and Progress*, [privately published], London, 1906, p. 26.

[12] Humanitarian League, *Fifth Annual Report, 1895–96*. [British Library]

[13] Isabella Ford, 'The Woman's Movement', *Humanity*, Vol. III, No. 47, January 1899, 99.

enter into Peace Conferences, however genuine may be the desire for peace among humane people.[14] Members of the League at the time included Lib-Lab MP Henry Broadhurst, Irish nationalists Michael Davitt, Justin McCarthy and John Dillon, peace activist J. Passmore Edwards and the Radical Liberal C. A. V. Conybeare. Other prominent members and anti-war critics included Frederic Harrison, Edward Carpenter, W. T. Stead, Elizabeth Wolstenholme Elmy, Charlotte Despard, Ramsay MacDonald and Mrs Cobden Sanderson.

Opposition to war in South Africa

To opponents of the war in South Africa the government and the people had been hoodwinked by a cabal of insidious special interest groups, 'a conspiracy of financiers and ambitious politicians', according to Frederic Harrison.[15] They quickly worked up the war into a desultory tale of thuggish aggression, with peaceable and free-born Republics left cowering in the wake of British imperial greed. The Unionist government's claim to be defending the citizenship rights of the British-born 'Uitlander' in South Africa and offering British protection to natives in the region was dismissed summarily as a façade. Instead, anti-war protestors argued the reverse to be true: the rights and duties of humanity were being vitiated and the bonds of human solidarity torn asunder by British actions in South Africa. It was here that the new scientific humanitarianism fused so well with an emerging liberal politics of rights and duties: for it would be through the vigour of 'spontaneous' moral convulsions such as this that the liberal polity would be periodically revived and the struggle for moral evolution advanced. Foreign affairs, sufficiently distant from divisive domestic concerns, offered a testing ground of ethical intent. At the core of L. T. Hobhouse and his circle's opposition to the war stood the necessity of promoting an ethical polity – both at home and in South Africa – and it was in the vision of self-determining republics conjured by Guiseppe Mazzini that the ideal of an ethical polity seemed most likely to be realised.

Mazzini's letters and pronouncements featured heavily in the reading of Hobhouse, his *Manchester Guardian* colleague J. A. Hobson and their peers, just as they had for W. T. Stead at the time of the 'Bulgarian atrocities'. Democratic republics, they averred, were the true expression of a people's conscience, which, free of the selfishness of elite rule and special interests, had a natural propensity for altruism. Republics were the smallest serviceable units of humanity, but they were, in turn, embedded in wider networks of international co-operation. As L. T. Hobhouse remarked in 1904, national rights 'have their assigned place in the democratic system'. For 'the world advances by the free, vigorous growth of divergent types' which preserve their vitality in an organic order of life 'resting on the spontaneous

---

[14] 'Notes', *Humanity*, Vol. III, No. 54, August 1899, 153.
[15] Harrison, *Autobiographic Memoirs*, p. 126.

co-operation' of its parts.[16] Here, then, were the principles upon which the independence of the Boer Republics was lauded, free speech in Britain was claimed to
be a test of moral vigour and solidarity with the victims of oppression was deemed
an expression of co-operative humanity.

Many of those opposed to war in South Africa were veteran campaigners against
the Ottoman treatment of Christians, as well as against British conduct in Afghanistan, and many would reunite after the war to protest the plight of the Macedonians.
This did not mean that they were always unanimous. Thus, for example, for some,
support for a people 'struggling to be free' extended to Irish Home Rule, while for
others, basic liberties and freedom from clericalism in Ireland were best secured
through direct union with Britain.[17] Of these, Leonard Courtney, known as the
'conscience of the House of Commons', and his wife, Kate, were two prominent 'pro-
Boer' Liberal Unionists. The war in South Africa saw them retreat from the Unionist
position – but without wishing to forfeit their long-standing friendship with fellow
Unionist and supporter of the war Millicent Garrett Fawcett. Likewise, 'self-
determination' could mean a number of things: sympathy for Ottoman Christians
saw calls for the independence of Bulgaria, Armenia and Macedonia that ranged
from ethnic nationalism to greater autonomy within the existing Ottoman Empire,
and the case for the white settler population in the British Empire was similarly
divisive. Even less straightforward was what constituted a 'unit' of humanity – and
what was to be the fate of those individuals who were excluded. Concern for
the freedom of the Boer Republics did not, as a rule, extend to the freedoms of
the 'native races' in South Africa. Those who venerated the Boer states as peaceable,
self-determining polities resolved this contradiction, rather uncomfortably, by
arguing that Boer self-government, so evidently a manifestation of liberty, would
ensure the freedom of other races (brushing aside the evidence of the Aborigines
Protection Society to the contrary).[18]

Threat of war in South Africa brought many of these progressives together in a
new campaigning organisation, the South African Conciliation Committee (SACC).
The SACC included among its members *Manchester Guardian* writers, Positivists,
Quakers and members of the Humanitarian League, as well as groups that Frederic
Harrison deemed were Positivist in all but name, such as the South Place Ethical
Society and the Rainbow Club.[19] 'This war makes all the good people kin', Harrison
noted with satisfaction.[20] By mid-1900, its president, Leonard Courtney, oversaw

---

[16] Quotation and text taken from Howard Weinroth, 'Radicalism and Nationalism: An Increasingly Unstable
Equation', in A. J. A. Morris (ed.), *Edwardian Radicalism 1900–1914: Some Aspects of British Radicalism*, Routledge,
London, 1974, p. 219.

[17] Biagini, *British Democracy*, p. 326.

[18] Claire Hirshfield, 'Blacks, Boers and Britons: The Anti-War Movement in England and the "Native Issue,
1899–1902"', *Peace and Change*, Vol. 8, 1982, 24–25.

[19] 'Harrison once defined "ethicists" as "simply Positivists *minus* the definite dogmas and formulae of
Comte"', Martha Vogeler, *Frederic Harrison: The Vocations of a Positivist*, Clarendon Press, Oxford, 1984, p. 220.

[20] Quoted in *ibid.*, p. 236.

more than 33 branches around the country, comprising 1,056 members and 22 Groups of Women.[21] Frederic Harrison, H. W. Massingham and the publisher Mr T. Fisher Unwin were members of the Executive Committee. Courtney's wife, Kate, joined Emily Hobhouse, the Reverend and Mrs Barnett, Lady Carlisle and her son-in-law Gilbert Murray and H. J. Wilson MP on a General Committee. This exemplary cross-section of the liberal avant garde was accompanied by Keir Hardie, J. A. Hobson, H. N. Brailsford, Edward Carpenter, Henry Salt, J. L. Hammond and Isabella Ford.[22] A pamphlet campaign was launched to counter the bluster of the pro-war party and to educate the public on the true causes and progress of the war. Outcry over the imperilment of free speech by a tainted press and jingoistic 'mobs' was twinned with faith in the virtue of the masses, should the facts be known. Thus the intention was to disseminate

> accurate information on the whole dispute, and for the consideration, as soon as a proper opportunity arises, of some peaceable settlement of the great conflict between this country and the Boer Republics . . . In view of the now recognised facts of the past, we think it to be not less contrary to reason than abhorrent to humanity to wage war for aggressive purposes beyond the point which may be necessary either for the protection of the Queen's subjects or for the preservation of the integrity of her dominions.[23]

W. T. Stead, presiding over the abrasive 'Stop the War Committee' – with its unequivocal 'Stop the War and Stop It Now' slogan – had little time for the SACC's measured attempt at public enlightenment. Leonard Courtney, however, was not to be cajoled into more demonstrable protest, and was careful to maintain a courteous distance from Stead's campaign. But other links were forged. Within the SACC's orbit were Cobdenite non-interventionists, observant pacifists and existing party associations (Liberal Associations, Women's Liberal Associations and Reform Clubs).[24] Of the latter, Claire Hirshfield has noted the consistent, sometimes radical, defiance of the Women's Liberal Federation (chaired by Lady Carlisle), which she characterises as an 'unprecedented feminine assault' by an organised party auxiliary.[25] Within the peace movement, the war saw older organisations, such as the International Arbitration League and the Quaker-backed Peace Society,

---

[21] See S. H. Swinny, 'The Work of the South Africa Conciliation Committee, 1900', [The Committee], London, 1900.

[22] See the following SACC publications: 'Minutes of the General Committee Meeting at the Westminster Palace Hotel, Thursday April 5th 1900'; 'Receipts and Payments Account from 12 October 1900 to 12 October 1901'; 'Receipts and Payments Account from 21 July 1899 to 12 October 1900'; 'List of Names and Addresses', H. S. Swinny (Sec.), 'The Work of the South African Conciliation Committee, 1901.' All published in London, by the Committee.

[23] SACC, '"The Committee's Manifesto" as issued to the public press on 15 January 1900', [The Committee], London, 1900.

[24] Paul Laity, 'The British Peace Movement and the War', in David Omissi and Andrew S. Thompson (eds), *The Impact of the South African War*, Palgrave, Basingstoke, 2002, p. 154.

[25] Claire Hirshfield, 'Liberal Women's Organisations and the War against the Boers, 1899–1902', *Albion*, 14:1 (1982), 27–49.

become increasingly moribund.[26] Partly, the difficulties were internal, but a change in the commitments underpinning an anti-war stance was also making itself felt. From within overlapping 'advanced' Liberal and Quaker circles emanated a desire to place the abolition of war within a wider progressive agenda. As the editor of the Humanitarian League's *Humanity* put it,

> It is impossible, looking at this war, to doubt that the growth of humane sentiment must be seriously, perhaps fatally, retarded by an episode of this sort in a nation's history . . . And the chief lesson of the war will perhaps be seen to be this – that it is not sufficient for reformers to denounce the barbarities of warfare *alone*, as the advocates of peace have too often done in the past. A humane spirit can only be developed by a consistent protest against *all* forms of cruelty and oppression; it is only by cultivating a whole-minded reverence for the rights of all our fellow-beings that mankind can hope to rid itself of that inheritance of selfish brutality of which the 'imperialist' mania is but a symptom and a part.[27]

Among more radical Quakers, the outbreak of hostilities in South Africa coincided with a questioning of conventional evangelical pieties and the quest for a more rigorous spiritual engagement with the world. However, despite the formation of the Friends' Peace Committee in 1889, the majority of Friends continued to undertake merely customary observance of the Quaker peace testimony. Some even supported British action in South Africa. John Bellows, an influential publisher and veteran of Quaker relief work in the Franco-Prussian War and Armenia, vented views on the righteousness of British policy and the vulnerability of 'the natives' under Boer rule. Bellows' stance confounded those at the forefront of the 'new Quakerism', such as the teacher and writer (and, from 1901, editor of the *British Friend*), Edward Grubb.

Instead, Grubb wished to place the Quakers' opposition to the conflict in South Africa, and to war in general, on the universal fatherhood of God and the fundamental brotherhood of man, rather than abstruse scriptural teachings.[28] He was part of an assault on evangelicalism which, by the turn of the century, had culminated in a resurgent and self-assured 'Quaker renaissance' and a commitment to a revived Peace Testimony. This saw the rise of a generation committed to liberal theology and the importance of the 'Inward Light', the presence of which had been originally attested to in the seventeenth century by the sect's founding father, George Fox. The 'Inward Light' was understood as the chink of God within, giving rise to individual acts of service and witness that dispensed with the need for strict doctrinal guidance, biblical instruction and theories of predestination, and vivifing claims to a common humanity. The persecution and incarceration of George Fox in

[26] Laity, 'British Peace Movement', p. 141.

[27] Editorial, 'Some Lessons of the War', *Humanity*, Vol. IV, No. 67, September 1900, 69; see also Edward Carpenter, *Boer and Briton*, Labour Press, Manchester, 1900.

[28] For a history of the Quakers' pacifism in the late nineteenth century, see Margaret Hirst, *The Quakers in Peace and War: An Account of their Peace Principles and Practice*, The Swarthmore Press Ltd, London, 1923.

1650, and his renunciation of arms, was appropriated as an important precedent at a time when these internal transformations rendered the rediscovery of Quaker history a key source of theological inspiration and authority.[29] Spearheading this inquiry into Quaker origins was Grubb's friend, the young John Wilhelm Rowntree, of the well-known family of chocolate manufactures in York. With a vigorous, creative mind and considerable personal charisma, John Wilhelm was the closest Quakers let themselves come to a guru figure. Though he was only in his mid-thirties when he died in 1905, his influence on young Friends infused all aspects of the Quaker renaissance. His was an uncompromising quest to challenge Quaker complacency and grapple with the implications posed by biblical criticism, changing attitudes to poverty and fears for the militarisation of society.

For John Wilhelm Rowntree and Edward Grubb, the conflict in South Africa represented an important test of conscience and called forth the kind of public action and, if need be, controversy that made more conservative Quakers nervous. Alongside many progressives at this time, they shared a commitment to scientific method: the answer to social problems lay in fusing Christian ethics with a discriminating model of research and intervention. Quakers, of course, had a long history of yoking spiritual ends with rational administrative means; yet the impetus of the Quaker renaissance called forth both a reanimation of ethical principle and a more explicit commitment to public service in place of the vagaries of philanthropy. In a paper read at the annual Scarborough Summer School in 1897, Edward Grubb addressed his audience on the problems of industrial relations and political economy, in terms which sought to marry the 'Inward Light' with empirical investigation:

> Christianity we may allow, provides sound principles of action; but how to *apply* those principles, in the wholly new conditions of present industrial society – that is the problem. Hence, the definite study of social problems becomes, for some at least, a Christian duty.[30]

Nevertheless, while sharing a commitment to alleviating social problems and opposing militarism, some Quakers found uncongenial the economic socialism and anti-imperialism propounded by a minority of progressives. Within Quaker circles were prominent men of business with extensive colonial trading connections.[31] Here the influence of Cobden and Bright still held sway over those eager to refute J. A. Hobson's analysis of the interplay between modern capitalism, imperialism and war first put forward during the Boer War. H. S. Newman, editor of the *British Friend*'s more staid cousin *The Friend*, reassured them that the protection of foreign

---

[29] This was the period in which the charismatic John Wilhelm Rowntree, leading spokesman of the new theology, inaugurated an influential chronicle of Quaker history. Thomas Kennedy, *British Quakerism 1860–1920: The Transformation of a Religious Community*, Oxford University Press, Oxford, 2001, pp. 168–169.

[30] Edward Grubb, *Social Aspects of the Quaker Faith*, Headley Brothers, London, 1899, p. 74.

[31] For Quaker attitudes to trade, philanthropy and empire, see Kevin Grant, *A Civilised Savagery: Britain and the New Slaveries in Africa, 1884–1926*, Routledge, London, 2005.

securities was generative of peace rather than of incitement to war.[32] Most Quakers could, however, unite over the importance of civic enterprise. Corporate wealth, Grubb reminded them, had supported good works among their workers at home and in the colonies, and enhanced social, industrial and imperial relations as a result: '[W]e shall judge that it is not wealth or property in itself, but the *use we make* of wealth and property . . . which is really the subject of our Lord's praise or blame.'[33] Quakers took satisfaction in a vision of thoroughgoing service funded by an ethical capitalism. Methodological investigation into the causes of distress, measured giving and the fostering of 'self help' and industriousness were all to be promoted. Here lay the path not only to domestic harmony but also to international peace and friendship. It is instructive to find Quakers quietly providing behind-the-scenes support for the South Africa Conciliation Committee through the provision of funds, premises and committee members; later, their Meeting Houses would host Emily Hobhouse's lecture tour exposing conditions in the concentration camps.[34]

Initially, the hopes of the SACC were pinned on disputing government claims of a 'just' war in South Africa, cutting through official rhetoric with a direct appeal to the British public's moral sense. The khaki election of October 1900, which returned Lord Salisbury as prime minister, seemed depressing confirmation of an electorate infected by jingoism and of the grievous imperilment of free speech. Now from the battlefields of South Africa came news that the limits of civilised conduct were being breached. Lord Roberts and his successor, Lord Kitchener (the commander of the British army following Roberts's jubilant but premature departure in October 1900), were deploying methods of colonial warfare used by Roberts in Afghanistan but never before against a 'civilised' people. These included the forced internment of Boer women and children as part of a 'scorched earth' policy. In the meantime, the tenor of opposition in Britain was beginning to change. The question of a 'just' war was increasingly tied to that of a 'just' and workable peace, and the appeal to the British people's moral sense was made reliant on more than detailed refutation. For the public's compassion was now made the subject of a concerted appeal: one which evoked the abject Boer suffering to question not only the legitimacy of the war but also its conduct. Even before the full details of civilian internment were known, critics grasped the potential to embarrass the newly elected government and launch a new line of attack. Here lay the prospect of galvanising the fractured Liberal Party and providing a fillip to the anti-war protest. In the weeks following the election L. T. Hobhouse wrote to C. P. Scott, his editor at the *Manchester Guardian*, to acquaint him with some new developments:

[32] Laity, 'The British Peace Movement', p. 153.
[33] Grubb, *Social Aspects of the Quaker Faith*, p. 184. Emphasis in original.
[34] Greenwood, *Quaker Encounters*, p. 151.

Two things are going on of which I should like you to know. One is a movement in London towards getting up a memorial protesting against the present methods of war, and taking the line as the alternative, negotiations with the Boer leaders. Hammond is working, in consultation with the Courtneys, Reid, Captain Pirie, and Lloyd George (who is doubtful). He is going to try to get Morley to draft the memorial . . .

Secondly: my sister is organising a relief fund for the Dutch women and children whose farms have been burnt, and for those who are imprisoned. She is trying to get a certain number of non-party people into it, on humanitarian grounds. Probably she will very shortly go out to South Africa herself to help in administering it. . . . I think it would be extremely desirable that she should write letters – which she can do very graphically – to the English papers, describing what she finds. I think she ought to offer such letters to several papers, sending more than one copy of them; . . . it could not then be suggested that she appealed to the anti-war press only . . . I think much might be done by this method.[35]

He was not to be disappointed. With her revelations of atrocity, Emily Hobhouse and her supporters transformed the question of government policy in South Africa from a minority cause into a pressing humanitarian issue necessitating immediate redress.

The threat of annexation and the beginnings of a feminine critique

Raised in a secluded Cornish rectory and only a few years older than Leonard, Emily Hobhouse shared many of the attributes of her younger brother, notably an uncompromising sense of public morality and a deft ability to convert moral indignation into rousing prose. But more demonstrative in temperament, and lacking the leader writer's ready platform, she surpassed him in both her single-minded activism and her flair for provocative publicity. Emily, rather than L. T. Hobhouse, took the more vigorous role in the anti-war agitation. The more circumspect Leonard, it was said, 'showed limited interest in people, while remaining passionate about humanity'.[36] The same could not be said of Emily: driven by a febrile energy and emboldened by a self-assurance born both of her class and of her steely idealism, she embarked upon a mission to expose military misconduct in South Africa and bring succour to the afflicted. Her defiant sense of entitlement – she did not hesitate to press her case either with High Command in South Africa or with government officials at home – would win her many admirers, but rankled critics and friends alike.

As with many progressives, the substance of L. T. Hobhouse's convictions rested less on objective scrutiny than on his intellectual and moral inheritance, an inheritance shared with his sister. Emily Hobhouse recorded her convictions in fragments of her unpublished autobiography. Quoting admiringly from the Gladstonian writings

[35] L. T. Hobhouse to C. P. Scott, 7.11.1900, JRL, C. P. Scott papers, 132/102.
[36] Stefan Collini, entry for Hobhouse, Leonard Trelawny, Dictionary of National Biography Online.

of her uncle, the Liberal peer Lord Arthur Hobhouse, she argued the importance of making

> people see that a nation does not become great by increasing the number of subjects without regard to quality or proximity; that extension of dominion by military force brings weakness and not strength . . . that the truest and bravest patriots are those who dare to warn their countrymen when hurrying in ignorance or passion to do wrong . . . that free thought and speech are, with occasional friction and inconvenience, the very life-blood of mankind without which they dwindle into insignificance.[37]

These convictions animated Emily's social activism at home and abroad. Her first experiences were in temperance work, which she, along with her brother and radicals such as his friends Lady Carlisle and Gilbert Murray, approached as an entwined social and political problem. The issue was not simply individual drunkenness, but the sapping effects of drink on public morality and freedom of political expression (observed, not least, in the rowdiness and violence faced by 'pro-Boer' speakers), and the iniquity of a brewery special interest in parliament. Temperance work, for these individuals, formed part of a wide-ranging commitment to moral and social reform, including female emancipation. This led on to Emily's work for the Women's Industrial Council (she was elected to the executive in 1898), where the focus of her interests lay in the effects of child labour. Her work for the Council continued alongside that for the SACC, but was eventually relegated by the more pressing need of protesting the war. Emily's colleagues at the Council included Barbara Bradby, former student of L. T. Hobhouse and wife of Lawrence Hammond (editor of 'pro-Boer' weekly *The Speaker*). Barbara's sister, Dorothy Bradby, would become a stalwart of the relief fund inaugurated by Hobhouse to assist Boer women and children. Emily Hobhouse thus had at her fingertips an influential intellectual, journalistic and political network – and soon provided grounds for a moral convulsion which would galvanise them to action.

In April 1900 Emily Hobhouse and her good friend Kate Courtney organised a women's branch of the SACC. Under the Committee's auspices, they then convened a women's protest meeting at the Queen's Hall, London, held on 13 June 1900. The platform that evening boasted radical aristocracy and the co-activist spouses of well-known liberal luminaries. Kate Courtney presided in the presence of Lady Mary Hobhouse (Lady Hobhouse and her husband, Lord Arthur Hobhouse, Emily's aunt and uncle, were her chief backers), the indomitable Countess of Carlisle (Home Ruler, President of both the North of England Temperance League and the Women's Liberal Federation), Mrs S. A. Barnett, Mrs Bryce (chair of the Women's National Liberal Association and wife of Armenophile, 'pro-Boer' MP and historian,

---

[37] Quoted in Ryrie Van Renan (ed.), *Emily Hobhouse: Boer War Letters*, Human & Rousseau, Cape Town, 1984, p. 14. Emily Hobhouse's autobiography, written in the style of a series of letters to her friend Mrs Steyn, was never published but sections have been reproduced in Ruth Fry, *Emily Hobhouse: A Memoir*, Jonathan Cape, London, 1929, and in Van Renan, *Emily Hobhouse*.

James Bryce) and Mrs Frederic Harrison.[38] Emily Hobhouse had earlier been incensed by the exclusion of women from the Liberal conference in Manchester at which the wrongs of the war were discussed. They had eventually gained admittance by offering to serve the tea. '[F]or over two hours,' she chided,

> we were lapped in the luxury of absolute unanimity of feeling; Liberals to the right of you, Liberals to the left of you, Liberals in front of you volleyed and thundered . . . Nevertheless, I have one thing against that Liberal conference in that they were so far luke-warm, so far *bad* Liberals, that *they did not invite a single woman* to share their deliberations.[39]

'We [female liberals] longed to protest', she recalled, 'and it occurred to me that women, at least, might make a public protest without rousing undue criticism.'[40] Thus it was that Hobhouse sought both to counter and to take advantage of women's formal political exclusion. On the one hand, her attempt to keep her protest aloof from politics failed. On the other, the anti-war protest significantly influenced the suffragist campaign, though in ways not necessarily anticipated. In general, the anti-war protest offered a fillip to suffragist arguments, particularly radical ones, though these led to greater, rather than less, estrangement from the established political parties, Liberal as well as Conservative. Claire Hirshfield has noted the radicalising effect of the anti-war campaign (and especially Emily Hobouse's concentration camp exposé) on both the Women's Liberal Federation (WLF) and, to a lesser extent, the more reticent Women's National Liberal Association.[41] Women, it seemed, must be urgently enfranchised if male bluster and aggression was to be checked, and to this end the WLF cemented its war-time independence from the Liberal Party by taking a decision in 1902 to refuse its support to anti-suffrage Liberals. That a WLF activist could reflect, when faced with male political vacillation, that women had come 'to represent the moral conscience of the Liberal Party' seemed both confirmation of Gladstone's estimation of women's unique moral character and the basis of a far more radical critique than he had imagined.[42] Many found the relationship between 'popular consent and legitimate government' wanting: anti-war suffragists began forcefully to posit a 'moral force' qualification for citizenship, resting on democratic rights and ethical duties rather than on physical force or military service.[43] For women such as Emmeline Pankhurst, E. C. Wolstenholme Elmy, Emmeline Pethick-Lawrence and Charlotte Despard, active in radical and

---

[38] *The Times*, 14.6.1900.

[39] Quoted in Van Renan, *Emily Hobhouse*, p. 17 (original italics).

[40] Quoted in *ibid.*, p. 18.

[41] Eugenio Biagini notes that the women's Liberal associations had also been among the first to take up the issue of Armenian atrocities in 1895; Biagini, *British Democracy*, pp. 317–318.

[42] Hirshfield, 'Liberal Women's Organisations', 48.

[43] Laura E. Nym Mayhall, 'The South African War and the Origins of Suffrage Militancy in Britain, 1899–1902', in Ian C. Fletcher, Laura E. Nym Mayhall and Philippa Levine (eds), *Women's Suffrage in the British Empire: Citizenship, Nation and Race*, Routledge, London, 2000, p. 4.

socialist circles and the committees of the Humanitarian League, the denial of women's democratic voice in debates over the war rankled. For some, the spectacle of a British display of arms in South Africa in the name of securing 'Uitlander' citizenship rights legitimated similarly direct tactics in pursuit of the female vote at home – that many then went on to found the militant Women's Social and Political Union in 1905 was a direct link with this war-time examination of citizenship rights.[44] Hobhouse, however, rejected their militancy. She emphasised instead peaceful conciliation and democratic control of foreign policy. In this manner, she would contribute to early twentieth-century radical critiques of secret diplomacy and to a rigorous, if initially less popular, feminist pacifism.

The Queen's Hall meeting of June 1900 took place in the shadow of an expected British victory and the annexation of the Boer Republics. Thus it was resolved not only to condemn the 'bad policy' of the British government but also to protest a settlement which would lead to the 'extinction of the two Republics'. Emily Hobhouse voiced a resolution to convey 'sympathy with the women of the South African Republic and Orange Free State' and 'profound sorrow at the thought of their suffering' at this time.[45] Her expression of sorrow found ready accord, for accounts of farm burnings in South Africa were now beginning to intensify. For Emily Hobhouse, however, an expression of sorrow was insufficient: she wished for a practical demonstration of sympathy, such as would embody the cause of conciliation between Boer and Briton in South Africa, and both illuminate and mitigate the evils of brute imperialism. With Kate Courtney and other prominent opponents of the war, Hobhouse founded the South African Women's and Children's Distress Fund in September 1900. This, they declared, was to be a philanthropic agency, by virtue of which it was non-party and strictly neutral, although certainly, on writing to the sympathetic weekly *The Speaker*, the Fund's Honorary Secretary Miss Bradby thought nothing of elucidating its links with the anti-war party and its founding intention of prioritising aid to Boer civilians:

> Under the auspices of the Women Workers of the South Africa Conciliation Committee, a scheme has lately been set on foot for helping to provide clothing for the distressed Boer women and children, now in destitution.[46]

Those with the temerity to refuse her appeal Hobhouse deemed deficient in humanity, such that she could profess herself shocked at 'the chilling attitude of some accounted most saintly'.[47] Unsurprisingly, the vast majority of her supporters were already in the anti-war camp: Mrs Bryce, Canon Barnett, the Quaker Sir Edward Fry, and Lord and Lady Hobhouse. Later, Emily Hobhouse would recall her impetus to action in the following terms:

[44] *Ibid.*, p. 11.
[45] *The Times*, 14.6.1900.
[46] Miss E. D. Bradby, letter to the editor, *The Speaker*, 26.1.1901.
[47] Van Renan, *Emily Hobhouse*, p. 28.

[f]rom the first, I, and indeed all whom I knew, had been concerned primarily about our *own* country and whether or not she was acting upon the highest principles of Justice and Humanity. . . . But now, as . . . every post brought news of the effects of English policy and actions upon an innocent population of women and children, when one saw the concrete results of our policy upon human life, I was filled with indignation and a passionate desire to show concrete sympathy to these unfortunates by taking them material relief to soften their suffering.[48]

If Hobhouse's relief mission was an urgent attempt to mitigate suffering, it was also an attempt to address the causes of suffering through a campaign of political advocacy and public education. Her aim was a transformation of the national and international order, the better to reflect the ethical values of humanity and justice that, timeless, universal and tied to an immutable gendered order, would enrich and extend liberal traditions both at home and abroad. As Emily Hobhouse herself understood, the realisation of her ethical vision, however apolitical in conception, depended upon political action. Yet did Hobhouse's political convictions lead her to erroneously conceptualise the causes of bodily suffering in South Africa and to overstate its extent when conditions began to be ameliorated? As will be seen in the following chapter, it was over her portrayal of abject Boer suffering that controversy flared, not only between Hobhouse and pro-war critics such as Millicent Garrett Fawcett, but also within Quaker circles.

[48] *Ibid.*, p. 25.

6

The rational application of compassion?
Relief, reconstruction and disputes over civilian
suffering in the Anglo-Boer War, 1899–1902

In a long line of women who attested to a 'calling' in situations where their presence was considered improper, Emily Hobhouse spoke of the mystical, seemingly irresistible, draw of suffering strangers. This she later described as 'a mission under compulsion of some inward force which cannot be conveyed to others and which merely rests on one's own faith for achievement'.[1] In feeling this calling she was not alone. Individual Quakers, frustrated at the corporate hesitancy of the Society of Friends, felt compelled personally to investigate news of hardship in the Boer Republics. Sailing south to Cape Town on the same ship as Emily Hobhouse were Joshua and Isabella Rowntree and their nephew Harold Ellis, of the Scarborough branch of the Rowntree family, about to begin a self-appointed three months' investigation of civilian distress. Though they were at the time unknown to one another, this would mark the beginning of an association between Emily Hobhouse and the Society of Friends which would outlast the war. Their circles, in fact, already overlapped. Joshua Rowntree, a solicitor by profession and considered an expert in social problems, had played host to a 'pro-Boer' peace rally in Scarborough, and this 'shrewd, kindly Quaker' had consulted Hobhouse's friends the Courtneys in the weeks preceding his voyage.[2] Rowntree returned to publish reports of his investigation in the *Manchester Guardian* and *The Friend* and to furnish information for Lloyd George to ask awkward questions in the House of Commons. This chapter follows these English visitors to South Africa, examining disputes over Hobhouse's portrayal of abject Boer suffering and some of the ramifications of British efforts at relief and reconstruction at this tumultuous juncture in South African history.

Before departing, Hobhouse had denounced the British army's policy of farm burning. But only on arrival did she become fully aware of the problems caused

[1] Van Renan, *Emily Hobhouse*, p. 29.

[2] The description of Rowntree is Kate Courtney's, see her Diary, 3.12.1900, British Library of Political and Economic Science, Courtney papers /30.

by housing the displaced families in temporary camps. She at once made an urgent appeal to improve conditions for the internees, many of them families of men on commando. In testifying to the hardships of Boer women and children, Hobhouse hoped to hold the British government to account. But the British authorities, fearful that Hobhouse's allegations of cruelty risked increasing Boer militancy, barred her from returning to South Africa and appointed the well-known Liberal Unionist and female suffragist Millicent Garrett Fawcett to head an official inquiry. Garrett Fawcett combined this with a rival relief mission on behalf of the pro-imperialist Victoria League. Differences in how they apportioned relief, and blame, if not their actual findings, prompted Garrett Fawcett to argue that Hobhouse's sympathies had forfeited her claim to impartiality; Hobhouse countered that Garrett Fawcett had extinguished feminine pity with cold calculation. Quakers, meanwhile, were torn over their support for Emily Hobhouse's anti-war protest and evidence from their own relief workers that conditions were gradually improving. This chapter ends with relief workers' segregation of concern in South Africa, which meant that the black concentration camps were largely ignored, and an examination of the assumptions that underpinned Emily Hobhouse's post-war collection of Boer women's testimony and work of reconstruction. Here, as in the Balkans, in a situation where suffering was heralded as the birth-pangs of the nation, British relief workers became unwitting heroines in the brutal cause of 'national freedom'.

Relief in the concentration camps

Arriving at Table Bay in late December 1900 and anticipating the war soon to be over, Emily Hobhouse and the Rowntrees intended to provide comforts to soften the severity of annexation and to act as agents of *post bellum* reconciliation. Emily Hobhouse had arranged to illustrate the human cost of British imperialist policy for the readers of the *Manchester Guardian*. The Rowntrees undertook no such promise. Their altogether more circumspect reports were testaments not simply of personal reticence, but also of the more quiescent role of the Society of Friends. However, in place of imminent peace, this small band of English visitors arrived at the inauguration of British martial rule in the subdued but still restive Boer Republics and a 'scorched earth' policy involving farm burning and systematic civilian internment in military-controlled camps. Some of those threatened with farm burning had been given warning to pack belongings; others were herded onto railway trucks with no time to gather useful possessions, or indeed, amongst the poorest, had few possessions to gather. Enduring midday sun, storms of dust and plummeting night-time temperatures, they arrived, tired and bewildered, at canvas encampments – some among the more inhabitable situated near transport links and fresh water, others tethered to the windswept veldt, cut off and exposed. 'Imagine the heat outside the tents, and the suffocation inside', Emily Hobhouse urged, 'the flies lay thick and black on everything; no chair, no table, nor any room for such.'[3]

These camps, hastily erected, ill-appointed and often lacking basic sanitary arrangements, had distressingly high levels of disease and mortality. In total, it is estimated that 20,000 black South African and 28,000 Boer civilians died in the camps, the majority of whom were children. Elizabeth van Heyningen makes a useful comparison with the effects of rapid industrialisation, describing the camps as 'a temporary urbanisation of the Boer peasantry'.[4] It is therefore fitting to find that the English visitors approached conditions in the camps in the light of their own experiences of public health and poverty in urban Britain. Their attitude towards voluntary giving also owed a debt to domestic concerns. Nor is it surprising that British civilian administrators and Millicent Garrett Fawcett's officially appointed committee would recommend preventative public health measures of the sort advocated by reformers in late nineteenth-century Britain (but at the time uncommon in South Africa). All urged practical reform of the camps. But divergent attitudes to the origin of the war and the moral status of the camps saw correspondingly varied stress placed upon the importance of personal sympathy, impartial methods and moral instruction. And thus it was too that the proffering of commodities such as school books, medicine and milk became highly charged, dividing English agents and giver and recipient alike.

At the time, Lord Roberts asserted that 'scorched earth' methods were part of a reactive measure against Boer irregular warfare, and this assertion has long held sway. Now it seems that the reverse was true: land clearance and arson were a deliberate policy of intimidation borrowed directly from colonial warfare and responsible for prompting the Boers to adopt guerrilla methods.[5] Lord Arthur Hobhouse, Frederic Harrison and L. T. Hobhouse had all protested Lord Roberts's policy of 'scorched earth' in his campaigns on the Indian frontier. But it was the use of 'uncivilised' methods against the descendants of Europeans that was now considered so controversial (by comparison, the treatment of interned black South Africans received little attention). The first camps were established for captured burghers who refused to take an oath of neutrality and became prisoners of war. When these camps were then extended to house an increasing number of women and children from the zones of British military operations, Roberts and the War Office presented this as offering 'protection' to destitute 'refugees'. The camps were

---

[3] Emily Hobhouse, *Report to the Committee of the Distress Fund for South African Women and Children*, Friars Printing Assoc., London, 1901, p. 4.

[4] Elizabeth van Heyningen, 'A Tool for Modernisation? The Boer Concentration Camps of the South African War, 1900–1902', *South African Journal of Science*, 2010, Vol. 106, Nos 5–6, online version not paginated.

[5] Helen Bradford, 'Gentlemen and Boers: Afrikaner Nationalism, Gender and Colonial Warfare in the South African War', in G. Cuthbertson *et al.* (eds), *Writing a Wider War: Rethinking Gender, Race and Identity in the South African War, 1899–1902*, Ohio University Press, Cape Town, 2002, pp. 56–58.

always intended as a military measure, however – a fact that Kitchener, for one, consistently upheld – operating as punishment camps for irreconcilable women after the intimidation of arson had not only failed but had strengthened civilian resolve.[6] Writing in the *Westminster Gazette*, Millicent Garrett Fawcett argued that women's contribution to the war effort rendered them legitimate targets, for 'no one can take part in war without sharing in its risks'.[7] Lack of clarity over the status of civilians in international law meant that those supporting the war effort could appeal to a minimalist reading of the law to justify the camps as a military necessity.[8] Field Marshall Lord Wolseley, now Commander-in-Chief at the War Office, argued that the Boers' failure to sign the 1899 Hague Conventions (they had been refused an invitation for fear of antagonising the British) invalidated any claims under international law:

> I know the Boers of all classes to be most untruthful in all their dealings with us and even among themselves. They are very cunning, a characteristic common to all untruthful races . . . To attempt to tie our hands in any way, no matter how small, by the 'Laws and Customs of War' proposed for *civilised* nations at the peace Conference, would be in my opinion suicidal, for the Boers would not be bound by any such amenities . . . I can imagine many positions and circumstances where any such one-sided adherence to those laws could be prejudicial to our military interests of the moment.[9]

Yet, for Emily Hobhouse and supporters such as W. T. Stead, the question of Boer ratification was merely a technicality and ought not to obscure Britain's duty to uphold the principles of justice and humanity. By gendering international law (civilians were uniformly rendered female, combatants male), they attempted to elucidate what, in guerrilla war especially, remained indistinct categories, and in doing so sought to emphasise the British government's moral duty. This became not merely an obligation to treat non-combatants with humanity, but the far more emotive duty to protect vulnerable women and children from abuse. Boer women were routinely depicted as defenceless and passive. Rarely was the presence of male burghers in the camps – or female militarism – mentioned. The result was a moral outcry against government policy that was far more influential than the SACC's cerebral anti-war stance. W. T. Stead, in typically bombastic fashion, compared the British army's treatment of civilians to Ottoman persecution of the Armenians. The British government stood accused of

---

[6] *Ibid.*, p. 55.

[7] *Westminster Gazette*, 13.7.1901.

[8] Article II of the Hague Convention stipulated that the treaty applied only to signatories. However, the preamble to this convention, the Martens' Declaration', held that 'Populations and Belligerents remained under the protection and empire of the principle of international law, as they resulted from the usages established between civilised nations'. See S. B. Spies, *Methods of Barbarism? Roberts, Kitchener and Civilians in the Boer Republics January 1900–May 1902*, Human & Rousseau, Cape Town, 1977, pp. 10–11; Geoffrey Best, *War and Law since 1945*, Clarendon Press, Oxford, 1994, pp. 43–44. For the more 'Idealist' reading of The Hague Conventions, see W. T. Stead, 'The Progress of the World', *Review of Reviews*, Vol. XX, July–December 1899, 115.

[9] Quoted in Spies, *Methods of Barbarism?* p. 13 (original italics).

deeds of rapine and of outrage which recall the conduct of the Huns of Attila, and of the Bashi Bazouks of Abdul the Damned . . . famine and lust are employed against the women to crush the spirit of the race whom our Generals are unable to subdue . . . if these things, now but half brought to light, are permitted to continue without protest . . . we shall stand condemned as a nation, the Pharisaism of whose pretensions is only outdone by the atrocity of its crimes.[10]

For Frederic Harrison, farm burning was 'merely part of a far larger whole', a 'barbarous, vindictive, systematic attempt to terrorise and crush a brave enemy in arms', while the camps were, in the words of Emily Hobhouse, symptomatic of 'a wholesale cruelty'.[11] She made explicit the connection between bodily suffering and the 'injustice' of the war. 'Imprisonment of the women and children in any shape or form beyond that to which the whole civil population is subjected, grates against the mind and conscience of Liberal English people', the author of an SACC pamphlet (most probably Hobhouse) wrote; and again, '[w]e are deliberately keeping in prison the wives and children of men who are fighting for their country and independence'.[12] Though conditions in individual camps were acknowledged to vary, the camp system as a whole embodied the heavy-handed, obdurate short-sightedness that characterised the British *modus operandi* in South Africa and placed future relations between Boer and Briton in jeopardy. In consequence, the bodily effects of concentration and bad management on the Boer internees required not only practical reform but also moral redress and conciliation. In her Report to the South African Women's and Children's Distress Fund, Hobhouse urged the authorities to appoint a band of philanthropic women to reform the camps (all their reserves of 'mother wit and womanly resources' would, she thought, be needed to improve conditions and soften bitter hearts), but argued ultimately for the camps to be disbanded.[13]

There is no doubt that the general discomfort could be vastly alleviated . . . but it should be clearly understood that [reforms] are suggested only by way of amelioration. The main thing is to let them go. . . . Above all one would hope that the good sense, if not the mercy, of the English people will cry out against the further development of this cruel system which falls with such crushing effect upon the old, the weak, and the children.[14]

To condemn as unwise and illiberal the camp policy and the war of brutality of which it was a symptom, Hobhouse evoked, in prose and pen drawings, the tears

---

[10] W. T. Stead, *Hell Let Loose! What Is Now Being Done in South Africa*, broadside printed by Speaight & Sons, London, c.1900.

[11] Frederic Harrison, 'An Appeal to English Patriotism', *Manchester Guardian*, 31.5.1901; Emily Hobhouse, *Report to the Committee of the Distress Fund*, p. 4.

[12] 'Some Comments on the Report of the Ladies' Commission on the Concentration Camps', SACC pamphlet No. 93, [The Committee], London, 1902, pp. 8 and 14.

[13] Hobhouse, *Report to the Committee of the Distress Fund*, p. 15.

[14] *Ibid.*, p. 14.

of grieving mothers and the wasted bodies of suffering children (the 'murdered innocents' of her subsequent Report). Her denunciations rang out in the pages of sympathetic weeklies such as *The New Age* and *The Speaker*, and were repeated in the daily press. Her line drawing of a skeletal child, Lizzie van Zyl, one of a number of so-called 'faded flowers', was one of the most graphic images of Boer suffering to reach the British public. (Lizzie van Zyl was one of a number of children to inexplicably waste away in the camps, probably dying as a result of the dairy-rich diet intended to aid recovery).[15]

In January 1901, when Emily Hobhouse and the Rowntrees first started upon their inquiries, 11 camps were in existence. Hobhouse visited the camps at Bloemfontein, Norval's Pont, Aliwal North, Springfontein, Kimberley and Mafeking, finding Bloemfontein the worst. Her visit coincided with the military administration of the camps passing into the civilian hands of the High Commissioner, Alfred Milner, and with a rapid influx of internees following British failure to subdue the restive population of the two Boer Republics. She observed, in horror, the suffering attendant upon a period of disorganisation and transition, with rapidly expanding numbers left without sufficient facilities or provisions. Meanwhile, the Rowntrees embarked upon an inquiry into the optimum way of alleviating Boer and British 'Uitlander' suffering alike, envisioning their mission as facilitating 'appeasement'. They travelled across the two British colonies, taking in the towns and countryside of Natal, the Eastern Cape and the districts around Cape Town, and predicting famine if the situation there remained unabated.[16] Where Hobhouse had ventured into the newly annexed Transvaal and Orange Free State (now the Orange River Colony), the Rowntrees restricted themselves to the Cape Colony and Natal, where they concentrated their investigation on the camps at Pietermaritzburg and Port Elizabeth, the latter of which had seen a reduction of internees during the Rowntrees' stay. Finding that the funds to aid English refugees, such as the Lord Mayor's Fund, were well administered, the Rowntrees recommended that Quaker monies be best spent on assisting Boer women and children in the camps. They called for a small number of Quaker women to visit South Africa to minister to this need. The lack of school equipment in Pietermaritzburg concerned them in particular. Agreeing with Hobhouse on the need to prioritise relief to Boer internees, they then returned home. The tone of their findings – reported to *The Friend* throughout their stay – was circumspect, reflecting their different experiences, but also the Quakers' rather more diffident sense of mission.

Arriving back in England in May 1901, a month after the Rowntrees, Emily Hobhouse immediately began to publicise conditions in the camps. Travelling on her ship this time was Milner, High Commissioner of all four South African colonies,

---

[15] Stanley, *Mourning Becomes*, p. 130.
[16] Minute of Pickering and Hull Monthly Meeting, 21.11.1900, quoted in Greenwood, *Quaker Encounters*, p. 154.

on his way to London to confer urgently with government colleagues, not least upon the problem of the camps. Hobhouse's campaign of public education met with hostility and derision, but she gained a hearing at Friends' Meeting Houses in areas known for their liberalism and non-conformity. Here she repeated her charge of 'wholesale cruelty'.[17] Joshua Rowntree also spoke out, though in terms rather more conciliatory. He arraigned 'the indelible stain that always and must ever attach to war', rather than the British government. But he publicly endorsed the integrity of Hobhouse's findings.[18] Hobhouse berated the Secretary of State for War, Brodrick, over conditions in the camps, and sympathetic MPs drew upon both Hobhouse and Rowntree's investigations to harangue the government. If one of Emily Hobhouse's intentions in visiting South Africa had been to galvanise Liberals to action, then she scored a notable success. Liberal leader Campbell-Bannerman and rising star Lloyd George now took up the issue with gusto. 'When is a war not a war?' Bannerman famously thundered, following an interview with Hobhouse; 'When it is carried on by methods of barbarism in South Africa.'[19] The phrase quickly entered the lexicon of anti-war protestors such as W. T. Stead, who rushed 'Methods of Barbarism: The Case for Intervention' into print.[20]

The threat of a sustained protest prompted the government to action. Broderick hand-picked Millicent Garrett Fawcett to lead an investigation, impressed by her article in the *Westminster Gazette*. The imperative was to deflect mounting accusations of 'cruelty'. Nevertheless, this was not an exercise intended to side-track genuine inquiry, for, having finally gained full civilian control of the camps, Milner was convinced of the necessity for fundamental reform. Like Chamberlain, the Colonial Secretary, he worried that outcry over the camps was beginning to dominate public attitudes to the war and jeopardise his hopes of reconciling the Boers to British supremacy. For Milner the need was vital and pressing: to change public perception, especially in South Africa, and to ensure that the camps exemplified, rather than threatened, his policy of Anglicisation. On the importance of reconciling Boers to the value of British rule, Millicent Garrett Fawcett and fellow members of the newly formed Victoria League were in full accord. The Victoria League, a pro-imperialist publicity bureau for the white settler colonies, had a number of prominent women members, such as Violet Markham. Such was the Victoria League's commitment to impressing upon the Boer population the benevolence of British rule that it launched its own relief committee, the Dutch Women's Fund, to do so. Garrett Fawcett oversaw its administration in South Africa. Milner, who had urged the formation of

---

[17] Report of speech to the Huddersfield Society of Friends, *Huddersfield Examiner*, 23.7.1901.

[18] For example, see report of his Manchester and Lancaster speeches in *Manchester Guardian*, 21 and 22.6.1901.

[19] Bannerman was addressing a National Reform Union dinner of 14.6.1901. Quoted in Hewison, *Hedge of Wild Almonds*, p. 192.

[20] W. T. Stead, *Methods of Barbarism: The Case for Intervention*, Mobray House, London, July, 1901.

a 'neutral committee – not pro-Boer', gave his blessing and directed sympathetic inquirers to the fund.[21] An advertisement in *The Times* in June 1901 appealed for subscriptions to fund 'additional comforts' (not wishing to imply a lack of necessities) and sought to rally those who, 'in entire sympathy with the policy of the war', wished to 'soften the rigours to women and children of camp life' but felt alienated by the partisan nature of existing funds.[22] Presenting it as a natural feminine concern, the women of the Victoria League were anxious to stress that their fund was, 'purely philanthropic, absolutely non-political'.[23] At the same time, the League instigated (far more successful) funds for British war graves and British refugees fleeing for the safety of the coast. Garrett Fawcett and her government committee, comprising medical women, a factory inspector and a general's wife and quickly dubbed the 'Ladies Commission', sailed in August 1901.

Emily Hobhouse, smarting at her exclusion from the government committee, also departed for South Africa, intent on resuming her work for the South African Women's and Children's Distress Fund. However, barred from disembarking by the authorities, she was forced to return to England, where she stood on her rights and castigated the authorities for 'tyrannical and lawless' behaviour.[24] In the months that had passed since Hobhouse's last visit, an unobtrusive band of Quaker women had arrived in South Africa. Heeding Joshua Rowntree's call, Frances Taylor and Anna Hogg offered their services to the Friends' South African Relief Fund Committee, it now having set its mind to prioritising relief to the camps. They went, according to the accreditation documents provided by their committee, 'to assist those who have suffered through the present war and to aid in the work of appeasement as they may be able and to comfort the sufferers, irrespective of nationality'.[25] Accompanying them was Helen B. Harris, a veteran of Armenian relief. Though not at the time a member of the Religious Society of Friends, she was willing to act under its auspices to offer 'loving service' among war victims.[26]

The Boer women and children internees of British concentration camps now became the subject of considerable investigation and intervention. Their illnesses, emotional states and levels of deprivation, first invoked by Emily Hobhouse, were the focus of attention once again. But now the nature and meaning of their suffering was disputed and the appropriate British response was called into question. After an investigation of all but one of the camps, Garrett Fawcett's committee of inquiry

---

[21] Details of letter to Mrs Ward recorded in letter from Milner to Chamberlain, 24.6.1901, quoted in Paula M. Krebs, '"The Last of the Gentlemen's Wars": Women in the Boer War Concentration Camp Controversy', *History Workshop Journal*, Vol. 33, 1992, 38.

[22] *The Times*, 26.6.1901.

[23] *The Times*, 16.7.1901. Quoted in Eliza Riedi, 'Women, Gender, and the Promotion of Empire: The Victoria League, 1901–1914', *The Historical Journal*, Vol. 45, No. 3, September 2002, 578.

[24] Emily Hobhouse, *A Letter to the Committee of the South African Women's and Children's Distress Fund*, The Argus Printing Co., Ltd, London, 1901, p. 11. She attempted to mount a campaign with her friend H. J. Wilson to challenge the legality of her deportation, Sheffield City Archives, H. J. Wilson papers, MD, 2513: 1–18.

[25] Hewison, *Hedge of Wild Almonds*, p. 207.

[26] *Ibid.*, p. 207.

proposed three explanations for the high death rates: general conditions associated with the effects of war, factors in the control of the camp authorities and factors in the control of the camp population. Many of the committee's detailed findings and recommendations endorsed Emily Hobhouse's earlier report. But their tone was deliberately that of a public health inquiry, avoiding Hobhouse's conclusions regarding the justice or otherwise of the camp policy. One of the committee's members, Lucy Deane, a factory inspector (her salary merely transferred for the purposes of the inquiry), captures something of this outlook in her frequent letters home.[27] The British authorities, she wrote, had done nothing other than create '33 London slums' on the South African veldt, so she 'felt quite at home going from tent to tent, like visiting "workers" at home and inspecting Water supply, Hospital and Sanitary arrangements, for all the world like the old days!'[28] The general findings of the Ladies Commission's report stressed the ignorance and neglect of Boer mothers, leading to the unnecessary deaths of those such as Lizzie van Zyl. The individual inquiries into each camp were thorough, however, and did not hesitate to enumerate deficiencies in administration and facilities, where they were found. If, among others, Emily Hobhouse found it difficult 'to reconcile the tone of the General Report with that of the separate Reports [into each camp] which follow[ed]', Lucy Deane's letters reveal the lack of agreement which explains why.[29] Unable to concur with her colleagues on the causes of morbidity, but unwilling to risk a minority report, Deane 'struggled and fought and pleaded and argued', and though she 'couldn't prevent all the jam and blarney at the beginning', was able to

> have got put in (a) all the 'recommendations' we made and these by their own showing give a picture of the Camps. (b) The points in which I thought the Government had failed ... The only thing I have failed over is the Rations, which are in my opinion one of the causes of the death-rate, too scanty and very unsuitable. .... I only hope a discriminating public will see between the lines about it![30]

Something of the attitude that so rankled Deane is captured in an article by her fellow committee member, Miss Katherine Brereton of Guy's Hospital (former head of a South African yeomanry hospital). Writing in *The Pall Mall* magazine, Brereton eschewed the term 'concentration camp' in favour of the more amenable 'canvas towns', and wrote neutrally of the 'indirect hardships of war', while praising superintendents 'chosen from the best men at hand'. Conditions in each tent were made to reflect the qualities of their inhabitants, with some so dirty 'that one says "how can any one ever live in a tent?"', but the next 'clean and orderly ... all pointing to the clever, careful woman'. Far from coerced, many of the inhabitants

---

[27] For her details of employment, including salary see, TNA, WO 32/8061/32.
[28] Lucy Deane, letter to sister, Ladysmith 23.12.1901, and Kimberley 18.8.1901, British Library of Political and Economic Science, Streatfeild papers, 2/11/45195.
[29] 'Some Comments on the Report of the Ladies Commission', p. 2.
[30] Streatfeild papers, letter to sister, Ladysmith 23.12.1901.

had volunteered themselves, 'one man because he wanted his children educated, others because their children were worn out, trekking with the commandoes'.[31] Here, the camps were places of refuge offering the advantages of medical and educational modernity to a rural, rather ignorant, people: precisely the image of practical advancement and friendly guidance which Milner and his friends at the Victoria League sought to propagate. In private, however, both Milner and the women on Garrett Fawcett's committee of inquiry conceded that the camp policy had been a blunder. Lucy Deane could point to a rare unanimity of feeling on this question: 'We all feel that the policy of the "Camps" was a huge mistake ... It has made people hate us, it is thoroughly unnatural and we were not able to cope with the hugeness of the task', though, of course, 'this opinion is outside the terms of reference of our Commission'.[32] Milner concurred. 'The whole thing ... has been a mistake', he wrote to Chamberlain in December 1901, '[i]f we can get over the Concentration Camps, none of the other attacks upon us alarm me in the least.'[33]

The meaning of the gift

The arrival in South Africa of the Ladies Commission coincided with a concerted effort by the civilian authorities to address deficiencies in the camps' health services, sanitation, food and water supply, as well as to educate the camp children.[34] Nevertheless, the autumn months of 1901 saw death rates peak as the measles epidemic present in South Africa before the war ravaged the closely populated camps, before eventually abating in the first two months of 1902 (weaned infants and children were especially vulnerable, as life on the sparsely populated veldt had resulted in low immunity rates).[35] Millicent Garrett Fawcett made over a portion of the Dutch Women's Fund's £1,925 at her disposal to establish soup kitchens in the camps and to buy tinned milk, baby food and flannel. However, her committee's report was scathing about 'indiscriminate charity'; indeed, Milner had now banned all unsolicited aid not distributed through recognised channels.[36] The £1,400 remaining, Garrett Fawcett recommended to be spent on schooling in the camps – making a grant of £800 to E. B. Sargant, the director of education, for the purpose. Though voluntary, these camp schools 'were the first step of Milner's Anglicisation scheme

---

[31] Katherine Brereton, 'Life in the Concentration Camps', *The Pall Mall Gazette*, Vol. 27, 1902, pp. 36–38, 40.
[32] Streatfeild papers, letter to sister, Ladysmith 23.12.1901.
[33] Milner to Chamberlain, 7.12.1901, quoted in Paula M. Krebs, *Gender, Race and the Writing of Empire: Public Discourse and the Boer War*, Cambridge University Press, Cambridge, 1999, p. 39.
[34] Eliza Riedi, 'Teaching Empire: British and Dominions Women Teachers in the South African War Concentration Camps', *English Historical Review*, CXX, 489, December 2005, 1316–1347.
[35] Van Heyningen concludes that measles was the largest single cause of death (42–43% of deaths), 'A tool for modernisation'.
[36] Quoted in Riedi, 'Women, Gender and the Promotion of Empire', 581.

for the Boer Republics'. Their financial support was outside the advertised remit of the Dutch Women's Fund.[37]

Responding to the Ladies Commission's report in February 1902, the author of SACC pamphlet No. 93 (from its tone, likely to be Emily Hobhouse) denounced the tenor of its findings and the picture of neglectful Boer motherhood that emerged. By now, Hobhouse had no recent first-hand knowledge of conditions in the camps to draw upon; meanwhile, Garrett Fawcett and Milner's recommendations were taking effect, and the incidence of measles was falling. Maintaining an emphasis on the dejection and suffering of Boer women and children in the camps, the pamphlet decried the absence of 'any spark of womanly feeling' in Garrett Fawcett's inquiry.[38] It was this emphasis upon the importance of demonstrable compassion that marked out Hobhouse's efforts from those of the Commission. In her own report, Hobhouse stressed the time spent listening to and commiserating with the Boer internees, and placed special emphasis on the collection of women's first-hand accounts. It was, she believed, these acts of empathy, acknowledgement and catharsis that would aid reconciliation and act as testaments against future war. Elsewhere, of course, her activities in this line were far from welcome. For it was precisely Hobhouse's spirit of sympathetic engagement, her mediation of the 'voice' of the interned women, that Milner and Garrett Fawcett sought to exorcise. Encouraging Boer women to consider themselves victims of a brutal incidence of war-time criminality made the publication of their testimony seem an act of dangerous politicisation and risked their assimilation to superior British rule. Yet Hobhouse was emphatic about the need for cultural sensitivity and dialogue, and this also informed her methods of delivery.

It was no good providing British-style hospitals or preserved and condensed foodstuffs to people suspicious of the unfamiliar and wary of enemy intentions. Aid, whether official or voluntary, had to be negotiated in order to be effective, and the 'spirit' in which it was bestowed was crucial. Commodities could have culturally specific meanings, be as much a threat as a blessing, and attempts at 'modernisation' might not necessarily be welcomed as heralding progress. Thus it was unsurprising that a farming population which valued fresh meat was suspicious of the canned variety – or that a camp myth arose of metal hooks concealed in preserved meat. This meant that, even when meat provision increased (to one million pounds every month by 1902 in the Orange River Colony camps alone), suspicion remained.[39] Similarly, as Hobhouse pointed out, given the prevalence in Boer families of home nursing with traditional remedies, camp hospitals, which enforced restricted diets for dysentery cases and limited visiting hours, were viewed as unnatural if not cruel; when run by enemy British doctors and nurses, they seemed dangerous places to

---

[37] *Ibid.*, p. 580.
[38] SACC, 'Some Comments on the Report of the Ladies Commission', p. 3.
[39] Van Heyningen, 'A Tool for Modernisation', 8.

which to send loved ones.[40] The result was, in van Heyningen's apt phrase, 'a confrontation between different cultures of healing'.[41] Thus, where Garrett Fawcett's commission criticised Boer practices as primitive, the South African Women's and Children's Distress Fund, though by no means favouring traditional medicine, understood the need to convince Boer women of the virtues of British medical practices.[42]

Nevertheless, a sympathetic Hobhouse was still keen to emphasise her 'scientific methods' when it came to the investigation of distress, particularly the use of questionnaires to ascertain need. As if to signal this, the section of her report given over to her findings saw an abrupt switch to the third person:

> The necessity of such inquiries will be obvious to anyone who has had the smallest experience of administering relief, whether in London or elsewhere. Miss Hobhouse has fortunately enjoyed a good deal of such experience.[43]

Yet, however impartial, she averred, needs-based relief did not equate to 'indiscriminate charity' or cold calculation. In fact, Hobhouse distinguished her recipients by social status: the higher their standing, the more brutal their current dejection and the more pressing its amelioration, 'much care being taken to bestow relief where it was most needed relatively to the condition of life enjoyed by the recipient in happier days'.[44] Hobhouse wished to take the 'best class of girls' out of the camps and place them in boarding schools, fearful of the effects of enervating, unoccupied days in the camps.[45] 'Official' relief was also decried. Garrett Fawcett's administration of the Victoria League fund she compared to the doling out at a 'pauper institution'. For '[i]n this way the better half of the gift is destroyed, only the material aid remains, and that to be measured out by the will of an official'. Of the concentration of Victoria League funds upon schooling, she was particularly scathing: 'the Victoria League might do well to use their own judgement rather than that of the Commission as to which is the greater necessity, beds or books'.[46]

Meanwhile, the three women affiliated to the Friends South African Relief Fund Committee began to report back their impressions of the camps. They arrived in June 1901 and were joined by a further Friend, Georgina King Lewis (another veteran of Armenian relief), in July, their visit coinciding with the controversy

---

[40] Hobhouse, *Report to the Committee of the Distress Fund*, pp. 5–6; SACC, 'Some Comments on the Report of the Ladies Commission', p. 12.

[41] Elizabeth van Heyningen, 'Women and Disease: the Clash of Medical Cultures in the Concentration Camps of the South African War', in Greg Cuthbertson et al. (eds), *Writing a Wider War: Rethinking Gender, Race and Identity in the South African War 1899–1902*, Ohio University Press, Chicago, 2002, p. 186.

[42] Van Heyningen, 'Women and Disease', p. 197; SACC, 'Some Comments on the Report of the Ladies Commission', p. 12.

[43] Hobhouse, *Report to the Committee of the Distress Fund*, p. 18.

[44] SACC, 'Some Comments on the Report of the Ladies Commission', p. 5; and see Emily Hobhouse, *The Brunt of War and Where it Fell*, Methuen & Co., London, 1902 p. 119.

[45] Hobhouse, *Report to the Committee of the Distress Fund*, p. 7.

[46] SACC, 'Some Comments on the Report of the Ladies Commission', pp. 5 and 15.

aroused by Hobhouse's revelations and with the new sense of official urgency; but it also took place against a backdrop of climbing death rates as the measles epidemic took its greatest toll. The letters of these Quaker women presented Friends at home (by now united and energised by indignation at civilian suffering) with something of a dilemma. Quaker meeting houses had become one of the few venues open to Emily Hobhouse on her speaking tour, and many Friends, Joshua Rowntree included, publicly endorsed both her revelations and her right to free speech. Relief for the internees now became a priority, the Friends South African Relief Fund Committee putting the collection and shipment of clothes into the hands of a dedicated women's sub-committee in London.[47] Controversy centred on the question of whether the letters of women Friends in South Africa ought to be published. This was not a question of jeopardising access by displeasing the authorities. The problem rested, rather, in the ambivalence of the letters themselves.

Visiting Pietermaritzburg, the women Friends documented improvements since the Rowntrees' visit and praised official action, but nevertheless reported on-going need and the soaring death rate. Much of this detail lent weight to Hobhouse's findings, but the women Friends' criticism of Boer women's habits seemed to confirm Garrett Fawcett's summations. In September 1901 Helen Harris returned home and suggested prioritising the purchase of milk. The Quakers' Relief Fund Committee, distressed at child mortality rates, contacted the two remaining women Friends later that autumn. However, their urgent offer of £1,000 for milk for all camp children was rejected on the grounds that provisions were now plentiful and extra milk would do little to halt the measles epidemic.[48] In October, Frances Taylor, writing from South Africa, criticised Friends for 'accepting everything' that Hobhouse had claimed, for 'we have not found things as Miss Hobhouse described them and goes on describing them . . . things may have been very bad at the start . . . [but] [a]ll her statements seem to have been more or less exaggerated'.[49] By December, the two remaining women Friends could report no further need of Quaker aid. In London, difficult questions began to be asked about the non-publication of these later letters.[50] In her correspondence Frances Taylor had expressed her incomprehension at Friends unwillingness to publish her findings, and prominent Quakers argued that full exposure should be given to Taylor and Hogg's impressions. If genuine 'appeasement' was to be facilitated, it was only fair to counter claims of deficient care

---

[47] Hewison, *Hedge of Wild Almonds*, p. 209; in total £4,275 would be raised, of which £2,342 remained unspent during the course of the war, see Friends South African Relief Fund, 'Report of the Committee to the Yearly Meeting, Fifth Month, 1902', in *Yearly Meeting Proceedings, 1902–1906*, London, [The Society], 1906, p. 140.

[48] Eventually a donation of £500 was agreed upon for concentrated milk powder for the most exposed camps, Hewison, *Hedge of Wild Almonds*, p. 213.

[49] Frances Taylor to Elsie Cadbury, 14.10.1901, Balmoral Camp, South Africa, quoted in Hewison, *Hedge of Wild Almonds*, p. 216.

[50] On the relief committee's unease, see Friends South African Relief Fund, 'Report of the Committee to the Yearly Meeting, Fifth Month, 1902', p. 139.

and government indifference with evidence of the efficacies of official interventions. Others argued that mere impressions did not constitute a full investigation and their publication was unmerited. Joshua Rowntree, for one, was against publication. Emily Hobhouse put Hogg's advice against extra donations of milk down to a 'war neurosis'. The secretary of the Friends South African Relief Fund Committee felt that need still remained, noting the lack of milk for children over five.[51]

To some Friends, it appeared that information favourable to the government was being deliberately suppressed by those seeking to maintain the credibility of Hobhouse's findings of 'cruelty' once the situation in the camps had improved: in denying just treatment and publicity to the British government's scheme of reform, more radical Friends, it seemed, risked the constructive work of peace and friendship then afoot in South Africa, through the deliberate distortion and politicisation of camp conditions.[52] Yet for others, sympathetic to the views of Hobhouse and the SACC, it was impossible to approach suffering in the camps without reference to their fundamental injustice, which they considered to be the most important impediment to reconciliation. In addition, they wished it not to be forgotten that morbidity in the camps must first and foremost be attributed to the greater risks of infection attendant upon a concentrated population – over and above the relative merits of remedial medical provision or cultural practices. If their co-religionists at work in the camps were representative, then the question of the camps' moral status risked receding into irrelevance when faced by material amelioration (indeed, when mortality rates fell dramatically in early 1902, so too did public interest in the matter). Thus it was crucial to emphasise that it was the principle of civilian internment which was at issue and that ultimate responsibility for suffering in the camps rested with the British government: deliberation solely upon practical need risked the exoneration of brutal military policy. At the root of the problem was British belligerence, that 'Imperial policy of self-aggrandizement and lust after gold'.[53] This ought to be confronted even if it took Quakers into the cross-fire of controversy.

This bitter conflict suggests a perennial dilemma: how did one keep a moral injustice at the forefront of the public's mind when practical reforms had substantially (though not completely) ameliorated the physical suffering that was so ready an exemplar and source of indignation? For some Quakers it also suggested another: to what extent were questions of injustice to be publicly addressed through images of abject suffering, at risk, on the ground, of jeopardising access or opportunities for reconciliation and of exacerbating existing enmities? However, if, for Quakers, the appropriate response to these dilemmas proved divisive, it also proved generative. Quaker values were in flux, and not only over this particular war. Debates over

---

[51] Van Renan, *Emily Hobhouse*, p. 425; Hewison, *Hedge of Wild Almonds*, p. 213.
[52] For instance, Friends in Reading, detailed in Hewison, *Hedge of Wild Almonds*, p. 216.
[53] William Charles Braithwaite, May 1902, quoted in Kennedy, *British Quakerism*, p. 265.

appropriate activity in South Africa became a site for the elaboration of wider commitments. In particular, as pacifist values became increasingly central to Quaker identity in the early twentieth century, so too did the provision of relief as a constructive act of international friendship. Peace on earth may indeed be a goal held in common, but, to most Quakers, peace meant more than the absence of armed conflict. Yet what was to be the nature of Quaker pacifism? And how was a Godly kingdom of Christian fellowship to be realised in place of war?

In the 1870–71 conflict between France and Prussia, and a few years later in the Ottoman Empire, those providing aid had sought a 'softening of hearts' to the Quaker message of Christian tolerance and harmony. It was hoped that the spreading of Quakerly values of thrift, co-operation and self-reliance would engender social progress and dampen the spirits of war. This exemplar of Quaker charity and spiritual service among groups of warring strangers sat alongside more formal attempts to influence governments to adopt international arbitration. But the war in South Africa, where Britain was herself a belligerent, presented more of a challenge. It also coincided with the decline of the evangelicalism which had infused earlier efforts at relief, and the scriptural injunction against war had given way to a revived interest in the 'Inward Light', that chink of Godliness which rested in all. For Quaker consciences were called to account over the Boer War in a way that they had not been in earlier conflicts. John Wilhelm Rowntree, pained at Quaker hesitancy in the early days of the war, felt that one lesson of the war 'is the need for proper instruction of our *own* people. Each generation has to recapture for itself its spiritual heritage, and we need to seize upon the opportunity the war gives us for the restatement of our principles in terms which will appeal to a new generation.'[54] In these circles, Quaker responses to war were increasingly represented as a gesture of brotherly love and a recognition of the sacredness of all human life.[55] Edward Grubb urged Friends to take up relief work in the camps, aghast that they had prevaricated in the face of mounting death rates. In this way, relief assumed a special significance for a younger generation of Friends whose ethical commitment to defeat state-sponsored militarism became increasingly fervent. In this way too, an opposition to armed conflict came to be experienced as a deeply personal struggle for peace and test of conscience. This did not, of course, preclude future controversies and compromises; and accusations that Friends' opposition to war was merely conventional would continue. For 'progressives', the dilemma of loyalty to a belligerent state and the risk of political controversy in South Africa forced greater consideration of the ethics of Quaker action in war and in the making of a just peace. Quaker values continued to be tested and forged by the manifold dilemmas of providing relief whilst serving as a witness for peace; yet, while the public image of the Quakers was increasingly identified with pacifism and relief work, Thomas Kennedy's work has shown that this was the result not of growing

---

[54] Quoted in Hewison, *Hedge of Wild Almonds*, pp. 132–133.
[55] See for example, Hirst, *Quakers in Peace and War*.

corporate unanimity (indeed the Great War would see Quakers once again divided), but of the hardening of conviction amongst a younger generation committed to freedom of conscience in these matters.

Testimonies of suffering; degrees of concern

While the Quakers deliberated, for Emily Hobhouse there was little question that the publication of her testimony of suffering in the camps was a moral duty, one which surpassed qualms that her privileged right of access might be jeopardised.

> To me it is clear as the weeks passed on that it was the publication of the facts in the two Houses of Parliament which had so angered the Government. Had I *not* done so probably they would have let me return to the camps. On the other hand, would they (without the public stimulus) ever have made the supreme efforts necessary for the reformation of the camps and for bringing them up to the level safe for the Whitewashing Committee to visit and report on them? My Uncle believed not, and though, inexperienced in governmental ways as I then was I sometimes wavered in opinion, I have long ceased to have any doubt but that the line I was advised to take was the best to effect the good we so desired for the people concerned.[56]

But there were other consequences to invoking the suffering of women and children in South Africa. By enumerating domestic hardship and maternal grief, Hobhouse intended to give voice to the little-heard trials of women in war time and to bring home the domestic suffering which accompanies war. In doing so, she hoped to dismantle the political fences that lay in the way of co-operation between Boer and Briton in South Africa and to foster an ethical polity free to determine its own future. Yet the spirit in which relief was bestowed did not guarantee that it was received in kind, and her delivery of aid and collection of testimony lent themselves to sentiments both less universal and less conciliatory. Hobhouse insisted that she was inspired by timeless principles of justice and humanity. But for some recipients, her inquiry into Boer suffering validated political aspirations that were racially divisive and far from just. In this context, the racially selective representation and ministration of suffering by all the British relief workers in South Africa lent itself, intentionally or not, to a political narrative of imperilled nationhood last seen at the time of the 'Bulgarian atrocities' agitation. Hobhouse's relief mission, and that of Quakers, operated according to a segregation of concern that was subsequently replicated in Garrett Fawcett's governmental inquiry. Attention was fixed on Boer suffering but largely ignored that of the black camp inmates. Some blacks had accompanied their former masters to live as servants in the Boer camps, but the majority were housed in separate camps, until rehoused in August 1901 on empty Boer farms, for the purpose of producing food for the British army.[57] The black

---

[56] Fry, *Emily Hobhouse*, pp. 162–163.
[57] Stanley, *Mourning Becomes*, p. 6.

camps, largely written out of history in subsequent Afrikaner accounts of the war, are now thought to have endured mortality rates comparable to those of the Boer camps. This selectivity attested to a notable moral ambivalence at the heart of the humanitarian outcry over South Africa.

This segregation of concern arose in part from the origins of the initial indignation over the war and its conduct, specifically, the outcry over attempts to coerce politically mature and self-determining people of European extraction. Nothing seemed to exemplify this moral morass more than the suffering of civilised women and children who were subject to methods last used against Afghans, and this explains the emotional charge generated by the encounter with the physical hardships of the Boers. Hobhouse and the Rowntrees did express sincere concern for the 'Kaffirs'.[58] But theirs was a physical suffering of an already abject race. It could not be equated with the moral injury inflicted by the political subjugation of a superior and free-born people. Thus, just as Hobhouse differentiated the needy according to their social status (and hence the greater or lesser their fall into destitution), the low political and social status of the blacks made their current plight less immediately pitiable. For Hobhouse, the specific charge against the British authorities was not that they had interned blacks but that, in arming natives and rendering Boer civilians, especially women, vulnerable to attack, they had upset the racial order, one, that is, in which the childlike 'Kaffirs' ought to be protected and improved by their white superiors. Thus her report into the camp included the recommendation 'That, considering the growing impertinence of the Kaffirs, seeing the white women thus humiliated, every care shall be taken not to put them in places of authority.'[59]

Many of those currently championing the rights of the Boer people to political autonomy had previously expressed concern over the Boers less than paternalistic treatment of blacks. Reconciling the claims of the Boer to live in freedom with the protection of black civil rights proved an uncomfortable moral conundrum. To this end, concern for blacks tended to be subjugated according to a moral calculus which set greater store in protesting the corrupting effects of British coercive practices. 'While we are sinning so deeply in South Africa', wrote Kate Courtney, 'it seems to me more hypocrisy to be considering other people's sins.'[60] In light of this, the fact that the majority of blacks were loyal to the British and looked to them for emancipation from Boer rule was somewhat awkward. Equivocation continued even when evidence of British mistreatment of blacks presented an opportunity to reveal the hypocrisy of government claims to be fighting a war for democratic rights in South

---

[58] Hobhouse called upon the Aborigines Protection Society, whose members included such 'pro-Boer' luminaries as Leonard and Kate Courtney, to take up the cause of the native camps. This they did in rather desultory fashion, owing, as Claire Hirshfield argues, to general prevarication on the question of native rights amongst opponents of the war.

[59] Hobhouse, *Report to the Committee of the Distress Fund*, p. 15; on this issue see also Krebs, *Gender, Race and the Writing of Empire*, pp. 62–66.

[60] Quoted in Hirshfield, 'Blacks, Boers and Britons', 26.

Africa. Emphasis instead was placed upon championing the Boer's right to autonomy and, when peace looked imminent, on ensuring a swift and equitable settlement between Boer and Briton, even when this denied the civil rights of natives. 'A moral lapse', writes Hirshfield, 'which allowed well-meaning men with impeccably liberal and humanitarian credentials to acquiesce in a settlement clearly destructive of the prospects of the nonwhite majority'.[61]

Hobhouse was not guilty of the idealisation of the Boers found among some anti-war critics. It was, rather, she trusted, that reconciliation of the white races in South Africa, grounded in fraternal co-operation rather than coercion, would be a progressive force, improving the Boers, uplifting the British and breeding the harmony and political liberty which would secure the rights of the 'lower' races in South Africa. Invited to make a speech at the unveiling of the Women's Monument to commemorate Boer women and children's sufferings in the camps, she implored the Afrikaners to reflect that their women and children had 'died for freedom', a 'sacrifice' which must not now be tarnished by 'withholding from others in your control the very liberties and rights which you have valued and won for yourselves'.[62] Hobhouse was prevented by ill health from appearing in person, and her script (written under her friend Olive Schreiner's meticulous guidance and containing flashes of Schreiner's greater radicalism) was read out on her behalf. The irony was that, in the years that followed, Hobhouse's collection of first-hand testimonies of Boer women's suffering would be appropriated less as cries for fraternal peace and reconciliation than as clarion calls for a racially segregated South Africa. Perhaps unwittingly, she had captured the articulate pronouncements of the upper echelons of Boer society, with whom she had the most ready sympathy and contacts, and given voice to relatively cogent, though not necessarily representative, nationalist political aspirations.[63] Hobhouse's publication of these testimonies in *Tant' Alie of the Transvaal* (1923) and *War Without Glamour, or Women's War Experiences Written by Themselves* (1927) coincided with a spate of Boer war-time reminiscences and a period of escalating Afrikaner nationalism. In this context, the suffering of the women and children in the camps attained a transcendental significance. Contained within these accounts, it seemed, was the heart of the nation, united in suffering and a contraction of grief, and now buoyed by the need for unity and vigilance against external – and internal – threats.

Peace work

The years following the Peace of Vereeniging in May 1902 are known as the period of 'reconstruction' in South African history. Saul Dubow has noted the inappropriateness

[61] Hirshfield, 'Blacks, Boers and Britons', 30.

[62] Quoted in Fry, *Emily Hobhouse*, p. 262; A letter from Olive Schreiner to her brother Will in November 1913 reveals that Schreiner spent two days working on the speech. The letter (along with all other extant Olive Schreiner letters) appears on the Olive Schreiner Letters Project website (www.oliveschreiner.org).

[63] Helen Dampier, 'Women's Testimonies of the Concentration Camps of the South African War, 1899–1902 and after', PhD thesis, Newcastle University, 2005, chapter 1.

of a term which implies restoration of existing conditions: in reality, he writes, 'post-war South Africa was being created for the first time, both as a nation-state and in the realm of public imagination'.[64] If this was true of the official modernisation schemes instigated by Milner, now ensconced as governor of the defeated Boer states, it was true also of the voluntary schemes of reconstruction undertaken by Emily Hobhouse, her supporters and her Quaker friends. For, in the defeated states of the Transvaal and Orange River Colony, Hobhouse set to work establishing domestic textile industries designed to replace essential household goods lost in the war and to weave together the fabric of a new South Africa founded on self-reliance, co-operation and autonomy. If she shared with Milner a desire for *rapprochement* between whites in South Africa, she rejected outright his vision of a modern capitalist society under British control. Her war-time relief work thus segued into attempts at regeneration, or what we would now recognise as 'development work' – not, that is, an attempt to return to the *status quo ante bellum* but a desire to engineer the future prospects of a people upon the models that she deemed most enlightened. In this way, Hobhouse made her own contribution to the period of 'reconstruction', offering a challenge to Milner's policy, certainly, but also encapsulating many of the ambiguities of British intervention in this period of South African history.

For Milner, the reorientation of the political economy of the two existing and two new British colonies in South Africa was predicated on cultural as well as political supremacy. His policies operated in continuum not only with his pre-war thinking on these matters but also with his war-time policies of Anglicisation in the concentration camps. His priorities were to rebuild the mining industry and resolve labour shortages (controversially, through the importation of central African and Chinese labour), to develop an efficient administration geared towards the greater unity of the four colonies and to encourage British immigration. 'The establishment in South Africa of a great and civilized and progressive community, one from Cape Town to the Zambesi', would be, he hoped, 'independent in the management of its own affairs, but still remaining, from its own firm desire, a member of the great community of free nations gathered together under the British flag'.[65] Milner was assisted by his 'kindergarten' of young British policy makers, and by channels of voluntary association and endeavour. The Victoria League, for instance, donated its remaining war-time funds to its 'sister' society, the Guild of Loyal Women of South Africa, for philanthropic projects in Bloemfontein and Pretoria. It also collected £1,000 worth of donations to aid returning Uitlander refugees, while League member Violet Cecil raised £9,000 for returning Boer loyalists.[66] League members were also active in post-war emigration schemes, though they were to be disappointed by the low take-up rate. One of the most controversial aspects of Milner's Anglicisation

---

[64] Saul Dubow, 'Imagining the New South Africa in the Era of Reconstruction', in David Omissi and Andrew S. Thompson (eds), *The Impact of the South African War*, Palgrave, Basingstoke, 2002, p. 77.

[65] Quoted in Saul Dubow, 'Colonial Nationalism, The Milner Kindergarten and the Rise of "South Africanism", 1902–10', *History Workshop Journal*, Vol. 43, 1997, 57.

[66] Riedi, 'Women, Gender and the Promotion of Empire', 580–582.

policy concerned educational reforms overseen by the former inspector of the camp schools, E. B. Sargant. These stipulated that, as in the camps, the language of instruction was to be English rather than Dutch, and that British values were to be further imbibed through the teaching of British history. Three hundred teachers were recruited from Britain for this purpose. Philippa Fawcett, who had accompanied her mother, Millicent Garrett Fawcett, on her inspection of the camps, pursued this work for the Transvaal education department. In 1902 she welcomed her mother on a Victoria League-sponsored lecture tour of South Africa that was dedicated to celebrating British achievements past and present.

A few months later, in May 1903, Emily Hobhouse returned to South Africa and cast a rather more jaundiced eye upon British accomplishments. She set out to investigate conditions in the rural districts, following in the footsteps of Ramsay MacDonald the previous summer. As correspondent for the *Leicester Pioneer* (its readership covering a constituency that he coveted on behalf of the new Labour Representation Committee), MacDonald reported on a land of devastation and the unreconciled hearts of the Boers. During her visit, Hobhouse established a life-long friendship with Jan Smuts, the former Boer War commander and architect of the eventual political union of South Africa, and was feted for her work during the war at large public gatherings throughout the defeated territories. The letters and printed reports that she sent to sympathisers in Britain detailed the broken health of families reunited after time spent in concentration and prisoner of war camps and now living amidst burnt-out farms, ruined crops and the bleached skeletons of their cattle.[67] Under the auspices of the South African Women's and Children's Distress Fund once more she distributed food and clothes to the destitute, funded by royalties from the publication of *The Brunt of War* a year earlier and donations from sympathisers such as her friend the radical MP H. J. Wilson. She was particularly concerned with two classes of children: those of formerly well-off families 'where the parents are still alive, but too impoverished to pay for the schooling which is needed', and 'the lower class of bijwoners' [tenant farmers'] daughters'

> with nothing to do and eating their parents' heads off, and whom in England we should at once send to service. But service never enters their heads, that is Kaffir work. Yet the Kaffirs are so tiresome and the whole country is crying out for good servants, and here are just the girls for it. . . . These people I wholly refuse to help, because I am sure their old customs *must* be altered owing to the great upheaval the country has undergone, and pressure of circumstances must drive them to take service. . . . In consequence (as they all agree) those bijwoner families are sinking to a condition far below respectable Kaffirs.[68]

[67] Emily Hobhouse, 'After the War', Nos 1 and 2, South African Women's and Children's Distress Fund, London, 1903.
[68] Emily Hobhouse to unidentified recipient (letter intended for circulation), 12.6.1903, Sheffield City Archives, H. J. Wilson papers, MD 2515/2.

Hobhouse was at pains to point out the bitterness which was accruing. Delays in honouring receipts for animals requisitioned by the British army and in administering compensation claims were a particular bone of contention. 'Now they feel the whole thing is British', she wrote of the frustrations over requisitioning, 'and that means unjust, dishonest, grasping.'[69] In the midst of rising indignation in South Africa and Britain over the question of indentured Chinese labour in South African mines, Campbell-Bannerman, for one, found it congenial to listen. The conciliatory tone of South African policy following the 1906 Liberal election victory (which brought an unprecedented 29 Labour Representation Committee members into government, including Ramsay MacDonald for Leicester) owes something to this lobbying.

November 1904 saw the winding up of the South African Women's and Children's Distress Fund and its replacement by the Boer Home Industries scheme. Familiar figures present at the opening of the new fund included Leonard and Kate Courtney, and subscriptions came from, among others, Mrs J. R. MacDonald, H. J. Wilson and Mr and Mrs Hammond, and it was warmly greeted by women's organisations and politicians in South Africa. However, Hobhouse's consistent pitch of concern for the domestic and personal fall-out of the conflict in South Africa met with fluctuating political interest in both South Africa and Britain. In South Africa, her endeavours met with the approval of Boer leaders concerned for the fate of the 'poor whites'. Nevertheless, her linking of the suffering of the concentration camps and present-day destitution was inconvenient, given their desire to inaugurate a new chapter in Anglo-Boer relations. Thus it was that Hobhouse's early attempts to combine post-war relief with collating women's concentration-camp testimonies was met with evasion from Smuts and other Boer leaders (her testimony arousing interest only with the growth of Afrikaner nationalism in the 1920s, as Helen Dampier's work shows). Meanwhile, for radicals in Britain, the moral indignation over war-time 'methods of barbarism' in South Africa that had so convulsed progressive opinion had by now lost its urgency and a large part of its political function. Nevertheless, foreign affairs continued to stimulate moral conviction and shared ideals: many 'pro-Boers', including James Bryce, the Hammonds, the Buxton brothers and H. N. Brailsford, remobilised as the Balkan Committee, preoccupied with shaping British responses to fresh allegations of Ottoman cruelty, this time in Macedonia.

The new Boer Home Industries Fund sought to develop domestic textile production. Orphaned and impoverished girls were to be trained in the crafts of carding, spinning, dyeing and weaving. Instruction would take place in schools funded for the purpose by subscribers, equipping the girls to carry on this work when they returned to their farms. This was 'self-help' rather than relief (though the scheme would never achieve financial self-sufficiency). Initially, Hobhouse favoured lace

---

[69] Emily Hobhouse to unidentified recipient (letter intended for circulation), 10.6.1903, Sheffield City Archives, H. J. Wilson papers, MD 2515/1.

production, deeming it 'refining and educative' and musing that 'a girl gains in moral qualities as well as skill'.[70] But, on the advice of her friend Alice Stopford Green, she decided to concentrate on wool as more suited to local conditions. Green, Irish nationalist, champion of Gaelic craft heritage and critic of colonialism in Africa and elsewhere, had visited Boer prisoners of war on St Helena, and lambasted British imperial 'arrogance' in articles written upon her return.[71] In advocating wool, Green was more mindful than the genteel Hobhouse that lace was a luxury affordable by the few. She pointed out another merit to critics of capitalist overproduction: 'that the women of every nation in the Old World had spun and had woven, they had been through the educative processes entailed in producing all the textile necessities of their peoples till within the comparatively short period that machinery had replaced them'.[72] Hobhouse duly chose spinning and weaving for her schools as the more practical and egalitarian option. However, this was not an attempt to reinstate a domestic economy disrupted by the war: instead, she laboured to establish home industries in 'traditional' handicrafts with no real precedent among the Boers. Tenuously, she tried to establish a connection with the pioneering days after the Great Trek, when women were forced to make their own dyes, for lack of shops.[73] Early days saw the girls taught from scratch with spindles and looms rendered obsolete by modern textile manufacturing. They practised on antique spinning wheels donated by European sympathisers in Switzerland and Germany, and toiled to dig up roots from the parched veldt to experiment with natural dyes. At first producing rugs and blankets, then, as their work became more refined, fabric for garments, the girls made goods of immediate value to families that were attempting to replenish war-depleted homes. But self-sufficiency in material goods was not the only thing to which Hobhouse aspired.

In this period of flux in which a new imperial bond and the possibility of a union of the four South African territories was being probed, Hobhouse attempted to fashion the new relationship between Boer and Briton after her own pattern: values of trust, co-operation and the nobility of labour were to be revived with each yard of arduously spun cloth. Hand-crafted textiles met a desire for a South African cultural 'heritage' able to reconcile a sense of old European aesthetics and new colonial nationalist aspirations. On these grounds she made an appeal for funds 'to all who value a work so plainly calculated as this to restore unity and goodwill between British and Dutch'.[74] This, she hoped, would contribute to a growing sense of national self-sufficiency and autonomy:

---

[70] Hewison, *Hedge of Wild Almonds*, p. 237.

[71] Alice Stopford Green, 'A Visit to the Boer Prisoners at St Helena', *The Nineteenth Century*, Vol. 48, December 1900, 983.

[72] Emily Hobhouse to Mrs Steyn, quoted in Van Renan, *Emily Hobhouse*, p. 328.

[73] *Ibid.*, p. 6.

[74] Hobhouse, Emily, *The Report of the Boer Home Industries and Aid Society, March 1905–May 1906*, June 1906, p. 3.

I think a step forward was made last week when we finished a certain red rug. It was not a very pretty one in colour or design, but the triumph lay in the fact that it was the first one made with warp and weft of the country, as well as pile, and thus was wholly without European influence. We hope before long to make them all from local products.[75]

As a model of liberal development that equated industriousness with dignity and moral fibre, material self-sufficiency with the virtues of independence, and trade and co-operation with fellow feeling, the Boer Home Industries scheme found ready accord with Quakers. This mix of moral instruction and material provision was familiar from the days of the Franco-Prussian War, and the Home Industries provided constructive peace work around which Quakers could unify now that the war was over. When Hobhouse sought an assistant, it would be the Quaker Margaret Clark who would answer the call. Clark helped to open schools in Philippolis and Langlaagte. She was joined later by Quakers Marion Rowntree and Anna Ruth Fry. After a number of false starts, these schools began to foster something akin to the 'arts and crafts' movement in Britain (Hobhouse noted a debt to William Morris). But they also aped the more conservative Home Industries movement in Britain, run by philanthropic individuals such as Mrs Leopold de Rothschild at Wing in Buckinghamshire and Tye Jebb in rural Shropshire, who organised tuition in 'useful skills' for the labouring classes.[76] Anna Ruth Fry had earlier founded, and funded, another such example: a young men's leatherworking class in her home-town of Failand near Bristol.[77] But an emphasis on preservation and revivalism meant that those embracing small-scale cottage industry in post-war Philippolis were undertaking activities which, increasingly obsolete in Britain, were equally economically retrogressive in South Africa. It is difficult to imagine Quaker industrialists (the Clark family of shoe manufacturers, to which Margaret Clark belonged, or those such as the Rowntrees, with large commercial interests in African cocoa) advocating a return to these quaint manufacturing practices for their own businesses. Olive Schreiner, for one, though also a critic of Milnerite political economy, aspired to a different vision for a modernised South Africa: of progressive education for girls, unionised solidarity between all races and full social and political equality within a federal system.[78]

For Hobhouse, the humble spinning wheel had become emblematic of independence and rejuvenated national pride (much as it would for her friend and fellow South African resident M. K. Gandhi). Her evocations of 'traditional' ways of life, suggesting a spiritual and aesthetic yearning for alternatives to modern capitalist

---

[75] *Ibid.*, p. 12.

[76] For reference to de Rothschild see Jan Marsh, *Back to the Land: The Pastoral Impulse in Victorian England from 1880 to 1914*, Quartet Books, London, 1982, p. 163. Eglantyne (Tye) Jebb founded the 'The Home Arts and Industries Association' in the 1880s; see Clare Mulley, *The Woman Who Saved the Children: A Biography of Eglantyne Jebb Founder of Save the Children*, Oneworld, Oxford, 2009, pp. 23–5.

[77] Jan Marsh, *Back to the Land*, p. 163.

[78] Carolyn Burdett, *Olive Schreiner and the Progress of Feminism: Evolution, Gender, Empire*, Palgrave, Basingstoke, 2001, p. 176.

production, spoke to those in Britain and South Africa who were of a radical disposition, and to those espousing a vision of pastoral paternalism. Thus, the liberal South African Women's Federation sponsored a number of pupils at Hobhouse's schools, while Botha, Smuts and other members of the newly formed Het Volk party, as well as Hertzog of the Orangia Unie, took to wearing clothes made of Boer Industries fabric and to patronising Hobhouse's stalls at fairs around the two colonies. Though reportedly feeling like a peacock in his Boer Industries suit, Smuts described Hobhouse's work as 'a landmark of their history'.[79]

Hobhouse hoped that the Home Industries would be taken up by a government department, once responsible government had been achieved. In December 1908 this hope was fulfilled when the Orange River Colony and the Transvaal appointed committees to oversee the schools as part of their new education ministries. Yet, in championing 'revivalism', her schools chimed with a contemporary veneration of the pre-war Boer 'way of life' (a coded reference to its racial order).[80] Contrary to the urgings of her friend Olive Schreiner, Hobhouse continued to prioritise Boer–British relations over the fate of blacks, just as she had in the concentration camps. War, Hobhouse thought, had disrupted the racial order; 'Kaffirs', freed from Boer farms during the conflict, were becoming increasingly self-confident, but also disruptive. Only with a liberal settlement and reconciliation between the white races would the 'native question' find generous resolution, and the gradual unfurling of political rights see a restoration of the social order. Hobhouse tended to elide race with class: her major preoccupation was with preventing respectable Boer girls from slipping down the social ladder, passed by entrepreneurial blacks on the way up, and with training lower-class Boers – the 'poor whites' – to do jobs which relied on imported Asian labour. Here, the vision of an enlightened vanguard driving forward an increasingly democratic political system was to guide her thinking. For Hobhouse, the articulation of a 'separatist' agenda was wholly antithetical, and she was grieved by growing Afrikaner ethnic nationalism, but her sense of an inherent social hierarchy and her faith in progress meant that in neither her practical work nor her written reports did she challenge the gendered and racial order in South Africa. This is captured, in passing, in passages of her reports in which she describes gratifying acts of reciprocation, and the role of black servants:

> The girls' mothers, and many besides, continue to pour upon us gifts in kind. I come in one hour and find a new-baked loaf laid on the table; later on, a jug of milk is brought by some bare-footed Kaffir girl to the door; again, a basket of vegetables or fruit, water melon or spring-bok venison.[81]

Segregationist attitudes had their origins in this period of 'reconstruction' and the quest for greater Union, and arose from the prejudices and priorities of the Milnerite

[79] Emily Hobhouse, *The Third and Final Report of the Boer Home Industries and Aid Society, Dec., 1908*, p. 18.
[80] Stanley, *Mourning Becomes*, p. 90.
[81] Hobhouse, *The Report of the Boer Home Industries and Aid Society, March 1905–May 1906*, p. 5.

'kindergarten' and the assumptions of the liberal minded but racially bounded Smuts and his circle.[82] Hobhouse would deeply regret the rise of racial supremacist ideology in the Afrikaner nationalism of the 1920s. Yet one of the ambiguities of her role as relief worker lay in the implicit 'reconstruction' of existing racial divisions in social and productive relations even while she gave voice to a vision of a racially inclusive polity. But a deeper ambivalence lay in the (mis-)appropriation of her legacy in the first decades of the twentieth century by Boer nationalists keen to trace the contours of a white Afrikaner history in which the hardship of the Boer War featured as a test of the 'national' spirit. Rather than being received in the spirit of progress and conciliation in which they were conferred, Hobhouse's war-time gifts and attempt at 'reconstruction' contributed, unintentionally, to a nationalist mythology of suffering, restitution and deliverance.

[82] Mark Legassick, 'British Hegemony and the Origins of Segregation in South Africa, 1901–14', in W. Beinart and S. Dubow (eds), *Segregation and Apartheid in Twentieth Century South Africa*, Routledge, London, 1995; Dubow, 'Colonial Nationalism'.

7

Neutrality, proficiency and the feminisation of aid: from the 'scramble for Africa' to the Great War

Attempts may have been made to dismiss Emily Hobhouse as a loose cannon, but she was not the only woman whose arrival in South Africa annoyed the authorities. Milner complained bitterly of 'the frivollings of the fashionable females' and the 'mutual jealousies, feuds, back-bitings' of women desperate to share in the war's excitement.[1] Many expressed their intention of caring for sick and wounded British troops. One society lady, on being fitted for her Red Cross uniform, insisted she be made to 'look effective on a battlefield'.[2] Apocryphal or not, such stories of vanity and meddlesome social influence abounded. Hobhouse, therefore, was not alone in her effort to transfer voluntary aid from Britain to South Africa, much of it unsolicited, and some of it deeply unpopular. Yet, within this temporary expatriate community existed networks of affiliation which barely touched one another. While Hobhouse and her friends concerned themselves with conciliating Boer civilians, the personnel of the new Central British Red Cross Committee (CBRCC, founded in 1899) directed their efforts exclusively to British wounded.

The CBRCC oversaw a controversial attempt during this period to systematise the provision of paramedical services and bring it under War Office supervision. Original committee members passed away (having continued to dominate the movement into old age), and old familial connections were replaced by greater bureaucratisation. For many at the Order of St John this offered a golden opportunity to enshrine the 'founding spirit' of voluntary aid in war. Those at the NAS disagreed. But, as the brio of freelancers in earlier conflicts gave way to attempts at regulated and increasingly regimented civilian aid work – reflected in new provisions in the Geneva Convention – a watershed occurred in the management and organisation of the Red Cross movement, although one accompanied by considerable wrangling. This was exemplified in the experience of the female-dominated Red Cross VADs,

---

[1] Quoted in J. Lee Thompson, *A Wider Patriotism: Alfred Milner and the British Empire*, Pickering and Chatto, London, 2007, p. 58.
[2] *Ibid.*, p. 58.

inaugurated to provide dependable auxiliary medical support following the debacle of the Boer War. For the VAD, an agency reliant upon the vagaries of voluntary assistance and gifts of money, time and labour – gifts which the wealthy and leisured woman had more readily at her disposal – would never fully assume the place of a corps of disciplined reservists. Like many volunteers who welcomed the sense of independence and adventure offered by relief work, VADs chafed at rules and routines, some because they felt these to be an affront, others because they felt that the professionalisation of care lessened the quality of mercy.

This chapter considers the strained, sometimes acrimonious, negotiations that attended the systematisation of voluntary aid in Britain in this period of colonial conflict and fears of an impending German invasion. Of particular interest here is how neutrality, civilisation and progress came to be the parochial values of a vigorously patriotic, and increasingly feminised, British Red Cross movement, and how, in a period of internal dispute and the greater politicisation of voluntary aid, the beatific Red Cross 'ministering angel', her eyes raised above political considerations, came to be celebrated as the idealised conduit of the public's compassion.

Voluntary aid and the 'scramble for Africa': the Sudan

The Boer War of 1899–1902 was one of a cluster of colonial campaigns at the end of the nineteenth century in which the Red Cross movement provided aid to British soldiers for the first time. This is not to say that aid in foreign war ceased, as the rather more freelance assistance of the British Red Cross to all sides in the Balkan Wars of 1912–13 testified, but there was now a distinct bifurcation of Red Cross work. Indeed, when war broke out in the Balkans, an explanation for intervention in a foreign conflict was deemed necessary: the rationale that was offered captured something of the British Red Cross's dual role, and its dual appeal.

> What had the British Red Cross Society to do with the Balkan War at all? . . . For it is generally known that the invested funds of the Society may only be used for the purpose of rendering assistance in wars in which British troops are engaged. But though this is true, the Red Cross stands for something more than that: it stands for brotherhood, the spirit of which is ready to do what it can to alleviate suffering wherever it exists. Limitations of natural boundary, and questions of nationality, cannot affect this spirit, and the call from the blood-stained, man-strewn battlefields of the Balkans fell on willing ears and responsive hearts: the Society became the medium of the benevolence of the British public.[3]

Despite this image of brotherhood, aid for combatants in the colonial wars of the 1880s and 1890s was reserved exclusively for British troops and their allies. Providing this assistance brought fresh challenges, as well as fresh opportunities.

---

[3] *The British Red Cross in the Balkans: A Series of 106 Reproductions of Photographs Taken By Members of the British Red Cross Society's Units*, [BRCS], Cassel & Co. Ltd, London, 1913, p. v.

This provoked renewed conflict between the grandees of the NAS and their ambitious but poor relations at the Order of St John. Both had a seat on the CBRCC (and its successor, the BRCS, established in 1905) and, though all were agreed on the need for efficiency, the level of co-operation with the medico-military authorities, indeed the exact operational mandate for voluntary aid provision, was still far from settled. Wrangling took place on a number of levels: over who could claim to be the historic custodians of the Geneva Convention and embody the true spirit of battlefield chivalry; over the demarcation between 'comforts' and 'necessities'; over the optimum balancing of compassion and efficiency and the relative virtues of the amateur and the professional; and over the fluctuating boundary dividing philanthropic and military agencies which was jealously guarded by the army medical services. In a period of imperial expansion and the greater militarisation of state and society (this was the era of the National Service League), colonial rivalry and invasion fears, these tensions became ever more acute. But something else had changed and the implication for the Red Cross movement was profound: the ear of the War Office was now fully open to the advantages of an on-demand and low-cost system of auxiliary medical provision. Members of the Order of St John could expect a receptive hearing for their scheme of war-time paramedics, and chafed more than ever at the fiscal stranglehold exerted by the NAS. Meanwhile, the founders of the NAS felt their existing sense of mission to be under threat, and some, at least, felt that the Order of St John was exploiting patriotic support for the British army to pursue its own agenda of expansion and greater financial security.

These tensions first came to prominence in the Sudan. The British army's Sudan campaign to relieve Egyptian army garrisons held under siege by the rebellious Sudanese became famous for its failure to save General Gordon at Khartoum. Though under nominal Ottoman control, Cairo had in practice passed into the hands of a British 'advisor', the Consul-General, following fears of bad debts. One observer likened Gladstone's indirect responsibility for Egypt to a 'silent annexation à la Bosnia.'[4] To the south was the Egyptian Sudan, a region known for slave trading and now convulsed by the rise of Muhammad Ahmad, calling himself El Mahdi (Messiah), and attempts by his *jihadist* followers to throw off Egyptian rule. The attempt by Gordon to not only relieve the garrisons but also quash the rebellion had resulted in his capture. Influential figures, W. T. Stead prominent among them, urged rescue of this colourful hero. In September 1884 Gladstone, after much prevarication, sanctioned Wolseley's scheme for an audacious rescue mission down the uncharted Nile.

The prime minister, champion of the European Concert and self-determination and famous for his fulminations against Ottoman tyranny, now found himself ordering unilateral action against the insurgent Mahdists to rescue Gordon, evacuate the

---

[4] Quoted in Shannon, *Heroic Minister*, p. 305. The ensuing discussion of Gladstone's thinking on these matters is indebted to Richard Shannon's biography.

garrisons and pacify this troublesome area in the interests of the security of Egypt and its titular ruler, the Ottoman Khedive. Gladstone was able, after some accommodation, to declare that Britain's actions in stabilising Egypt fulfilled the intentions of the Concert of Europe and to stress his principled consistency in relation to the Sudanese. 'I have from the first regarded the rising of the Sudanese against Egypt as a justifiable and honourable revolt. The Cabinet have I think never taken an opposite view . . . We sent Gordon on a mission of peace and liberation.' He 'never understood how it was that Gordon's mission became one of war'.[5] When it came to Gladstone's expression of 'responsibility' for Egypt, even his supporters had qualms. The more sceptical warned about intervening in the country for the sake of bondholders. In a piece which prefigured critiques of the Boer War, his own among them, Frederic Harrison pointed to the financial interests at play in this act of imperialism.[6] Surviving a motion of censure in parliament following Gordon's death, even Gladstone was forced to register the piquant irony of receiving the sultan's congratulations on retaining office.[7]

It was during the Sudan campaign that the NAS developed one of its defining roles in British war: providing convoy links and in-transit care between field and base hospitals. This assistance represented a milestone. Since the end of the Russo-Turkish War in 1878, the NAS had provided assistance in two conflicts involving British soldiers (against the Zulu and Sekukuné in 1879 and the Boers in 1881), but this was limited to crediting the account of a government officer, Deputy-Commissary J. S. Young, for the purpose of purchasing extra medical 'comforts' and equipment.[8] The Sudan, in contrast, was the first British conflict in which an NAS contingent worked alongside the army medical services. In the face of considerable derision, Wolseley, accompanied by Brackenbury and the rest of the 'Wolseley ring', had settled on a route that took his men down the Nile (rather than sailing down the Red Sea to the port at Suakin and then going across to Khartoum by land, as his critics advocated). He faced a difficult task of navigation, a task compounded in the dry spring and summer months by a drop in the water level. After Aswan, cataracts made for shallow rapids and perilous rock protrusions. Wolseley's prodigious solution was to commission a flotilla of shallow craft, constructed and dispatched from England in record time. The NAS, heeding Wolseley's request for assistance, faced similar obstacles. It responded with initiative and alacrity, purchasing a special steamer 'which drew only two feet six inches of water, and was capable of steaming five miles an hour against the stream'. At a cost of £12,156, this launch and its staffing costs represented by far the single biggest outlay of the Society, followed at £3,223 by pay

---

[5] Shannon, *Heroic Minister*, p. 327.
[6] Taylor, *The Trouble Makers*, p. 90. Shannon, *Heroic Minister*, p. 303.
[7] Shannon, *Heroic Minister*, p. 351.
[8] £1,727 was expended by the NAS in the Zulu and Sekukuné Campaigns, £1,100 during the war with the Boers. NAS, *Report of the Operations of the British National Society for Aid to the Sick and Wounded in War during the Egyptian Campaign, 1884–85*, London, 1885, p. 8 [hereafter NAS, *Report* (Egypt)].

and allowances for other NAS staff. Christened the *Queen Victoria* in honour of the Society's patron, the steamer rendered 'excellent service . . . by transporting on her upward journeys on the Nile comforts for the use of patients in hospitals on the line of communications, and on her downward journeys by conveying, and by towing dahabeahs also conveying, invalids, for whom every comfort was provided on board.'[9]

J. S. Young was again seconded from the government for the purpose of liaising with the military and was appointed the Commissioner of the Society on the Nile in charge of a small team of doctors and Nursing Sisters. Spring 1885 saw the NAS embark on a new venture, this time at Suakin in support of the army of Sir Gerald Graham. Graham was under orders to secure this strategic area of Eastern Sudan at a time when the British government had contracted a private engineering company to construct a railway from Suakin to Berber and thus link the Red Sea to the Nile. At Suakin the NAS turned once again to the talented Mr Kennett-Barrington to manage its affairs. By now an experienced manager of relief operations and a respected member of the Order of St John, Kennett-Barrington oversaw a small medical team, hand-picked by NAS Committee member and senior army surgeon Sir William MacCormac. Once again, Kennett-Barrington chafed against the workings of a distant and, he felt, unaccountable NAS Committee, especially Sir William MacCormac's 'patronage' of 'the confounded doctors' who were 'so jealous of each other. Next time I go out', he rued, 'I shall select *all* my staff.'[10] MacCormac, having first come to prominence in the voluntary aid movement as surgeon and chronicler of the Anglo-American ambulance during the Franco-Prussian War, was now one of the leading medical men in Victorian Britain. As surgeon and lecturer at St Thomas' Hospital he was known as an expert on antiseptic surgery and, at the NAS, for his allegiance to Loyd Lindsay's vision of voluntary aid to the battlefield – a disposition that did nothing to mollify Kennett-Barrington and his colleagues at the Order of St John.[11]

Kennett-Barrington and his fractious staff cared for the wounded upon the *Ganges*, and the *Princess*, the latter bought specially, as they sailed down the Red Sea. To much press fanfare, the Society was also loaned the use of the *Stella*, a yacht owned by wealthy expatriate businessman and Wolseley ally Sir Allen Young, for the purpose of transporting wounded from Suakin 'and in suitable cases taking patients short trips in the Red Sea &c'. Young was honoured with the grand title of 'Commissioner Afloat attached to the Suakin Ambulance'. NAS surgeons also served at the army's Base Hospital at Suakin and Kennett-Barrington could report with pride that, '[t]he most important operations are performed at this hospital . . . it was no doubt a compliment to the Society's staff that these surgeons were selected

[9] *Ibid.*, p. 10.

[10] Vincent Kennett-Barrington to his wife, 26.4.1885, quoted in Morris, *First Aid to the Battlefront*, p. 185.

[11] For biographical information on MacCormac, published to coincide with his knighthood, see *The Star*, 10.9.1881; Hutchinson, *Champions of Charity*, p. 350.

for the posts which they occupy'.[12] The NAS's Dr Squire was appointed Administrator of Anaesthetics, and in addition was given charge of a division of 80 beds at the Suakin Base Hospital. Some of Kennett-Barrington's staff also accompanied the troops in skirmishes at Tamai, though 'happily there were but few losses on our side'.[13] A small number of NAS nurses were attached to the Auxiliary Hospital on Quarantine Island, Suakin, and travelled with the worst cases to England on hospital ships.

Lists of stores dispatched to the Sudan reveal the range of comforts the Society deemed necessary. Twenty-four ambulance stretchers, 4 bottles of Valentine's meat juice and 24 dozen tins of calves' feet jelly, 6 dozen bottles of port wine, 32 ounces of lettuce seeds, and 40 camels for the purpose of transporting the wounded, are included in long lists of medical conveyances, tonics and nutritious foodstuffs. Excerpts from the letters of the Society's medical officers record the care taken to make the Citadel hospital in Cairo as cheerful and comfortable as possible, with screens, bookcases and chairs. Meanwhile, the walls of temporary hospitals, including the terminus of the Sudan Railway, were decorated with mottoes and pictures taken from illustrated journals, and patients enjoyed a ready supply of newspapers, tobacco, skittles, draughts and chess boards. From the Society's report, we learn that the officers were given soda water – the men, ginger-beer and lemonade – and that at Abu Fatmeh a successful cottage garden flourished, planted by doctors and tended by locals. Radish, peas, mustard, cress and a variety of herbs grown from seed provided fresh greens to the hospital, excluding lettuce, which 'the natives don't understand'. Regrettably, the camels arrived at Halfa with bad colds; 50 government camels also had to be hospitalised.

Equipment and stores, purchased from Messrs Ross & Co. (one of several medical merchants flocking to the area) at cost price included a number of cows, on the discovery that patients were not supplied with fresh milk. However, in general, the 'hospitals and the field ambulances being really well supplied', Kennett-Barrington directed attention to the supply of fresh limes, oranges, tobacco and other comforts.[14] He described to his wife how

> The tired and worn out men are so grateful for their presents. Perhaps I may be criticised for this in the press but I consider that what I am doing carries out the spirit of adding to the comfort of our forces in the field. The poor fellows come in *loaded* with dust and thirsty, so parched. An orange is indeed a blessing to them. The limes I sent out on the Tamai march were greedily sought after . . .[15]

The supply of 'comforts' to men not on the sick list crossed a fine line first established during the Franco-Prussian War, when preventative treatment such as immunisation, building up reserve medical supplies or providing fresh food to

[12] Letter from Kennett-Barrington to Loyd Lindsay, 1.4.1885, NAS, *Report* (Egypt), p. 64.
[13] Letter from Kennett-Barrington to Loyd Lindsay, 8.4.1885, NAS, *Report* (Egypt), p. 67.
[14] NAS, *Report* (Egypt), p. 67.
[15] Kennett-Barrington to his wife, 7.4.1885, in Morris, *First Aid to the Battlefront*, p. 179.

fighting troops were ruled out on the grounds that they enhanced military capacity and could impinge upon the outcome of a conflict.[16] In British wars, this distinction was quickly eroded, and in the Sudan in 1885 the lack of emergency cases gave considerable scope to NAS activities. Here, the provision of medical 'comforts' knew no bounds when funded by a private organisation and measured against civilian standards, and in hot and trying conditions the provision of ice, soda water and lime juice was deemed acceptable for those on the sick list and those deemed in danger of appearing on it.

Letters and reports sent by NAS staff to their parent committee confirm that there were relatively few battlefield casualties but describe heat exhaustion and diarrhoea during long marches in the early part of the campaign, followed by the spread of enteric fever (typhoid) when later the troops were contained in camps. The army's medical supplies were considered sufficient and the facilities well organised. Vincent Kennett-Barrington noted that the feted *Stella* barely saw service.[17] The conclusions of one doctor, working at the Suakin Base Hospital, were typical:

> As a civilian, who had exceptional opportunities for observing the medical arrangements for the force, I cannot resist mentioning the admirable nature of the preparations made. I found a hospital, almost in the desert, arranged and provided in a manner which would have done credit to a hospital at home; while nothing in the way of medical and surgical necessaries or comforts for the sick was wanting. A well-founded operating tent made it possible to perform operations without distraction, while it saved the other patients the misery of seeing what might have added to their own sufferings.[18]

A concern not to antagonise the regular army medical services may account for the fulsomeness of some of this praise. Others who saw service at Suakin were not as complimentary and saw grounds instead for their own reformist schemes. For Surgeon-Major George Joseph Hamilton Evatt, of the Army Medical Service, the campaign confirmed his impression that the medical corps required a larger reserve force, including trained female nurses.[19] Yet Vincent Kennett-Barrington's private correspondence corroborates a favourable analysis. Likewise, the NAS's aid to the sick and wounded on the Nile and Red Sea ran gratifyingly smoothly. The comparison with NAS extemporisation in the Franco-Prussian War could not be more striking. Nevertheless, a small gust of controversy came to ruffle these calm waters, for the publicity courted by the NAS, and felt a necessary form of accountability, was interpreted by the officers of the army medical services as an attack upon their cap-abilities. An agency dedicated to the voluntary relief of combatant casualties trod a difficult line between being seen to co-operate closely with the regular medical services and demonstrating the need for its own existence. For Loyd Lindsay, the

[16] NAS, *Report* (Franco-Prussian War), pp. 151–152.
[17] Kennett-Barrington to his wife, 13.5.1885, in Morris, *First Aid to the Battlefront*, p. 193.
[18] Dr J. Edward Squire to Loyd Lindsay 26.6.1885, NAS, *Report* (Egypt), p. 81.
[19] Summers, *Angels and Citizens*, p. 154.

very *raison d'être* of the voluntary aid movement was its public mandate to speak out independently against, and to ameliorate, abuse or inadequacy. But it was one thing to criticise the provision of a foreign army, quite another to hint that British military-medical provision was deficient. Crucial working relationships risked being jeopardised. Kennett-Barrington confided to his wife that Loyd Lindsay, a dogged champion of soldiers' welfare, was 'dislike[d] . . . immensely' among the medical officers whom he met on campaign.[20] Loyd Lindsay's recent questions in parliament concerning allegations of abuses by the Army Hospital Corps in the 1881 Natal campaign were no doubt fresh in their minds. This had resulted in a War Office inquiry on which Loyd Lindsay sat as an assertive Commissioner.[21]

Press interest in the NAS's adventure on the Nile garnered support and established the organisation as the leading authority in the provision of voluntary aid. But NAS commissioners on the ground found the degree of favourable coverage uncomfortable. Great stress was thus placed on the provision of 'comforts' rather than essentials, on granting supplementary gifts rather than on plugging gaps. For Kennett-Barrington, such discretion was as necessary an attribute as his prodigious organisational skills; without the trust and co-operation of the army medical services his work was impossible. He was aghast, therefore, when Loyd Lindsay implied in the national press that the NAS was providing critical services, by means of a steam launch evacuating the wounded between Wady Halfa and Cairo, which the regular medical services were unable to match.[22] He was further appalled at an 'exaggerated summary' of his work in *The Times*. 'One creates so much jealousy by being brought too prominently forward.'[23] Meanwhile, officers of the army medical services had the ear of *The Standard* and retaliated in a series of anonymous letters to the editor in which they slammed 'such unnecessary interference and such lavish, wasteful, and indiscriminate expenditure.'[24] This brought forth a spirited rejoinder from one of Kennett-Barrington's colleagues, an anonymous 'H. St. J. G.' (coded reference to the Order of St John's headquarters at St John's Gate), who, in an analogy that said much about the yoking of patriotism, imperialism and the heroic knight-errant, compared the spirit of chivalry that marked voluntary aid to that of 'the martyred Gordon'. Their elaboration of the need for battlefield philanthropy exemplified the extent to which the common soldier was now considered the repository of the nation's honour:

---

[20] Kennett-Barrington to his wife, 9.5.1885, in Morris, *First Aid to the Battlefront*, p. 192.

[21] Summers, *Angels and Citizens*, p. 135; Loyd Lindsay was a member of the Committee Appointed by the Secretary of State for War to Inquire into the Army Hospital Corps, Hospital Management and Nursing in the Field, and the Sea Transport of Sick and Wounded, 1883, [Cd 3607]. The resulting report, covering operations in the first Egyptian campaign against Arabi, was critical, concluding that, among other things, the training and supervision of hospital orderlies were defective.

[22] Loyd Lindsay, letter to national press, 9.3.1885, reprinted in NAS, *Report* (Egypt), pp. 92–94.

[23] Kennett-Barrington to his wife, 20.5.1885, Morris, *First Aid to the Battlefront*, p. 195.

[24] 'A Much Needed Protest', *The Standard*, 24.4.1885. See also Letters to the Editor, *The Standard*, 27, 28 and 29.4.1885.

The soldier is no longer the hired mercenary, mere food for cannon; he is our comrade, who exposes his life for the protection of our interests, in grateful recognition of which we at home are willing to do what we can for his comfort in camp and hospital.[25]

Such views had advocates elsewhere. Gordon himself had recognised the necessity of improving medical services to troops if public goodwill, and army recruitment, were to be secured. '[T]he truest way to gain recruits to our army would be, by so remedying the defects, and alleviating the suffering of soldiers,' he wrote to Florence Nightingale.[26] Meanwhile, military reformists such as Wolseley and his ally, Order of St John member Col Brackenbury, had been quick to recognise the potential for a flexible, trained volunteer corps providing supplementary medical care and an outlet for the public's concern and generosity, even if medical staff further down the ranks were less than convinced.

For Kennett-Barrington, describing himself self-deprecatingly as 'Half-Commissariat Sergeant and Half light porter', and now a veteran of 20 years of relief work, the kind of ingenuity required in marshalling aid to the sick and wounded had become routine. 'One war is just like another', he reflected from the Sudan, 'and so I felt quite at home.'[27] The adrenaline appears to have been no less addictive. Bemoaning his absence at the birth of his second child, Kennett-Barrington promised his wife that the Sudan would be his last venture for the NAS. A few months later he was to be found tending the wounded in the Servo-Bulgarian War. His letters home document a constant conflict between the pull of his home-life – 'I am not happy away from you dearest and long to get back' – and the drama and fulfilment of a role that he had created and in which he felt himself to be irreplaceable.[28] In the Sudan, Kennett-Barrington's path crossed once again with that of another experienced relief worker, Lady of the Order of St John, Viscountess Strangford, last encountered in such circumstances in the hill villages outside Philippopolis after the 'Bulgarian atrocities'. Strangford's relief work was but one front of a wider campaign: an extension of the training of hospital nurses and the admission of qualified female nurses into the Army Medical Department. To this end she had advocated a number of schemes, none of which had got off the ground, and found herself crossing Florence Nightingale – which may account for why.[29] Strangford had long wished to found a permanent Hospital of the Order of St John in the Near East. An earlier offer of a 'considerable sum' to establish a hospital in Damascus having been turned down by the Order (it being unable to find sufficient matching funds), she now found an outlet for her

---

[25] Letter to the Editor, *The Standard*, 25.4.1885.

[26] Gordon to Nightingale, 22.4.1880, quoted in Summers, *Angels and Citizens*, p. 134.

[27] Kennett-Barrington letter to his wife, 7.4.1885, in Morris, *First Aid to the Battlefront*, pp. 193 and 178.

[28] Kennett-Barrington letter to his wife, 13.5.1885, in Morris, *First Aid to the Battlefront*, p. 193.

[29] The exception was a milestone scheme for district nursing under the auspices of the Order of St John, on which she worked with Nightingale ally and Franco-Prussian War veteran Florence Lees. See Summers, *Angels and Citizens*, p. 120.

ambitions in Egypt.[30] Initially travelling to the region in 1882 as commissioner of
the Order's Egyptian Relief Fund, Strangford was under instruction to provide aid
to refugees in Alexandria during Wolseley's first Egyptian campaign, the successful
suppression of Col Arabi's military rebellion against the Khedive. Wolseley's
victory was so perfunctory that the anticipated refugees failed to materialise; Lady
Strangford devoted her energies instead to the newly established Victoria Hospital
in Cairo, where she nursed the British and Egyptian troops hospitalised following
the campaign.[31]

With Wolseley's second Egyptian campaign in the Sudan ending rather less
successfully, despite – critics said because of – his audacity, NAS affairs were wrapped
up following the withdrawal of British troops in May 1885. Wolseley expressed his
gratitude in a letter to Loyd Lindsay, one of several published endorsements inserted
into the NAS's subsequent report. He dwelt in particular on the effectiveness of the
female nurses who had accompanied the NAS team – 'it would be impossible to
over estimate the boon these nurses have been to every force in the field' – before
making one telling recommendation: 'my experience leads me to believe that the
higher the social position of the nurses, the greater their usefulness.'[32] Readers of
Loyd Lindsay's report were encouraged to draw a number of lessons: that the NAS
had amply fulfilled a niche role in war, providing additional comforts alongside the
medical necessities of the Army Medical Service; that it was reasonable to assume that
future conflicts were going to be similarly 'small wars' with a disparity of weaponry
between the British and their opponents; and that flexibility of response and independence of action had won the day for the NAS – after all, could assistance for
Wolseley's Nile adventure ever have been predicted and planned for in advance?

The 1883 government inquiry into army hospital provision which followed
accusations of deficiencies in the Natal campaign had recommended, no doubt
under Loyd Lindsay's guidance, that voluntary aid would act as a stimulus to the
regular medical corps, which would vie to emulate the innovations of the NAS. 'The
rivalry produced both in the medical and nursing departments between the civil
and the military spirit, could not fail to produce beneficial results.'[33] Now, following the fractious response of army medical officers, and chastened perhaps by his
commissioner's response on the ground, Loyd Lindsay adopted a more conciliatory
tone. He even found it necessary to use the pages of the NAS report to retract his
earlier statement on the superiority of NAS services: 'any such inference was
unintentional and would have been unjustified.'[34] Nevertheless, Loyd Lindsay, like
his friend Florence Nightingale, upheld the need for a clear boundary between the

[30] Order of St John, *Report of the Chapter, 1874*, Harrison and Son, London, 1874, p. 8.
[31] 'The Victoria Hospital Cairo', in Order of St John, *The Egyptian Relief Fund Report 1883*, Harrison and
Son, London, 1883, p. 3.
[32] Wolseley to Loyd Lindsay, 28.4.1885, NAS, *Report* (Egypt), p. 23.
[33] NAS, *Report* (Egypt), p. xl.
[34] *Ibid.*, p. 14.

regular medical services and voluntary aid if soldiers' welfare was to be championed and the War Office made to feel its responsibilities. And in fact, although it was not always tactful to say so, from the days of the Franco-Prussian War there had existed a precedent for the army's invitation of NAS technologies and methods.

For Loyd Lindsay and his supporters at the NAS, the Sudan campaign counted as a success for the independent and responsive model of voluntary aid that they had long championed. His achievements were honoured by Lord Salisbury, the incoming prime minister, and in 1885 he was created Baron Wantage of Lockinge. It must have rankled, therefore, to find John Furley using the occasion of the war in Egypt to reignite his attack on the 'spasmodic fussiness and philanthropic insanity' of an unaccountable NAS in the pages of *The Nineteenth Century* and make an unfavourable comparison with the work of Continental Red Cross societies 'more or less under official control'. Furley ended his diatribe with the by now familiar plea of the Order of St John for 'a perfect understanding' to be fostered between 'benevolent neutrals' and the official army medical services, and for voluntary medical preparation for war to be placed upon a permanent footing.[35] He repeated these criticisms in 1887, following the Servo-Bulgarian War, this time with a warning that a great European conflict would not be long in coming, and called once again for the creation of Red Cross branches throughout the Empire, devoted to war preparation.[36] His articles, less reflections on the actual quality of NAS provision in Egypt than attempts to forward the agenda of the Order of St John, sought to bring Loyd Lindsay into line and close the breach with the army medical services. Innovative members of the British army's High Command such as Wolseley may well have recognised the virtues of philanthropic involvement, but it would take the medico-military debacle of another colonial conflict for the War Office to grasp the true value of voluntary aid. By this time, Loyd Lindsay (died 1901) and most of the earlier generation of NAS founders, including Sir William MacCormac (died 1901), had passed away. And the Order of St John, with a network of influential contacts, even if with less impressive financial leverage, could shape the increased interest of the War Office to its advantage. It was left to Loyd Lindsay's nephew, Archie Loyd, to fight a rear-guard action. This would take place in the pages of official reports and in rival attempts to establish an authoritative version of Red Cross history.

Reform and regulation: the South African debacle and the question of neutrality once more

In 1897–98 the NAS provided aid during the Turco-Greek War, including, with little fanfare or comment, a novel extension of its work to care for civilian refugees in Thessaly, the numbers of which far exceeded sick and wounded combatants. This

---

[35] John Furley, 'The Red Cross', *The Nineteenth Century*, vol. 18, December 1885, 879, 891–892.
[36] John Furley, 'The Red Cross', *The Standard*, 3.2.1887.

was followed by aid to British soldiers during the successful re-annexation of the Sudan. This assistance, though initially declined by the British army, commenced in August 1898 on a small but significant scale, for it saw the inauguration of official co-operation between the Society's Commissioner (Col J. S. Young once again) and the new Royal Army Medical Corps (RAMC), established that same year.[37] Thus was entrenched the distinct bifurcation of NAS activity in these years, which saw, on the one hand, impartial aid in foreign war (in practice limited to the Balkans) and, on the other, exclusive aid to the British army in its conflicts in Africa and, in 1914, in Europe. These years were marked by formal co-operation between the various voluntary aid societies (the new CBRCC inaugurated in 1899 comprised the St John Ambulance Association, the Princess Christian's Army Nursing Reserve and, under duress, the NAS) and greater supervision by the War Office, now under Lord Landsdowne. They also saw the commencement of recruitment and fund-raising drives, for the Boer War of 1899–1902 was the first conflict in which the NAS had to appeal to the public for funds. Official and unofficial publicity ranged from Loyd Lindsay's modest request for donations in the press, to a sheaf of jovial songs and verse celebrating the work of the Red Cross nurse. Yet, despite formal co-operation, these years were distinguished by an intensification of the rivalry between the Order of St John and the NAS over control of the new Red Cross Committee, by a lack of co-ordinated activity on the ground between the RAMC and the Red Cross and by tension between the old spirit of autonomy and amateurism and a new emphasis on discipline and professional proficiency.

South Africa in 1899 found NAS officials reprising their role in the Sudan, particularly the provision of transport links for the evacuation of British wounded. To this end was commissioned, again with remarkable speed, the *Princess of Wales* hospital ship and a fully functioning hospital train, complete with dispensary, kitchens and nurses' quarters. Familiar names took to the helm: first Col J. S. Young, then John Furley acted as NAS commissioners, overseeing the running of the hospital train and the supply of stores to military and civilian hospitals.[38] The South African War also saw the beginnings of what Furley had long championed: an imperial British Red Cross movement. The Canadian Red Cross accompanied Canadian troops to their first overseas war. A Good Hope Red Cross Committee, under the presidency of Milner, and likewise affiliated to the British Red Cross in London, took its orders from the women of the Victoria League. The problems faced by those looking after civilians in the concentration camps were faced likewise by those in charge of troop welfare in camps and hospitals for British soldiers. Enteric fever took its toll, particularly in 1900. Urgent calls were made for fresh milk, which the NAS endeavoured to supply, along with condensed and preserved

---

[37] *The Daily News*, 26.12.1898.

[38] *Report by the British National Society for Aid to the Sick and Wounded in War of its Operations in Connection with the Transvaal War, 1899–1902*, [The Society,] London, 1902 [hereafter, NAS *Report* (South African War)].

foodstuffs. Between April and June, with typhoid rampant in the town, the Red Cross Committee supplied Bloemfontein with, among other things, 1,600 pillows, 65,000 fresh eggs and 130 cases of preserved meat. The contrast with provision for the concentration camps – which the Committee did not see as its responsibility – is instructive. Nevertheless, problems of transport and an overstretched military-medical service hampered the care of the wounded combatant, as they did that of the interned civilian. Publicly, the NAS reported that the authorities in South Africa were quick to act under the instruction of a General Commanding the Lines of Communication (General Sir F. Forestier Walker), who secured the transportation of Red Cross items via Military Railway Staff and the Cape Government Railway.[39] But, in a war in which military surgeons had access to innovations in X-ray technology and sterilisation, the hospital fatality rate remained notably high, as were deaths from disease.[40] The care of the sick and wounded quickly became a national scandal. William Burdett-Coutts MP, correspondent of *The Times*, wired back shocking stories of exhausted nursing staff, unsanitary conditions and a lack of medical supplies in the hospitals. The radical *Reynolds's Newspaper* was quick to take the side of the humble Tommy, exposing the 'Hospital Horrors' of an exploitative military system and stoking indignation over a war unusually reliant on reservists and volunteers.[41]

Sir John Furley (knighted in 1899), at work amidst the confusion of sabotaged railways lines and the crush of volunteers, was less than favourable in his appreciation of the new CBRCC. In common with a plethora of voluntary agencies at the seat of the conflict, the CBRCC had come under attack for inefficiencies and duplication. Though it was largely exonerated in a public inquiry, to which Loyd Lindsay gave evidence of co-operation and competence, in private Furley expressed his frustration that the military authorities in South Africa had little knowledge of the CBRCC's existence. He also added his voice to a now familiar refrain: the careful planning and prior accreditation of Red Cross staff was being jeopardised by the audacity of amateurs, particularly society ladies and their vanity projects:

> [E]very man and woman who thought that they could do something, determined *to run his or her own show*: the result in waste and overlapping was truly appalling, whilst self-advertisement was carried to an extent which was the envy of traders.[42]

For Furley, of course, such stories of amateurism were grist to his mill, especially as the offer of service by the women's division of the St John Ambulance Brigade had been declined. But now the War Office was inclined to listen.

Royal commissions conducted during and after the war reiterated the devastating effects of siege war, disrupted transportation systems and insufficient preventative

---

[39] NAS, *Report* (South African War), pp. 57–58.

[40] Of 22,000 deaths, only half were on the battlefield. A further 75,000 soldiers were shipped home with serious injury or illness. Summers, *Angels and Citizens*, p. 173.

[41] *Reynolds's Newspaper*, 1.7.1900.

[42] Furley to Loyd Lindsay, 29.10.1900, quoted in Hutchinson, *Champions of Charity*, p. 243.

measures such as water purification and inoculation against typhoid. They also uncovered a hospital system overburdened by the unexpected demands of the conflict. An absence of in-built flexibility meant that trained reserves were lacking and the army had to rely instead upon impromptu recruitments of surgical, nursing and orderly staff in South Africa and Britain, and an influx of volunteers. A wholesale review and reorganisation of military provision followed. The result was the creation of an Expeditionary Force in 1907 and a merger of the Yeomanry and Volunteers into the new Territorial Force, complete with dedicated medical teams. Furley saw his opportunity. Working closely with fellow Order of St John members Sir Alfred Keogh, Director-General of the Army Medical Service, and Lord Knutsford, Loyd Lindsay's replacement as Chair of the Red Cross Committee, he stamped his vision of a trained paramedical corps upon proceedings. Commissioned to report on the expansion of voluntary aid work throughout the country, he recommended that the Committee become the headquarters and co-ordinating agency for Red Cross branches throughout the provinces and the Empire. Despite objections from leading members of the NAS, who justifiably felt that such a scheme jeopardised their independence and rendered them at the beck and call of the War Office, the reforms had the support of the king and queen. A merger of the CBRCC and a reluctant NAS was affected by royal command in July 1905 and a new BRCS was inaugurated.

This new agency was charged with creating trained corps of VADs, to be attached to the Territorial Force at county level and prepared to oversee the transportation of the wounded from field ambulance to base hospital. Initially, given current invasion fears, such a scheme was envisioned as part of home defence; VADs were not to accompany the army overseas. Far from smoothing relations between the NAS and the Order of St John, these arrangements provided new grounds for conflict. The twists and turns of these tussles have been amply documented by John F. Hutchinson; particular sticking points included the suggestion that the NAS should sign over its funds to the new BRCS, which did not apply to the considerably less well-off St John Ambulance Association, and the agreement that the St John Ambulance Association would be responsible for all the examining and certificating of fee-paying VAD recruits. This prompted the BRCS Council to seek other, cheaper providers in order to break the stranglehold, to which the War Office responded by allowing the Territorials to independently commission their VAD units from the St John Ambulance Association and thus bypass the BRCS altogether.

Behind these disputes lingered an on-going cleavage over the role of voluntary aid in war, as well as the emotional pull of family loyalty. Archie Loyd, elected as one of the three NAS representatives on the CBRCC (and after 1905 a Vice-Chairman of the BRCS), felt keenly the responsibility of consecrating his uncle's memory within the organisation. Bearing testament to Loyd Lindsay's conviction that aid to the wounded ought to be prompted by public sympathy rather than by War Office directives, he objected to being corralled into an organisation that placed emphasis on peace-time preparation and military discipline. He was also incensed by the lobbying of the well-connected Order of St John, and what he took to be the bad faith of the War Office in allowing the Order to maintain special privileges. For Loyd, this culminated outrageously in 1914, when, after behind-the-scenes manoeuvring by the St John hierarchy, *The Times* was led to publish an appeal for funds that were to be distributed equally between the BRCS and the Order of St John. This despite the Order's being a member of the BRCS and, according to its constitution, unwarranted in assuming an autonomous position. The Order thereby gained a degree of financial security and public prestige which Loyd felt unable to protest without jeopardising public goodwill. The Order had secured a triumph. Established as a permanent, highly visible fixture of the voluntary aid movement, it was no longer forced to accede to the demands of its richer relation. Its members could feel satisfied that the real spirit of battlefield chivalry would now be allowed to flourish.

The contest for control of the voluntary aid movement took place politely in official meetings. There was also much informal pulling of strings. Civilised swords clashed too in the writings of the various participants. Memoirs and official reports were turned to use to establish 'founding principles'; attempts were made to produce a definitive history of the movement – and were just as quickly overwritten in rival publications. Ensuring that one was seen to be protecting the true spirit of voluntary relief was vital, and establishing the authority of historical precedent was key. The historian is left, therefore, not to trace the genealogy of a founding ideal, but to sift the documents of an on-going feud. From the time of the Franco-Prussian War, the Order of St John had maintained that the NAS 'oligarchy' had acted outside of the Geneva Convention. In place of regulation it had sanctioned a range of ad hoc activities and unaccountable volunteers. As Sir Thomas Longmore had insisted, 'The treaty nowhere contains reference to the neutralisation of any one not forming part of the Staff originally employed in the service of the ambulances and hospitals of the belligerents; there are no stipulations in it regarding private persons.'[43] Meanwhile, by the early twentieth century, members of the Order were deftly side-stepping the recency of its origins. Aggrandising claims to be the historic custodians of 'Hospitaller' work in war abounded; Red Cross societies were but belated adherents to traditions that the Order had long cherished. Sir Herbert Perrott, chief secretary of the St John Ambulance Association, extolled the Order as

> a body which for nearly 900 years has borne the device of a white eight-pointed cross, and carried on the work for the benefit of the sick and wounded in war, while the device of the Red Cross Society, which represents merely the democratic and socialistic arms of the city of Geneva, was adopted at a conference held there in the early sixties, and has scarcely the antiquity of half a century.[44]

---

[43] Longmore, 'On the Geneva Convention of 1864', p. 7.
[44] Quoted in Loyd, *An Outline of the History of the British Red Cross Society*, and reproduced in Hutchinson, *Champions of Charity*, p. 252.

It was no coincidence that these years saw concerted attempts by the British government to revise the Geneva Convention. It, like other Great Power signatories who had fought a war since the ratification of the first Geneva Convention in 1864, had found it wanting. The disputed role of the Red Cross ambulances of neutral states, such as the Netherlands in the Boer War, and the need to ascertain the exact remit of voluntary aid vis-à-vis the Army Medical Service made the need for clarification particularly pressing. At issue was the autonomy of voluntary agencies and the need to resolve the troubling question of neutrality. At the international conference of the Red Cross societies held in Geneva in 1906, these negotiations were pursued by a team of delegates, each with experience of viewing the workings of the Convention through the lens of British military provision. The senior member was Major-General Sir John Ardagh, a distinguished expert in military intelligence at the War Office. He was accompanied by Surgeon-Major W. G. Macpherson RAMC, who, like Ardagh, was fresh from observing the exemplary medical arrangements of the Japanese Red Cross in the Russo-Japanese War (1904–5), as well as by the distinguished professor of academic law, Sir Thomas Erskine Holland (author of *Laws and Customs of War on Land*, which was issued to the British forces in 1904), and that veteran of international Red Cross conferences, Sir John Furley, who now was finally to have his moment.

Amidst the trying heat of a Genevan summer the British delegates reported from the halls of the Hotel de Ville on rather desultory proceedings and 'a certain amount of impatience and intolerance'. Their confidential assessments of the role of the ICRC were damning. A preliminary report dismissed its members as 'an irresponsible Committee of Swiss gentlemen', and noted 'the desire of the more influential and well-organised Societies to cut themselves adrift from any interference on the part of the International Committee of Geneva'. Frustration was then expressed when 'it became evident that few of the delegations had had any experience of the workings of the Geneva Convention in war, and that most of them had come to Geneva for the purpose of introducing into the Convention larger humanitarian ideals, which are not always possible of realisation in war'.[45]

The final text of the revised 1906 Geneva Convention bore the 'many evidences of hasty draftsmanship' of delegates eager to finish and leave. Nevertheless, the British representatives took satisfaction that 'the articles . . . in the main agreed with those contained in the British project' (the *Projet de Convention Revisée* was an advance draft sent by the plenipotentiaries). They noted two welcome revisions. Firstly, 'the words neutral, neutrality and neutralised are not found in the Convention and are replaced by "entitled to be respected under the articles of the Convention"'. With this revision, the status of a wounded combatant in enemy hands was changed from 'neutral' to prisoner of war. Secondly, the ambiguous status of voluntary

---

[45] Ardagh, 'Geneva Convention 1906, The Procedure of the Conference', confidential report, TNA, Foreign Office, Ardagh papers, Papers Relating to Geneva Convention, PRO 30/40/3.

medical workers was also clarified. Now mentioned in the Convention for the first time, voluntary agencies, 'duly recognised and authorised by their governments', ought to be 'accorded the same privileges as that of the regular medical service'.[46] For, as the British delegates commented, 'there are grave objections to any organisations which tend to compete or interfere with the regular military service'.[47] If wishing to proffer assistance in a foreign war in which their own army was not a party, they had now to gain the assent of their government and of the belligerent army to which they offered their services. The British regretted that the new Convention did not cover civilians in time of war (this would not happen until after the Second World War).[48] They were prosaic also in their assessment of the limitations of the laws of war. Indeed, their report following a preliminary 1902 Conference had ended with a telling augury: 'Whether a conqueror will consider the fulfilment of the pledges given in the Convention as more valid than the complete defeat of his adversary, remains to be seen.'[49]

With these revisions, the meaning of Red Cross neutrality was modified. A red cross on the battlefield no longer signified a blanket of immunity for the wounded and their carers but, rather, that, fully integrated into their own army medical services, members of the RAMC and battlefield volunteers, together with their patients, would be 'protected and respected' if captured by an opposing army. But another meaning of Red Cross neutrality – the claim of the ICRC in Geneva to be the objective codifiers and guardians of the Western conscience – persisted. Nevertheless, only after the Great War was this position widely taken to betoken a moral stance. As will be seen, this attempt in 1906 at legal clarity notwithstanding, the red cross remained a symbol open to multifarious interpretation and hazy appropriation. For many, Red Cross work remained neutral by dint of its being 'above the fray': the feminisation of the BRCS in fund-raising and publicity images of beatific Red Cross nurses would only amplify this impression.

For the Order of St John, however, the revised Geneva Convention seemed to promise an end to the ballooning of neutral freelancers on the battlefield and brought international law into line with Furley and Longmore's vision of regulated voluntary aid. For these individuals, humanity in war meant maximising the numbers of (British) lives saved. This required planning and, above all, systematic co-operation with the military authorities. But for family and supporters hoping to secure the legacy of Loyd Lindsay, the prospect of a fully integrated Red Cross organisation was anathema. Only an autonomous agency would prioritise soldiers' welfare and correct deficiencies in accordance with civilian standards. Giving vent

---

[46] *Ibid.*

[47] *Papers relating to the Geneva Convention 1906, Presented to both Houses of Parliament by Command of His Majesty*, Cd. 3933, London, HMSO, 1908.

[48] *Ibid.*, p. 34.

[49] 'Report on the Seventh International Conference of Red Cross Societies', confidential report, TNA, Ardagh papers, Papers Relating to Geneva Convention, PRO 30/40/3.

to indignant concern in the heat of a campaign might risk jealousy and sour working relationships, even saving fewer lives in the short-term, but it might also widen the scope of concern (to areas or cases not considered a priority by the military) and replenish the fount of public sympathy. Pre-concerted attempts to organise peace-time provision would, it was feared, have little such purchase on the British public's moral imagination or its flair for voluntary endeavour. This view had found its way into the CBRCC's report at the close of the South African War:

> At the time war broke out the Central Red Cross Committee could not foresee the direction in which voluntary aid would manifest itself, nor even approximately the extent to which it would develop as the war progressed. Judging, however, by the experience of this campaign it is evident that voluntary aid organisations such as exist in connection with Continental armies are not applicable to the genius and spirit of the British nation. It is manifestly impossible that an army that is recruited entirely on voluntary principles should in time of peace excite that interest in the homes of the country, which the compulsory system of military service does on the Continent . . .[50]

The report ended by praising private ventures, such as the Portland Hospital, whose offer of assistance was accepted and overseen by the CBRCC, and whose presence in South Africa had caused the likes of Furley and Milner to grumble about 'lady amateurs'. In 1907 Harriet Loyd Lindsay (Lady Wantage) published a dutiful memoir of her husband's life. She paid tribute to the vigour of private philanthropy in South Africa, which was able to

> break through the trammels of 'red tapism,' to avoid the overlapping of rival Societies, to secure flexibility and elasticity together with community of action, while retaining the advantages of systematic organisation and official recognition, these were the ideals which the Society, under Lord Wantage's guidance, ever kept in view.[51]

Such views had currency. 'There is something so prosaic in expressing one's love and gratitude to the nation's defenders in writing a cheque only', editorialised the *Nursing Record*,

> . . . the very narrow limits of the Central Red Cross Committee, as at present constituted, savour too much of the War Office bureaucracy to appeal to the general public, and to be told constantly that this is the only channel by which the public are *permitted* to aid the sick and wounded, has a distinctly discouraging effect upon the British public, which is a self-governing animal.[52]

That proponents of these ideals were losing the upper hand is evident in Archie Loyd's desperate attempt to set on record the founding principles of the British Red Cross and to forensically document developments in its constitution. 'It was urged

---

[50] 'Conclusion', in Central British Red Cross Committee, *Report on the Voluntary Organisations in aid of the Sick and Wounded during the South African War*, HMSO, London, 1902, p. 60.

[51] Wantage, *Memoir*, p. 414.

[52] *The Nursing Record*, Vol. XXIII, No. 604, 28.10.1899.

that recent misunderstandings had been largely caused and increased by the want of any such consecutive record.'[53] His account simmers with ill-concealed resentment of War Office duplicity. This history, published in 1917 and accompanied by reams of documentary evidence, provided an introduction to the work of the branch committees in the First World War. Digs at the 'abuse of social influence' by the Order of St John and the 'advantage taken of the nation's crisis to push on with an attack upon our legitimate status and position' proliferated.[54] But if Loyd hoped to have the last word, he was to be disappointed. The new Chair of the BRCS, Arthur Stanley MP, deeming imprudent the timing of such a history, withdrew it from circulation.

'Ministering angels'? The feminisation of relief work, 1899–1918

The Royal Commission appointed to consider the care and treatment of the sick and wounded during the Boer War was clear in its praise of the trained female nurse. It recommended that 'for enteric and other fever patients and such-like, they would appear to be far better than orderlies, and their general employment in fixed hospitals ought to be now generally recognised by the authorities, and be provided for future wars'.[55] The recommendation was adopted and plans for a reserve band of trained female volunteers got under way. There lingered, however, an assumption that women were especially suited to sick nursing in base hospitals, rather than treatment of the wounded on the front line. The government now sponsored not one but three different bodies: the Queen Alexandra's Imperial Military Nursing Reserve, the Territorial Force Nursing Reserve, and the VAD. The newly formed BRCS took responsibility for providing trained hospital nurses and for overseeing the creation of the VAD. Established in 1909, the VAD was divided into men's and women's divisions and the most suitable tasks were allotted accordingly. Men were to take charge of converting buildings into war hospitals and organising transport facilities, women were to be responsible for catering, housekeeping and nursing in rest stations, and clearing hospitals between field and base.[56]

The official history of the VAD was published in 1917, and doubled as an induction manual for war-time recruits. New members were advised that they would not be 'untrained, but trained in a different way [to the qualified nurse], must be willing to do all the smaller tasks, build up, improvise, be capable of making "the best of a bad job", and, above all, accept discipline unquestioningly'.[57] This body of 'trained amateurs' had become the largest of the three new women's reserves. It had been assumed that they would support the Territorial Force Nursing Reserve in the event

[53] Loyd, Loyd, *An Outline of the History of the British Red Cross Society*, prefatory note, unpaginated.
[54] *Ibid.*, p. lxxx.
[55] *Report of the Royal Commission Appointed to Consider and Report upon the Care and Treatment of the Sick and Wounded during the South African Campaign*, Cd. 453, London, HMSO, 1901, p. 7.
[56] Summers, *Angels and Citizens*, pp. 203 and 212.
[57] Thekla Bowser, *The Story of British V.A.D. Work in the Great War*, Andrew Melrose, London, 1917, p. 23.

3 First World War fundraising poster designed by Alonso Earl Foringer for the American Red Cross and distributed in Britain in 1918.

of invasion. Inspiration in official circles came from the achievements of the Japanese Red Cross in the recent Russo-Japanese War (1904–5), the infrastructure and organisation of which exemplified the benefits of integrating voluntary aid into the military medical services. However, if Lord Haldane at the War Office, and his chief advisors, Viscount Esher (Chair of the reformist War Office reconstitution committee) and Sir Alfred Keogh at Netley, were now fully alive to the possibilities of voluntary aid, the lifeblood of these new organisations came unsolicited from women involved in local initiatives up and down the country.[58] A climate of invasion fear allowed numerous schemes to train women in voluntary aid to flourish. The War Office was inundated by those offering courses in first aid, drill, signalling and stretcher bearing. Statistics from the inaugural years of the VAD bear out the preponderance of female interest in this work: while the Territorial Force benefited from an influx of male recruits, the VAD scheme drew mostly women to its ranks, its numbers being two-thirds female in the years 1910–14. The female membership rose from 8,000 in 1910 to 50,000 on the eve of war in 1914.

The public image of aid work was now shorn of the associations with masculine chivalry that had been favoured by the NAS in the Franco-Prussian War. It was now feminised to such an extent that Katherine Furse, war-time Commandant of the VADs, could contend that 'V.A.D. work is entirely for the sick and wounded. All such work is eminently work for women.'[59] Fund raising, recruitment and fictional images styled the Red Cross as the feminine counterpoint to battle-scarred masculinity. Intuitive, compassionate and selfless, the Red Cross nurse appeared to operate in a neutral realm that was the reverse of political or military exigency – just at a time when any genuine claim to neutrality had been sacrificed to formal incorporation into the medico-military services and written out of international law.

The intrepid 'lady amateur' of the Franco-Prussian and Russo-Turkish wars, whose upper-class intonations and imperious manner had brought male patients and Medical Officers alike to heel, no longer occupied quite the same place in hospital wards or nursing literature. In her place was a new breed of Red Cross nurse, variously celebrated for her demure worthiness or biddable coquettishness. The heroine of L. T. Meade's *A Sister of the Red Cross: A Story of Ladysmith* was suitably gratified to find that her nurse's uniform 'set off her clear complexion and graceful figure to the best possible advantage' and was 'just pining to be doing, and helping, and saving lives. Oh, mine is a grand mission!'[60] Likewise, the heroine of Edith C. Kenyon's *Pickles a Red Cross Heroine* was 'really a beautiful picture in the picturesque Red Cross uniform', having set out on her 'noble Red Cross work . . . to

---

[58] Summers, *Angles and Citizens*, pp. 213–217.
[59] Quoted in Henriette Donner, 'Under the Cross – Why V.A.D.s Performed the Filthiest Task in the Dirtiest War: Red Cross Women Volunteers, 1914–1918', *Journal of Social History*, Vol. 30, No. 3, 1997, 692.
[60] L. T. Meade, *A Sister of the Red Cross: A Story of Ladysmith*, Thomas Nelson and Sons, London 1901, pp. 14 and 11.

do our bit for dear old England and our king.'[61] Meanwhile, popular songs of the time ranged from the reverential to the sentimental. The decorous and dutiful 'Queens of the Red Cross' inspired veneration:

Fair daughters of our race, devoted, true
A song of praise we sing, we sing to you.
When duty calls, you warfare's dangers dare,
To tend our sons with sisterly, sweet care.
We loudly sing of your devoted band,
True hearted, kind, with ever gentle hand;
Angels of comfort, our brave soldiers prize
The words from your lips, the pity in your eyes.

Elsewhere, more light-hearted lyrics captured flirtatious banter and hospital passions. In one song, a mischievous 'Little Irish Red Cross Nurse' was to be found casting a spell over her patients:

Soon our wounds began to heal, but Cupid played his wonted part
And his little arrows did disperse
Till a score or more were stricken and each brought a wounded heart
To our dainty Irish Red Cross nurse.[62]

A favoured image of poster art and verse was the 'ministering angel', an ethereal figure unsullied by political concerns or the violence of war. The most iconic of these images, combining piety with maternal pity, depicted a Red Cross nurse cradling a wounded soldier in the manner of a *pietà*. Designed as a fund-raising poster by Earl Foringer, it was used first in America before being adopted by the British Red Cross in 1918 (and resurrected in the Second World War). Nurses themselves, enduring chilblains and with their legs swaddled against the cold, were rarely recorded as feeling angelic. Whether from maternal feeling, an assertion of social precedence or necessary emotional distancing, voluntary nurses did, however, refer frequently to their patients from the rank and file as 'pets' or 'boys', and to the hospital wards as 'nurseries'.[63] 'I am the mother of my division and the pivot round which everything revolved,' declared one nurse in the Great War.[64] Wounded officers were accorded rather more respect.

Fund-raising images of ministering angels aside, Director-General of the Army Medical Service Sir Alfred Keogh readily acknowledged that the work of the nurse in war 'is not purely humanitarian. Their importance to efficiency is greater than

[61] Edith C. Kenyon, *Pickles a Red Cross Heroine*, Collins' Clear Type Press, London, 1916, pp. 43 and 9.

[62] J. Ward Moseley and Ralph Sanders, 'Queens of the Red Cross', Grosvenor Chambers, Manchester, 1915; Kenneth Clear and John Mackie, 'The Little Irish Red Cross Nurse', Charles Sheard & Co, London, 1915. [British Library]

[63] Albinia Wherry, typed recollections, Brotherton Library, University of Leeds, Liddle Collection, WO 131; see also, Donner, 'Under the Cross', 697.

[64] Anon., *Letters from a French Field Hospital*, Constable and Co. Ltd., London, 1917, p. 95.

they themselves know.'[65] Nevertheless, feminised images of instinctual compassion, invoking a long tradition of female voluntary work as a 'calling', obfuscated the extent to which an independent voluntary organisation had become a necessary part of national war planning and rendered ambivalent the extent to which women could claim the rights and privileges usually attendant on military service. The War Office could take advantage of the fact that the Red Cross was at once a vital adjunct of the war-time medical services and a voluntary agency for the self-sacrificing bestowal of 'comforts'. But it was forced to deal with some of the organisational and administrative difficulties that such ambivalence posed, nonetheless.[66] The line between 'comforts' and 'necessities' that had been traversed by the Red Cross in the Sudan was, by the time of the Great War, rendered meaningless by the extent of the critical services that it provided. These ranged from crucial communication and transport services to the skill of medical auxiliaries at work in operating theatres and hospital wards in all the major theatres of war. In May 1918 Surgeon-General Sir Anthony Bowlby, formally senior surgeon in charge of the independent Portland Hospital during the war in South Africa and now overseeing the care of the whole of the British forces in France, complained that the BRCS ought not to be liable for hospital huts and motor ambulances or other vital infrastructure. In response, the editor of *The Red Cross* reassured readers that the original 'spirit' of the Red Cross remained, even if strained temporarily by the demands of the current war:

> the circumstances of this war, and of most wars, prescribe limits to what the State can do without voluntary assistance. And voluntary assistance is claimant and insists on coming forward to make things more comfortable for its heroes. This is the Red Cross role. . . . [After the war] The Government . . . must be asked to take over all its original duties, leaving the Red Cross to stand by and provide the comforts and luxuries which cannot be expected of the 'Department'; and which, if they could, would probably be less appreciated than those which are the result of unofficial kindness and gratitude.[67]

In a war of attrition in which 89% of soldiers recovered from their wounds or illnesses, a certified, regulated and reliable volunteer nursing and paramedical staff proved to be a necessity.[68] Far from being confined to the home front, as initially anticipated, female VADs accompanied the troops to France, Serbia, Malta, Mesopotamia, Salonika and Egypt. They could be found working in hospitals close enough to the front to be vulnerable to shell fire. Miss K. Hodges, an ambulance driver with the Scottish Women's Hospital Unit, recalled an 'intense excitement, the feeling of "we're going to the War, isn't it marvellous! We're going to the War!"' Joining the First Serbian Division, she encountered chaos on the Romanian front: 'I am sitting in a barn waiting for wounded as I write, only a few miles from the firing

[65] Quoted in Summers, *Angels and Citizens*, p. 197.
[66] See Donner, 'Under the Cross', 687–689.
[67] Editorial, 'Red Cross Luxuries v Army Necessities', *The Red Cross*, Vol. V, No. 4, May 1918, 54; letter from Sir Anthony Bowlby, *ibid.*, p. 58.
[68] Donner, 'Under the Cross', 687.

line. The guns are booming away all the time and have been for the last few days, a very big battle raging, thousands of wounded and not nearly enough hospitals for them.'[69] VAD Commandant Katherine Furse lauded the commitment of those who 'have worked patiently and indefatigably without advertisement and with no thought of self'.[70] But she was mindful of the profitable ambiguity by which such self-sacrificing labour was idealised at the expense of adequate remuneration or professional status. To rectify a situation which tended towards both exploitation and inefficiency, she proposed incorporating the VAD into a centralised National Service scheme. This, she argued, would inspire longer terms of service and prevent overlap and seepage between the various women's agencies. The War Office and her colleagues at the BRCS disagreed. Exasperated, she resigned her post, riled that 'our co-operating with other services or VADs being recruited through a Government Department [was] *infra dig*. In some minds there seems to be a fetish about nursing being on a higher plane than other work for women, and therefore almost holy.'[71] The phrase is a telling one. It meant that while some women experienced a degree of emancipation, these 'ministering angels' were also subject to a 'scandalous manipulation of their good will'.[72]

Meanwhile, the dilemmas of relying upon a 'donor mentality' while insisting on standardisation of provision are no more apparent than in debates over uniform. Uniform required the disciplining of the self to the strictures of the institution, and the significance of this for the voluntary nurse in war time was not lost on Furse, who was keen to ensure a stringent dress code. For some women, this was itself a welcome emancipation from the middle-class home. 'No one felt prouder of her uniform than I did,' recalled VAD Marguerite Fedden.[73] Yet a uniform also connoted the obedience and subservience of domestic service. Furse decried those volunteers who not only felt at liberty to assert their taste and class by customising their uniforms with fur and pearls, but also tailored their hours and duties to suit.[74] Her troubles were compounded by professional nursing bodies that insisted on the sartorial differentiation of trained nurse from amateur. In an attempt to appease all, Furse commissioned a dress designer from Debenham and Freebody's to draft a brochure 'showing the VAD uniforms, as fashionable dresses were shown in their advertisements'.[75]

A series of etiquette guides for VADs, penned by luminaries of the first-aid movement such as Sir James Cantlie, sought to resolve the problem of discipline into one

[69] Imperial War Museum, Documents and Sound Section, Papers of Miss K. Hodges, transcript of recollections written in 1934, 92/22/1.

[70] Dame Katherine Furse, 'The VADs', draft letter to *The Times*, Imperial War Museum, The Women at War Collection, Furse papers, Reel 27 10/1, HM 1108.

[71] Katharine Furse, *Hearts and Pomegranates: The Story of Forty-five Years, 1875–1920*, Peter Davies, London, 1940, p. 352.

[72] Donner, 'Under the Cross', 688.

[73] Marguerite Fedden, *Sister's Quarters Salonika*, Grant Richards Ltd., London, 1921, p. 19.

[74] Furse, *Hearts*, p. 352.

[75] Furse, *Hearts*, p. 352.

of feminine propriety. 'Many who are "taking up work in connection with the Red Cross because it is voluntary" have the idea that they will do what they can in the way they consider best or more agreeable to themselves', Cantlie commented in the pages of *The Red Cross*, 'and each one be a law unto himself or herself', the more so, he thought, since women were used to running their own households.[76] His preface to the handbook *Hints to VAD Members in Hospitals* showed how 'enthusiastic and well-meant help is no longer mere sporadic enthusiasm, but is converted into sustained and disciplined endeavour'.[77] This extended to regulation of leisure time and the banning of romantic entanglements, for, as Furse explained, 'we had to make our reputation as we went along, and, with the gossip of the South African War at the back of our minds, we determined to prove how serious and discreet we could be'.[78]

These ladies of the South African War, who, in the words of Sir John Furley, thought that they had 'a right to walk about the hospitals as they please', joined the dissolute 'camp follower' as the antithesis of the new breed of VAD nurse.[79] Where previously cosmopolitan Lady Strangford figures had been esteemed for their aristocratic pluck, these same qualities now seemed redolent of the 'masquerade nurse' all 'silk gowns and the flimsiest caps and aprons', who were taking the place of 'real nurses'.[80] Attacks upon the 'lady-amateur' were given added impetus at the turn of the century by campaigns for the state registration of nurses. These were led by the recently established British Nursing Association and the *Nursing Record*. Though Thekla Bowser, author of the official history of the VAD movement, was quick to stress unity rather than discord – the 'real and splendid socialism' that arose from 'paying a debt' to the 'men who are defending us' – the unregulated amateur presented a double threat, challenging both professional standards and calls for the creation of an obedient and fully integrated reserve of female volunteers.[81] As one correspondent noted caustically, '[n]o doubt the South African "nurses" have done much to direct public attention to the necessity of differentiating between the true and the false [nurse], and after all we may perhaps have something to thank the Society lady for'.[82]

[76] Sir James Cantlie, 'Etiquette in Voluntary Aid Detachments', *The Red Cross*, Vol. II, No. 9, September 1915, 196.

[77] Sir James Cantlie, preface to E. C. Barton, *Hints to VAD Members in Hospitals*, Macmillan and Co. Ltd., London, 1915.

[78] Furse, *Hearts*, p. 307.

[79] John Furley to Loyd Lindsay, 16.4.1900, BRCS Archive, Wantage papers, D/Wan/15/5/12.

[80] Anon., '"A Plague of Women": Views of an Army Nurse at the Front', quoted in the *Daily Graphic* and republished in an untitled and undated newspaper cutting preserved in BRCS archive, Wantage papers, D/Wan/15/5/15.

[81] Bowser, *The Story of British V.A.D. Work*, pp. 16–17.

[82] Anonymous letter, 'Registration', *Nursing Record*, Vol. XXV, No. 641, July 1900. For debates surrounding the campaign for state registration and the related campaign for a professional corps of nurses to be deployed in war time, see Summers, *Angels and Citizens*, pp. 152–162.

Not all, however, were willing to equate professionalisation and standardisation with optimum care of the wounded. In the memoirs of Lady Jessica Sykes, volunteer nurse at the private Portland Hospital during the South African War, there surfaced the imperious class-confidence of one who could circumvent regulations and 'red tape' with aplomb. Sykes countered both the idealisation of ministering angels and the campaigns of the pro-registrationists by protesting that unmarried career nurses were, in general, inferior physical specimens unable to cope with the rigours of war nursing. Meanwhile, strictly voluntary hospitals protected patients 'from all those forms of annoyance and petty tyranny which are so rampant'.[83] Sykes devoted many pages to descriptions of the picturesque local scenery and native tribes and, in doing so, recalled the 'lady amateurs' of the Franco-Prussian War, able to demonstrate the superior quality of mercy that came from an uncommon refinement. As this suggests, debates regarding the relative virtue of professional training versus accomplished amateurism were frequently rendered in class-based and gendered terms. In the Great War, Furse noted how recruitment patterns exacerbated such tensions, for 'the dregs of the Nursing Profession are now being used owing to insufficiency of the best type of Trained Nurses. The result is that you get very inferior women put in charge posts while you have highly educated cultured women serving as VAD members.'[84]

Though the war in South Africa saw the ballooning of female war-time nursing, few personal accounts of service in this conflict exist; perhaps they smacked too much of the self-publicising amateur. In the Great War, however, the surge of middle-class women into the ranks of the Red Cross was accompanied by a profusion of VAD reminiscences. Many were morale-boosting tales of plucky nurses and chipper amputees. The British public could be reassured that '[m]en on crutches or with one arm disabled find croquet a very suitable game, as it does not require any violent exertion.'[85] Others stressed camaraderie and adventure, though they did not stint on detailing the suffering of wounded troops. The more self-consciously literary of these accounts exposed the myth of the ministering angel, portraying days spent in undertaking proficient but impersonal hospital routines. Here the virtue of a cultured sensibility was again extolled and set against the troubling nature of routine care, which at once cauterised pity and became a psychological and practical necessity. 'The general atmosphere of inhumanness', VAD nurse Vera Brittain wrote to her fiancé, disturbed her more than did mutilated causalities. In particular, the spectacle of

---

[83] Lady Jessica Sykes, *Side Lights on the War in South Africa: Being Sketches Based on Personal Observation during a Few Weeks' Residence in Cape Colony and Natal*, Fisher Unwin, London, 1900, pp. 28 and 152; see also the memoir of Dosia Bagot, who helped to found the Portland Hospital, *Shadows of the War*; for further details of Sykes, see Summers, *Angels and Citizens*, pp. 166–167.

[84] Katharine Furse, 'Draft Copy: Foundations of the Present Difficulties in VAD Service', Imperial War Museum, Women at Work Collection, Reel 27 10/1, HM 1108.

[85] E. M. Spearing, V.A.D., *From Cambridge to Camiers under the Red Cross*, W. Heffer & Sons Ltd, Cambridge, 1917, p. 18.

Bart's Sisters, calm, balanced, efficient, moving up and down the wards self-protected by that bright immunity from pity which the highly trained nurse seems so often to possess, filled me with a deep fear of merging my own individuality in the impersonal routine of the organisation.

Aloof and somewhat condescending from her vantage-point of middle-class accomplishment and literary poise, she mocked the mispronunciations of the sisters-in-charge and disdained their apparent fussiness. But she soon found her own actions becoming habitual, decrying 'the baffling contrast between the ideal of service and its practical expression – a contrast that grew less as our ideals diminished with the years while our burden of remorseless activities increased'.[86] Conversely, for Enid Bagnold, another aspirant novelist, hospital routine served to grant her the 'exhilaration of liberty' to express herself free of the stifling expectations of civilian life, but she too was to find that 'pity is exhaustible' and that the sisters' 'attitude towards the patients, which began by offending me, ends by overtaking me'.[87]

Despite their differences of tone and purpose, nursing novels of the period shared a conviction that a duty of care was owed to the British soldier, those heroic representatives of the nation's glory. Not for the first time, the insignia of the Red Cross doubled as a religious symbol, here by way of sanctifying service to the wounded soldier and, through him, to king and country. 'Our Red Cross Prayer', which appeared in VADs' pocket books in 1914, beseeched the

Lord, who once bore your own Cross shoulder high to save mankind, help us to bear our Red Cross banner high with clean hands unafraid. . . . Teach us no task can be too great, no work too small, for those who die or suffer pain for us and for their Country.[88]

Sharon Ouditt likens this to a 'devotional glamour' that transformed the mundane and the repellent into the sublime.[89] This was, though, an exclusive duty of care to the British soldier, rather than fraternal recognition of the brotherhood of all wounded. Here the duality of the Red Cross's role saw the internationalism and impartiality of aid in the Balkan wars replaced seamlessly a year later with the patriotic mobilisation of voluntary aid in a British war. In this period, far more so than after 1945, the Red Cross was 'an open, abstract symbol . . . many of those wearing it during the [1914–18] war had no direct affiliation to Geneva whatsoever'.[90] It was not that the Geneva Convention was unknown. Rather, its meaning was rendered parochial and malleable, being a symbol both of the pro-registrationist nurse's

[86] Vera Brittain, *Testament of Youth*, Virago, London, 1992 [1933], pp. 211, 212.

[87] Enid Bagnold, *A Diary without Dates*, Virago, London, 1978 [1918], pp. 17, 60, 75.

[88] 'Our Red Cross Prayer', printed on back cover of K. Furse, *Notes for VADs to Keep in Their Pocket Books*, Imperial War Museum, Women at Work Collection, Reel 27 10/1, HM 1108.

[89] Sharon Ouditt, 'Nuns and Lovers: Voluntary Aid Detachment Nurses in the First World War', in *Fighting Forces, Writing Women: Identity and Ideology in the First World War*, Routledge, London, 1994, p. 34.

[90] Heather Jones, 'International or Transnational? Humanitarian Action during the First World War', *European Review of History*, Vol. 16, No. 5, October 2009, 707.

professional impartiality and of British civility in a war against barbarism. Thus it was that at the outbreak of the South African War *The Nursing Record* stressed the natural affinity between the trained nurse and the ideals of the Red Cross:

> The work of the nurses, in caring for the sick and wounded, is one which must commend itself to all, whatever their politics may be, and however strongly they may disapprove of the reasons which have led to the present crisis. The mission carried on under the shelter of the Red Cross flag is one which seeks, as far as possible, to alleviate the horrors of war, and . . . strives, only to render assistance wheresoever it may be needed.[91]

Likewise, during the Great War, the publicist Mary Billington remarked that,

> Women can be proud today of the share that is theirs in this war for national freedom . . . To help to win that peace, they place at the Empire's service all that self-sacrifice, all that devoted duty, all that disciplined endurance, which in the trained nurse is symbolised in the Red Cross of Geneva.[92]

The commendable, but rather remote, aspirations of the ICRC in Geneva were repeatedly subsumed into England's war-time mission to defend European civilisation – they were also taken to endorse a variety of activities which had little bearing on the Geneva Convention. 'We wanted to prove our readiness to do anything which could be done under the Geneva Convention', Furse recalled, and when asked to test gas masks, 'we analysed this suggestion very conscientiously and finally satisfied ourselves that protection and prevention were part of Red Cross work, a theory which has held good in other directions since then.'[93]

The remit of the VAD was to work alongside the regular medical services in the rear of the British army, where it was inevitable that most casualties were British. The protocols of the Geneva Convention governing the treatment of wounded foreign nationals were generally upheld, however. Vera Brittain records the 'efficiency but never compassion' with which German prisoners were treated in the wards.[94] Overall, care to wounded prisoners of war was satisfactory, with little abuse.[95] But this did not preclude derogatory references to patients as 'filthy Hun', nor dissipate the 'the instinctive loathing of the enemies of one's country' felt by one voluntary nurse in South Africa.[96] Accusations that enemy states had transgressed codes of civilised conduct served to heighten such animosities. Stories of atrocity and military misconduct abounded. One song from the time of the Boer War cheered the Red Cross nurse who had

---

[91] *The Nursing Record*, Vol. XXIII, No. 603, 21.10.1899.
[92] Billington, *The Red Cross in War*, p. 190.
[93] Furse, *Hearts*, p. 319.
[94] Brittain, *Testament*, quoted in Jones, 'International or Transnational?' p. 707.
[95] Jones, 'International or Transnational?' p. 707.
[96] Bagot, *Shadows of the War*, p. 9.

One aim a head – her duty – and to do that duty well
Nor cares she of the risk she runs, from shot or bursting shell
One thought alone her patients and the means to see them through
In spite of Boer fire upon Red Cross and White flag too[97]

Perceived or actual breaches of international law thus entered into the cultures and mythology of war-making, galvanising troop morale and public opinion behind the 'necessity' of defeating a barbaric opponent and preserving civilisation, by whatever means. Following the Franco-Prussian War, contraventions of the newly minted Geneva Convention had led Moynier at the ICRC to advocate renewed effort to codify and rationalise the laws of war. The expectation, as Sigmund Freud reflected in 1915, had been that war would be a 'chivalrous passage of arms' in which 'all the international undertakings and institutions in which the common civilization of peace-time had been embodied would be maintained'.[98] For Freud, of course, war-time transgression was unsurprising, given civilised man's underlying barbarism. But more common at the time of the Great War, as Stéphane Audoin-Rouzeau and Annette Becker note, was a congealing of the alleged transgressions of 1870–71 into mutual myths of the singular and insatiable barbarism of the enemy. The breaches of 1914–18 offered further confirmation of such barbarity. The 'scientific' neutrality of the kind institutionalised by the ICRC had become, for many, increasingly incomprehensible: 'On each side, people were so convinced of the legitimacy of their struggle for law and civilisation that neutrality, or aloofness from combat, was inconceivable to them – except to conceal a secret partiality.'[99]

For many involved in war-time philanthropy in Britain the ICRC had been seen as a near-irrelevance. And yet, there, emblazoned on British ambulances and VAD personnel, was to be found the internationally celebrated emblem of the Red Cross movement. For this was a symbol that had been rendered parochial and patriotic, exemplifying, never more so than when adorning the uniform of a devoted 'ministering angel', all that was honourable and worth fighting for. These sentiments found expression in the wartime song 'Noble Women of the Grand Red Cross':

There is a sign, the sign of the Cross
And is painted flaming red
Borne on the breast of women so true
Tending they who fought and bled . . .
Fierce be the fight, the struggle be long,
Still the work goes bravely on
Healing the sick and helping the sore

[97] Ada Giles and Walter W. Hedgcock, 'The Red Cross Nurse', J. B. Cramer & Co. Ltd., London, c.1900. [British Library]
[98] Sigmund Freud, 'Thoughts for the Times on War and Death', (1915), www.panarchy.org/freud/war.1915.html (accessed 2.6.2010).
[99] Audoin-Rouzeau and Becker, 14–18: Understanding the Great War, p. 139.

Caring for each mother's son
Martyred women too have died
True to country, cross and pride
God protect and keep watch o'er the Grand Red Cross.[100]

Transgressions of international law were justified in the name of defending such inimitably British values. In 1918, the journal of the British Red Cross offered two rather telling insights into how such contraventions were understood: as cynical transgressions of the laws of war for reasons of military advantage (attributed to the enemy); and as the necessary breaching of international law, in keeping with noble efforts to defend civilisation (the British case):

> The International Red Cross Committee has issued a strong appeal to all belligerents against the use of poisonous gas. There seems to be little practical use in this otherwise well-justified step. The practice was begun by the Germans, and self-protection compelled their opponents to meet it with the same weapon. As it happens, our measures of defence and our gas have turned out better than those of the Germans. Five days out of six the wind, too, is in our favour. This may be the time to make a change from the enemy point of view. But poison gas is one of those breaches of international law which the war is being prosecuted in order to put an end to for all time.[101]

Only with the end of the Great War would the ICRC gain credibility as the neutral guardian of the Western conscience; though of course, this did not prevent similar breaches.

---

[100] Odette Wellmon and H. M. Wellmon, 'Noble Women of the Grand Red Cross', Dedicated to the Allied Red Cross, Henderson & Spalding Ltd., London (undated, acquired by the British Library in 1919).
[101] *The Red Cross*, Vol. V, March 1918, 34.

Conclusion: humanity and relief in war and peace

Saving the Children

The Armistice in November 1918 and the opening of peace negotiations two months later found apostles of humanity such as Edward Carpenter in despondent mood. Not only was the human wreckage in the backwash of war there for all to see, but hopes for the immediate progress of civilisation were cast adrift. The Humanitarian League, and progressive opinion more generally, had foundered and split over the justness of the war. January 1919 found the editor of *The Humanitarian* lamenting that 'As a result of the war . . . the humanitarian "movement", if it has moved at all during the past four years, has moved in a backward direction.'[1] Three months later the League disbanded. Sombrely, the journal's final editorial noted that the 'general and comprehensive principle of humaneness', which sought not merely an end to human cruelty but also to effect an evolution in ethics, had gained few adherents. Far from galvanising the moral vanguard, 'the advocacy of Rights, leading as it does into ethical and philosophical disputation, demands much more thought than a simple question of humane treatment.'[2] The on-going peace negotiations and even the promise of a new international order did little to dissipate the mood. The League of Nations was to be welcomed, for it offered the 'machinery for the settlement of international disputes', but what was sorely needed was 'a change of heart' to rid war of its 'romance'.[3] Under a photograph of the German delegation to the London Reparations Conference, the *Manchester Guardian* of 2 March 1921 published a gloomy letter from Edward Carpenter and his old 'pro-Boer' allies Kate Courtney and Marian Ellis (Lady Parmoor). 'Civilisation itself seems to be on the wane', they decried. 'The nations are filled with mistrust and antipathy for each other, the classes have rarely been

---

[1] 'After the War', *The Humanitarian*, Vol. VIII, No. 193, January 1919. *The Humanitarian* was the successor of the journal *Humanity*.

[2] 'Annual Report', *The Humanitarian*, Vol. VIII, No. 194, April 1919, 160.

[3] 'Some Thoughts on War', *The Humanitarian*, Vol. VIII, No. 188, August 1918, 124.

so antagonistic, while the relation of individual to individual has rarely been so frankly selfish.'[4]

Unsurprisingly, the Council of the BRCS saw things rather differently. The war had brought untold suffering, but it had also called forth innumerable acts of 'devotion and self-sacrifice'.[5] On the date of the Armistice, the Red Cross and the Order of St John could count 90,651 female and 35,342 male VADs.[6] A total of £14,000,000 had been donated through *The Times* appeal alone.[7] This had funded life-saving necessities, as well as the advertised 'comforts'. Indeed, the staff of the BRCS, far from being limited to the dutiful mopping of brows, had, in the course of half a century, contributed to a transformation in medico-military practices. Providing aid in foreign conflicts had offered the opportunity to observe developments in Continental warfare, to hone appliances and techniques for evacuating the wounded and to test new theories in rapid-response medicine. As a result, by the time of the Great War, the British army had developed an effective model for the emergency care of its sick and injured, treating them in portable hospitals in the field rather than in static hospitals miles behind the lines, and able to draw upon a flexible reserve of trained paramedics. For those at the BRCS with no wish to stand down its operations in peace time, new international bodies offered opportunities for expansion and co-operation. In fact, the BRCS never returned to its pre-war role: it now became a permanent institution for voluntary work in peace as well as war. A new Royal Charter of January 1919 granted an unprecedented extension of its remit. It was now 'authorised to include in its objects and purposes the improvement of health, the prevention of disease, and the mitigation of suffering throughout the world'.[8] Hospital auxiliary work, the long-term care of injured veterans and infant welfare work, in particular, were all considered.[9]

Old anxieties lingered, however. Sir Frederic Treves felt strongly 'the need of keeping our personnel together and alive ... some such kind of peace work is absolutely necessary to ensure preparedness in case of war'. But on the proper relationship of voluntary work to new statutory bodies there was little agreement. Sir Anthony Bowlby, having grumbled during the war over the state's reliance on the Red Cross for vital hospital infrastructure, now 'deprecated any action that might infringe on the work of the Ministry of Health, in connection with maternity and child welfare'. Queen Alexandra, President of the BRCS Council, repeated Loyd Lindsay's mantra that the Society's independence would be jeopardised by a

---

[4] 'The Danger to Civilisation', Letters to the Editor, *Manchester Guardian*, 2.3.1921.

[5] '£14,000,000: End of *The Times* appeal', *The Times*, 1.1.1919.

[6] *Reports by the Joint War Committee and the Joint War Finance Committee of the British Red Cross Society and the Order of St. John of Jerusalem in England on Voluntary Aid Rendered to the Sick and Wounded at Home and Abroad and to British Prisoners of War 1914–1919*, [The Society], London, HMSO, 1921, p. 190.

[7] '£14,000,000: End of *The Times* appeal', *The Times*, 1.1.1919.

[8] *The Red Cross*, Vol. VII, No. 1, 15.1.1920, p. 1.

[9] The question of its post-war role dominated the Society's journal and Council meetings; see, for example, *The Red Cross*, Vol. VI, No. 2, 15.3.1919, 13 and 15.

permanent commitment to peace-time work. 'Its greatest attraction to the public', was that it was '*the* organisation to which the people can turn with a firm belief that it will help out our soldiers in a more tender and sympathetic, and if you like, a less "red tape" way than any Department under the Government'.[10] Unsurprisingly, the BRCS's endorsement of the new American-backed League of Red Cross Societies (established in 1919) was partial at best, the League's vision of permanent international collaboration being embraced by only some of its Council.

Domestic infant welfare soon became the post-war BRCS's main preoccupation. Child-development milestones and 'behaviourist' approaches had come into fashion following the war.[11] In 1918, state legislation provided for nation-wide mother and baby clinics at which advice was given and 'normal' behaviour and growth were measured. During the 1920s and 1930s the BRCS participated in this 'mothercraft' movement, training VADs in the hygienic care of young children. Publications such as Mabel Liddiard's *British Red Cross Society Infant Welfare Manual* (first published in 1928) advocated the methods of the renowned behaviourist Truby King and extolled a modern approach to child rearing. Instructions for feeding and weaning accompanied the sensible advice that restrictive infant clothing be removed and babies' cribs be rid of their Victorian drapery. These methods contributed to a dramatic reduction in infant mortality.[12] Vera Brittain, for one, attributed the survival of her first-born to such interventions. At the same time, clear parallels were drawn between child development and the fitness of the race to defend itself and govern others.[13] '[T]he happy contented child is the pillar of the State', and the BRCS was to help ensure that these contributions to national and imperial stock were properly nurtured.[14]

As Anna Davin has shown, the coupling of child welfare and concerns about the moral fibre of the nation-state had wide appeal in early twentieth-century Britain. It also entailed precisely the kind of national service for women of which Millicent Garrett Fawcett and many of her fellow suffragists approved. Garrett Fawcett's 1924 autobiography, *What I Remember*, reviewed her experiences in war and peace and drew an explicit link between women's war-time contribution to the care of Belgian refugees, voluntary nursing and infant welfare work (all of which her National Union of Women's Suffrage Societies had helped to organise), and the right – and necessity of – women's political participation.[15] In retrospect, she also made a similar claim for her work in the South African War, something she had not pressed at the time. These examples of voluntary work at home and in the colonies provided a model of women's active citizenship now that the vote had been secured. Indeed, as this book has repeatedly shown, relief work was a prominent arena for promoting

[10] BRCS Minutes of Council, 29.4.1919. Original italics.

[11] Christina Hardyment, *Dream Babies: Childcare from Locke to Spock*, Oxford University Press, Oxford, 1984, chapter 4.

[12] Hardyment, *Dream Babies*, p. 159.

[13] Anna Davin, 'Imperialism and Motherhood', *History Workshop Journal*, 1978, Vol. 5, 9–65.

[14] Gwen St Aubyn's *Family Book* (1935), quoted in Hardyment, *Dream Babies*, p. 159.

[15] For a discussion of suffragists' work with Belgian refugees see, Katherine Storr, *Excluded from the Record: Women, Refugees and Relief 1914–1929*, Oxford, Peter Lang, 2009.

national rejuvenation, furthering England's role overseas and enacting the ideals of participatory citizenship. This latter was not a connection that the BRCS had traditionally been keen to endorse, however – Red Cross dignitaries such as Lady Loyd Lindsay were well known anti-suffragists. Indeed, Garrett Fawcett had been reproved in the war-time pages of *The Red Cross* for recommending that nurses and VADs place before their patients the arguments for women's suffrage. This she indignantly denied; after all, she retorted, 'doing good to people was better propaganda'.[16]

By this time, infant welfare had also become the focus for a revival of optimism among disheartened humanitarians of the liberal Left. Protestors against the British blockade of German ports during the peace negotiations, many of whom were old 'pro-Boer' allies, were to be found exhibiting the suffering body of the 'enemy' child once again. Pamphlets and photographs documented malnourished and under-developed German children with wasted bodies and disproportionate heads. The effect of a lack of milk, flannel and other essentials was brought home in reports of the wailing of hungry babies with chapped and inflamed skin. The British public's exposure to such suffering would, it was hoped, raise money to 'fight the famine'; but it would also bring British government and society to their moral senses. Already, this work with the defeated and famished populations of central Europe had begun to occupy the attention of Quakers, relieved to find common cause after divisions over the justness of the war. Sceptical of a League of Nations that rested on military sanctions as a last resort, many Quakers saw relief work as a way of building the international friendships which would result in a durable peace.[17] For Quakers in post-war Europe, as in previous conflicts in France, the Balkans and South Africa, the personal act of giving was an important part of the gift. But their work in post-war Europe also represented the culmination of a period of tumultuous change for the Society of Friends, which, over the years covered in this book, had seen relief work become a significant test of Quaker conscience and a gesture of recognition of the brotherhood of man. In Germany, donated food and goods for infants and nursing mothers became known as *Liebesgaben* (gifts of love), a name prized by Quakers for evoking that 'outward expression of the spirit of love from man to man which refused to be turned into hatred at the bidding of Governments'.[18] Ruth Fry, Emily Hobhouse's assistant in the Boer Home Industries scheme, was among the first to volunteer for post-war Quaker relief, subsequently serving as General Secretary of the Friends War Victims' Relief Committee between 1921 and 1923.

Emily Hobhouse, meanwhile, was occupying herself with raising funds for a Swiss charity to aid the children of Central Europe and for the Russian Babies Fund, of which she was Chair. The intention, as always, was to supersede militarism with

---

[16] *The Red Cross*, Vol. II, No. 4, April 1915, 84.

[17] See for example, 'The League of Nations', *The Friend*, March 1918, 167–169; Edward Grubb, *What is Quakerism?* Headley Bros. Ltd., London, 1917, p. 136; Kennedy, *British Quakerism*, pp. 401–404.

[18] Ruth Fry, *A Quaker Adventure: The True Story of Nine Years' Relief and Reconstruction*, Nisbet and Co. Ltd., London, 1926, p. 304. The Quakers may have overlooked the fact that the same word was used for the gifts to soldiers from the über-patriotic German Red Cross, see Jones, 'International or Transnational?' p. 704.

co-operation and trust. Again, this required more than a League of Nations; it neces-
sitated the creation of ethical polities and an end to what Hobhouse diagnosed as a
collective 'war neurosis'. This was of the sort which, on reading her old antagonist's
autobiography, she felt Millicent Garrett Fawcett to be suffering.[19] Like Garrett
Fawcett's, the thoughts of Emily Hobhouse, busy translating and editing Boer women's
testimonies of the concentration camps, had returned to South Africa and, like
Garrett Fawcett again, she had, by the close of the Great War, developed an explicit
connection between her attitude to this earlier war, war in general and her views on
democracy and citizenship. As was to be expected, her thinking on these matters
differed substantially from that of her erstwhile adversary; but they did, however,
have in common many of the ambient assumptions of their day concerning women's
innate maternal qualities and the virtues of exporting British civilisation. Following
the cessation of the Boer Home Industries scheme and her return from South Africa
in 1908, Hobhouse had been active in the People's Suffrage Federation, alongside
Charles Roden and Noel Buxton, Margaret Llewelyn Davies and most of the Parliamentary Labour Party. This, unlike Garrett Fawcett's National Union of Women's
Suffrage Societies, sought to align progressives of all stripes in a campaign for an end
to both property and sex qualifications for the vote.[20] For Hobhouse, as for many in
the People's Suffrage Federation, full democracy and equal citizenship would allow
humanity truly to flourish and to determine an open and moral foreign policy – and
only when this was true of all nations would war become an anachronism. To this
end, Hobhouse was to be found at the outbreak of war in 1914 in neutral Holland,
combining relief work with Belgian refugees with participation in various feminist-
pacifist peace meetings. Her foreword to the *Report of the International Congress of
Women's Suffrage Societies*, which had taken place in The Hague in 1915, is testimony
to her expansive hope that female enfranchisement would give expression to the
maternal instinct in international affairs:

> From the very moment of the declaration of War . . . the hearts of women leapt to
> their sister women, the germ of the idea, nameless and unformed, that the women of
> the world must come to that world's aid, was silently and spontaneously conceived and
> lay in embryo in the hearts of many . . . the women of the Hague Congress . . . aim
> [at] . . . a World in Permanent Peace founded on the new order of a complete and dual
> citizenship – women with men – their field, the nation and the world.[21]

---

[19] Van Renan, *Boer War Letters*, p. 423.

[20] Sandra Stanley Holton, *Feminism and Democracy: Women's Suffrage and Reform Politics in Britain, 1900–1918*, Cambridge University Press, Cambridge, 1986, p. 64.

[21] Jennifer Hobhouse Balme, *To Love One's Enemies: The Work and Life of Emily Hobhouse Compiled from Letters and Writings, Newspaper Cuttings and Official Documents*, Hobhouse Trust, Cobble Hill, Canada, 1994, p. 547; see L. B. Costin, 'Feminism, Pacifism, Internationalism and the 1915 International Congress of Women', in *Women's Studies International Forum*, Vol. 5, 1982, 301–315. Hobhouse also spent the war years investigating the German treatment of occupied Belgians and attempting to refute the image of German barbarity, see John V. Crangle and Joseph O. Baylen, 'Emily Hobhouse's Peace Mission, 1916', *Journal of Contemporary History*, Vol. 14, No. 4, October 1979, 731–744.

For Hobhouse, voluntary aid empathetically bestowed formed an important part of this constructive work for peace and freedom, quelling 'war neurosis' and opening people's hearts to the suffering caused by war. Spring 1919 saw her participating in a new relief organisation. Conceived as the charitable wing of the anti-blockade and anti-Versailles protest, the new SCF encompassed a familiar tally of progressives: Liberals, socialists, Quakers, radicals, feminist-pacifists and humanitarians. Whatever the fate of the Liberal Party in parliament, here was evidence of the tenacity of progressive liberal values in international affairs and the continuity of activist networks from the days of the Bulgarian and Armenian 'atrocities' and the Boer War onwards. The inaugural meeting of the SCF was blessed by Kate Courtney. Emily Hobhouse undertook relief work under its auspices in Liepzig in 1919 and Ruth Fry worked with the SCF in post-war Austria. Other members from this time included Charlotte Despard, Charles Roden Buxton, Margaret Llewelyn Davis, Emmeline Pethick-Lawrence, L. T. Hobhouse, J. A. Hobson, Vera Brittain and the Victoria Leaguers Lady Lyttleton and Violet Markham. Its linch-pins were two sisters, Eglantyne Jebb and Dorothy Buxton (daughters, incidentally, of Mrs Tye Jebb, stalwart of the domestic Home Industries schemes which had so inspired Emily Hobhouse in South Africa). The work of the SCF would soon extend from ameliorating the effects of the blockade to succouring those starving in the Russian famines and winning international accord for its Declaration of the Rights of the Child. Full-page press advertisements with prominent pen-and-ink drawings of ragged women and beseeching children stressed the urgency of the situation – and launched a blatant assault upon the reader's conscience:

> While you are reading these words some poor starving child is dropping by the wayside – fleshless – almost – a mere bag of bones! These poor, helpless, starving, and disease-stricken children cry aloud for food and succour. They see grim death all around them – they face famine and pestilence – they succumb to untold horrors while we go about our daily duties enjoying life, seeking pleasure, and living just as we wish. Every hour – every MINUTE, a weakened, broken human being gives up its grip on life and goes to face its Maker.[22]

In internal histories and recent treatments, Dorothy Buxton and her husband, Charles Roden Buxton's, extensive contribution to committee work and policy development at SCF has been overshadowed by the figure of Eglantyne Jebb, who, with her burning intensity of purpose and astute grasp of publicity, quickly became the public face of the new organisation.[23] Much like Henri Dunant, Jebb has come to occupy the place of a visionary – the story was told of her receiving inspiration for the Declaration of the Rights of the Child atop Mont Blanc – but, as with the

---

[22] 'Grim Tragedy of Famine-Stricken Russia. Millions of Babes Slowly and Painfully Dying from Starvation', SCF appeal, *Manchester Guardian*, 4.8.1921.

[23] See Mulley, *The Woman Who Saved the Children*; Linda Mahood, *Feminism and Voluntary Action: Eglantyne Jebb and Save the Children, 1876–1928*, Palgrave Macmillan, Basingstoke, 2009.

Geneva Convention, it is always worth inquiring into why certain ideals win accord at any one time. It is also worth placing those with a spontaneous 'calling' – whether Dunant, Jebb or Emily Hobhouse – into the context of their wider social networks and their concerns.

Jebb's initiation into the challenges of aid work had come during the Second Balkan War of 1913, when, as a young Oxford History graduate, she had volunteered to distribute aid on behalf of the Balkan Committee's Macedonian Relief Fund. Prior to this she had worked for the Charity Organisation Society in Cambridge. It was under the Balkan Committee's auspices that liberal campaigning networks had regrouped after the close of the Boer War. Founded in 1903 by Charles Roden Buxton and presided over by historian and Armenian scholar James Bryce MP, the Committee interpreted recent bloodshed in the Balkans as yet further evidence of Ottoman venality.[24] Their publication of disturbing photographs of slaughtered Macedonians in a fund-raising brochure reinforced this impression. These were taken by Victoria de Bunsen, Charles Roden Buxton's sister. Arranged in a slender album displaying one photograph per page with a title and a few words of explanation, these could be easily mistaken for snapshots of a bucolic late-summer holiday, peasants captured dozing in the haystacks. A closer examination reveals their subtle horror. For the accompanying text tells a much darker story: these are the murdered bodies of families, slumped amidst their harvesting. The impression is of an industrious and pastoral people, kin to the British peasant of yore, cut down by a merciless tyrant. No suggestion is made that they are part of a regional conflict, and only obliquely do we learn that their deaths may not have been at Turkish hands. 'The real fact is that most of the outrages are actually organised by the Turks, and that general chaos allows the Sultan's agents to stir up bloodshed even among European peoples.'[25] The Balkan Committee blamed this situation on Disraeli's equivocations at the 1878 Berlin Congress, and called on the Liberal government to offer redress.

Eglantyne Jebb, however, while learning well the value of the arresting image, found it harder to apportion blame in a region where atrocities were committed on all sides and claims to nationhood contested the same territory.[26] Her response on visiting the region in 1913 was correspondingly less Gladstonian than that of most of her Balkan Committee colleagues: the sufferers she encountered were less the victims of a particular oppressor than universal 'victims of war'. But she was also disappointed with the Macedonian Relief Fund, of whose philanthropic dilettantism she despaired, and with the refugees themselves for their failure to

---

[24] Other members of the Balkan Committee included Leonard Hobhouse, George Cadbury, Octavia Hill, Herbert Gladstone, H. N. Brailsforth, J. L. Hammond, Canon Barnett and the international lawyer John Westlake (who replaced James Bryce as chair in 1905). See Davide Rodogno, *Against Massacre: Humanitarian Interventions in The Ottoman Empire 1815–1914*, Princeton University Press, Princeton, NJ, 2012, pp. 235–236.

[25] Victoria de Bunsen, *Macedonian Massacres: Photos from Macedonia*, The Balkan Committee, London, c.1907, p. 6.

[26] Mulley, *The Woman Who Saved the Children*, pp. 148–158.

Photos from Macedonia

The Harvest.
A Family Stabbed
while at Work.

WE publish these pictures with much reluctance. We would gladly forget the horrid sights we
have seen, and avoid harrowing our friends. But before evil can be conquered it must be faced,

4 First page of the Balkan Committee's pamphlet depicting murdered
Macedonian peasants.

'self-help' according to Charity Organisation Society principles.[27] In her frustration
with ethnic-nationalism there were echoes of Emily Hobhouse's disappointment
with the direction of contemporary South African politics, as well as a more general
ambivalence in progressive circles over the traditional equation of national self-
determination with freedom and humanity. Increasingly, calls were being made
for greater mediation by international bodies, legal safeguards and tolerant provision for minorities (some also advocated population transfers). The instability
and injustice of the international order, militarism and 'war neurosis' were deemed
the enemy; barbarity, atrocity and ethnic-nationalism symptoms of these deeper
forces. 'It is in war itself', Jebb reflected in 1913, 'not in its victims, that . . . barbarity
lies.'[28] Thus the response must be correspondingly universal: sympathy for the victim
of one side over another would only exacerbate levels of suffering. The challenge was
to reassert the virtues of Western civilisation in the face of the barbarism of war.[29]
This formed the basis of Arnold J. Toynbee's contemporary critique of the selectivity
of Gladstone's humanitarian politics in the 1870s and, like Toynbee, Jebb advocated
impartial international regulation as well as greater cross-cultural dialogue. Here, in

[27] Mahood, *Feminism and Voluntary Action*, pp. 148–149, 154.
[28] Mulley, *The Woman Who Saved the Children*, p. 167.
[29] Emily Baughan, '"Every Citizen of Empire Implored to Save the Children!" Empire, Internationalism
and the Save the Children Fund in Interwar Britain', *Historical Research*, Vol. 8, No. 213, 2013.

an expansive vision of internationalism which hailed the League of Nations, but also sought to surpass it in its emphasis on building ethical polities through grass-roots activism and education, were some of the idealistic origins of the SCF.

By generating genuine international solidarity and undertaking a universal commitment to save all the world's children, SCF members hoped to thwart war and mitigate its cruelty.[30] Their relief practices enshrined the principles of self-help and participatory citizenship; they also adopted the new child-development milestones then in vogue to compare international rates of child welfare.[31] Ultimately, the hope was for temporary relief programmes to be taken up and incorporated into state welfare departments once political stability had been achieved in post-war Europe, just as Emily Hobhouse had sought a similar transition of the Boer Home Industries once representative government had been granted in South Africa. This was first achieved in Vienna in the 1920s. Again, as has been seen time and again throughout this book, relief workers' practices and priorities were not only enmeshed with emancipatory projects to advance the national and international order, but developed in step with trends in the domestic charitable and welfare sector. Again, stress on physical and psychological development, and the contemporary behaviourist emphasis on training the child in the habits of self-reliance and good citizenship, segued into wider social and political aspirations.[32] For the SCF, however, the hope was less for a crop of military and imperial heroes than for a generation of peace-loving internationalists. For critics, of course, this amounted to saving the enemy. Nevertheless, the SCF gained a level of public support from across the political spectrum that had been denied to Emily Hobhouse's campaign in the Boer War.[33] The universal care and protection of children, and the prevalence of the ideal of childhood innocence (at a time when 'total war' rendered women complicit), was broad enough to allow for members' different emphases and interests. Certainly it was congenial to liberal imperialists, such as Violet Markham, drawn by existing interests in infant welfare and approving, no doubt, the rapid expansion of SCF affiliates in the settler colonies.[34]

---

[30] Patricia Sellick, 'Responding to Children Affected by Armed Conflict: A Case Study of Save the Children Fund (1919-99), PhD thesis, Bradford University, 2001, pp. 216-267; Dominque Marshall, 'Humanitarian Sympathy for Children in Times of War and the History of Children's Rights, 1919-1959', James Marten (ed.), *Children and War: A Historical Anthology*, New York University Press, London, 2002.

[31] These milestones of development featured in SCF's publication *All the World's Children*.

[32] By the 1930s, the behaviourist consensus was being challenged by psychodynamic practices which focused frequently on child aggression – a phenomenon that Elaine Sharland and Cathy Urwin link to international events and concerns over the 'individual's contribution to war'; see 'From Bodies to Minds in Childcare Literature: Advice to Parents in Inter-war Britain', in Roger Cooter (ed.), *In the Name of the Child: Health and Welfare, 1880-1940*, Routledge, London, 1992, pp. 191-195.

[33] The sum of £1 million had been raised by the SCF by the end of 1919; see Mulley, *The Woman Who Saved the Children*, p. 271.

[34] Members of the Victoria League such as Markham participated in infant welfare work in the interests of 'national efficiency'; see Riedi, 'Gender and the Promotion of Empire', 591.

The post-war focus on peace-time welfare work, much of it directed towards children, also characterised the expanded vision of the ICRC. It was in this period that Geneva came to stand for an untarnished internationalism and principled neutrality and, alongside the League of Nations (though not necessarily under its auspices), a new generation of aid organisations chose to open their headquarters and bureaux in the city. These included the Save the Children International Union, the League of the Red Cross Societies and the Women's International League. The ICRC presented itself as both patron of such ventures and custodian of the 'sacred fire' of impartiality and independence, seeking to distance itself from the patriotic fervour displayed by national Red Cross societies during the war and the rival League of Red Cross Societies, which could appear less than autonomous.[35] Though for years seen by many of the larger national Red Cross societies as a near irrelevance, the ICRC now successfully emphasised its neutrality in order to position itself as the moral conscience of the Red Cross movement, outflanking the ambitions of the League of Red Cross Societies to lay claim to its 'real' spirit. As ever, such a position of principled neutrality was also a necessary one: its existence and its authority depended upon its claim to represent all of the signatories of the Geneva Convention. It refused to jeopardise this claim by alienating any one nation, especially as it now wished to revise the Convention to encompass prisoners of war and civilians. Arguing that it was preserving the authentic and historic Red Cross ideal, and in keeping with the times, it now reoriented itself as a universal agency for the promotion of world peace, committed to 'a generalised struggle against the evils which attack humanity from the very cradle of the infant' and working not just in war and peace 'but also *for peace*'.[36] In the words of historian John F. Hutchinson, the post-war era of permanent ICRC standing committees devoted not just to relief in war but also to welfare and development in times of peace seemed to offer a 'panacea for all the sufferings of Humanity'.[37] But with such permanence and universalism also came the permanent institution of existing practices, habits of mind and old networks of influence and association. Moreover, the reliance on donations and public appeals, not now as forthcoming as during the patriotic heyday of 1914–18 or the period of flux and hope that followed, curtailed the reach of this new generation of relief organisations, leading to little immediate deviation from existing circuits of sympathy and gift giving.[38] For the moment, the SCF, ICRC and League of Red

[35] John F. Hutchinson, '"Custodians of the Sacred Fire": The ICRC and the Postwar Reorganisation of the International Red Cross', in Paul Weindling (ed.), *International Health Organisations and Movements, 1918–1939*, Cambridge University Press, Cambridge, 1995. Gustave Ador, ICRC president, sat on the Honorary Committee of Save the Children International Union. The two organisations had strong links.

[36] 'Activité internationale de la Croix-Rouge en temps de paix', *Revue Internationale de la Croix Rouge*, Vol. 3, No. 26, February 1921 and contemporary ICRC sources, quoted in Hutchinson, *Champions of Charity*, pp. 339 and 343.

[37] Hutchinson, *Champions of Charity*, p. 319.

[38] On the League's funding shortfall see Hutchinson, 'Custodians of the Sacred Fire', p. 29. The SCF saw a similar drop in revenue after public subscriptions peaked during the famines in Eastern Europe and Russia in the early 1920s.

Cross Societies concentrated their ambitions on the usual Christian populations of
Europe and the Near East.

Spontaneity, urgency – and the place of history

Compassion that eschews sentimentalism, practical and humane care that avoids
becoming routine or patronising: relief workers today are as likely to be heard invoking the importance of balancing head and heart as Sir John Furley was a century
ago. A desire to come to the aid of those in need is certainly a virtue – the world
would be a bleaker place without acts of kindness and sympathy and efforts at
human amelioration. But the image of a ministering angel, if still as potent, is as
inappropriate now as it was then to describe the gruelling and occasionally dangerous task of providing aid in war. It obscures too the very varied motivations and
aspirations that continue to underpin relief work. An individual's decision to join
an aid agency may be as much a product of ideological commitment as it was in the
past, just as war's opportunities and peculiar glamour remain a compelling draw.
The NAS surgeon implementing theoretical knowledge during the Franco-Prussian
War, the middle-class woman sailing to South Africa to proffer aid and expand her
horizons or the Quaker eager to inculcate the value of industriousness and self-help
in the Balkans, all share something in common with those in search today of
gap-year escapades, pay and occupational skill or an arena for religious conversion and the spreading of a 'social gospel'. Likewise, relief work remains female
dominated at the operational level, mostly by nurses who stand to earn more
working for an international aid agency than they would in a domestic hospital. But
if the ministering angel's halo of self-sacrificing concern illuminates the virtue of
a spontaneous response to suffering, it also casts into shadow the rise and workings of a distinctive occupational field. This field's origins and its legacies, rarely
addressed other than through reference to founding fathers and inaugural ideals,
repay historical scrutiny.

Today an argument is heard for humanitarian ideals to be extricated from the
corrupting effects of too close a relationship with political agencies and the media.
Those denouncing the politicisation of aid and the unwitting complicity of aid
organisations in sustaining conflict have led a call for a return to humanitarian first
principles. For some, this means the ethical clarity of founding visionaries such as
Henri Dunant and his standard of neutrality, for others, a rejection of neutrality
when the fundamental principle of humanity is at stake – and the possibility of
withdrawal if this principle is compromised. A golden thread of consistent humanitarian ideals is conjured up, which, if now somewhat tarnished, ought to be clasped
before it corrodes. Thus will the paradoxes of relief in war be mitigated (if never
fully resolved). There is confidence that an ethical position that is suitably robust
will enable free and sincere interaction with recipients and an objective and compassionate response to human need. Here lies Fiona Terry's hope that relief 'given in

accordance with its intention' to respond to the needs of the most vulnerable will foster a 'free exchange and dialogue' between aid agencies and populations in distress.[39]

Yet there have always been competing claims to these founding ideals, and these claims ought to be treated less as an expression of timeless compassion or institutional consistency than as strategic calls upon history to legitimate a particular ethical position. This was as true for contests over the 'spirit' of the Red Cross movement at the beginning of the twentieth century, as it was true for reclamation of the historic but far from unequivocal 'Peace Testimony' by the Society of Friends. Moreover, if the veneration of founding fathers and inaugural ideals sets the parameters of ethical debate, then this debate in turn, however critical, reinforces the legitimacy of 'urgentist' aid work in principle. That a golden thread of consistent humanitarian ideals does not exist is one conclusion of this book. Instead, the origins of relief work in war rest on a mix of idealism and anxiety, ethical conviction and compromise, external pressure and new professional expertise. Thus, invocations of neutrality, impartiality, humanity and universality, principles that we might today consider foundational, can be caught sight of in the past, but their meaning and status were far from consistent and are harder to grasp. For instance, neutrality was at once a defining feature of the emerging protocols of relief in war, and something lacking a fixed definition. It could refer to the technically neutral status of the wounded combatant and their authorised carer under the 1864 Geneva Convention; to operational impartiality and the distribution of aid to all sides; to the role of the ICRC as objective codifier of the Western conscience; to assistance that was non-political; or derived from the identity of the recipient – childhood, in the words of Eglantyne Jebb, represented a 'neutral ground . . . where all could most easily meet'.[40] And rather than an end in themselves, it might be observed further that these principles and protocols were often a means – a *modus operandi* – in the service of a range of 'higher' (and not always now fashionable) ends: for some, the realisation of the Kingdom of God on earth, for others, the civilisation of war to the point of anachronism, for still others, the duty of the vanguard to exemplify Western progress and foster self-determination according to degrees of political maturity.

Relief work, then, was never simply a flowering of the Western conscience as many at the time – and subsequently – liked to imagine, but arose in symbiosis with the growing professionalism of allied sectors, with the rise of the 'new' journalism and in specific response to contemporary military, theological and political anxieties and aspirations. Moreover, relief agencies, whether promoting the spread of British Red Cross branches throughout the Empire, or highlighting the plight of 'victim nations' in the Balkans, contributed to both the formulation and the projection of

---

[39] Terry, *Condemned to Repeat?*, pp. 242–243.
[40] Quoted in Mulley, *The Woman Who Saved the Children*, p. 276.

British interests overseas. Current calls for aid organisations to eschew political entanglements (the Balkans in the 1990s being the usual case in point) simply by refusing funding from political bodies or by upholding organisational autonomy ignore these deeper relationships. If, then, the need to be attentive to the teleological manner in which ideals are presented is one finding of this book, another points to the need for a genuine investigation of the history of vocational conventions and practices.

The tangled origins of relief work present a complex legacy: institutional prerogatives, occupational protocols and unspoken assumptions are as consequential as acknowledged ideals and ethical resolutions. Undertaking such an inquiry requires reckoning with this field of endeavour in its fullest extent, and a focus that spans the politics of humanity and relief in Britain, as well as at the point of delivery. Committee reports, 'self-help' schemes, surgical handbooks and sentimental images of 'ministering angels' invite analysis. Administrative procedures, recruitment and fund-raising campaigns, the logistics of dispatch and distribution, all are relevant if the apparently intuitive is to be reconciled with relief workers' habits of mind. This *habitus*, emerging first in the context of military modernisation, progressive and social-democratic campaigns and the heyday of British colonialism, continues to generate perceptions and influence practice. Here can be highlighted the reliance upon fund-raising and campaigning conventions which use children to evoke 'victims of war', and an 'urgentist' credo by which aid work is perceived as a purely spontaneous response to human suffering. Also important are the assumptions governing international law, domestic welfare and overseas relief which were current when aid organisations were first established. Specifically, on the one hand, that 'scientific' impartiality was thought possible and prized for the collective advance in moral consciousness and human amelioration that it promised and, on the other, that traditional philanthropic moralising and class and racial hierarchies governed who was deemed 'worthy' of discretionary aid.

The fund-raising image of the victim of war and disaster is now most usually that of the helpless child: immiserated, degraded, terrified and vulnerable. These are powerful and moving. They can generate sorrow and indignation. In this way, Susie Linfield writes, each document of suffering is also a document of hope.[41] Hand in hand with the war correspondent and the rise of investigative journalism, these images have provided knowledge of suffering in distant places, whether the result of war or of political violence, for over a century. As such, they have repeatedly stretched the British public's imagination, conscience and sense of responsibility and cannot simply be written off as voyeuristic or exploitative. Emily Hobhouse's harrowing illustration of an emaciated Boer child is only one in a chain of images of suffering children that, across the course of the twentieth century, seared themselves

[41] Susie Linfield, *Cruel Radiance: Photography and Political Violence*, University of Chicago Press, Chicago, IL, 2010, p. 33.

upon the British public's imagination (Vienna in 1919, Biafra in 1967–70, Bosnia in 1992–95). For many, it was Hobhouse's depiction of grieving mothers and dying children, rather than the SACC's reasoned arguments of the rights and wrongs of the war, that galvanised the public to protest British action in South Africa. Paradoxically, Linfield notes, it is images of debasement and suffering such as these, rather than abstract discussions of the rights and duties of humanity, that make palpable the idea of having rights, by virtue of their absence. Their power is at their strongest when they present us with a 'specific, *individual*, experience of suffering'.[42] The appeal that they make to a universal shared humanity is one of the key premises of liberal interventionism and non-governmental organisation action. But this kind of knowledge about suffering is not above being disputed or ignored, nor without certain other ramifications.

As suggested by the British public's mixed reception of images of suffering in prose, pen-and-ink drawing and photography, in the Franco-Prussian War, Rumelia, South Africa or Macedonia, not all felt moved to action, nor were those with a 'calling' necessarily responding to knowledge of suffering. And, just as Hobhouse's critics argued that Lizzie van Zyl's suffering resulted from unsanitary Boer habits, rather than from British incompetence, knowledge of suffering can be contested. Moreover, when these images are undifferentiated, or become conventional, or are divorced from explanatory text, they tend to condition certain responses. This does not negate the power of these images, but it does suggest implications in their use to represent the 'victims of war' in fund-raising campaigns. The war correspondent Linda Polman has observed the potential for beneficiaries to manage their self-representation in conformity with fund-raising images. In addition, the repeated use of the image of the child tends not only to equate child development with the 'fitness' of a society more generally but also to infantilise and render all recipients, including soldiers, guerrilla fighters and even war criminals, 'helpless innocents'. This decontextualises and dehistoricises the causes of suffering, and the production and selection of knowledge about such suffering, to the extent that recipients become nothing other than their corporeal bodies or 'bare' humanity.[43] As anthropologist Lisa Malkii comments,

> At first it is difficult to see what might be so problematic in seeing the suffering of people with the eyes of 'humanitarian concern' and 'humanitarian compassion'. It is surely better than having no compassion or simply looking the other way. But this is not the issue. The issue is that the established practices of humanitarian representation and intervention are not timeless, unchangeable, or in any way absolute. On the contrary these practices are embedded in long and complicated histories of their

---

[42] *Ibid.*, pp. 34 and 39.

[43] Lisa Malkii, 'Speechless Emissaries: Refugees, Humanitarianism, and Dehistoricization', *Cultural Anthropology*, Vol. 11, No. 3, August 1996, 388; see also, *idem*, 'Children, Humanity, and the Infantilization of Peace', in Ilana Feldman and Miriam Ticktin (eds), *In the Name of Humanity: The Government of Threat and Care*, Duke University Press, Durham, NC, 2010, pp. 58–85.

own . . . These humanitarian representational practices and the standardized interventions that go with them have the effect, as they currently stand, of producing
anonymous corporeality and speechlessness. That is, these practices tend actively to
displace, to muffle, and pulverize history . . .[44]

Of course, this does not mean to say that the staffs of aid agencies are themselves
unaware of the political situation into which they intervene, and some have a long
history of political advocacy work, such as SCF UK, starting with its campaign
against the British blockade in 1919. But this, in turn, raises another issue: what
are the specific implications of using images of abject suffering to publicly address
questions of abuse, war criminality or tyranny? Reliance upon physical suffering to
exemplify political oppression, injustice or cruelty, as in the exposé of conditions in
the Boer War concentration camps, poses a particular kind of dilemma. For, though
political injury may remain, any amelioration of physical suffering can result in a
decline of public concern. Moreover, an emphasis on bodily suffering can occlude
the question of political responsibility (including the international responsibility
of foreign states) by limiting responses to questions of nutrition and sanitation.
This was precisely Milner's intention in attempting to extract the politics from
the spectacle of suffering in South Africa (and precisely the impetus behind Emily
Hobhouse's countervailing intention to keep this suffering in the public eye –
risking, for some, an exaggeration of the severity of conditions). It was also the
situation nearly a century later when representations of a 'humanitarian crisis' in the
Bosnian War obscured the failure of European states to intervene and kept attention
focused on numbers of victims rather than numbers of murderers.[45] Elsewhere,
pressing human need, particularly if it is a less ready exemplar of political or
ideological imperatives – or is experienced by those not deemed full members
of humanity, or as amenable to stereotypes of childlike innocence – can be ignored
(as was the case of concentration camps for blacks in the Boer War). The result
is that the elaboration of crisis depends upon knowledge of suffering that can be
compromised, partial or selective: relief, therefore, is never simply predicated on an
impartial or universal assessment of human need alone.

These images of abject suffering sustain a vocation that prioritises the urgency to
save and protect. This 'urgentist' credo places particular stress upon spontaneity. At
an operational level, this suggests flexibility and innovation and an unpremeditated
and intuitive response to human need. Evidence abounds of relief workers' personal
ingenuity, energy and skilled extemporisation. Whether draughts boards and
oranges in the Sudan, beef tea and a clean pair of pyjamas on a Boer War hospital
train or the critical care provided by VAD nurses in the 'flying' hospitals of the Great
War, the rapid, responsive, expert provision of emergency care has brought untold

[44] Malkii, 'Refugees', 389.
[45] This was something that many aid agencies decried at the time, see Brendan Simms, *Unfinest Hour:
Britain and the Destruction of Bosnia*, Penguin, London, 2002, pp. 34–37.

comfort and saved innumerable lives, often at great personal cost. But there are other consequences of this 'urgentist' credo. From the start, emergency relief was yoked to a military imperative. In an era of quick-fire weaponry and increasingly 'total' war, aid agencies provided niche services in rapid-response evacuation procedures, paramedical support and the maintenance of interned or displaced civilians. Wittingly or not, at an operational level, this credo can still serve military objectives, providing the logistical support necessary to treat the wounded or feed people deliberately displaced. This is not a corruption of an initially 'pure' ideal, nor at the time was this considered a paradox. Many voluntary aid societies sought openly to enhance British military capabilities. For those that did not, and opposed war, qualms as to unintended consequences stood for less than confidence in the effects of moral uplift and a civilised example: the 'war spirits' would, they trusted, be abated and friendly international co-operation would ensue. Only now, when relief work is more likely considered the reverse of an inevitable militarism, does aid in war time present itself as an agonising paradox.

There are still other implications to this spontaneity. Much of the legitimacy and authority of the field of relief work derives precisely from an image of its being a spontaneous gesture of sympathy and solidarity with the vulnerable and victimised, of its existing as the converse of militarism and political exigency, and of its confronting abuses of power.[46] There is profitable ambiguity in reducing the field of organised relief work to a personal act of intuitive moral service. It obscures the relations of power that exist between aid worker and recipient, international aid organisation and local service provider, and between funding bodies, donor governments and 'host' countries.[47] Fund-raising campaigns, the support of donor governments and the recruitment of volunteers all rely upon this image of a pure, untrammelled compassion. Yet spontaneity – when aid efforts are viewed as repeated acts of conscience and are self-regulated – can result in proliferation and lack of co-ordination, give free reign to incompetents and cranks, and breed a cavalier insouciance in those with absolute power over the sick and wounded.

In response to these concerns, Janice Gross Stein stands for many when she pleads the need for greater accountability, particularly to the recipients of aid. Aid agencies in the past, it is assumed, by-passed the need for accountability by virtue of a taken-for-granted assurance that they were doing good.[48] Stein concludes, however, that while accountability is the new watchword, it is to donors alone that aid agencies report. 'A radical handover of responsibility to local partners is

---

[46] Michael Barnett and Thomas G. Weiss, *Humanitarianism Contested: Where Angels Fear to Tread*, Routledge, London, 2011, p. 55.

[47] David Kennedy, *The Dark Side of Virtue: Reassessing International Humanitarianism*, Princeton University Press, Princeton, NJ, 2004, pp. 348–349.

[48] Janice Gross Stein, 'Humanitarian Organizations. Accountable – Why, to Whom, for What, and How?' in Michael Barnett and Thomas G. Weiss (eds), *Humanitarianism in Question: Politics, Power, Ethics*, Cornell University Press, Ithaca, NY, 2008, p. 138.

unlikely . . . as long as humanitarian organisations are held accountable by donors for their operational performance and are dependent on a funding structure that emphasizes what they themselves have accomplished.'[49] This, though, is not quite the modern phenomenon supposed. Nineteenth-century relief workers were not above scrutiny or suspicion, however secure in their own worthiness. The war correspondent took aid agencies to account: accusations of wastage, pilfering, dilettantism and even espionage abounded in the nineteenth-century press. (Something of this tradition of public scrutiny is evident today in hard-hitting books by journalists Linda Polman and David Rieff.) From the outset, relief organisations were required to persuade interested parties, whether journalists, donors, military officials or governments, that their actions were at once benevolent and effective. As today, individual relief workers and their committees stressed that their intentions were unpremeditated – they were, they emphasised, merely the conduits of a spontaneous public outcry – but also that their actions were accountable to their donors, their conscience and, for some, to God (hence the meticulously kept records of Quaker relief workers, and the financial accounts and tables of recovery rates in NAS reports). What we see today, therefore, are notions of accountability that perpetuate traditional philanthropic priorities.

These priorities make stark the discretionary power inherent in any decision to give aid in times of vulnerability and strain. At the turn of the nineteenth century individuals such as Kate Courtney and Joshua Rowntree moved between attempts at 'scientific' charity and social investigation at home and involvement in relief work overseas, convinced that they occupied the moral vanguard and confident that a cloud of ignorance and vested interest was all that stood in the way of public enlightenment, an ethical polity and peaceful international relations. The public may react to their efforts with incomprehension or accusations of faddism, but this could be attributed to their occluded vision; *Seventy Years among the Savages*, the title of the memoir by the Humanitarian League's Henry Salt, was only partly tongue in cheek. However impartial the aid worker or domestic social worker at an operational level, this was a role that *required* discretionary power: how otherwise was recidivism to be overcome than by the leadership of elevated individuals prepared to sacrifice their own time and comforts? Selections had to be made; aid was not to be given indiscriminately; dependency had to be avoided.

Courtney and Rowntree, as well as Loyd Lindsay and his colleagues at the NAS, viewed discretionary domestic welfare and overseas relief as complementary attempts at human amelioration, and their practices and priorities spanned domestic and foreign relief. But this changed over the course of the twentieth century as greater emphasis was placed on a citizen's right to welfare (though not necessarily an end to public moralising on the question of worthiness) and a whole sector grew up, dedicated to arbitration, appeals and public accountability. This was part of a long

---

[49] *Ibid.*, p. 141.

renegotiation of the social contract that had involved many of those active in philanthropy at home and overseas and which encompassed many of their models of
delivery. The SCF, for instance, not only collaborated with government services in
the provision of infant welfare centres in Britain throughout the inter-war period
(staffed, in several cases, by those with experience of relief in the Balkans and elsewhere) but, in keeping with the social-democratic roots of many of its founders, had
long campaigned for greater state provision as a right. But greater disparity now
existed between the domestic welfare sector and overseas relief missions – which
remained discretionary and largely unregulated interventions. Today domestic
welfare work and foreign relief missions are rarely spoken of in the same breath.

Though the government continues to contract aid agencies to provide domestic
welfare services (Save the Children remains active in domestic infant welfare work,
for example), overseas relief work is not subject to the same public regulation and
accountability (press scrutiny aside), nor tied to meeting recipients' enforceable
rights to certain services. Indeed, one consequence of linking the right to security
and welfare to citizenship was that, lacking the ethical international order that
many progressives envisaged, it denied these rights to the displaced and stateless.[50]
In the twentieth century, refugees (many in permanent camps) became the largest
category of humanitarian subject, an illustration of the failure of aid agencies' early
internationalism, but also now the site of their greatest endeavour. Indeed the more
general point may be made that it is in the breach between the nineteenth-century
relief workers' expansive ideals and the present-day reality that their *modus operandi*
remains, and thrives. What was once conceived as a temporary 'stop gap' has
become a permanent field dedicated to raising money to fund philanthropic interventions overseas. This has given rise to a disparity in the representation of human
need in domestic and overseas contexts. In Britain public discussion of need or
neglect rarely relies upon images of abject suffering. Of course, this more muted
tone may well be a facet of the necessity of maintaining state funding and collaboration on domestic projects. But it is surely true that Linfield's insight into the role of
images of human immiseration operates here in reverse: human need in a domestic
context is more likely to be addressed publicly through reference to a failure of social
policy (or military covenant) than to images of abjection precisely because enforceable rights exist. To which might be added Rosalyne Rey's observation that while
pain is a physical phenomenon, suffering assumes a moral quality – and conditions
a 'humanitarian' response.[51]

This also means that aid agencies have the discretionary power, in overseas
projects at least, to select 'worthy' subjects. As such, they place a condition
upon intervention that makes pronounced the difference with the universality of

---

[50] This point was drawn out by Hannah Arendt, *On Totalitarianism*, Harcourt Brace Jovanovich, New York, 1973 (1951), p. 293.
[51] Roselyne Rey, *The History of Pain*, Harvard University Press, London, 1995, pp. 2–3.

provision that is understood to exist within statutory welfare services. As Erica Burman notes, '[h]idden within' relief practices 'is a tacit assumption of conditionality . . . where the help "we" offer "them" is on "our" own terms'.[52] Thus, for example, ostensibly egalitarian notions of empowering others to help themselves, thereby avoiding dependency, long favoured in the kinds of 'self help' practices developed by Quakers and progressives, overlook how relevant such a concept is to those with no choice but to enter internment camps, or left struggling to feed children on reduced rations. Specific issues also attach to the bestowal of commodities where traditions of healing differ or cultural meanings are not bridged: here Emily Hobhouse, witness to the imposition of Western clinical practices upon the inmates of the Boer concentration camps, was astute in her need for sensitivity and the *quality* of the relationship between giver and recipient.

Yet Hobhouse was herself to exemplify another common feature of the discretionary nature of aid: the opportunity to implement experimental models of treatment and forms of 'rescue'. Often, exposure to innovative practice can improve the comfort of patients and enhance rates of recovery. Thus, for example, the experimental use of antisepsis and the latest design of stretcher in the Franco-Prussian War improved the condition of French troops (it also informed standards of rapid-response medicine at home, both in the military medical service and in provision for domestic accidents). But opportunity can also be taken to exercise hobby-horses and give free reign to domestic preoccupations which may be of little benefit to recipients. Here Hobhouse's attempt to introduce spinning wheels into communities devastated by war in South Africa reflected more the fashion for William Morris among her progressive friends than any inherent usefulness of such quaint manufacturing practice to destitute Boer families. Experiments in ethical 'fair-trade' capitalism and the production of ethnic trinkets for sale to Western consumers continue. Here, Dinah Rajat and Jock Stirrat's concept of 'parochial cosmopolitanism' captures well this distinguishing and long-lived feature of relief workers' *habitus*:

> 'cosmopolitan' in the sense that they attempt to deny the local and the parochial. But on the other hand, what is equally apparent is that the world of development people is frequently extremely parochial in the sense that it is based on a particular set of ideas as to what development is and how it should be attained, and in the sense that the people involved are often trying to recreate forms of life which, far from stressing the inclusivity of 'true' cosmopolitanism, are based on the exclusivity of parochialism. This in turn . . . is linked to a sense of nostalgia for an imagined home, a recreation of that home in a foreign land. Yet this is not the only nostalgia to be found in the world of development. If one form of nostalgia looks back to an imaged homeland, another looks back to an imagined world of 'pre-development' similar to Rosaldo's 'imperial nostalgia' where, 'people mourn the passing of what they themselves have transformed'

[52] Erica Burman, 'Poor Children', 34.

(Rosaldo, 1989). So if, . . . cosmopolitanism is in many ways a denial of parochial pasts, the cosmopolitanism of the development world coexists – indeed, perhaps depends upon – the nostalgic creations of imagined past parochialisms.[53]

This was the essence of Hobhouse's Boer Home Industries scheme, at once a nostalgic creation of an 'imagined' (white) South African craft heritage and a vision of a cosmopolitan ideal of future co-operation between peoples of an independent nation and between nations. Yet Hobhouse's assistance, given in the spirit of fraternity and emancipation, was received among some in South Africa as an endorsement of the Boer 'way of life', implicitly and unintentionally underscoring an exclusionary ethnic-nationalism. For all that relief workers prioritise their own ethical responses, it is important to remember that recipients have their own ethical values and political imperatives. Ilana Feldman underlines this point in her astute analysis of the ethical scrutiny to which Quakers subjected their relief work in Gaza in the years 1948–50, and their troubled encounter with attempts by recipients to inflate the refugee ration rolls. For Quakers this amounted to fraud; for those in refugee camps the impetus, it seems, was to maintain the impression of their community's numerical preponderance at a time when ideas about Palestinian citizenship were forming.[54] Here, then, were examples of ethical rigour – but not the 'free exchange' hoped for between aid workers and populations in distress. Indeed, whatever this book has demonstrated about the spirit in which relief agencies bestowed their gifts in war (and this was as varied as relief agencies were numerous), as much remains to be written about the (not always reciprocal) spirit in which they were received.

[53] Dinah Rajak and Jock Stirrat, 'Parochial Cosmopolitanism and the Power of Nostalgia', in David Mosse (ed.), *Adventures in Aidland: The Anthropology of Professionals in International Development*, Berghahn Books, Oxford, 2011, pp. 161–162.

[54] Ilana Feldman, 'The Quaker Way: Ethical Labor and Humanitarian Relief', *American Ethnologist*, Vol. 34, No. 4, November 2007.

Bibliography

Archives and manuscripts

Bodleian Library, University of Oxford, Department of Western Manuscripts
Bryce papers
Disraeli papers
British Library, London, Archives and Manuscripts
W. E. Gladstone papers
British Library of Political and Economic Science, London School of Economics
Courtney papers
Streatfeild papers
British Red Cross Society, London, Museum and Archives
British Red Cross Society papers, 1905–1923
Central British Red Cross Committee papers, 1899–1905
Wantage papers, 1870–1901
Brotherton Library, University of Leeds
Liddle Collection
Imperial War Museum, London, Department of Printed Books and Manuscripts
Private papers
The Women at War Collection
John Rylands Library, University of Manchester, Special Collections
E. A. Freeman papers
C. P. Scott papers
Library of the Society of Friends, London
Friends South African Relief Fund papers, 1899–1906
Friends War Victims' Relief Fund papers, 1870–1873
London Yearly Meeting Proceedings
Manchester Central Library, Local Studies and Archives
Religious Society of Friends, Minutes of the Manchester Preparatory Meeting, 1871
The National Archives, London
Foreign Office, Ardagh papers, papers Relating to Geneva Convention, PRO 30/40/3
Foreign Office, Correspondence Respecting Geneva Convention, FO 83/760
Foreign Office, General Correspondence Respecting Atrocities in Bulgaria, FO 78/2551–2556

War Office, Reports from Medical Officers on the War between France and Germany in
    1870–1871, WO 33/23
War Office, Reports, Accounts and Recommendations Concerning Concentration Camps,
    WO 32/8061/32–182
Sheffield City Archives
H. J. Wilson papers
Wellcome Library and Archives, London
Florence Nightingale papers
Sir James Cantlie papers
Sir Thomas Longmore papers
Surgeon-Major J. H. Porter papers
Thomas Weldon Trench papers

Newspapers and periodicals

Blackwood's Magazine
British Medical Journal
Daily News
Good Words
Huddersfield Examiner
Humanity
Jewish Chronicle
Manchester Guardian
Morning Post
Northern Echo
Nursing Notes: A Practical Journal for Nurses
Nursing Times
Pall Mall Gazette
Review of Reviews
The Freeman's Journal
The Friend
The Humanitarian
The Nation
The Nursing Record
The Speaker
The Standard
The Star
The Times
Westminster Gazette

Official sources

Hansard Parliamentary Debates.
*Papers relating to the Geneva Convention 1906, Presented to both Houses of Parliament by
    Command of His Majesty*, Cd 3933, London, HMSO, 1908.

Report on the Concentration Camps in South Africa by the Committee of Ladies appointed by the Secretary of State for War, containing reports on the camps in Natal and the Orange River Colony and the Transvaal, 1902, Cd 893, London, HMSO, 1902.

Royal Commission Appointed to Consider and Report upon the Care and Treatment of the Sick and Wounded during the South African Campaign, Cd. 453; Minutes of evidence, Cd. 454, London, HMSO, 1901.

Published minutes and reports etc. of societies and committees

Balkan Committee (Macedonian Relief Fund)

de Bunsen, Victoria, *Macedonian Massacres: Photos from Macedonia,* London, The Balkan Committee, c.1907.

Boer Home Industries and Aid Society

Hobhouse, Emily, *The Report of the Boer Home Industries and Aid Society, March 1905–May 1906,* June 1906.

Hobhouse, Emily, *The Third and Final Report of the Boer Home Industries and Aid Society, Dec., 1908.*

British National Society for Aid to the Sick and Wounded in War

Loyd Lindsay, Robert (Col), 'Lecture to Royal United Service Institution: "On Aid to the Sick and Wounded in War"', London, Harrison and Sons, 1871.

Loyd Lindsay, Robert (Col), 'Letter to the Local Committees and to the Subscribers of the National Fund for Aid to the Sick and Wounded in War, By Col. Loyd Lindsay', London, [The Society] 1871.

Questions on the Operations of the British National Society for Aid to the Sick and Wounded in War, and Replies Thereto, by Various Members of the Society's Staff and Others: Being the Result of Their Experiences in the Franco-Prussian War, 1870–1871, London, Harrison & Sons, 1871.

Red Cross Operations in the North of France, 1870–1872, Printed for the Boulogne English Committee for Aid to the Sick and Wounded in War, London, Spottiswoode & Co., 1872.

Report by the British National Society for Aid to the Sick and Wounded in War (The British Red Cross Society) of its Operations in Connection with the Transvaal War, London, [The Society], 1899.

Report of the Operations of the British National Society for Aid to the Sick and Wounded in War during the Egyptian Campaign, 1884–85, London, [The Society], 1885.

Report of the Operations of the British National Society for Aid to the Sick and Wounded in War During the Franco-Prussian War, 1870–71, Together with a Statement of Receipts and Expenditure and Maps, Reports and Correspondence, London, Harrison and Sons, 1871.

Report of the Operations of the British National Society for Aid to the Sick and Wounded in War During the Servian War against Turkey, 1876, together with a Statement of Receipts and Expenditure and a Map, Reports, and Correspondence, London, [The Society], 1877.

British Red Cross Society

Anon., *East Lancashire Branch, British Red Cross Society, An Illustrated Account of the Work of the Branch During the First Years of the War,* Manchester, Sherrat & Hughes, 1916.

Central British Red Cross Committee, *Report on the Voluntary Organisations in Aid of the Sick and Wounded during the South African War*, London, HMSO, 1902.

Loyd, Archie K., *An Outline of the History of the British Red Cross Society from Its Foundation in 1870 to the Outbreak of War in 1914*, London, [The Society], 1917.

Reports by the Joint War Committee and the Joint War Finance Committee of the British Red Cross Society and the Order of St John of Jerusalem in England on Voluntary Aid Rendered to the Sick and Wounded at Home and Abroad and to British Prisoners of War 1914–1919, London, [The Society], HMSO, 1921.

The British Red Cross in the Balkans: A Series of 106 Reproductions of Photographs Taken by Members of the British Red Cross Society's Units, London, [The Society], Cassel & Co., Ltd., 1913.

Bulgarian Peasant Relief Fund

Strangford, Viscountess, *Report of the Expenditure of the Bulgarian Peasant Relief Fund with a Statement of Distribution and Expenditure*, London, Hardwicke & Brogue, n.d.

Humanitarian League

Annual Reports, 1895–96.

Order of St John in England

Annual Report of the Order of St John of Jerusalem in Anglia, London, Basil Montagu Pickering, 1871.

Annual Report of the Order of St John of Jerusalem in Anglia, London, Basil Montagu Pickering, 1877.

Anon, 'The proper sphere of volunteer societies for the relief of sick and wounded soldiers in war. A paper read before the General Assembly of the Order, 25 June 1977', London, Harrison and Co., 1877.

Brackenbury, H., 'Aid to the Injured', Proceedings of a public meeting of the Knights of St John of Jerusalem, Woolwich, A. W. and J. P. Jackson, 1878.

Report of the Chapter, 1874, London, Harrison and Son, 1874.

Report of the Chapter, 1877, London, Harrison and Son, 1877.

The Egyptian Relief Fund Report 1883, London, Harrison and Son, 1883.

The Statutes of the Sovereign and illustrious order of St John of Jerusalem, Anglia, London, printed by John E. Taylor, 1864.

Religious Society of Friends

Friends South African Relief Fund, 'Report of the Committee to the Yearly Meeting, Fifth Month, 1902', in *Yearly Meeting Proceedings*, 1902–1906, London, [The Society], 1906.

Friends War Victims' Relief Fund, *Executive Committee Report*, December 1870, London, [The Society], 1870.

Friends War Victim Relief Fund, 'Report from the Committee of the War Victims' Fund for Non-Combatant Sufferers in Eastern Europe, 1877', *Yearly Meeting Proceedings*, London, [The Society] 1877.

General Report of the Committee of the War Victims' Fund to the Meeting for Sufferings, London, [The Society], c.May 1871.

South African Conciliation Committee

'Minutes of the General Committee Meeting at the Westminster Palace Hotel, Thursday April 5th 1900', London, [The Committee], 1900.

'Receipts and Payments Account from 21 July 1899 to 12 October 1900', London, [The Committee], 1900.

'Receipts and Payments Account from 12 October 1900 to 12 October 1901', London, [The Committee], 1901.

'The Committee's Manifesto as Issued to the Public Press on 15 January 1900', London, [The Committee], 1900.

Swinny, S. H. (sec.), 'The Work of the South African Conciliation Committee, 1901', London, [The Committee], 1901.

'List of Names and Addresses', London, [The Committee], 1901.

'Some Comments on the Report of the Ladies' Commission on the Concentration Camps', London, [The Committee], 1902.

South African Women's and Children's Distress Fund

Hobhouse, Emily, *A Letter to the Committee of the South African Women's and Children's Distress Fund*, London, The Argus Printing Co., Ltd., 1901.

Hobhouse, Emily, 'After the War', Nos 1 and 2, London, South African Women's and Children's Distress Fund, 1903.

Hobhouse, Emily, *Report to the Committee of the Distress Fund for South African Women and Children*, London, Friars Printing Assoc., 1901.

Stafford House Committee

Kennett-Barrington, Vincent, *Report of the Record and the Operation of the Stafford House Committee for the Relief of Sick and Wounded Turkish Soldiers*, London, Spottiswoode & Co., 1879.

The Turkish Compassionate Fund

Burdett-Coutts, W. (ed.), *The Turkish Compassionate Fund: An Account of Its Origin, Working, and Results*, London, Remington & Co., 1883.

Secondary works

Adler, Judith, 'The Origins of Sightseeing', *Annals of Tourism Research*, Vol. 16, 1989.

Alderman, Geoffrey, *The Jewish Community in British Politics*, Oxford, Clarendon Press, 1983.

Allen, M. A. M., *Simple Sketches of Christian Work and Travel*, London, Headley Bros., 1911.

Anderson, Dorothy, *The Balkan Volunteers*, London, Hutchinson & Co., Ltd., 1968.

Andrews, Malcolm, *The Search for the Picturesque: Landscape Aesthetics and Tourism in Britain, 1760–1800*, Aldershot, Scholar Press, 1989.

Anon., *Letters from a French Field Hospital*, London, Constable and Co. Ltd., 1917.

Anon., *The Ceaseless Challenge: Souvenir of the Red Cross Centenary 1863–1963*, London, [The Society], 1963.

Argyll, Duke of (Sir George Campbell), 'The Resettlement of the Turkish Dominions', *Fortnightly Review*, April, 1878.

Audoin-Rouzeau, Stéphane and Becker, Annette, *14–18: Understanding the Great War*, London, Institut français du Royaume-Uni, 2004.

Bagnold, Enid, *A Dairy without Dates*, London, Virago, 1978 [1918].

Bagot, Dosia, *Shadows of the War*, London, Edward Arnold, 1900.

Balme, Jennifer Hobhouse, *To Love One's Enemies: The Work and Life of Emily Hobhouse Compiled from Letters and Writings, Newspaper Cuttings and Official Documents*, Cobble Hill, Canada, Hobhouse Trust, 1994.

Barnett, Michael and Weiss, Thomas G. (eds), *Humanitarianism in Question: Politics, Power, Ethics*, Ithaca, N.Y., Cornell University Press, 2008.

Barton, E. C., *Hints to VAD Members in Hospitals*, London, Macmillan and Co. Ltd., 1915.

Bass, Gary J., *Freedom's Battle: The Origins of Humanitarian Intervention*, New York, Alfred A. Knopf, 2008.

Baughan, Emily, '"Every Citizen of Empire Implored to Save the Children!" Empire, Internationalism and the Save the Children Fund in Interwar Britain', *Historical Research*, Vol. 8, No. 213, 2013.

Baylen, Joseph O. and Crangle, John V., 'Emily Hobhouse's Peace Mission, 1916', *Journal of Contemporary History*, Vol. 14, No. 4, October 1979.

Bayly, C. A., and Biagini, Eugenio (eds), *Guiseppe Mazzini and the Globalisation of Democratic Nationalism, 1830–1920*, Proceedings of the British Academy, Oxford, Oxford University Press, 2008.

Beinart, William and Dubow, Saul (eds), *Segregation and Apartheid in Twentieth Century South Africa*, London, Routledge, 1995.

Bell, Duncan, *The Idea of Greater Britain: Empire and the Future of World Order, 1860–1900*, Princeton, NJ, Princeton University Press, 2007.

Bell, Duncan (ed.), *Victorian Visions of the Global Order: Empire and International Relations in Nineteenth-Century Political Thought*, Cambridge, Cambridge University Press, 2007.

Bellows, John, *The Track of War around Metz and the Fund for the Non-Combatant Sufferers*, London, Trubner & Co., 1871.

Bellows, John, *The Truth about the Transvaal War and the Truth about War*, Gloucester, John Bellows, 1900.

Best, Geoffrey, *Humanity in Warfare: The Modern History of the International Law of Armed Conflict*, London, Methuen, 1983.

Best, Geoffrey, *War and Law since 1945*, Oxford, Clarendon Press, 1994.

Biagini, Eugenio, *British Democracy and Irish Nationalism 1876–1906*, Cambridge University Press, Cambridge, 2007.

Billington, Mary Frances, *The Red Cross in War: Woman's Part in the Relief of Suffering*, London, Hodder and Stoughton, 1914.

Blunt, Fanny, *The People of Turkey: Twenty Years' Residence among Bulgarians, Greeks, Albanians, Turks and Armenians by a Consul's Daughter and Wife*, 2 vols, London, John Murray, 1878.

Bonar, H., *The White Fields of France; or, The Story of Mr McAll's Mission to the Working Men of Paris and Lyons*, London, James Nisbet & Co., 1880 (2nd edn).

Bourdieu, Pierre, *The Field of Cultural Production: Essays on Art and Literature*, Cambridge, Polity Press, 1993.

Bowser, Thekla, *The Story of British V.A.D. Work in the Great War*, London, Andrew Melrose, 1917.

Brackenbury, Henry (Sir), 'Philanthropy in War', *Blackwood's Magazine*, February 1877.

Bradford, Helen, 'Gentlemen and Boers: Afrikaner Nationalism, Gender and Colonial Warfare in the South African War', in G. Cuthbertson *et al.* (eds), *Writing a Wider War: Rethinking Gender, Race and Identity in the South African War, 1899–1902*, Cape Town, Ohio University Press, 2002.

Braithwaite, M., *Memorials of Christine Majolier Alsop*, London, S. Harris & Co., 1881.

Braithwaite Turner Buckle, Elizabeth, *Triumphant over Pain*, London, Longmans, Green & Co., 1923.

Brereton, Katherine, 'Life in the Concentration Camps', *The Pall Mall Gazette*, Vol. 27, 1902.

Briggs, Asa, *Saxons, Normans and Victorians*, Hastings and Bexhill Historical Association, 1966.

Brittain, Vera, *Testament of Youth: An Autobiographical Study of the Years 1900–1925*, London, Gollancz, 1978 [1933].

Brown, Heloise, *'The Truest Form of Patriotism': Pacifist Feminism in Britain 1870–1902*, Manchester, Manchester University Press, 2003.

Bryce, James, *Impressions of South Africa*, London, Macmillan & Co., Ltd., 1899 [1897].

Burdett, Carolyn, *Olive Schreiner and the Progress of Feminism: Evolution, Gender, Empire*, Basingstoke, Palgrave, 2001.

Burman, Erica, 'Poor Children: Charity Appeals and Ideologies of Childhood', *Changes: Journal of Psychology and Psychotherapy*, Vol. 12, 1994.

Burrow, J. W., *A Liberal Descent: Victorian Historians and the English Past*, Cambridge, Cambridge University Press, 1981.

Buzard, J., *The Beaten Track: European Tourism, Literature and the Ways to Culture, 1800–1918*, Oxford, Clarendon Press, 1993.

Cantlie, James (Sir), 'Etiquette in Voluntary Aid Detachments', *The Red Cross*, Vol. II, No. 9, September 1915.

Cantlie, Neil (Sir), *A History of the Army Medical Department*, Vol. 2, London, Churchill Livingstone, 1974.

Capper, Samuel, *Wanderings in War Time. Being the Notes of Two Journeys taken in France and Germany in the Autumn of 1870 and the Spring of 1871*, London, Richard Bentley & Son, 1871.

Carpenter, Edward, *Boer and Briton*, Manchester, Labour Press, 1900.

Chesson, F. W., *Turkey and the Slave Trade. A Statement of Facts*, The Eastern Question Association, Papers on the Eastern Question, no. 7, London, Cassell, Petter & Galpin, 1877.

Cirakman, Asli, *From the 'Terror of the World' to the 'Sick Man of Europe': European Images of Ottoman Empire and Society from the Sixteenth Century to the Nineteenth*, Oxford, Peter Lang, 2002.

Claeys, Gregory, *Imperial Sceptics: British Critics of Empire, 1850–1920*, Cambridge, Cambridge University Press, 2010.

Clayton Windscheffel, Ruth, *Reading Gladstone*, Basingstoke, Palgrave Macmillan, 2008.

Cobbold, Lorna, *In Blue and Gray*, Cambridge, W. P. Spalding, 1917.

Cole-Mackintosh, Ronnie, *A Century of Service to Mankind: A History of the St John Ambulance Brigade*, London, Century Benham, 1986.

Collini, Stefan, *Liberalism and Sociology: L. T. Hobhouse and Political Argument in England 1880–1914*, Cambridge, Cambridge University Press, 1979.

Collini, Stefan, *Public Moralists: Political Thought and Intellectual Life in Britain, 1850–1930*, Oxford, Oxford University Press, 1993.

Collins, Wilkie, *The New Magdalen*, Stroud, Sutton Publishing, 2001 [1873].

Cooter, Roger (ed.), *In the Name of the Child: Health and Welfare, 1880–1940*, London, Routledge, 1992.

Cooter, Roger, 'The Moment of the Accident: Culture, Militarism and Modernity in Late-Victorian Britain', in Roger Cooter and Bill Luckin (eds), *Accidents in History: Injuries, Fatalities and Social Relations*, Amsterdam, Rodopi, 1997.

Cooter, Roger and Luckin, Bill (eds), *Accidents in History: Injuries, Fatalities and Social Relations*, Amsterdam, Rodopi, 1997.

Costin, L. B., 'Feminism, Pacifism, Internationalism and the 1915 International Congress of Women', *Women's Studies International Forum*, Vol. 5, 1982.

Crampton, R. J., *Bulgaria*, Oxford, Oxford University Press, 2007.

Creswell Hewett, F., *Recollections of Sedan*, Halifax, NS, Fowler & Co., 1877.

Cuthbertson, G. et al. (eds), *Writing a Wider War: Rethinking Gender, Race and Identity in the South African War, 1899–1902*, Cape Town, Ohio University Press, 2002.

Dampier, Helen, 'Women's Testimonies of the Concentration Camps of the South African War 1899–1902 and After', PhD thesis, University of Newcastle, 2005.

Davey, Arthur, *The British Pro-Boers, 1877–1902*, Cape Town, Tafelberg, 1978.

Davin, Anna, 'Imperialism and Motherhood', *History Workshop Journal*, Vol. 5, 1978.

Donner, Henriette, 'Under the Cross – Why V. A. D.s Performed the Filthiest Task in the Dirtiest War: Red Cross Women Volunteers, 1914–1918', *Journal of Social History*, Vol. 30, No. 3, 1997.

Dubow, Saul, 'Colonial Nationalism, the Milner Kindergarten and the Rise of "South Africanism", 1902–10', *History Workshop Journal*, Vol. 43, 1997.

Dubow, Saul, 'Imagining the New South Africa in the Era of Reconstruction', in David Omissi and Andrew S. Thompson (eds), *The Impact of the South African War*, Basingstoke, Palgrave, 2002.

Dunant, Henri, *A Memoir of Solferino*, London, Cassell & Co., 1947.

Ensor, Robert, *England 1870–1914*, Oxford, Clarendon Press, 1992 [1936].

Evans, Arthur, *Through Bosnia and Herzegovina on Foot during the Insurrection, August and September 1875, with an Historical Review of Bosnia and a Glimpse at the Croats, Slavonians, and the Ancient Republic of Ragusa*, London, Longmans, Green & Co., 1877.

Farah, Caesar, 'Protestantism and British Diplomacy in Syria', *International Journal of Middle East Studies*, Vol. 7, No. 3, July 1976.

Fedden, Marguerite, *Sister's Quarters Salonika*, London, Grant Richards Ltd., 1921.

Feldman, Ilana, 'The Quaker Way: Ethical Labor and Humanitarian Relief', *American Ethnologist*, Vol. 34, No. 4, November 2007.

Feldman, Ilana and Ticktin, Miriam (eds), *In the Name of Humanity: The Government of Threat and Care*, Durham, NC, Duke University Press, 2010.

Ferguson, Niall, *The House of Rothschild: The World's Banker, 1849–1999*, New York, Viking, 2000.

Fletcher, Ian C., Mayhall, Laura E. Nym and Levine, Philippa (eds), *Women's Suffrage in the British Empire: Citizenship, Nation and Race*, London, Routledge, 2000.

Freeman, E. A., 'Race and Language', *Contemporary Review*, Vol. 29, March 1877.

Freeman, E. A., *The Eastern Question in Its Historical Bearings*, Manchester, National Reform Union, 1876.

Freeman, E. A., *The Ottoman Power in Europe: Its Nature, Its Growth and Its Decline*, London, Macmillan & Co., 1877.

Fry, Ruth, *A Quaker Adventure, The Story of Nine Years' Relief and Reconstruction*, London, Nisbet & Co., 1926.

Fry, Ruth, *Emily Hobhouse: A Memoir*, London, Jonathan Cape, 1929.

Furley, John, *In Peace and War: Autobiographical Sketches*, London, Smith, Elder & Co., 1905.

Furley, John, 'The Red Cross', *The Nineteenth Century*, Vol. 18, No. CVI, December 1885.

Furley, John, 'The Red Cross', *The Standard*, 3 February 1887.

Furse, Katharine, *Hearts and Pomegranates: The Story of Forty-five Years, 1875–1920*, London, Peter Davies, 1940.

Garrett Fawcett, Millicent, *The Martyrs of Turkish Misrule, Containing a Supplement by Miss Irby Detailing the Work of the Bosnian and Herzegovinian Fugitives and Orphan Relief Fund*, The Eastern Question Association, Papers on the Eastern Question, no. 11, London, Cassell, Petter & Galpin, 1877.

Garrett Fawcett, Millicent, *What I Remember*, London, T. Fisher Unwin Ltd., 1924.

Gladstone, William, 'Aggression in Egypt and Freedom in the East', *The Nineteenth Century*, Vol. 2, No. VI, August 1877.

Gladstone, William, *Bulgarian Horrors and the Question of the East*, London, John Murray, 1876.

Gladstone, William, 'England's Mission', *The Nineteenth Century*, Vol. 4, No. XIX, September 1878.

Gladstone, William, 'Montenegro', *The Nineteenth Century*, Vol. 1, No. III, May 1877.

Gladstone, William, 'The Paths of Honour and Shame', *The Nineteenth Century*, Vol. 3, No. XIII, March 1878.

Grant, Kevin, *A Civilised Savagery: Britain and the New Slaveries in Africa, 1884–1926*, London, Routledge, 2005.

Green, Alice Stopford, 'A Visit to the Boer Prisoners at St Helena,' *The Nineteenth Century and After*, Vol. 48, No. CCLXXXVI, December 1900.

Green, Alice Stopford, 'Our Boer Prisoners: A Suggested Object-Lesson', *The Nineteenth Century and After*, Vol. 49, No. CCXCI, May 1901.

Greenwood, John Ormerod, *Quaker Encounters: Friends and Relief*, Vol. 1, York, William Sessions Ltd., 1975.

Grubb, Edward, *Social Aspects of the Quaker Faith*, London, Headley Brothers, 1899.

Grubb, Edward, *What Is Quakerism?* London, Headley Bros. Ltd., 1917.

Hardyment, Christina, *Dream Babies: Childcare from Locke to Spock*, Oxford, Oxford University Press, 1984.

Harrison, Frederic, *Autobiographic Memoirs*, Vol. II (1870–1910), London, Macmillan & Co. Ltd., 1911.

Harrison, Frederic, 'Cross and Crescent', *Fortnightly Review*, December 1876.

Hatton, Helen, *The Largest Amount of Good. Quaker Relief in Ireland, 1654–1921*, London, McGill–Queen's University Press, 1993.

Henty, G. A., *A Tale of Two Sieges of Paris*, London, S. W. Partridge & Co., 1895.

Hewison, Hope Hay, *Hedge of Wild Almonds: South Africa, the 'Pro-Boers' and the Quaker Conscience*, London, James Currey Ltd., 1989.

Hirshfield, Claire, 'Blacks, Boers and Britons: The Anti-War Movement in England and the "Native Issue", 1899–1902', *Peace and Change*, Vol. 8, 1982.

Hirshfield, Claire, 'Liberal Women's Organisations and the War against the Boers, 1899–1902', *Albion*, Vol. 14, No. 1, 1982.

Hirst, Margaret E., *The Quakers in Peace and War: An Account of Their Peace Principles and Practice*, London, The Swarthmore Press Ltd., 1923.

Hobhouse, Emily, *The Brunt of War and Where It Fell*, London, Methuen & Co., 1902.

Hobhouse, Emily, *War without Glamour or Women's War Experiences written by Themselves 1899–1902*, Bloemfontein, Nasionale Pers Beperk, 1924.

Hobson, J. A., *Imperialism: A Study*, London, James Nisbet & Co., 1902.

Hobson, J. A., *The War in South Africa: Its Causes and Effects*, London, James Nisbet & Co., Ltd., 1900.

Holmes, Colin, 'Goldwin Smith: A "Liberal" Anti-Semite', *Patterns of Prejudice*, Vol. 6, No. 5, September/October 1972.

Holton, Sandra Stanley, *Feminism and Democracy: Women's Suffrage and Reform Politics in Britain, 1900–1918*, Cambridge, Cambridge University Press, 1986.

Horne, John and Kramer, Alan, *German Atrocities: A History of Denial*, New Haven, CT, Yale University Press, 2001.

Hupchick, Dennis, *The Balkans from Constantinople to Communism*, Basingstoke, Palgrave, 2002.

Hutchinson, John F., *Champions of Charity: War and the Rise of the Red Cross*, Oxford, Westview Press, 1996.

Hutchinson, John F., '"Custodians of the Sacred Fire": The ICRC and the Postwar Reorganisation of the International Red Cross', in Paul Weindling (ed.), *International Health Organisations and Movements, 1918–1939*, Cambridge, Cambridge University Press, 1995.

Irby, Paulina, 'Bosnia in 1875', Foreign Office Pamphlets, No. 76, London, 1876.

Irby, Paulina and Mackenzie, G. Muir, *Travels in the Slavonic Provinces of Turkey-in-Europe*, London, Daldy, Isbister & Co., 1877 (1st edn 1867).

Jones, H. S., *Victorian Political Thought*, Basingstoke, Macmillan, 2000.

Jones, Heather, 'International or Transnational? Humanitarian Action during the First World War', *European Review of History*, Vol. 16, No. 5, October 2009.

Jones, William, *Quaker Campaigns in Peace and War*, London, Headley Brothers, 1899.

Julius, Anthony, *Trials of the Diaspora: A History of Anti-Semitism in England*, Oxford, Oxford University Press, 2010.

Kennedy, David, *The Dark Sides of Virtue: Reassessing International Humanitarianism*, Princeton, NJ, Princeton, University Press, 2004.

Kennedy, Thomas, *British Quakerism 1860–1920: The Transformation of a Religious Community*, Oxford, Oxford University Press, 2001.

Kenyon, Edith C., *Pickles a Red Cross Heroine*, London, Collins' Clear Type Press, 1916.

Koskenniemi, Martii, *The Gentle Civilizer of Nations: The Rise and Fall of International Law 1870–1960*, Cambridge, Cambridge University Press, 2001.

Koss, Stephen, *The Rise and Fall of the Political Press in Britain*, London, Hamish Hamilton, 1981.

Koven, Seth, *Slumming: Sexual and Social Politics in Victorian London*, Oxford, Princeton University Press, 2004.

Krebs, Paula M., *Gender, Race and the Writing of Empire: Public Discourse and the Boer War*, Cambridge, Cambridge University Press, 1999.

Krebs, Paula M., '"The Last of the Gentlemen's Wars": Women in the Boer War Concentration Camp Controversy', *History Workshop Journal*, Vol. 33, 1992.

La Motte, Ellen, *The Backwash of War: The Human Wreckage of the Battlefield as Witnessed by an American Hospital Nurse*, London, G. P. Putnam's Sons, 1916.

Laity, Paul, 'The British Peace Movement and the War', in David Omissi and Andrew S. Thompson (eds), *The Impact of the South African War*, Basingstoke, Palgrave, 2002.

Laqueur, Thomas, 'Bodies, Details and the Humanitarian Narrative', in Lynn Hunt (ed.), *The New Cultural History*, Berkeley, University of California Press, 1989.

Lees, Florence, 'In a Fever Hospital before Metz', *Good Words*, 1873.

Legassick, Mark, 'British Hegemony and the Origins of Segregation in South Africa, 1901–14', in W. Beinart and S. Dubow (eds), *Segregation and Apartheid in Twentieth Century South Africa*, London, Routledge, 1995.

Levene, Mark and Roberts, Penny (eds), *The Massacre in History*, Oxford, Berghahn, 1999.

Lilliard, Mabel, *British Red Cross Infant Welfare Manual: 'The Mothercraft Manual'*, BRCS Manuals No. 9, London, [The Society], 1928.

Lloyd, David, *Battlefield Tourism, Pilgrimage and the Commemoration of the Great War in Britain, Australia and Canada, 1919–1939*, Oxford, Berg, 1998.

Longmore, Thomas (Sir), *Gunshot Injuries*, 2nd edn, London, Longmans, Green and Co., 1895 [1861].

Longmore, Thomas (Sir), 'On the Geneva Convention of August the 22nd 1864', A Lecture Delivered at the Royal United Service Institution, London, Harrison and Sons, 1866.

McCarthy, Justin, *Death and Exile*, Princeton, NJ, Darwin Press, 1995.

MacCormac, William (Sir), *Notes and Recollections of an Ambulance Surgeon. Being an account of work done under the Red Cross during the campaign of 1870*, London, J. & A. Churchill, 1871.

MacLaughlin, Louisa and Pearson, Emma, *Our Adventures during the War of 1870*, 2 Vols, London, Richard Bentley & Son, 1871.

MacLaughlin, Louisa and Pearson, Emma, *Service in Servia under the Red Cross*, London, Tinsley Brothers, 1877.

Maclean, Norman, 'The English Military Ambulance 1870 (The First Field Ambulance?)', typescript of article for *British Army Review*, Wellcome Library.

Mahood, Linda, *Feminism and Voluntary Action: Eglantyne Jebb and Save the Children, 1876–1928*, Basingstoke, Palgrave Macmillan, 2009.

Makdisi, Ussuma, 'Reclaiming the Land of the Bible: Missionaries, Secularism and Evangelical Modernity', *The American Historical Review*, Vol. 102, No. 3, June 1997.

Malkii, Lisa, 'Children, Humanity, and the Infantilization of Peace', in Ilana Feldman and Miriam Ticktin (eds), *In the Name of Humanity: The Government of Threat and Care*, Durham, NC, Duke University Press, 2010.

Malkii, Lisa, 'Speechless Emissaries: Refugees, Humanitarianism, and Dehistoricization', *Cultural Anthropology*, Vol. 11, No. 3, 1996.

Manji, Firoze and O'Coill, Carl, 'The Missionary Position: NGOs and Development in Africa', *International Affairs*, Vol. 78 (2002).

Marsh, Jan, *Back to the Land: The Pastoral Impulse in Victorian England from 1880 to 1914*, London, Quartet Books, 1982.

Marshall, Dominique, 'Humanitarian Sympathy for Children in Times of War and the History of Children's Rights, 1919–1959', in James Marten (ed.), *Children and War: A Historical Anthology*, London, New York University Press, 2002.

Marten, James (ed.), *Children and War: A Historical Anthology*, London, New York University Press, 2002.

Matthew, H. C. G. (ed.), *The Gladstone Diaries*, Vol. IX, January 1875–December 1880, Oxford, Clarendon Press, 1986.

Mayhall, Laura E. Nym, 'The South African War and the Origins of Suffrage Militancy in Britain, 1899–1902', in Ian C. Fletcher, Laura E. Nym Mayhall and Philippa Levine (eds), *Women's Suffrage in the British Empire: Citizenship, Nation and Race*, London, Routledge, 2000.

Meade, L. T., *A Sister of the Red Cross: A Story of Ladysmith*, London, Thomas Nelson & Sons, 1901.

Meininger, Thomas, A., *The Formation of a Nationalist Bulgarian Intelligentsia, 1835–1878*, London, Garland Publishing Inc., 1987.

Melman, Billie, 'Claiming the Nation's Past: The Invention of an Anglo-Saxon Tradition', *Journal of Contemporary History*, Vol. 26, Nos 3–4, September 1991.

Modiano, Raimonda, 'The Legacy of the Picturesque: Landscape, Property and the Ruin', Stephen Copley and Peter Garside (eds), *The Politics of the Picturesque: Literature, Landscape and Aesthetics since 1770*, Cambridge, Cambridge University Press, 2010.

Moore, Sandford, *Notes with a Prussian Sanitats Detachment in the Loire Campaign, 1870*, London, Pardon & Son, 1872.

Morris, A. J. A., *Edwardian Radicalism 1900–1914: Some Aspects of British Radicalism*, London, Routledge, 1974.

Morris, Peter (ed.), *First Aid to the Battlefront: Life and Letters of Sir Vincent Kennett-Barrington (1844–1903)*, Stroud, Alan Sutton, 1992.

Mosse, David (ed.), *Adventures in Aidland: The Anthropology of Professionals in International Development*, Oxford, Berghahn Books, 2011.

Moyn, Samuel, *The Last Utopia: Human Rights in History*, London, Harvard University Press, 2010.

Mulley, Clare, *The Woman Who Saved the Children: A Biography of Eglantyne Jebb, Founder of Save the Children*, Oxford, Oneworld, 2009.

Nassibian, Akaby, *Britain and the Armenian Question 1915–1923*, New York, St. Martin's Press, 1984.

O'Brien, D. P. (ed.), *The Correspondence of Lord Overstone*, Vol. 3, Cambridge, Cambridge University Press, 1971.

Oliver, Beryl (Dame), *The British Red Cross in Action*, London, Faber and Faber, 1966.

Omissi, David and Thompson, Andrew S. (eds), *The Impact of the South African War*, Basingstoke, Palgrave, 2002.

Ouditt, Sharon, 'Nuns and Lovers: Voluntary Aid Detachment Nurses in the First World War', in Sharon Ouditt, *Fighting Forces, Writing Women: Identity and Ideology in the First World War*, London, Routledge, 1994.

Ouditt, Sharon, *Fighting Forces, Writing Women: Identity and Ideology in the First World War*, London, Routledge, 1994.

Parker, C. J. W., 'The Failure of Liberal Radicalism: The Racial Ideas of E. A. Freeman', *The Historical Journal*, Vol. 24, No. 4, December 1981.

Perkins, R., 'The Life and Times of Lt Col Sir Nicolai Elphinstone Bart', unpublished manuscript, British Red Cross Society, Archive.

Polman, Linda, *War Games: The Story of Aid and War in Modern Times*, London, Viking, 2010.

Poovey, Mary, *Making a Social Body: British Cultural Formation, 1830–1864*, Chicago, University of Chicago Press, 1995.

Porter, J. H., *The Surgeon's Pocket Book: Being an Essay on the Best Treatment of Wounded in War*, London, Charles Griffin, 1875.

Price, M., 'The Picturesque Moment', in Frederick Hilles and Harold Bloom (ed.), *From Sensibility to Romanticism*, Oxford, Oxford University Press, 1965.

Quataert, Jean H., 'German Patriotic Women's Work in War and Peace Time, 1864–90', in Stig Förster and Jörg Nagler (eds), *On the Road to Total War: The American Civil War and the German Wars of Unification, 1861–1871*, Cambridge, Cambridge University Press, 1997.

Rajak, Dinah and Stirrat, Jock, 'Parochial Cosmopolitanism and the Power of Nostalgia', in David Mosse (ed.), *Adventures in Aidland: The Anthropology of Professionals in International Development*, Oxford, Berghahn Books, 2011.

Rey, Roselyne, *The History of Pain*, London, Harvard University Press, 1995.

Riedi, Eliza, 'Teaching Empire: British and Dominions Women Teachers in the South African War Concentration Camps', *English Historical Review*, Vol. CXX, No. 489, December 2005.

Riedi, Eliza, 'Women, Gender, and the Promotion of Empire: The Victoria League, 1901–1914', *The Historical Journal*, Vol. 45, No. 3, September 2002.

Rieff, David, *A Bed for the Night: Humanitarianism in Crisis*, London, Vintage, 2002.

Rodogno, Davide, *Against Massacre: Humanitarian Interventions in The Ottoman Empire 1815–1914*, Princeton, NJ, Princeton University Press, 2012.

Rose, Sonya, 'Women's Rights, Women's Obligations: Contradictions of Citizenship in World War II Britain', *European Review of History*, Vol. 7, No. 2, 2000.

Ross, Ellen, *Slum Travellers: Ladies and London Poverty, 1860–1920*, Berkeley, University of California Press, 2007.

Rubinstein, David, *A Different World for Women: The Life of Millicent Garrett Fawcett*, London, Harvester Wheatsheaf, 1991.

Rundle, Henry, *With the Red Cross in the Franco-German War 1870–1871*, London, Werner Laurie, n.d.

Ruskin, John, *The Seven Lamps of Architecture* (5th edn), Orpington, George Allen, 1886 [1849].

Ryan, Charles, *Under the Red Crescent: Adventures of an English Surgeon with the Turkish Army at Plevna and Erzeroum, 1877–1878*, London, John Murray, 1897.

Ryan, Charles, *With an Ambulance during the Franco-German War: Personal Experiences and Adventures with Both Armies, 1870–1871*, London, John Murray, 1896.

Saab, Ann Pottinger, *Reluctant Icon: Gladstone, Bulgaria and the Working Classes, 1876–1878*, Cambridge, MA, Harvard University Press, 1991.

Saab, Anne Pottinger, 'The Doctor's Dilemma: Britain and the Cretan Crisis of 1866–69', *Journal of Modern History*, Vol. 49. No. 4, December 1977.

Salt, Henry, *Humanitarianism: Its General Principles and Progress*, London, [privately published], 1906.

Sandwith, Humphrey, *England's Position with Regard to Turkey and the Bulgarian Atrocities*, Liverpool, D. Marples & Co., n.d.

Sandwith, Humphrey, *Shall We Fight Russia? An Address to the Working Men of Great Britain*, London, Cassell, Rebler & Galpin, n.d.

Segesser, Daniel Marc, '"Unlawful Warfare is Uncivilised": The International Debate on the Punishment of War Crimes, 1872–1918', *European Review of History*, Vol. 14, No. 2, June 2007.

Sellick, Patricia, 'Responding to Children Affected by Armed Conflict: A Case Study of Save the Children Fund (1919–1999)', PhD thesis, University of Bradford, 2001.

Session, W. K., *They Chose the Star. An Account of the Work in France of the Society of Friends War Victims Relief Fund from 1870–1875, during and after the Franco-Prussian War*, Friends Relief Services, 1944.

Seton-Watson, Robert, *Disraeli, Gladstone and the Eastern Question: A Study in Diplomacy and Party Politics*, London, Macmillan & Co., Ltd., 1935.

Shannon, Richard, *Gladstone and the Bulgarian Agitation 1876*, London, Thomas Nelson & Sons Ltd., 1963.

Shannon, Richard, *Gladstone: Heroic Minister 1865–1898*, London, Penguin, 1999.

Shannon, Richard, *Gladstone: Peel's Inheritor 1809–1865*, London, Penguin, 1999.

Sharland, Elaine and Urwin, Cathy, 'From Bodies to Minds in Childcare Literature: Advice to Parents in Inter-war Britain', in Roger Cooter (ed.), *In the Name of the Child: Health and Welfare, 1880–1940*, London, Routledge, 1992.

Shults, R. L., *Crusader in Babylon, W. T. Stead and the Pall Mall Gazette*, Lincoln, University of Nebraska Press, 1972.

Simms, Brendan, *Unfinest Hour: Britain and the Destruction of Bosnia*, London, Penguin, 2002.

Smith, Angela, *The Second Battlefield: Women, Modernism and the First World War*, Manchester, Manchester University Press, 2000.

Smith, Goldwin, 'Can Jews Be Patriots?', *The Nineteenth Century*, Vol. 3, No. XV, May 1878.

Soffer, Reba, 'Nation, Duty, Character and Confidence: History at Oxford, 1850–1914', *The Historical Journal*, Vol. 30, No. 1, March 1987.

Spearing, E. M. (V.A.D.), *From Cambridge to Camiers under the Red Cross*, Cambridge, W. Heffer & Sons Ltd., 1917.

Spence Watson, Robert, *The Villages around Metz*, Newcastle, J. M. Carr Printing Works, c.1872.

Spies, S. B., *Methods of Barbarism? Roberts, Kitchener and Civilians in the Boer Republics January 1900–May 1902*, Cape Town, Human & Rousseau, 1977.

Stanley, Liz, *Mourning Becomes . . . Post/Memory and Commemoration and the Concentration Camps of the South African War*, Manchester, Manchester University Press, 2006.

Stead, W. T., *Hell Let Loose! What Is Now Being Done in South Africa*, London, Speaight & Sons, c.1900.

Stead, W. T., *Methods of Barbarism: The Case for Intervention*, London, [privately published], 1901.

Stead, W. T., 'The Progress of the World', *Review of Reviews*, Vol. XX, July–December 1899.

Stein, Janice Gross, 'Humanitarian Organizations. Accountable – Why, to Whom, for What, and How?' in Michael Barnett and Thomas G. Weiss (eds), *Humanitarianism in Question: Politics, Power, Ethics*, Ithaca, NY, Cornell University Press, 2008.

Stephens, W. R. W., *The Life and Letters of Edward A. Freeman*, London, Macmillan & Co., 1895.

Stoker, George, *With 'The Unspeakables', or, Two Years Campaigning in European and Asiatic Turkey*, London, Chapman & Hall, 1878.

Storr, Katherine, *Excluded from the Record: Women, Refugees and Relief 1914–1929*, Oxford, Peter Lang, 2009.

Summers, Anne, *Angels and Citizens: British Women as Military Nurses 1854 to 1914*, Newbury, Threshold Press, 2000.

Sykes, Jessica (Lady), *Side Lights on the War in South Africa: Being Sketches Based on Personal Observation during a Few Weeks' Residence in Cape Colony and Natal*, London, Fisher Unwin, 1900.

Sylvest, Casper, *British Liberal Internationalism, 1880–1930: Making Progress?*, Manchester, Manchester University Press, 2009.

Sylvest, Casper, 'The Foundation of Victorian International Law', in Duncan Bell (ed.), *Victorian Visions of the Global Order: Empire and International Relations in Nineteenth-Century Political Thought*, Cambridge, Cambridge University Press, 2007.

Taithe, Bertrand, *Defeated Flesh: Welfare, Warfare and the Making of Modern France*, Manchester, Manchester University Press, 1999.

Taithe, Bertrand, 'Reinventing (French) Universalism: Religion, Humanitarianism and the "French Doctors"', *Modern & Contemporary France*, Vol. 12, No. 2, 2004.

Taithe, Bertrand, 'The Red Cross in the Franco-Prussian War: Civilians, Humanitarians and War in the "Modern Age"', in Roger Cooter *et al.* (eds) *War, Medicine and Modernity*, Stroud, Sutton Publishing, 1998.

Taylor, A. J. P., *The Struggle for Mastery in Europe*, Oxford, Oxford University Press, 1971 [1954].

Taylor, A. J. P., *The Trouble Makers: Dissent over Foreign Policy 1792–1939*, London, Pimlico, 1993 [1957].

Templer, Mrs H., *A Labour of Love under the Red Cross during the Late War*, London, Simpkin, Marshall and Co., 1872.

Terry, Fiona, *Condemned to Repeat? The Paradox of Humanitarian Action*, Ithaca, NY, Cornell University Press, 2002.

Terry, Fiona, 'Humanitarian Action: Victim of Its Own Success?', *The Humanitarian Decade: Challenges for Humanitarian Assistance in the Last Decade and into the Future*, Vol. II, United Nations Office for the Coordination of Humanitarian Affairs, 2004.

Thacker, Anne, *The Narrative of My Experience as a Volunteer Nurse in the Franco-German War of 1870–1*, London, Abbott, Jones & Co., Ltd., 1897.

Thompson, J. Lee, *A Wider Patriotism: Alfred Milner and the British Empire*, London, Pickering and Chatto, 2007.

Toynbee, Arnold J., *The Western Question in Greece and Turkey: A Study in the Contact of Civilisations*, London, Constable and Co., 1922.

Tuke, James Hack, *A Visit to Paris in the Spring of 1871 on Behalf of the War Victims' Fund of the Society of Friends*, London, F. B. Kitto, 1871.

Van Heyningen, Elizabeth, 'A Tool for Modernisation? The Boer Concentration Camps of the South African War, 1900–1902', *South African Journal of Science*, Vol. 106, Nos 5–6, 2010.

Van Heyningen, Elizabeth, 'Women and Disease: The Clash of Medical Cultures in the Concentration Camps of the South African War', in Greg Cuthbertson *et al.* (eds), *Writing a Wider War: Rethinking Gender, Race and Identity in the South African War 1899–1902*, Chicago, Ohio University Press, 2002.

Van Reenan, Rykie (ed.), *Emily Hobhouse: Boer War Letters*, Cape Town, Human & Rousseau, 1984.

Varouxakis, Georgios, ' "Patriotism", "Cosmopolitanism" and "Humanity" in Victorian Political Thought', *European Journal of Political Theory*, Vol. 5, 2006.

Venables, Gilbert, *Is War Unchristian?*, London, Hodder & Stoughton, c.1872.

Vogeler, Martha, *Frederic Harrison: The Vocations of a Positivist*, Oxford, Clarendon Press, 1984.

Walkowitz, Judith, *City of Dreadful Delight: Narratives of Sexual Danger in Late-Victorian London*, London, Virago Press, 1992.

Wantage, Harriet (Lady), *Lord Wantage, V.C., K.C.B. A Memoir by His Wife*, London, Smith, Elder & Co., 1907.

Webb, Beatrice, *My Apprenticeship*, London, Longmans, Green & Co., 1926.

Weinbren, Dan, 'Against *All* Cruelty: The Humanitarian League, 1891–1919,' *History Workshop Journal*, Vol. 38, Autumn 1994.

Weindling, Paul (ed.), *International Health Organisations and Movements, 1918–1939*, Cambridge, Cambridge University Press, 1995.

Weinroth, Howard, 'Radicalism and Nationalism: An Increasingly Unstable Equation', in A. J. A. Morris (ed.), *Edwardian Radicalism 1900–1914: Some Aspects of British Radicalism*, London, Routledge, 1974.

Weissman, Frabrice (ed.), *In the Shadow of 'Just Wars': Violence, Politics and Humanitarian Action*, Ithaca, NY, Cornell University Press, 2004.

Westlake, John, *Memories of John Westlake*, London, Smith, Elder and Co., 1914.

Wheatcroft, Andrew, *Infidels: A History of the Conflict between Christendom and Islam*, London, Penguin, 2004.

Wohl, Anthony, 'Dizzi-Ben-Dizzi: Disraeli as Alien', *Journal of British Studies*, Vol. 34, No. 3, July 1995.

Sheet music

Clear, Kenneth and Mackie, John, 'The Little Irish Red Cross Nurse', London, Charles Sheard & Co., 1915.

Moseley, J. Ward and Sanders, Ralph, 'Queens of the Red Cross', Manchester, Grosvenor Chambers, 1915.

Vaughn, James and Makeham, John, 'England's Blazon; or, the Blood Red Cross', London, F. Pitman, 1871.

Wellmon, H. M. and Wellmon, Odette, 'Noble Women of the Grand Red Cross', London, Henderson & Spalding Ltd, (undated, acquired by the British Library 1919).

Websites and online resources

Bulgarian Red Cross, www.redcross.bg/history.html.
Bulgarian Red Cross, www.usd.edu/dmhi/brc/brchistory.html.
Dictionary of National Biography Online, www.oxforddnb.com.
Dossey, Barbara, 'Florence Nightingale, The Geneva Conventions and the International Red Cross', www.nightingaledeclaration.net/news/florence-nightingale-red-cross-geneva-conventions/.
Freud, Sigmund, 'Thoughts for the Times on War and Death' (1915), www.panarchy.org/freud/war.1915.html.
Olive Schreiner Letters Project, www.oliveschreiner.org.
Yugoslav Red Cross, www.jck.org.yu/foundation/found.htm.

Index

Literary and artistic works can be found under authors' names.
'n.' after a page reference indicates the number of a note on a page.
Page numbers in *italic* refer to illustrations.